The Psychologi‹

"*The Psychological Autopsy* is a powerful addition to the field and a fountain of knowledge for the reader. This book is destined to become a classic in the field! It is not only a topic that is needed, but it is an exceedingly well documented, well written, and theoretically sound book. This is truly a book that anyone who has an interest in suicide, homicide, or accidental death analysis simply must read!"

—Gerry Cox, PhD, emeritus professor of sociology
at University of Wisconsin–La Crosse

"Antoon Leenaars's *The Psychological Autopsy* is a clear-minded guide that combines the statistical and individual differences from which the lawyer, psychologist, and police investigator will gain much. This excellent guide brings a serious scientific approach about suicide and homicide to life. If you want to know the basics to the more complex components of this challenging and important area of forensic psychology, by all means get this book; it's an original and superb guide."

—Jack Kitaeff, JD, PhD, licensed psychologist, attorney at law,
author, and former major in the US Army

"This is essential reading for all of those professionally involved with the difficult task of establishing causes of death. Written by an internationally known expert, *The Psychological Autopsy* enriches our knowledge and way of thinking, especially on the psychological autopsy method and its theoretical and practical limitations. Corroborated by transcripts of a precious conversation with Edwin Shneidman, the volume distills the enormous expertise accumulated by the author's many years of forensic and clinical practice."

—Diego de Leo, DSc, MD, PhD, FRANZCP, emeritus professor
of psychiatry at Griffith University, Australia

The best way to grasp the essence of death scene investigation (DSI) is to witness its application, called the psychological autopsy, by an expert forensic scientist/ clinician. This remarkable book affords the opportunity to delve into the challenges that the forensic mental health specialist and public safety professional confront in DSI. Suicides, and often death, are complex, multidetermined events.

People, whether police investigators or mental health professionals, are generally perplexed, and even confused, when they are confronted by the equivocal case. Was it a suicide? Homicide? Accident? These are critical questions. Dr. Leenaars shows that DSI is, however, not mysterious; the reader can learn the generally accepted, evidence-based protocols of the psychological autopsy. Illuminated by individual (idiographic) case studies and general (nomothetic) research, this definitive guide allows the investigator to uncover the bare bones of a suicide or death.

Antoon A. Leenaars, PhD, CPsych, CPQ, a mental health, public health, and forensic psychologist, has conducted influential research on death and suicide, and was the founding editor in chief of the journal *Archives of Suicide Research*. Dr. Leenaars has provided forensic services in cases of wrongful death, suicide, homicide-suicide, homicide, and accidents.

The Psychological Autopsy

A Roadmap for Uncovering the Barren Bones of the Suicide's Mind

Antoon A. Leenaars

Routledge
Taylor & Francis Group

NEW YORK AND LONDON

First published 2017
by Routledge
711 Third Avenue, New York, NY 10017

and by Routledge
2 Park Square, Milton Park, Abingdon, Oxon, OX14 4RN

Routledge is an imprint of the Taylor & Francis Group, an informa business

Library of Congress Cataloging-in-Publication Data
A catalog record for this book has been requested

ISBN: 978-0-89503-918-7 (hbk)
ISBN: 978-0-89503-919-4 (pbk)
ISBN: 978-1-315-26621-3 (ebk)

Typeset in Times New Roman
by Apex CoVantage, LLC

Dedication

Perhaps the major pioneering forensic effort in modern death scene investigation is the works of Drs. Edwin Shneidman, Norman Farberow, and Robert Litman. They are the troika that started, named, developed, and standardized what became called *The Psychological Autopsy* (PA), the "general acceptance" empirical roadmap to understand the suicidal mind and to determine the mode of death, and why. I am honored to say, once more, they were my close mentors, teachers, and friends over decades. I was favored with not only learning from them but also consulting with them on individual (idiographic) cases. There is nothing like good consultation in this field. This book is for them.

And equally perhaps some of the major researchers on the PA, to my fellow members of the Division of Mental Health at the Norwegian Institute of Public Health, Drs. Gudrun Dieserud, Kari Dyregrov, and Heidi Hjelmeland. They are my fellow researchers, coauthors and friends. Our research in Oslo is one of the largest of general (nomothetic) psychological autopsy studies of suicide. I was honored to be a senior advisor. I was rewarded in Oslo not only with new illuminating insights but also lasting friendships. These new pioneers helped me to discover the evidence-based roadmaps to uncovering the barren bones of the mind's despair.

Table of Contents

Preface

The concept of investigating deaths that are uncertain as to mode of death—natural, accident, suicide, or homicide—is at least as old as the work of John Graunt of London, England in the 17th century. By that time, death records were kept; however, Mr. Graunt's genius laid in aggregating the mortality data into population estimates and constructed the first mortality tallies. Graunt was for the first time, in an accurate way, able to show the regularities (patterns) in the deaths, and thus showed that mortality data had great advantage for police, physicians, and the government in individual causes of death and death investigation. Yet death scene investigations (DSI) have always been shrouded in deep veils of mystery. Thus, a purpose of this book is to show that it is not that mysterious. It can, as Graunt already showed, be evidence based. This book, I believe, will teach you a tool to uncover the bare facts of suicides and other deaths. Not only Graunt, but also you can master it.

Allow me a digression: Like fingerprinting decades ago, DNA analysis has been revolutionary in forensic investigation and has applicability to DSI, such as suicide, homicide, accident, and even serial murder. The identification of human remains is of paramount importance and a difficult task in medicolegal investigations where both medicolegal experts and investigating agencies have to prove the correct identity of individuals in the court of law and for the relatives of the victims (claimants). In the serial killer case of Surinder Koli, in which I was involved, the exhibits (bones, skulls, and mutilated tissues) brought to the laboratory were degraded and highly contaminated, thus, of very poor quality. The case was equivocal.

The major problem was the assembly of the skeletal remains and skull/skull portions, and the identification of these body parts. The skeletal remains (627 pieces), including skull/skull portions (19), were recovered from the nearby sewer drain, sump, and the backyard of the house in which Mr. Koli was residing. In addition, soft tissues (51) were also recovered from the same sewer drain. The victims were killed over a two-year period. Some 19 sets were prepared by radiology/anatomical examination from the exhibits recovered. DNA profiling confirmed the correctness of these sets and also STR typing of nuclear DNA successfully identified eight individuals. Both DNA fingerprinting and radiography/anatomical examination played an important role in solving this complicated case.

The Koli case posed difficulties in identification, which were eventually tackled by systematic forensic methods. It was not mysterious; it was evidence based. However, it was difficult due to the poor quality of samples; it was, in fact, not possible to identify all the bodies. Furthermore, I believe that an interdisciplinary consulting approach (with forensic specialists from such disciplines as police, medicine, psychology, anthropology, odontology) for the identification of extremely fragmented human remains, such as also in mass disasters, has been proven to be most effective.

The impact of mortality data, fingerprinting, DNA analysis, and such on accurate death certification has been immense. Most relevant to our book is the interest regarding mode: "Accident, suicide, homicide, and undetermined (specify)."

The recent American history of DSI on suicide focuses around the Los Angeles Suicide Prevention Center (LASPC). In the 1950s the Chief-Coroner and Medical Examiner of Los Angeles County, Theodore J. Curphey, asked the leaders of the LASPC—Drs. Edwin Shneidman, Norman Farberow, and Robert Litman— to assist him with coroners' cases that were ambiguous as to the mode of death, usually between accident and suicide, although there were cases of homicide and suicide too. These were cases that depended on the decedent's *intention*. The center's three leaders were designated as deputy coroners and went to the scenes of death where they gently interviewed a number of key informants and then reported back to Dr. Curphey in a consultation setting that was strictly nonpartisan; that is, no one had a brief for one mode of death or another (e.g., homicide or suicide). Shneidman labeled this clinical-scientific procedure the psychological autopsy (PA). This book reflects Dr. Edwin Shneidman's (my mentor's) words and teachings. It is about the PA. The PA can be like DNA analysis, at least, like Dr. Shneidman, I believe so. It allows one to see for oneself. The PA is, at this time, the best roadmap to uncover the barren bones of the suicidal mind.

Since Graunt's work, there has been a sizable percentage of deaths that were equivocal as to precise mode because these psychological factors were unknown. Medical examiners, coroners, and police officers, throughout the country can be themselves, however, empowered when they employ the special skills of the behavioral scientists in case of equivocal deaths. The skills of behavioral scientists should be employed in the same way as the skills of biochemists, toxicologists, microscopists, and other physical scientists. It can be like fingerprinting and DNA analysis. The time has long since passed when we could take advantage of the luxury of disregarding the basic teachings of 20th century (and for that matter, the 21st century) psychology and psychiatry. DSI procedures (and the death certificates on which the mode of death are recorded) should reflect the role of the decedent in his own demise, and in equivocal cases this cannot be done without a PA.

As Dr. Shneidman notes:

> The retrospective analysis of deaths not only serves to increase the accuracy of certification (which is in the best interests of the overall mental health concerns

of the community), but also has the heuristic function of providing the serious investigator with clues that he may then use to assess lethal intent in living persons. (Leenaars, 1999a, p. 401)

The PA allows you to do DSI, not in a mysterious way. It will empower not only the coroner or medical examiner, but also you. Simply stated, that is the reason why I wrote this book.

Lake Louise, Alberta, Canada, 2015

Acknowledgments

Few people, like Edwin S. Shneidman, are vouchsafed the rare opportunity to create a new iconic forensic tool—to name it, to shape it, to contribute to it, and most importantly, to catalyze other competent investigators to invest in it: the psychological autopsy (PA). Dr. Shneidman investigated deaths; indeed, intensive, and psychological, death investigation. He has been my light in my studies in death and suicide, retrospective investigation and suicidology in general. He and his wife, Jeanne, called me, "son." Of course, I must also thank ("Dank U") Drs. Norman L. Farberow and Robert E. Litman, my teachers; they showed me the golden star.

I am most grateful to Chris Purcell's family, Mike, Helen, and Kristin, and his friend, Derek Ozawa, who were the informants in the psychological autopsy in Chapter 9, "A PA: A barren bones investigation." They tell a soldier's story. Equally, I am thankful to Myra Dell, mother; Laura McCarthy, aunt; Elsa Steenberg, friend; Sue Kwast, friend; and Dr. Paul O'Dell, physician; who were the informants in the PA of the Scott Dell case.

Sgt. Dr. Daniel Rudofossi encouraged the book and assisted in a number of aspects; like always, I am most grateful for his psychpolice wisdom. I'd like to also thank Drs. Gudrun Dieserud, Kari Dyregrov, and Heidi Hjelmeland, my co-researchers at the Norwegian Institute of Public Health, Oslo. Robert Olson (Center for Suicide Prevention, Calgary, Alberta, Canada) helped with the literature searches. Susanne Wenckstern, my wife and friend since age 14-15, helped me in unimaginable (well, some imaginable) ways and typed the manuscript. Finally, I would like to thank my co-investigators; police, psychiatrists, biologists, and so on, around the world, in the many forensic cases, who are the soul of this book; to name any is to miss some.

As is known, the case (legal) material in this book, such as court testimony, depositions, evidence, interviews, and such are in the public domain, and thus cannot be copyrighted. Yet the facts ("bare bones") are the heart of this book. I am especially grateful to Linda Pence, the defense lawyer for Bei Bei Shuai; and Peter Barnes, the prosecuting attorney in the Scott Dell case. Not only did they assist, but also they provided me with the personal documents. Thanks.

Appreciation is acknowledged to the following with permission, if needed, under the Copyright Act, to reproduce material that appears in this volume:

Leenaars, A., De Leo, D., Dickstra, R., Goldney, R., Kelleher, M., Lester, D., & Nordstrom, P. (1997). Consultations for research in suicidology. *Archives of Suicide Research, 3,* 139–151. With permission of Antoon A. Leenaars, Chair of IASR task force, lead author, and Editor-in-Chief of *Archives of Suicide Research.*

Shneidman, E. (1977). The psychological autopsy. In L. Gottschalk et al. (Eds.), *Guide to the investigation and reporting of drug-abuse deaths* (pp. 179–210). Washington, DC: USDHEW, U.S. Government Printing Office. With permission of David Shneidman.

Shneidman, E. (1993). An example of an equivocal death classified in a court of law. In E. Shneidman, *Suicide as psychache* (pp. 211–246). Northvale: Jason Aronson. With permission of David Shneidman.

PART ONE

Nomothetic Study

There should be discrete stages in our development of the understanding of the suicide's mind. There is a natural progression from conceptualization, to understanding, and then to application and practice. The two chapters in this section reflect on some basic conceptualizations on the general (nomothetic) that we need to begin, to draw a roadmap for uncovering the barren bones of the mind's pain. It presents what the mental health and public safety professionals need to know about suicide, and the many modes of death: homicide, homicide-suicide, self-harm, and accident, before practice; that is, death scene investigation (DSI).

I follow the WHO's recommendation to understand death—natural, accident, suicide, homicide—the NASH classification, as it is called. I take an ecological perspective: individual, relationship, community, and social factors. It is a system view. In the first chapter, I look at and answer: "What is a suicide?" Suicide is a complex, multidimensional event. It is not like water, where all water freezes at 32°F (if *only* it was that simple in our forensic undetermined deaths). I offer some reflections and present a way of understanding the suicides' mind, by detailing the most worldwide tested theory of suicide. There is nothing like sound evidence-based theory to sort out the booming, buzzing mess (flux) of the forensic unknown. The multidimensional theory answers the question, "How can we understand the barren bones of the suicidal mind's intention to die by suicide?" Indeed, *intention* is central in the bare howling facts. This chapter answers every investigators *a priori* question.

Chapter 2 looks beyond suicide; it examines, beyond the natural mode of the death, the other modes of death in the NASH classification: homicide and accident. It also examines homicide-suicide and self-harm, a must for the forensic and police expert. Dr. Norman Farberow, a pioneer in the psychological autopsy (PA), in a 1980 edited volume, *The Many Faces of Suicide*, speculated that there is a vast array of subintentioned deaths that occur beyond intended suicides. Accidental deaths (although there are many accidents that are intentional, vis-à-vis, suicide), self-harm, and some homicides can be seen through these markers. In this section I examine the many faces of violence and death. There are in fact a great many commonalities among the many modes of death—there is a stream of violence. Forensic investigation into death has to include a larger frame of violence and death. Suicide has to be a specific target, but also, to only understand suicide in psychological death investigations is too narrow. To uncover the howling tempest of the mind, a larger roadmap is needed.

CHAPTER 1
Suicide

Was it a suicide? Homicide? Accident? What was the mode of death? Those are the age-old questions for mental health, clinical, forensic, legal, police, and public safety professionals and students. This is "Death Scene Investigation" (DSI). Are there any guides that may assist us to answer our questions? Are there some tools? A roadmap? What can help us with the forensic unknowns?

Imagine we have a person who died by falling from a tall building. The question asked is the NASH question, "What is the mode of death?" Was it natural—did the person fall after suffering a fatal heart attack? Was it an accident—did the person slip due to a wet environment? Was it a suicide—did he intentionally jump? Was it homicide—did someone push him off the building? How do you decide? Our intent in this book is to make you think in NASH terms. It offers a Socratic method to allow you to answer the mode of death of the person who died falling off of the building. This is DSI.

The concept of investigating deaths that are uncertain as to mode of death—natural, accident, suicide, or homicide—is at least as old as the work of John Graunt (1620–1674) of London, England, in the 17th century. In 1662 John Graunt published a small book of observations on mortality that was of great social and medical significance. By that time, records were kept, however, Mr. Graunt's genius lay in aggregating the data into tallies. Once the data were obtained, Graunt focused on individual causes of death. He turned to population estimates and constructed the first mortality tallies. Graunt was for the first time, in an accurate way, able to show the regularities in the deaths when one is dealing in large numbers. Thus, he showed that mortality data had great advantage for police, physicians, and the government.

Although England has used standardized death records since the work of Graunt, the use of nonstandardized death records continued in the United States in the 19th century. In England records led to the formation of medicolegal investigations of deaths. It led to laws requiring recordkeeping. It mandated investigations using informants, not only to keep records but to prevent criminal practices after deaths. By 1874 personal information was required on each death, and by 1893 a death registration was required that called for an investigation into the mode of death. No standardization of registration was required in the U.S., until 1903. Prior to that date there was no federal standardization.

The impact of death certification was immense. Most relevant to our book is the interest regarding mode: "Accident, suicide, homicide, and undetermined (specify)." Since the beginning of the 20th century the certification and recordkeeping relating to deaths has implied that there are four modes of death. It needs to be said right away that the four modes of death have to be distinguished from the many causes of death listed in the International Classification of Diseases and Causes of Death (WHO). The four modes of death make up the acronym NASH. Thus, to speak of the NASH classification of death is to refer to the four traditional modes in which death is currently reported. Contemporary death certificates have a category that reads, "Accident, suicide, homicide, and undetermined"; if none of these are checked, then a "natural" mode of death, as occurs most often, is implied.

The recent American history of the procedure focuses around the Los Angeles Suicide Prevention Centre (LASPC). In the 1950s the Chief-Coroner and Medical Examiner of Los Angeles County, Theodore J. Curphey, asked the leaders of the LASPC—Drs. Edwin Shneidman, Norman Farberow, and Robert Litman—to assist him with coroners' cases that were ambiguous as to the mode of death, usually between accident and suicide, although there were cases of homicide and suicide too. These were cases that depended on the decedent's *intention*. The center's three leaders were designated as deputy coroners and went to the scenes of death where they gently interviewed a number of key informants and then reported back to Dr. Curphey in a setting that was strictly nonpartisan; that is, no one had a brief for one mode of death or another (e.g., accident or suicide). Shneidman labeled this clinical-scientific procedure the psychological autopsy (PA). Probably, their most famous case was Marilyn Monroe. On August 5, 1962, Marilyn died of a fatal drug overdose, shinning a very public light on ambiguous undetermined deaths. What was the actress' intention? Was it a suicide? Accident? Homicide? Farberow, Litman, and Shneidman were asked to investigate the death and they conducted a PA on Marilyn's state of mind. By reviewing the personal and other documents and conducting personal interviews with people who had recent and/or older contacts, they learned that she had made a previous attempt and had suffered with mood fluctuations. "Was she depressed?", they asked. After the DSI, they reported back to the coroner, and the team's verdict was "Suicide."

According to the *Oxford English Dictionary* (OED), autopsy is a Greek word, meaning, "seeing with one's own eyes." Like an autopsy in general, the PA procedure calls for the investigator to see him/herself. It is about "personal observation," a key task of both police officer and forensic specialist. This book reflects Dr. Edwin Shneidman's (my mentor's) words and teachings. It is about the PA. The PA is a roadmap to un-cover the barren bones of the suicidal mind.

Although there have been a few books on the topic (the last of Dr. Shneidman's is over 10 years old), there has been increasing research and opinions on the topic—Cavanagh, Carson, Sharpe, and Lawrie (2003), Pouliot and De Leo (2006), Conner et al. (2011, 2012), Gavin and Rogers (2006), Dyregrov, Dieserud, Hjelmeland, et al. (2011), Dyregrov, Dieserud, Straiton, et al. (2011), Hjelmeland, Dieserud, Dyregrov, Knizek, & Leenaars (2012). Indeed, it would be accurate to state that there is a growing number of publications on the topic, many, like the above, on what a PA is, how to standardize it, how to meet the Daubert ruling (this is discussed in full in chapter 11), and so on. Our book will go back to the beginning of the forensic technique and argue that the PA was well standardized and outlined. This book will make explicit what a PA is and how it can serve as a roadmap to uncovering the bare facts of a suicidal mind. We will also examine: What are the problems with the PA? How many informants are needed? What are the benefits for the informants? (As an aside, research shows that there are many.)

This book intends to meet some challenges that the forensic mental health and public safety professional confront. It is a guide. The reader will learn that suicide is complex, a multidetermined event. People, whether mental health professionals or police, are generally perplexed and even confused when they are confronted with the equivocal case. Was it an accident? Suicide? Homicide? These are critical questions, as John Graunt and Edwin Shneidman knew. There are at least two avenues to understanding: the general and the specific. The general or nomothetic approach deals with generalizations, using empirical, statistical demographic methods or techniques. And although the forensic and first responder specialist must be aware of this literature (knowledge), he or she needs to know the specific better. In our daily life, we are interested in a specific, unique case. Was Robin Williams' death a suicide? Why did, for example, Robin Williams, die by suicide? Why at that particular time? These are the real questions in the forensic unmapped. This is the specific or idiographic. The idiographic approach typically involves the intense study of the individual(s) (Allport, 1942, 1962). This book attempts to do both, a rarity in forensic suicide. It presents a literature review; it offers some generalities. Yet the barren bones are found in the unique case studies: Captain Joseph Campbell (a suicide that had been certified as a homicide), David Lucio and Kelly Johnson (a police homicide-suicide), Natalie (a gifted person who died by suicide), Christopher Lee Purcell (a soldier who died by suicide), Daniel Beckon (a case certified as suicide that was deemed in court to be undetermined), Scott Dell (a case certified as suicide that was a homicide), and Bei Bei Shuai (a pregnant woman, who attempted suicide, charged with murder of the fetus). The book is an educational tool. The book, we hope, meets the challenge—to dress down the psychological anomaly. We hope to thaw the hidden motive in suicide and homicide and some accidents.

UNDERSTANDING SUICIDE:
A FIRST STEP IN DRAWING A ROADMAP

A truism: Investigations begin with understanding (epistemology). Suicide is violence. Homicide is violence. They are lethal violence. Suicide, homicide, and other violence have always been part of the human experience. There are many possible ways of defining violence. The World Health Organization (WHO, 2002) defines violence as:

> The intentional use of physical force or power, threatened or actual, against oneself, another person, or against a group or community, that either results

in or has a high likelihood of resulting in injury, death, psychological harm, maldevelopment or deprivation. (p. 5)

Intentionality is central; one of the more complex aspects of the definition is the matter of intentionality. It is central to the definition of suicide, and other modes of death. *The Oxford English Dictionary* (OED) defines intentional as "done on purpose." Intentionality is the noun. It is to have as one's purpose. It is a conscious act. One intends suicide or homicide. At times an accident can be intentional violence too. One has a purpose—to kill, to induce annihilation.

It is estimated that 1.6 million people die by violence each year, although given that known rates are a fraction of the incidences, it is probably closer to 2 million. Almost half (800,000 to 1,000,000) of these are suicides; one third are homicides (530,000 to 660,000) and one fifth (320,000 to 400,000) are war related (WHO, 2002, 2014). (In 2014, the WHO reported a suicide number of 804,000). This is an enormous cost of violence (never mind the survivors). No single factor or event explains why so many people are violent. They are complex. Violence is multi-determined. Suicide, homicide, and also war-related deaths are not like copper or water, where *all* copper conducts electricity and *all* water freezes at 32 degrees Fahrenheit. They are multidetermined and need a multiaxal approach to understand them (Meehl, 1986)—this is very true about suicide. Suicide, homicide, and the like are the result of an interplay of individual, relationship, social, cultural, and environmental factors. This is sometimes called the *ecological model* (Bronfenbrenner, 1979; Dahlberg & Krug, 2002; Jenkins & Singh, 2000). The model takes a systems approach (von Bertalanffy, 1967, 1968). First applied to child abuse (Garbarino & Crouter, 1978), the model has been applied to a vast array of behaviors, most recently violence, including self-directed violence—suicide (WHO, 2002; see Figure 1).

The model simply suggests that there are different levels, that is, individual, relationship, community, and societal that influence deaths, suicide and homicide,

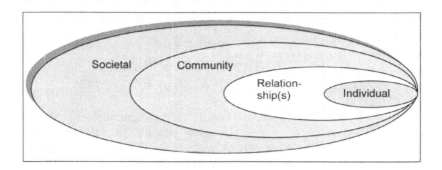

Figure 1. Ecological model for understanding suicide.

and thus, by implication, one can investigate behavior at various levels. Comprehensive (ecological) approaches, thus, would target not only the individual but also the factors beyond the individual. These approaches are also focused on the relationship (e.g., family members, relationships), community, societal, and environmental levels. Thus, suicide and suicidal behavior are multifaceted or multidimensional events (Farberow, MacKinnon, & Nelson, 1997; Leenaars, 1988, 2004; Lester, 1997; Shneidman, 1973a & b, 1985; Zilboorg, 1937).

Somewhat abbreviated here and there, the WHO (2002) believes that an ecological model helps us to best understand the multifaceted nature of death. It explores the relationship between individual and contextual factors and would call for investigating a death at multiple levels. It is not a shot in the dark approach to investigate it. To quote:

> Individual. The first level of the ecological model seeks to identify the biological and personal history factors that an individual brings to his or her behaviour. In addition to biological and demographic factors, factors such as impulsivity, low educational attainment, substance abuse, and prior history of aggression and abuse are considered. In other words, this level of the ecological model focuses on the characteristics of the individual that increase the likelihood of being a victim or perpetrator of violence.
>
> Relationship. The second level of the ecological model explores how proximal social relationships—for example, relations with peers, intimate partners and family members—increase the risk. . . .
>
> Community. The third level of the ecological model examines the community contexts in which social relationships are embedded—such as schools, workplaces and neighbourhoods—and seeks to identify the characteristics of these settings that are associated with being victims or perpetrators of violence. . . .
>
> Societal. The fourth and final level of the ecological model examines the larger societal factors that influence rates of violence. Included here are those factors that create an acceptable climate for violence, those that reduce inhibitions against violence. . . .
>
> The ecological framework highlights the multiple causes of violence and the interaction of risk factors operating within the family and broader community, social, cultural and economic contexts. . . .
>
> Complex linkages. While some risk factors may be unique to a particular type of violence, the various types of violence more commonly share a number of risk factors. Prevailing cultural norms, poverty, social isolation and such factors as alcohol abuse, substance abuse and access to firearms are risk factors for more than one type of violence. . . .
>
> It is also not unusual to detect links between different types of violence . . . associations have been found between suicidal behaviour and several types of violence, including child maltreatment . . . intimate partner violence . . . sexual assault . . . and abuse of the elderly. (WHO, 2002, pp. 12–15)

We will keep this system theory model in mind as we present a roadmap for our topic.

Therefore, there are biological, psychological, intrapsychic, interpersonal, sociological, cultural, and philosophical elements in many deaths. Suicide and suicidal behavior cannot be reduced to a single factor. This complexity of causation indicates the necessity of a parallel complexity of approaches to knowledge. Indeed, because suicide is a multifaceted problem, it needs to be understood on several different levels at once. This is equally true of homicide (Allen, 1980) and what presents to us too often in forensics—accidents. Was it a suicide? Homicide? Accident? Natural? We will explore these topics, but we will first discuss suicide in some detail. One, unequivocally, has to know suicide (or homicide, etc.) to understand a suicidal person, even if of a fellow officer (Leenaars, 2010a).

SUICIDE: A FEW OPENING THOUGHTS

Most frequently, people identify external causes (e.g., stress, ill health, being abandoned by the spouse, a demotion) as to why the person killed him/herself. This view is too simplistic, although often the suicidal person holds that perspective. This is not to suggest that a recent traumatic event (e.g., a divorce, a traumatic brain injury [TBI]) cannot be identified in many suicides. However, although there are always situational aspects in every suicidal act, they are only one aspect of the complexity, which we hope to demonstrate in this book.

Suicide is a multidimensional malaise (Shneidman, 1985). Suicide is not a sin. Suicide is not a crime. (It has been decriminalized in most of the world.) Within the larger frame of the ecological model, at the individual level, suicide is seen as a state of being, a human malaise. Malaise, according to the OED is "a condition of . . . discomfort, . . . a feeling of uneasiness." Malaise is PAIN. It is the deepest despair. There are biological, psychological, intrapsychic, logical, conscious and unconscious, interpersonal, sociological, cultural, and philosophical/existential elements in the suicidal pain, to name a few.

Any element of the malaise is a legitimate avenue to understanding suicide. Studies of serotonin have a place. Studies of culture have a place. Studies of the effect of gun control have a place. In fact, we oppose any reductionistic model in understating suicide. Suicide is a multifaceted event and is open to study by multiple disciplines. Herein we offer a psychological/psychiatric perspective. Let us begin with Shneidman's (1985) arboreal image to understand suicide. He wrote,

> An individual's biochemical states, for instance, are the roots. An individual's method of suicide, the contents of the suicide note, the calculated effects on the survivors and so on, are the branching limbs, the flawed fruit, and the camouflaging leaves. But the psychological component, the problem solving choice, the best solution of the perceived problem, is the main "trunk." (pp. 202–203)

From a psychological point of view, we would like to offer a few observations on the question, "why?"

DEFINITION OF SUICIDE

Understanding begins with definition. Briefly defined, suicide is the human act of self-inflicted, self-intentioned cessation (Shneidman, 1973b). Suicide is not a disease (although there are many who think so); it is not a biological anomaly (although biological factors may play a role in some suicides); it is not an immorality (although it has often been treated as such); and it is not a crime in the United States, Canada, and most countries around the world (although it was for centuries).

Suicide may today be defined differently depending on the purpose of the definition—medical, legal, administrative, and so on. In the United States and Canada (and most of the countries reporting to the World Health Organization [WHO]), suicide is defined (by a medical examiner or coroner) as one of the four possible modes of death. An acronym for the four modes of death is NASH: natural, accidental, suicidal, and homicidal. This fourfold classification of all deaths has its problems. The major deficiency is that it treats the human being in a Cartesian fashion, namely, as a biological machine rather than appropriately treating him or her as a motivated, intentional, biopsychosocial organism, That is, it obscures the individual's intentions in relation to his or her own cessation and, further, completely neglects the contemporary concepts of psychology regarding intention, including unconscious motivation.

The topic of the definition of suicide was the focus of an entire book by Edwin S. Shneidman (1985). Shneidman's book, *Definition of Suicide*, can be seen as a necessary step to more effective understanding and prevention of suicide. In the book, Shneidman argued that we desperately need a clarification of the definitions of suicide—definitions that can be applied to needful persons. He defined suicide as "Currently in the Western world, suicide is a conscious act of self-induced annihilation, best understood as a multidimensional malaise in a needful individual who defines an issue for which the suicide is perceived as the best solution" (p. 203).

We will be using Shneidman's definition here.

The two giants in the field of suicidal theorizing at the turn of the 20th century were Emile Durkheim (1858–1917) and Sigmund Freud (1856–1939). In *Suicide* (1897/1951) Durkheim focused on society's inimical effects on the individual, while Freud, eschewing the notions of either sin or crime, gave suicide back to the intentional man, but put the locus of action in man's unconscious. Since around 1900 a host of psychological theories aside from Freud's have focused on the individual; for example, those of Alfred Adler, Ludwig Binswanger, Carl G. Jung, George Kelly, Karl Menninger, Henry A. Murray, Edwin Shneidman, Harry Stack Sullivan, and Gregory Zilboorg, to name some of the best known (Leenaars, 1988). I first made the list, with Dr. Edwin Shneidman as my consultant to the roster, in the mid 1970s to early 1980s. From a 2016 perspective, there would be obvious additions. I would add, at least, Aaron T. Beck and David Lester, who reported a social-learning worldview. I will discuss Beck and Lester's theories in more detail below. These suicidologists have given us a rich history to understand suicide; thus, we will use the 10 suicidologists' theories to understand suicide better.

INTENTIONAL, SUBINTENTIONAL, AND UNINTENTIONAL

Freud (1901/1974), Shneidman (1963), Murray (1967), and others have specu-lated that beyond intentional suicides, there is a vast array of subintentional inimical behavior. The very lifestyle of some people, for example, seems to truncate and demean their life so that they are as good as dead. For example, a person, who drives his car recklessly against traffic may be seen through these lenses. In 1901, Freud stated,

> It is well known that in the severe cases of psychoneurosis instances of self injury are occasionally found as symptoms and that in such cases suicide can never be ruled out as a possible outcome of the physical conflict . . . many apparently accidental injuries that happen to such patients are really instances of self-injury. (pp. 178–179)

Freud further notes that such self-destruction is not rare. Often alcoholism, drug addiction, mismanagement of guns, unnecessary high-speed racing of a car, and masochistic behavior can be seen in this light (Farberow, 1980; Murphy, 1992). In this volume we will explore the many faces of suicide and death, as it is necessary in investigating and determining any mode of death (natural, accident, suicide, and homicide [NASH]).

A related concept is "subintentioned death" (Shneidman, 1963). This concept asserts that there are many deaths that are neither clearly suicidal nor clearly accidental nor, for that matter, natural. These are deaths in which the decedent played some covert or unconscious role in "permitting" his or her death to occur, either "accidentally" or by "inviting" homicide, or by unconsciously disregarding what could be a life-extending medical regimen and thus dying sooner than "necessary." Freud (1901/1974) speculated,

> Anyone who believes in the occurrence of half-intentional self-injury—if I may use a clumsy expression—will be prepared also to assume that in addition to consciously intentional suicide there is such a thing as half-intentional self-destruction (self-destruction with an unconscious intention), capable of making skillful use of a threat of life and of disguising it as a chance mishap. (pp. 180–181)

An important aspect of the issue at hand is that suicide is an intentional act. As Litman (1984) noted,

> The concept, which defines a death as suicide rather than an accident, is intention. For example, we assume that when a man shoots himself in the head with a gun, he intended to die. Therefore the death was a suicide. However, if in fact, he intended to survive, for example, if he thought the gun was not loaded, the death was accidental. (p. 88)

Thus, the concept that defines a suicide is intention. Suicidal intent can be defined as "understanding the physical nature and consequences of the act of self-destruction" (Nolan, 1988, p. 53). There is an understanding of the finality of the self-directed violence. What is the person's intention relating to his or her being dead? The verb "to intend" means to contemplate, to plan, to purpose. The noun, "intention" indicates a psychological exertion for a purpose, to an end (Litman, 1988). Intention is/was critical; in suicide, there must be intention to die. The person has, in his/her mind, the intent to be lethal. Litman (1988) stated, "The concept of suicide requires that the self-destructive action has, for at least one of its purposes or goals, the death of the person" (p. 71). Litman further stated,

> The concept "intentional" signifies to me that the individual in question understood, to some degree, his or her life situation and also understood, to some degree, the nature and quality of the self-destructive action (the proposed action representing to some degree, in the person's mind, killing one's self as a solution to the life situational problem). (p. 72)

Litman (1988) further noted,

> In suicide, a person has it in mind to end a distressing life situation by a self-destructive act, which carries a known predictability for causing death. Death is understood, in the mind of the person, as an end to his or her earthly existence. *When one's own death is being used instrumentally to solve life's problems, we are talking about suicide.* (author emphasis, p. 71)

Thus, the person who intends to die, by Litman's definition, would have to understand the finality of the act. A common question, often asked by people is, "How is suicide intent determined?" The question actually is "How can you reach an opinion about what was in the mind of a person who is now dead?" Of course it would be best to ask a person what he or she intended and/or understood; yet in all cases of suicide, we cannot. As Nolan (1988) stated, "Since the suicide victim is dead and unavailable for direct inquiry as to his intention, professionals charged with making such determinations have developed the standard investigatory technique now known as a psychological autopsy" (p. 56).

Litman (1988) makes the further obvious point about intention even in living people. He stated,

> Unfortunately, absolute certainty about human intentions is seldom achieved even with the living, including our patients, colleagues, and families. We constantly act upon our own evaluations of others' intentions based upon their verbal communications, their behaviors, their previous track records and the social context. (p. 78)

This is what a psychological retrospective study, a psychological autopsy (PA), does; it is "an excellent window for viewing and understanding intention" (Litman, 1988, pp. 78–79). We will discuss this topic in detail in a later chapter. The PA is a window into what the suicidal person had in mind.

As noted earlier, there are exclusions in any argument of intentionality. The most frequent exclusion is the question of "sane or insane." Suicide is an intentional, self-directed act, and many insane people—not all—cannot commit suicide since that person lacks "the requisite mental capacity to form intent to commit suicide" (Nolan, 1988, p. 52). There are insane people who kill themselves who do not understand the finality of the act. There are individual differences. Litman (1988) offers the example of a man who climbed into a lion's area of a zoo under the delusion that he was a biblical prophet with lion-taming powers, but the lion killed him. Often, there is no evidence that the person who died by suicide was insane, but we do know of some cases.

There are further exclusions, such as whether the person's blood alcohol level is at a significant level that would impair that person's ability to understand his or her act. Drug intoxication can be the same. Yet again they rarely apply. Suicide is an intentional act of self-directed violence.

Litman (1984) provides further striking insights on the topic and is a must read. The case of the actor Freddie Prinze is an example in point, Litman stated. Freddie Prinze shot himself in the head one night with his manager present. Mr. Prinze had called several people, stating, "I'm going to do it." He wrote a note in which he stated, "No one is responsible." The question here was, even if he left a note, was the death intentional? A few other facts were critical, according to Litman. Freddie Prinze was a drug user and had used drugs that night, and he often played with guns, often mimicking shooting himself. The decision, at least for insurance purposes, in that case was that he did not intend to kill himself. To conclude, the question to determine the mode of death as a suicide is, did the person intentionally kill him/herself?

Therefore, we are well advised to keep the concept of intentional, subintentional, and unintentional in mind, especially in forensic cases (Litman, 1988). For example, what was the intent of shooter Major Nidal Malik Hasan at the Soldier Readiness Center of Fort Hood, Texas, on November 5, 2009? He killed 13 people and wounded 30 more. No one predicted that trauma (and the deadly aftershocks). What was his intent? Did he intend homicide-suicide? Did he intend to be a martyr? Why would a major act that way? The courts decided that he indeed intended murder (Leenaars, 2013).

SUICIDE FACTS AND MYTHS

Lore about suicide contains a large number of interesting and esoteric items. People in general are not only perplexed and bewildered by self-destructive behavior, but they also believe a number of misconceptions about suicide. Here are some common fables and facts about suicide, formulated at his kitchen table by Shneidman around 1952 and incorporated into a number of publications (Shneidman & Mandelkorn, 1967):

1. Fable: People who talk about suicide don't commit suicide.
   Fact: Of any 10 persons who kill themselves, 8 have given definite warnings of their suicidal intentions.
2. Fable: Suicide happens without warning.
   Fact: Studies reveal that the suicidal person gives many clues and warnings regarding suicidal intentions.
3. Fable: Suicidal people are fully intent on dying.
   Fact: Most suicidal people are undecided about living or dying, and they "gamble with death," leaving it to others to save them. Almost no one commits suicide without letting others know how they are feeling.
4. Fable: Once a person is suicidal he or she is suicidal forever.
   Fact: Individuals who wish to kill themselves are suicidal only for a limited period of time.

5. Fable: Improvement following a suicidal crisis means that the suicidal risk is over.

   Fact: Most suicides occur within about 3 months following the beginning of "improvement," when the individual has the energy to put his morbid thoughts and feelings into effect.

6. Fable: Suicide strikes much more often among the rich; or, conversely, it occurs most exclusively among the poor.

   Fact: Suicide is neither the rich person's disease nor the poor person's curse. Suicide is very "democratic" and is represented proportionately among all levels of society.

7. Fable: All suicidal individuals are mentally ill, and suicide always is the act of a psychotic person.

   Fact: Studies of hundreds of genuine suicide notes indicate that although the suicidal person is extremely unhappy, he or she is not necessarily mentally ill.

ATTEMPTED SUICIDE

A previous attempt is one of the best clues to future attempts (Beck, Kovacs, & Weissman, 1975). However, not all previous attempters go on to attempt again (or kill themselves; about 15% do so versus 1.5% for the general population [Leenaars & Lester, 1995; Lester, 1992a]). Although it is obvious that one has to "attempt" suicide in order to commit it, it is equally clear that the event of "attempting suicide" does not always have death (cessation) as its objective. It is acknowledged that often the goal of "attempted suicide" (such as cutting oneself or ingesting large amounts of alcohol) is to change one's life (or to change the behavior of the "significant others" around one) rather than to end it. However, we wish to stress, as have others (e.g., Stengel, 1964; Diekstra, 1996), that it is useful to think of the "attempter" (sometimes referred to as the parasuicide) and the "completer" as two sets of overlapping populations: (a) a group of those who attempt suicide, a few of whom go on to commit it, and (b) a group of those who commit suicide, many of whom previously attempted it. A great deal has to do with *perturbation* and *lethality* associated with the event.

Perturbation refers to how upset (disturbed, agitated, sane-insane) the individual is—rated as low-medium-high (or alternatively on a 1 to 9 scale)—and may be measured by various means (e.g., self-reports, biological markers, psychological tests, observations). Lethality is roughly synonymous with the "deathfulness" of the act and is an important dimension in understanding any potentially suicidal individual. Lethality can be rated as low-moderate-high (or alternatively on a 1 to 9 scale). An example for measuring lethality is the following assessment item, derived from Shneidman (1967): "During the last 24 hours, I felt the chances of my actually killing myself (committing suicide and ending my life) were: absent, very low, low-medium, fifty-fifty, high medium, very high, extra high (came very close to actually killing myself)." A critical distinction in suicide (and often, for that matter, homicide) is that lethality, not perturbation, kills. All sorts of people are highly perturbed but are not suicidal. The ratio between suicide attempts and completions is about 4 to 1 to about 8 to 1—one committed suicide for every 4 to 8 attempts; however, in young people, some reports have the ratio at 50 to 1, even 100 to 1. The ratio, in fact, appears to vary a lot between nations and across risk groups, sex, age, and so on.

CONTEXTUAL OBSERVATIONS

Every investigation needs to recognize the contextual clues; the WHO's ecological model espouses such. Here I can only provide a summary. The keen investigator needs to understand so much more; yet, it is beyond the scope of this book.

From a vast potential list (see Hawton & van Heeringen, 2000), this section consists of six parts, sometimes called contextual clues, focused on clarifying suicide: biological roots, brain dysfunctions (with special reference to traumatic brain injuries), physical disabilities and illness, depression, specific precipitating events, and the family system. Remember, these are the background, the nomothetic ones.

Biological Roots

"No brain, no mind" is one of Henry Murray's, a Harvard psychiatrist, reminders to his student Edwin Shneidman (Shneidman, 2001). Dr. Shneidman's position is best presented in his 1985 book, *Definition of Suicide*. Therein he states his principles (see his Chapter V, "A Formal Definition, with Explication"). He writes, "Suicide is a multifaceted event and that biological, cultural, sociological, interpersonal, intrapsychic, logical, conscious and unconscious, and philosophical elements are present, in various degrees, in each suicidal event" (p. 202).

Stoff and Mann's (1997) edited volume begins to outline some understanding of the neurobiology of suicide. On a critical note, however, one could see Stoff and Mann's view as being too reductionistic. They reduce suicide to only biological roots. Stoff and Mann write,

> Efforts aimed at identifying the potentially suicidal individual using demographic, social developmental and psychological factors offer too weak a prediction to be of substantial clinical utility. It is believed that the biological perspective, which has grown out of the expanding research on the biological basis of mood disorders, is a predominant approach to suicide research. It can assist in the investigation of risk factors that predispose a person to suicidal behavior and that increase understanding of etiology, treatment, and ultimately, prevention." (p. 1)

Utilizing only this view will lead us astray. (A person is not simply a biological anomaly.) Once more, suicide is complex, more complex than most people are aware. It is not only the suicidal brain. It is not only the suicidal mind.

The classical study in suicidology of the biological roots was by Asberg, Traskman, and Thorien (1976). They identified 5-H1 AA in cerebrospinal fluid as a biochemical marker in some suicides. This study marked the beginning of empirical biological suicidology. Yet, although the Asberg study is almost 40 years old, there is relatively little well documented, verified knowledge regarding the neurobiology of suicide today (see Hawton & van Heeringen, 2000).

Despite the state of the knowledge, suicide must be seen as a biological event (and much more). Possible markers isolated to date include urinary 17-hydroxycortico-steroids (17-OHCS), cortisol in plasma and cerebrospinal fluid, cerebrospinal fluid 5-hydroxyindoleacetic acid, tritiated imipramine binding, 3-methoxy-4-hydroxyphenylglycol and homovanillic acid, urinary norepinephrine/epinephrine ratio; and thyroid-stimulating hormone response to thyrotropin-releasing hormone. Slaby (1995) and others (e.g., Maltsberger, 2002) are optimistic about our biological understanding of suicide in the future, especially in the relation of suicide to affective disorders (e.g., bipolar/manic-depressive disorder) and their neurobiological correlates. At least in some suicides, biological correlates may be strikingly relevant.

Brain Dysfunction and Traumatic Brain Injuries

The importance of brain dysfunction and its relation to cognitive deficits, learning disabilities, aggression (violence) regulation, impulsivity, and other abilities, are well documented. The relation of brain dysfunction and socioemotional problems in people is, however, a more neglected topic in the literature. Not only does a cognitive disorder (TBI or learning disability or even Alzheimer's) render a person at risk for socioemotional problems including suicide, but also there are particular subtypes of impairments/disabilities that may result in different levels of suicide risk. As a way of understanding this clue, I cite a brief literature review that comes from the extensive researched subfield on learning disabilities. Of course, there are great differences between sudden acute brain injuries, such as TBIs and long-standing, chronic general learning disabilities (LD). My main point is that it allows us to know the issue of the brain and suicide better.

Byron Rourke was a well-known neuropsychologist; Rourke and Fisk (1981) have documented that different patterns of cerebral dysfunction and their resulting disability(ies) render a person at risk for different types of socioemotional disturbances. They report three major subgroups: The first group has a right-brain dysfunction. These people are prone to learning problems with nonverbal, visual information. They may show the following socioemotional problems: not paying attention to visual objects, including other people; rarely expressing emotions appropriately in their facial expressions; having a voice that can be expressionless; being very talkative; talking to self; having flow problems in speech; and being awkward socially.

The second group has a left-brain dysfunction. These people are prone to learning problems with verbal information. They may show the following socioemotional problems: rarely initiating conversation; having problems paying attention, for example, in conversation; being brief and often concrete in their remarks; often stating "I don't know" to questions; and some are very impulsive, not thinking before they act. The third group has both left and right brain dysfunction and exhibit a conglomerate of symptoms.

Other more specific cerebral deficits render people at risk for other specific problems such as planning, sequencing social events, and so on. Sometimes there are problems in executive functioning (such as mood regulation, thinking before acting, and so on). Attention deficit/hyperactivity disorder (ADHD), in all its subtypes, is an example. There are people, of course, with ADHD, with very high IQs. There are diverse brain dysfunctions, some chronic, while some are acute. The acute may be due to strokes or to recovery after being hit with a bullet in the head in a shootout situation (or in self-inflicted shooting). Although further empirical studies need to be conducted in the neuropsychology of suicides these observations clearly warrant attention. Indeed, Rourke, Young, and Leenaars (1989) have shown that one possible outcome of childhood brain (central processing) deficiencies is suicidal behavior as well as other socioemotional problems, such as depression. They suggested that it is especially the first pattern associated with right-brain dysfunction that predisposes those afflicted to adolescent and adult suicide risk. This can all be true in acute cases of brain trauma in officers. The brain is so critical in risk.

Special Reference to Traumatic Brain Injuries

I must make special reference to traumatic brain injuries (TBI). It may well be a huge suicide risk factor. Too little is known about traumatic brain injury. TBI is the disruption of normal brain functioning that occurs secondary to any number of traumas, including a bump, blow, or jolt to the head or a penetrating head injury (CDC, 2009). Breshears, Brenner, Harwood, and Gutierrez (2010) undertook a study with the U.S. armed forces and note,

> Secondary to injuries sustained by U.S. military personnel in Iraq and Afghanistan, there has been increased focus regarding the assessment and treatment of deployment-acquired TBI, especially mild injuries caused by explosions/blasts (Warden, 2006). Estimates of deployment-acquired TBI range from 15% to 23% (Hoge, Auchterloine, & Milliken, 2008; Terrio, Brenner, Ivens, et al., 2009). Furthermore, there has been growing concern and debate regarding the psychiatric/emotional sequelae that is often associated with TBI in the military population (Hoge, Auchterloine, & Milliken, 2006). (p. 349)

TBIs have been identified as a very significant factor in suicides (Ritchie, 2010). Ritchie (2010) noted that there is a relationship between TBI and suicide. This may answer one of the main questions in a public health approach, "What is the cause(s) of the problem?" There are beginning answers. Yet very little is known about TBIs and suicide risk. Teasdale and Engberg (2001) presented the seminal population-based study on TBI and suicide. They found that the suicide rate among individuals with TBI was 2.7 to 4.1 times higher than that of the general population. Of course, it depended on the nature of the injury. Not all brain injuries or dysfunctions are alike; some present greater risk. Teasdale and Engberg further determined that the clear majority of individuals who attempted suicide postinjury had no history of suicide behavior, such as attempts predating TBI onset. The findings suggest that for at least a subset of TBI patients, injury status has the potential to independently pose increased risk for suicidal behavior (Breshears et al., 2010).

Breshears et al. (2010) in a study, "Predicting Suicidal Behavior in Veterans with Traumatic Brain Injury: The Utility of the Personality Assessment Inventory," published in the *Journal of Personality Assessment*, present one of the best studies to date. The questions were, What measures of psychopathology and suicidality can have functional utility and construct validity with respect to the individuals with a history of TBI and suicide risk? What evidence-based method can be used? Breshears et al. used an archival method. They utilized archival data from 154 veterans of the U.S. military who sustained TBI's. They obtained approval for the study. They note,

> Of the 154 subjects . . . a total of 11 (7.1%) subjects engaged in suicidal behavior within the 2-year follow-up period, and five (45.5%) of these had more than one documented incident, resulting in a mean number of suicidal behavior incidents of 1.8 ($SD = 1.1$). The severity of suicidal behavior among the 11 subjects encompassed highly lethal suicide attempts with injuries and explicit or implicit intent to die as well as suicide attempts without injury and one incident of self-harm behavior with injury (e.g., taking a medically serious overdose of medications reportedly in an attempt to incite hospitalization). (p. 350)

Of course, as stated in this chapter elsewhere, the prediction of suicide and related behaviors is inherently problematic (Miller, 1999; Pokorny, 1983). Yet there are certain risk factors that do suggest increased risk. Probably one of the best risk factors is a previous suicide attempt (Mann, Waternaux, Haas, & Malone, 1999; Rudd, Joiner, & Rajab, 1996; Shneidman, 1985). In Breshears et al.'s (2010) study, the medical archives of 29.25 % of subjects included histories of prior suicidal behavior, and of these, 24.4% engaged in suicidal behavior during the 2-year period. Most important, no soldiers who lacked such histories engaged in suicidal behavior during the 2-year period studied. They concluded that when a patient with a TBI had a history of suicidal behavior, the presence of high levels of psychological distress was associated with increased risk for future suicidal behavior. The risk was greater than that suggested by suicidal behavior alone. The TBIs increased, thus, the risk. The common timeline risk may range anywhere from 3 to 18 months. TBIs are an independent risk factor for suicide. I will go further: I believe a TBI, especially if associated with PTSD, is a very significant risk factor for suicide, both acute and chronic. This risk, I predict, continues throughout life.

Physical Disabilities and Illness

We would be remiss if we did not at least note the importance of physical problems in suicidal behavior in some people (Barraclough, 1986; Marzuk, 1994; Stenger & Stenger, 2000). Physical illness interacts with an individual's emotional functioning; indeed, some illnesses directly affect one's emotions. Empirical study regarding illness and suicide is urgently needed (see Koren, Hilel, Idar, Hemel, & Klein, 2007). Currently, research suggests that some physical illnesses are associated with suicidal behavior, including anorexia, bulimia, diabetes, epilepsy, traumatic brain injury (as we discussed above), and muscular dystrophia (Barraclough, 1986). Menstruation dysfunction and suicide are highly correlated (Dogra, Leenaars, Raintji, Lalwani, Girdhar, Wenckstern, & Lester, 2007; Leenaars, Dogra, Girdhar, Dattugata, & Leenaars, 2009). Some individuals with physical disabilities who are at risk are those with limb amputations or spinal injuries resulting in quadriplegia. Individuals with terminal illness such as AIDS appear also to be at high risk (Marzuk, 1989). However, it is important to realize that not all such people are suicidal and that research is needed to further substantiate these views.

Depression

It was once believed that all suicidal people were depressed, but this is a myth. The fact is that not all suicidal people are depressed and that not all depressed people are suicidal. Depression and suicide are not equivalent. Yet Lester (1992a) has noted that depression distinguishes many suicidal people from nonsuicidal groups. Depression can be noted in mood and behavior (ranging from feeling dejected and hesitancy in social contacts to isolation and serious disturbance of appetite and sleep), verbal expression (ranging from talks about being disappointed, excluded, blamed, etc., to talk of suicide, being killed, abandoned, helpless), and fantasy (ranging from feeling disappointed, excluded, mistreated, etc., to suicide, mutilation, loss of a significant person) (Pfeffer, 1986). Behavior such as excessive aggressiveness, change in work performance, and expressions of somatic complaints or loss of energy have all been associated with depression. However, not all depression is overt; some may be masked or guarded. Some people exhibit what has been termed masked depression. They dissemble. Anorexia, promiscuity, and alcohol abuse, for example, have been associated with depression, but also many other emotional disturbances or behaviors, too many to list. It is important to remember, however, that depression does not equal suicide in a simple one-to-one fashion. Most suicides experience *unbearable pain*—the pain of pain—but not necessarily depression (Shneidman, 1985). The unbearable emotion might be anxiety, despair, shame, guilt, dependency, hostility, hopelessness, or helplessness. Shame and disgrace may be especially unbearable pains. What is critical is that the emotion—pain—is unbearable. *Unendurable psychological pain* is the common stimulus in suicide (Shneidman, 1985), not depression alone. Having said that, depression is an important risk factor in many suicidal people.

Specific Environmental Precipitating Events

A current popular formulation regarding suicide is that suicide is simply due to an external event; for example, a rejection by a lover, the removal of a gun from a police officer, an investigation into sexual harassment, whatever. Of course, like all people, precipitating events (e.g., abuse of alcohol, sexual deviance, being bullied, being raped, divorce, a demotion) do occur in the suicides. That event is often difficult to discern. We are here reminded of a clinical example: A recent veteran was found dead in his car, having died in an intentional motor vehicle accident (MVA). People were perplexed: "Why did this person, a war-decorated soldier, having bravely fought and survived a major Iraq conflict, where many of his friends died, kill himself?" The parents found out that his girlfriend, who had waited years during his active military service, broke off the relationship and rejected him the day of his suicide. That was the reason: when a person gets rejected and is so in love, he may kill himself. A few friends and his old sergeant in the military knew that he had been having problems due to chronic pain from a wound that he suffered in the battle when he lost his friends. That was the reason. A few others knew that his father was an alcoholic and had been abusive during his childhood. That was the reason. His physician knew that he was suffering from posttraumatic stress disorder (PTSD), had not been taking his prescribed medication, and had been recently upset about that ("I'll be in the nut house next.") She knew the real reason. And others knew. I think you understand the message for your death investigation (see Chapter 6).

Shneidman (1985) has noted that the common consistency in suicide is not the precipitating event, but lifelong coping patterns. There are enduring characteristics. People who kill themselves, in fact, experience a steady toll of threat, stress, failure, challenge, and loss that gradually undermines their adjustment process, a dose response. Suicide has a history.

There are, of course, many threats, stresses, and so on in the suicidal person's mind. One further stimulus that has frequently been identified as a possible precipitating event is the death of a well-known (individual or community), much-publicized suicide (media). The discussion raises the issues of the contagion (copycat) effect. For example, in 2013/2014, the Canadian Forces (CF, DND) reported a rate of suicide (per 100,000) below the general population, which sets the community standard for comparison, albeit with serious error (Leenaars, 2013). The general population is then with a *nominal-level of measurement* at 100%. The rate in the CF was reported to be below 100% (in the U.S. soldiers, the suicide rate is now 200%, like the veterans). Yet there have been epidemics (i.e., a rate above normal expected rates and fluctuations [75–95 percentile]). At the end of November of 2013, in the CF, there were three suicides, a cluster. Since the start of the cluster, from November 25, 2013 to February 21, 2014, there were seven Regular Force members who died by suicide! There were three Reserve Force members. That would put the crude rate of suicide in those 3 months at four times the usual rate, so 400%. There was much media attention, contagion, and, I wonder, about copycat phenomena. And there were after wakes. Imagine the number of survivors; if we take a conservative estimate of 10 survivors for each death, that would mean 100 more survivors (I think that in the military culture, the number of survivors is greater than 10. What if the suicide was the Admiral, like Admiral Mike Boorda, who died by suicide on May 16, 1996?). Many years ago, the fine scientist David Phillips (1974, 1986) clearly documented the fact that such cluster suicides do occur in adults, unequivocally. Suicide clusters have, in fact, been reported in the United States, Canada, and across the world. Aside from clustering, the impact of suggestion (or some other dynamic factor) is also seen in the effect of media reporting of suicide. Furthermore, it has been noted that there may be particular characteristics of "contagion" suicides (Brent, 1992; Martin, 1998); yet further nomothetic study is needed. Be that as it may, for DSI practice, we already know that the media plays a role (a fact that suggests that, in a PA, you should look for yourself at the media, such as newspapers).

Family Background

A review of even the early literature and more current (e.g., Berman & Jobes, 1991; Goodyear-Brown, 2012; Hawton & van Heeringen, 2000; Leenaars & Wenckstern, 1991; Pfeffer, 1986; Richman, 1991; Toolan, 1981) suggests that the family system and its functioning is a central factor associated with suicide and suicidal behavior, although by no means do all families show these characteristics—some, none at all. Nevertheless, a few common observations of families can be provided:

1. There is, at times, a lack of generational boundaries in suicidal families. There is an insufficient separation of the parent from his or her family of origin. For example, a parent may take over the role of selecting and even being reinforcing of a career, such as being a police officer, well within adulthood.
2. The family system is often inflexible. Any change is seen as a threat to the survival of the family. Denial, secretiveness, dissembling, and especially a lack of communication characterize the family's interactions. Secrecy is valued and may often be lethal. One 8-year-old boy reported to me, "If I try to kill myself, maybe my dad will listen." Additionally in teenagers, such families have strong discipline patterns and limit setting that binds the individual in his/her identity development, which is critical at this time of a person's life. Parents may interfere in the romantic relationships of their children, even late adolescence.
3. At times, there is a symbiotic parent-child relationship. A parent, usually the mother, is too attached to the child, even the adult-child. Not only is such a relation disturbing, but the parent also does not provide the emotional protection and support that a parent usually provides intuitively to a person as he or she grows. Sometimes the parent treats the child as an "adult." One such teenager tried to break this bond by attempting to kill herself in her mother's prized car, while another (a straight-A student) intentionally obtained a B, resulting in a parent-child conflict and a suicide attempt by the youth. Additionally, it has been noted repeatedly in people that if such a parent dies, the person may kill him/herself to be magically reunited with that same parent.
4. Long-term disorganization (malfunctioning) has been noted in these families, for example, mother or father's control, divorce, domestic violence, alcoholism, or mental illness. In women, there is a very high rate of incest, sexual abuse, and such compared with the general population, and this has also been noted in men. Even in the suicides of adults, and even more so the elderly, these types of disorganization have been observed. One such 74-year-old female tried to kill herself, stating in a note that she had not seen her children for 20 years.

These observations raise further questions. Are the familial/interpersonal factors identified due to psychopathology not suicide risk per se? What are further familial risk factors? Are there observable protective factors? Can a family help? How?

BEHAVIORAL CLUES

In understanding suicide, we need to be aware of behaviors that are potentially predictive of suicide. However, there is no single definitive predictive behavior. The two concepts that have already been discussed, that may be helpful here are lethality and perturbation. The clues below are applicable to all age groups, although the mode of expression may differ depending on age and numerous other factors. We here present a few insights:

Previous Attempts

Although it is obvious that one has to "attempt" suicide in order to commit it, it is equally clear that the event of "attempting suicide" need not have death as its objective. As noted earlier, it is useful to think of overlapping populations: (a) a group of those who attempt suicide, a few of whom go on to commit it, and (b) a group of those who commit suicide, a few who previously attempted it. A previous attempt is a good clue to future attempts, especially if no assistance is obtained after the first attempt. However, not all previous attempters go on to attempt again (or kill themselves). Regrettably, despite the lethality of these risk factors, too frequently such behavior is not taken seriously, or minimized, even covered up by family members. "It was only an accident." Was it? (One has to be cautious about the credibility of one informant).

Verbal Statements

As with behavior, the attitude toward individuals making verbal threats is too frequently negative. Statements are seen as "just for attention." This attitude results in ignoring the behavior of a person who is genuinely perturbed and potentially suicidal. The important question is, "Why this way of getting attention when there are so many other constructive ways?"

Examples of verbal warnings are the following: "I'm going to kill myself" or "If they take my gun, I'll kill myself," both being very direct. Other more indirect examples are the following: "I am going to see my (deceased) mother" or "I give up" or "I can't cope with this stress."

Cognitive Clues

The single most frequent state of mind of the suicidal person is constriction (Hughes & Neimeyer, 1990). There is a tunnel vision, a narrowing of the mind's eye. There is a narrowing of the range of perception or opinions or options that occurs to the mind. Frequently the person uses words like "only," "always," "never," and "forever." The following are examples: "No one will ever love me. Only my wife loved me"; "Sam was the only one who loved me"; "The antigay attitude will always be that way"; and "Either I'll kill the sergeant or myself."

Emotional Clues

The person who is suicidal is often highly perturbed; he or she is disturbed, anxious, perhaps agitated. Depression, as already noted, is frequently evident. Suicidal people may feel boxed in, rejected, harassed, and unsuccessful. Some frequent feelings reported by patients are the following: anger, anxiety, emptiness, loneliness, loss, and sadness. A common emotional state in most suicidal people is hopelessness-helplessness. Statements like the following may signal hopelessness: "Nothing will change. Even my spouse rejected me. It will always be this way." Whereas helplessness may be verbalized as "There is nothing I can do. There is nothing anyone can do to make a difference."

Sudden Behavioral Changes

Changes in behavior are also suspect. Both the outgoing individual who suddenly becomes depressed and isolated and the normally reserved individual who starts being outgoing and drinking more may be at risk. Such changes are of particular concern when a precipitating painful event is apparent. Reckless behavior, such as inappropriate displays of a gun or drinking while driving, may be clues. Making final arrangements such as giving away unusual personal belongings such as a favorite firearm or other possessions may be ominous (but is by no means a common clue, but may be in a specific case, of course). A preoccupation with death, such as reading and talking about death, may be a clue. Some people, indeed, may suffer complicated grief; they do not overcome the loss of the dead person. They may be preoccupied with the death; they often identify with the dead person, and after the death long for, even magically, a reunion. This is especially so after a suicide. The death becomes the stimulus for believing that suicide is a solution, an escape from pain and grief. This loss is probably one of the most frequent common stimuli to suicide around the world. Nonetheless, constructive discussion or grief counseling after a death may not only be helpful for the individual but also essential. Education, a prevention, can help in the healing. There are so many possible behavioral cues and changes, not only about suicide, but also many red flags. One must evaluate the individual case, of course, too, the unique. (Science can only tell us what evidence to look for, not what is in *this* suicide.)

Life-Threatening Behavior

The following are examples of life-threatening behavior often found in suicide. A veteran who had killed himself had previously been seen leaning out of an open window at the VA hospital and at another time playing recklessly with a gun. Following the rejection by his girlfriend, a 24-year-old man died in a single-car accident on an isolated road after having had several similar accidents. A 70-year-old female with detailed knowledge of drugs as a nurse died from drug mismanagement despite the nurse in her residence controlling her medication. Self-destruction is not rare. Often alcoholism, noncompliance with treatment, and inappropriate use of firearms can be seen in this light, as previously discussed (see also Chapter 2).

Suicide Notes

Like previous attempts and verbal statements, suicide notes are important clues; however, they are often read but not listened to by the reader. About 18%–37% (40%) of adults leave notes (samples have varied greatly).

Here is a sample:

1. Adolf Hitler killed himself on April 30, 1945. Hitler is probably one of the great perpetrators of war in history worldwide—World War II. He wrote a last will on the 29th of April. He is believed to have died from a gunshot wound. There is no question in our mind that it is a genuine suicide note:

   As I did not consider that I could take responsibility, during the years of struggle, of contracting a marriage, I have now decided, before the closing of my earthly career, to take as my wife that girl who, after many years of faithful friendship, entered, of her own free will the practically besieged town in order to share her destiny with me. At her own desire she goes as my wife with me into death. It will compensate us for what we both lost through my work in the service of my people.

   What I possess belongs—in so far as it has any value—to the Party. Should this no longer exist, to the State; should the State also be destroyed, no further decision of mine is necessary.

   My paintings, in the collections which I have bought in the course of years, have never been collected for private purposes, but only for the extension of a gallery in my home town of Linz on Donau.

   It is my sincere wish that this bequest may be duly executed.

   I nominate as my Executor my most faithful Party comrade, Martin Bormann. He is given full legal authority to make all decisions.

   He is permitted to take out everything that has a sentimental value or is necessary for the maintenance of a modest simple life, for my brothers and sisters, also above all for the mother of my wife and my faithful co-workers who are well known to him, principally my old Secretaries Frau Winter etc. Who have for many years aided me by their work.

   I myself and my wife—in order to escape the disgrace of deposition or capitulation—choose death. It is our wish to be burnt immediately on the spot where I have carried out the greatest part of my daily work in the course of a twelve years' service to my people.

   Given in Berlin, 29th April 1945, 4:00 A.M.

   [Signed] A. Hitler

2. Kurt Cobain was a very famous, exceptionally talented rock star; his band, Nirvana, invented the grunge sound. Yet he painfully struggled; he had an emotional disturbance (psychopathology). On the 5th of April, 1995, he shot himself. Here is his note:

   To Boddah

   Speaking from the tongue of an experienced simpleton who obviously would rather be an emasculated, infantile complain-ee. This note should be pretty easy to understand.

All the warnings from the punk rock 101 courses over the years, since my first introduction to the, shall we say, ethics involved with independence and the embracement of your community has proven to be very true. I haven't felt the excitement of listening to as well as creating music along with reading and writing for too many years now. I feel guilty beyond words about these things.

For example when we're back stage and the lights go out and the manic roar of the crowds begins, it doesn't affect me the way in which it did for Freddie Mercury, who seemed to love, relish in the the love and adoration from the crowd which is something I totally admire and envy. The fact is, I can't fool you, any one of you. It simply isn't fair to you or me. The worst crime I can think of would be to rip people off by faking it and pretending as if I'm having 100% fun. Sometimes I feel as if I should have a punch-in time clock before I walk out on stage. I've tried everything within my power to appreciate it (and I do, God, believe me I do, but it's not enough). I appreciate the fact that I and we have affected and entertained a lot of people. It must be one of those narcissists who only appreciate things when they're gone. I'm too sensitive. I need to be slightly numb in order to regain the enthusiasms I once had as a child.

On our last 3 tours, I've had a much better appreciation for all the people I've known personally, and as fans of our music, but I still can't get over the frustration, the guilt and empathy I have for everyone. There's good in all of us and I think I simply love people too much, so much that it makes me feel too fucking sad. The sad little, sensitive, unappreciative, Pisces, Jesus man. Why don't you just enjoy it? I don't know!

I have a goddess of a wife who sweats ambition and empathy and a daughter who reminds me too much of what i used to be, full of love and joy, kissing every person she meets because everyone is good and will do her no harm. And that terrifies me to the point to where I can barely function. I can't stand the thought of Frances becoming the miserable, self-destructive, death rocker that I've become.

I have it good, very good, and I'm grateful, but since the age of seven, I've become hateful towards all humans in general. Only because it seems so easy for people to get along that have empathy. Only because I love and feel sorry for people too much I guess.

Thank you all from the pit of my burning, nauseous stomach for your letters and concern during the past years. I'm too much of an erratic, moody baby! I don't have the passion anymore, and so remember, it's better to burn out than to fade away.

Peace, love, empathy.

Kurt Cobain

Frances and Courtney, I'll be at your alter.

Please keep going Courtney, for Frances.

For her life, which will be so much happier without me.

I LOVE YOU, I LOVE YOU!

3. A 21-year-old male soldier had traveled to Detroit to bury his mother, who died by overdose on pills. He wrote,

Mary

I'm sorry I had to do this, but I had no choice. After Mom died, I no longer had any reason to go on. I've just realized it.

I have no future and life is entirely pointless. I've been deceiving myself all along and its time it stopped.

On the train on the way back from Detroit to Fort Bragg, I thought of this. Returning to the stinking Army made me realize al I was doing was wasting another 3 years. And then what was I going to do? Well, there isn't any positive answer.

I love you all very much and was glad you and Sharon and Mike and the kids and I got together.

Love,

Bill

4. Joe Smith, a homicide-suicide. He killed his children and wife, followed by his suicide. Here is his note:

Joe Smith, hold my father-in-law responsible for pressuring me to take the life of my wife and children. He is a killer. He plans and then causes trouble for us. I am taking the life of my wife and children because he is not worth that I should give my children to him.

I said to you that the money is of no use to me. Now, be happy with your money.

You bastard, you are a 3rd class person. You think that only the rich people speak the truth; sometimes you should see what you are doing.

I, Joe Smith, in my full senses, do will the death of my wife, children, and me.

5. A 37-year-old police officer, wanting to kill his sergeant, but killed himself, wrote,

Sergeant:

Goodbye you old prick and when I mean prick you are a prick. Hope you fall with the rest of us, you yellow bastard.

May precinct 25 get along without you.

Based on the discussion thus far, especially contextual observations and behavioral clues, how can these factors help us in investigation of death? However, before we begin to answer these questions, we need to discuss evaluation of risk in general.

INVESTIGATION OF SUICIDE RISK

No one really knows how to assess suicide risk perfectly. This limits your investigation. One of the most frequent questions asked about suicide risk is, How do you assess suicide risk? or more specifically, the question in front of us, How do you assess a person's suicide risk postdictively? Indeed, suicide risk assessment may well be the most complex clinical task that psychiatrists, psychologists, GPs, and other mental health professionals face. The same is true for health professionals working on forensic death cases. What is essential to learn is that assessment and prediction are interwoven with understanding.

In the 1960s and 1970s there was a focus on the prediction of suicide, and suicidologists believed that it would eventually be possible to predict which individuals out of a population would ultimately complete suicide (Beck, Resnik, & Lettieri, 1974). However, it was soon realized that the statistical rarity of suicide and the imperfection of the prediction instruments led to an enormously large number of false positives; so many, in fact, that the prediction instruments were of little use to clinicians or to those planning suicide prevention services (Lester, 1974).

In the 1980s and 1990s, the focus shifted to assessment (Maris, Berman, Maltsberger, & Yufit, 1992; Yufit & Lester, 2005). That is, rather than predicting the future occurrence of suicide in people, the intent was to assess potentially suicidal people in a more general sense, taking into account all of their life experiences, psychological characteristics, and specific contexts, which are relevant to future suicidal behavior (Maltsberger, 1986; Shneidman, 1985). Indeed, it is our belief that prediction and assessment are mutual processes and any separation is an artificial one. They are not separate categories.

Assessment requires clear definition. What is it that we are assessing? This is still true in retrospective investigation. This, as you have learned, is complex. In assessing suicide risk in people, we need to be aware of behaviors that are potentially predictive of suicide. However, there is no such definitive behavior. Suicide is a multidimensional event (Leenaars, 1988; Shneidman, 1980, 1985) and a multiaxal approach would be needed (Meehl, 1986; Millon, Krueger & Simonsen, 2010). Two concepts (which were introduced earlier) that are helpful are *lethality* and *perturbation* (Shneidman, 1973a & b, 1980, 1985, 1993a); they are like glasses that you look through at the data. This is very true in DSI.

The Minnesota Multiphasic Personality Inventory–2 (MMPI–2) is often considered the gold standard of psychological assessment instruments; yet there is no direct basis from the MMPI to assess, let alone predict, suicide risk. It will not assist us. There have been numerous attempts to construct tests for suicide prediction and related phenomena, most meeting with failure. In response to awareness of the inherent difficulties in assessing suicide some years ago, the National Institute of Mental Health (NIMH) of the United States organized a think tank in the assessment of suicidal behavior (Lewinsohn, Garrison, Langhinrichsen, & Marsteller, 1989). To date, it is still the largest review of predictive instruments, to my knowledge. They reviewed all available assessment instruments used to study suicidal behavior. Their conclusion: Few, if any, are useful. Like each clue, each test, by itself, has little utility (Garrison, Lewinsohn, Marsteller, Langhinrichsen, & Lann, 1991). Like each clue, each test, each criterion and such has thus to be placed into the context of a larger array of facts. That is the basis of sound science (and DSI). Maris, Berman, Maltsberger, and Yufit (1992) and Yufit and Lester (2005) made the same conclusion, namely that one could not reduce the richness and diversity of suicide and destructive behavior to the test. Pompili and Tatarelli (2010) offer the same conclusion in an updated evidence-based review. Would one test have solved the unknown, if a suicide? Homicide-suicide? (see section "How Can We Best Understand Suicide?") Therefore, if there is no test to accurately assess and predict suicide in the living person, then there is no definitive test to evaluate suicide in a dead person.

Based on the discussion to this point, I need to bring your attention to the fact that one can show very few behavioral clues and even score at a low level of lethality and still be highly suicidal (see below, Dissembling: Clues to Suicide Reconsidered). Often suicidal people show no clues. We often hear, "No one predicted the suicide," a very common situation. Nonetheless these clues may assist in many cases since a large percentage of people will give out clues; at least 80% in the general population. Of course there is the old problem in forensics (and science): evidence or clues, say a suicide note does not necessarily mean a suicide. There are false positives and true negatives (the real problem) (Leenaars, 1999b).

Comprehensive procedures such as the Thematic Guide for Suicide Prediction (TGSP) (Leenaars, 2004), to be presented later, may prove to be more useful in the future than specific measures, but there are no simple tools for your investigation—and keep in mind that your inquiry is retrospective. You cannot give a test, a questionnaire, or the like to the dead person. (Of course, this is common in all autopsies, to state the obvious.) Furthermore, can you give the same (unreliable) questionnaire to an informant (see Chapter 6)?

The more comprehensive procedures, such as the TGSP, are designed to assess a person's own narratives (stories), what the person says or writes in a suicide note or interview, or Internet writing (e-mails). Despite the need to be cautious, as discussed in detail in Chapter 6, survivors too can help with a retrospective investigation (a psychological autopsy). The TGSP is designed to measure the pain, lethality and perturbation, and the psychology of suicide. Thus, it should be obvious, from a forensic view, that tests should not be used as a single basis or test for suicide assessment, and an investigator, may have little utility for them in an individual death case.

It is likely that no one behavior, including a test score or an interview, will provide all of the information needed to assess suicide. A person's suicide risk could not and cannot be assessed at one time by one test, one interview, or such. Each bit of information (like a test score, an observation) will have to be placed in the context of that person's life. This is true in DSI. It is likely that a number of tests, contextual clues, interviews, and scales will be needed to classify such a complex human behavior as suicide, including retrospectively. No one test or behavior or observation may be the answer. This is not only because of the complexity, but also because of the low base (frequency) rate (Rosen, 1954). There is no one "bump on the head" that will tell us whether a person is (or was) suicidal or not, much less how suicidal that person is (or was). Furthermore, all predictions ultimately depend on the skill of the clinician and, retrospectively, of the investigator. In that sense, suicide evaluation is a task like many others that many of us face: a problem of understanding a number of observations of the same person.

All this pessimism should not be read to mean that no question, no risk questionnaire, no lethality evaluation, and so on, could be used. Besides the TGSP, there are useful measures, such as Beck's Suicide Intent Scale (BSIS) (Beck et al., 1975), Smith's Lethality of Suicide Attempt Rating Scale (LSARS) (Smith, Conroy, & Ehler, 1984), and Shneidman's list of predictive clues among the gifted Terman subjects who died by suicide (Shneidman, 1971). Can they help? I do not know; I think Shneidman's list can. Yet my own Thematic Guide for Suicide Prediction (Leenaars, 2004) has been used in nomothetic (general) study around the world and has helped solve individual forensic cases. The question asked is what scale would help us in forensic death investigation. Can a scale help? To begin to answer these questions, we need a detailed look at theory and suicide.

THEORY AND SUICIDE: A FOREWORD

As a crucial final point of introduction, there are, of course, views that theory should not play a role in understanding suicide. Suicidology should only be tabular and statistical. However, I believe that theory, explicit and implicit, plays a key role in understanding any behavior. Theory is the foundation in science (Kuhn, 1962) (and sound DSI). Newton, Einstein, Freud, Beck, and all great scientists are great because they were theorists. It is only through theory, Edwin Shneidman (1985) once noted, that we will sort out the booming buzzing mess (flux) of experience (William James). In fact, it can be argued that "sciences have achieved their deepest and most far reaching insights by descending below the level of familiar empirical phenomena" (Hempel, 1966, p. 77). Theory may well be in the eye of the beholder (Kuhn, 1962), but it is pivotal in scientific understanding whether one is a researcher, forensic investigator, police officer, or coroner; any of us. There is nothing as useful as good theory. People must make formulations about things to understand them (Husserl, 1907/1973). This does not mean that John Stuart Mill's (1806–1873) set of basic rules for science (and, for that matter, for forensic investigation) have to be abandoned. In his *System of Logic,* Mill (1892/1984) reported a set of canons for inductively establishing causality. These are the Methods of Difference, of Agreement and Difference, of Residues, and of Concomitant Variation. In our study of forensic suicide, for example, Mill's Method of Difference does not need to be abandoned; as we will see, in fact, it will be essential. John Stuart Mill has answered many questions. Thus, it would be wise to borrow the ideas of our leading theorists to answer empirically the question, "Why did the person kill herself? Why did the person kill his spouse, followed by his suicide?" What does psychological theory tell us?

PSYCHOLOGICAL THEORIES OF SUICIDE

The modern era of the psychological study of suicide began around the turn of the 20th century with the investigations of Sigmund Freud (1901/1974, 1909/1974, 1917/1974a, 1917/1974b, 1920/1974, 1921/1974, 1923/1974, 1933/1974, 1939/1974, 1940/1974). Freud's clinical research suggested to him that the root cause of suicide, within a developmental context, was the experience of loss or rejection of a significant, highly cathected object (e.g., a person). In 1920, Freud further developed what he termed a "deeper interpretation" of what leads someone to kill himself after such a loss or rejection. He stated,

> Probably no one finds the mental energy to kill himself unless, in the first place, in doing so he is at the same time killing an object with whom he has identified himself and, in the second place, is turning against himself a death wish which had been directed against someone else. (1920/1974, p. 162)

Freud, eschewing the two popular notions about suicide at the turn of the 20th century—sin and crime—placed the focus of blame on the person; specifically, in the person's unconscious. Since around 1900, there have been a host of psychological theories besides Freud's that have attempted to define suicide. Indeed, a (if not the) major advance in the psychology of suicide in the last century was the development of various models beyond Freud's that have attempted to understand this complicated human act, the most noteworthy of which has been that of Edwin Shneidman.

Here I have decided to present four points of view: psychoanalytic (Freud); cognitive-behavioral (Beck); social learning (Lester); and multidimensional (Shneidman). I hope in some way to clarify the central issue—understanding why people commit suicide. Let me begin with a few remarks by Shneidman on the topic of theory in general.

Shneidman (1985) suggests that a psychological theory regarding suicide begins with the question, What are the interesting common psychological dimensions of committed suicide?—not what kind of people commit suicide. This question, according to Shneidman, is critical, for they (the common dimensions) are what suicide is. Not necessarily the universal, but certainly the most frequent or common characteristics provide us with a meaningful conceptualization regarding suicide.

Most frequently, as mentioned earlier, nonprofessionals identify external causes (e.g., a TBI, being left by a lover, incarceration, etc.) as what is common in suicide. A recent downhill course (e.g., sudden acute alcoholism, loss of job, divorce or separation) can indeed be identified in suicide. However, although there are always situational aspects in every suicidal act, these are only the precipitating events. Suicide is more complex. Suicide, as discussed, is a multidetermined event. How can we understand these psychological complexities? This is a must in any investigation into a death (NASH).

Suicide is an intrapsychic drama on an interpersonal stage. From this psychological view, we can define suicide with the following key concepts and classifications of four suicidal theories: psychoanalytic (Sigmund Freud), cognitive behavioral (Aaron T. Beck), social learning (David Lester), and multidimensional (Edwin Shneidman):

The four perspectives will be presented in the form of concepts or protocol sentences. Protocol sentences are testable hypotheses—short statements stating a truth or concept; a concept expressed tersely in a few telling words. Although protocol sentences may be an "open concept," they must be testable (although some form of specificity is implied for the sentence to be testable). One must be able to determine the truth or falsity of the statement. They should also be subject to the possibility of verification (falsifiability), a must in any court case, of course. The protocol procedure was first introduced by Carnap (1931/1959) and applied in my own research in suicide for over four decades. Protocol sentences (or concepts) are one means of classifying an event.

Psychoanalytic

As I have already mentioned, Sigmund Freud first formulated the psychoanalytic perspective early in the 20th century. Other noteworthy suicidologists in this tradition are Karl Menninger, Henry A. Murray, and Gregory Zilboorg; probably the best current theorist is John T. Maltsberger. Erwin Stengel and Herbert Hendin are other theorists in this camp. Here are some protocol sentences (or concepts) derived from Freud's work.

1. Suicide is motivated by unconscious intentions. Even if the person communicates that he or she has consciously planned to kill him/herself, the focus of the action is in the unconscious.
2. The root cause of suicide is the experience of loss and rejection of a significant highly cathected object (i.e., a person)—the person, in fact, is singly preoccupied with this loss/rejection.
3. The suicidal person feels quite ambivalent. He/she is both affectionate and hostile toward a loss/rejecting person (or some other ideal).
4. The suicidal person is, in some direct or indirect fashion, identifying with a rejecting or lost person. Attachment, based upon an important emotional tie, is the meaning of identification.
5. The suicidal person exhibits an overly regressive attachment—"narcissistic identification"—with the object. He/she treats him/herself as if he/she were reacting to another person.
6. The suicidal person is angry at the object, although the feelings and/or ideas of vengefulness and aggression are directed toward him/herself.
7. The suicidal person turns back upon him/herself murderous wishes/impulses/needs that had been directed against the object.
8. Suicide is a fulfillment of punishment; that is, self-punishment.
9. The suicidal person experiences a sense of guilt or self-criticism. The person develops prohibitions of extraordinary harshness and severity toward him/herself.
10. The suicidal person's organization of experiences is impaired. He/she is no longer capable of any coherent synthesis of his or her experience.

Cognitive Behavioral

The cognitive behavioral (CBT) perspective is most widely associated with Aaron T. Beck and his colleagues (Beck, 1963, 1967, 1976; Beck & Greenberg, 1971; Beck, Beck, & Kovacs, 1975; Beck & Rush, 1978; Beck, Kovacs, & Weissman, 1979; Beck, Rush, Shaw, & Emery, 1979). George Kelly, Albert Ellis, Don Meichenbaum, David Rudd, and Mark Williams are also associated with this view; yet, Beck is the star. Here are 10 protocol sentences deduced from Beck's writings.

1. Suicide is associated with depression. The critical link between depression and suicidal intent is hopelessness.
2. Hopelessness, defined operationally in terms of negative expectations, appears to be the critical factor in the suicide. The suicidal person views suicide as the only possible solution to his/her desperate and hopeless, unsolvable problem (situation).
3. The suicidal person views the future as negative, often unrealistically. He/she anticipates more suffering, more hardship, more frustration, more deprivation, and so on.
4. The suicidal person's view of him/herself is negative, often unrealistically. He/she views him/herself as incurable, incompetent, and helpless, often with self-criticism, self-blame, and reproaches against the self (with expressions of guilt and regret) accompanying this low self-evaluation.
5. The suicidal person views him/herself as deprived, often unrealistically. Thoughts of being alone, unwanted, unloved, and perhaps materially deprived are possible examples of such deprivation.
6. Although the suicidal person's thoughts (interpretations) are arbitrary, he/she considers no alternative, accepting the validity (accuracy) of the beliefs.
7. The suicidal person's thoughts, which are often automatic and involuntary, are characterized by a number of possible errors, some so gross as to constitute distortion; for example, preservation, overgeneralization, magnification/minimization, inexact labeling, selective abstraction, negative bias.
8. The suicidal person's affective reaction is proportional to the labeling of the traumatic situation regardless of the actual intensity of the event.
9. Irrespective of whether the affect is sadness, anger, anxiety or euphoria, the more intense the affect the greater the perceived plausibility of the associated cognitions.
10. The suicidal person, being hopeless and not wanting to tolerate the pain (suffering), desires to escape. Death is thought of as more desirable than life.

Social Learning

The social learning view has been summarized by Lester (1987a); Albert Bandura and psychologists in the classical (Pavlov) and operant (Skinner) traditions are the best-known theorists of this view. Of late, Marsha Linehan is the best-known theorist in this tradition, with a CBT twist, the dialectical-behavioral view, I think. Others are Thomas Joiner and Roy Baumeister. The 10 concepts of this paradigm are as follows:

1. Suicide is a learned behavior. Childhood experiences and forces in the environment shape the suicidal person and precipitate the act.

2. Child-rearing practices are critical, especially the child's experiences of punishment. Specifically, the suicidal person has learned to inhibit the expression of aggression outward and simultaneously learned to turn it inward upon oneself.
3. The suicide can be predicted on the basic laws of learning. Suicide is shaped behavior—the behavior was and is reinforced in his/her environment.
4. The suicidal person's thoughts provide the stimuli; suicide (response) is imagined. Cognitions (such as self-praise) can be reinforcements for the act.
5. The suicidal person's expectancies play a critical role in the suicide—he/she expects reinforcement (reward) by the act.
6. Depression, especially the cognitive components, is strongly associated with the suicide. Depression goes far toward explaining suicide. For example, depression may be caused by a lack of reinforcement, learned helplessness, and/or rewarded.
7. Suicide can be a manipulative act. Others reinforce this.
8. Suicide is not eliminated by means of punishment.
9. The suicidal person is nonsocialized. He/she has not been sufficiently socialized into traditional culture. The suicidal person has failed to learn the normal cultural values, especially toward life and death.
10. The suicide can be reinforced by a number of environmental factors, for example, subcultural norms, suggestions on television, gender preferences for specific methods, suicide in significant others (modeling), a network (system) of family and friends, cultural patterns.

Multidimensional

The psychologist who has consistently argued for a multidimensional view is Shneidman (1967, 1973a & b, 1980, 1981, 1982a, 1985, 1991, 1993a—see Leenaars, 1999a). The other famous wisdom keepers in the tradition are Norman Farberow and Robert Litman. I would put my own evidence-based theory in this camp. It has also been called, an "ecological model." Here is a brief summary, utilizing our previous procedure, of Shneidman's work.

1. The suicidal person is in unbearable psychological pain. The person is focused almost entirely on this unbearable emotion (pain), and especially one specific (an arbitrarily selected) way to escape from it.
2. The suicidal person experienced a situation that is traumatic (e.g., poor health, rejection the spouse, being married to a nonsupportive spouse). What is implied is that some needs are unfulfilled, thwarted, or frustrated.
3. For the suicidal person, the idea of cessation (death, stopping, or eternal sleep) provides the solution. It permits him/her to resolve the unbearable state of self-destructiveness, disturbance, and isolation.
4. By the suicide, the person wishes to end all conscious experience. The goal of suicide is cessation of consciousness, and the person behaves in order to achieve this end.

5. The suicidal person is in a state of heightened disturbance (perturbation), for example, he/she feels boxed in, rejected, harassed, unsuccessful, and especially hopeless and helpless.
6. The suicidal person's internal attitude is ambivalence. The suicidal person experiences complications, concomitant contradictory feelings, attitudes, and/or thrusts (not only toward him/herself and other people but toward the act itself).
7. The suicidal person's cognitive state is constriction (tunnel vision, a narrowing of the mind's eye). He/she is figuratively intoxicated or drugged by his/her overpowering emotions and constricted logic and perception.
8. The suicidal person needs or wishes to egress. He/she wants to leave (the scene), to exit, to get out, to get away, to be gone, not to be around, to be "elsewhere"—not to be.
9. There is a serial pattern to the suicide. The suicidal person exhibits patterns of behavior that diminish or truncate his/her life, which subtract from its length or reduce its scope.
10. The person's suicide has unconscious psychodynamic implications.

To summarize, suicide is best understood as a multidimensional human event. What we have discovered so far is that suicide can be defined differently from various psychological theories. I do not mean to suggest that all these views are mutually exclusive or equally accurate or helpful. Some are clinically based theories, such as Freud or Shneidman's. Beck's is probably the most researched schema. We will next turn to a theory more in line with our discussion of what science is. It follows, among other individuals, Paul Meehl's ideas. We must have an evidence-based theory. But what is science? What does the investigator need to know before we can discern a good theory?

HOW CAN WE BEST UNDERSTAND SUICIDE?

Humans need to make meaning of things. It is a necessity. We not only want to understand but we need to. This is true about the topic that presents itself, suicide. The search for meaning is not new. We have developed reliable and useful theories and classifications long before modern science. Only science has done it better; the thought and logic is evidence based. There has been enormous value in developing explicit definition and methods (Millon, 2010; Millon et al., 2010). This systematic effort takes enormous time, not a few minutes of speculation. It has been worth the effort, and this is true in suicidology.

Thus, from science, what procedures have been most reliable and useful? What procedures, as opposed to the common everyday thoughts and methods, are best? There is an infinite number of ways. There are observations and sometimes controversies (Leenaars, 2006; Millon, 2010). There is much confusion to avoid. As Shneidman (1985) argued, the process of definition, and I would add, classification, are indispensable. Is that possible for suicide? Can we apply the scientific method to our topic? Suicide is complex and multidetermined. It is inexact. The classic writings of Hempel (1966) and Meehl (1978) are indispensable. I believe that our efforts in definition and classification in suicidology will be most fruitful in the future.

Let me ask the fundamental question: *Is it possible to understand suicide?* Is there logic that we can use? Is there evidence? Facts? Are there useful psychological experiences (e.g., pain levels, cognitions, behaviors, affects) that cluster together? Do they occur together; are there commonalities? Do they make sense? Do they make sense as clusters or patterns? Are they consistencies over time? Sex? Age? Culture? To answer these questions, calls for careful study.

The main problem at hand is that suicidology at the individual level is intrapsychic (i.e., existing or taking place within the mind or psyche). It is about intentionality. These mental processes are hidden and sometimes masked. Yet these introspective aspects have been for millennia central in defining and categorizing suicide. It is the unobservable process that results in the final act. The person intends to be dead. For example, if a clinical psychologist interviews a suicidal person, and the person, during the assessment, makes some statements, such as "I'm depressed all the time," "The pain is unbearable," and "I want to end it all," how would the psychologist classify the content, the patient's protocols. She/he needs to make meaning of the statements. The investigator wants to understand, predict, and control. The question is, Is the statement a particular or specific instance of a classification, say "depression" or "unbearable pain"? The psychologist will want to make observable observations, both subjective and objective. Of course, the trick in this difficult business is the question of how the specific instance fits into a more abstract classification. The psychologist, like all investigators, must make judgments about whether the content of a protocol is understandable within a given classification. The knack in suicide risk evaluation is concluding "yes" or "no." This, in fact, may well be the most difficult task that an investigator faces.

In science, intrapsychic concepts are known as "open concepts" (Millon, 2010; Pap, 1953). Like any concept, they must, however, be defined by some reliable and meaningful, albeit diverse, empirical facts or events. For example, the concept of *unbearable psychological pain* may be assessed by the person's own story, his penultimate note, a score on a psychology test, a history of previous attempts, a TBI, reckless behavior, and so on. Although the term *unbearable pain* of a person cannot be observed directly, it can be inferred and verified. One can conclude intentionality (see earlier discussion of Robert Litman's most insightful definition and classification on intention and suicide).

Of course, there are some people who object to terms like *unbearable pain*. It cannot be touched. It is not like water. Therefore, it does not exist; and if it did, it is background noise or surplus meaning. They argue that our science of suicidology is muddled. Of course, there are confusions, and problems; yet that is not a reason for eschewing a better empirical effort. One will, however, not be able to do it perfectly.

Open concepts have meanings with reference to theory—a theoretical network of variables and clusters. Absolute anchoring or verifying is not possible. At our current stage of knowledge on suicide, we still need creative methods. The very nature of our topic makes it so—we need open concepts (Millon, 2010; Shneidman, 1985).

What data from the stream of events and processes ought to be studied? What are the restrictions? "Is everything grist for the taxonomic mills?" (Millon, 2010, p. 153). What structural schema should we use to organize the elements of the event? Should we use formal statistical techniques such as empirically based clusters? Or should we just use clinical speculation?

Suicide has been studied from many vantage points. It has been legitimately defined and studied in different ways by psychiatrists, psychologists, criminologists, sociologists, anthropologists, and so on. No one person has the whole event. No observation or classification encapsulates all the complexities and multidimensional factors of suicide (Shneidman, 1985). There will be debates; yet it is also possible, if we classify the attributes in a taxa or commonality or pattern in clear and distinct ways. Or, to put it simply, if we have a suicidal patient, say Kurt Cobain, can two experts conclude the same risk? This is the question of replication. Can the two investigators classify the protocols and conclude the same: that is, Kurt Cobain's death was a suicide? If not, then we have a problem.

What elements must be chosen? How must they be classified? There are different formulations; yet I believe that multidetermined or multiaxal models offer the best fit. Suicide cannot be classified like SARS or cholera. In the infectious-disease (medical) model, we just observe, identify cases, disentangle confounders, and identify the cause. If only it were that simple! The disease model is too limited. Suicide is a multiaxal event. We need an ecological model. To quote Millon (2010): "The multiaxal structure aligns many of the potential relevant factors that can illuminate the nature of a clinical condition, and produce a means of registering their distinguishing attributes" (p. 160).

Thus, it should not be a surprise that defining suicide and assessing risk is demanding and often difficult. Schemas of unitary elements are a wishful fantasy. One cannot use Occam's razor. Complex systems or models, and thus, explorations are needed. This makes it more demanding. It requires a wide array of evidence or protocols and a great deal of forensic judgment. The task is more complex than most medical doctors and forensic investigators are accustomed to. The usual efficiency approach is useless and lethal. The task is more complex than often performed—it is not simply taking a sample of bodily fluids.

The question about suicide is how good are our schemas, generalizations, and classifications? Suicide is not a homogenous group. It is not like water (i.e., all water freezes at 32° Fahrenheit). It is not like copper (i.e., all copper conducts electricity). It is complex to classify, yes or no; however, it is also not as heterogeneous as "white things," few generalizations can be made. How do you classify then? People with similar expressions of suicide risk are neither like water nor white things. Regrettably, there are some who have attempted to classify suicide with robust generalizations, as if it were water or copper. There are even manuals and cookbooks to do so. Kendler and Zachar (2008) attributed this to the core belief that we, despite other scientists' good efforts before, have now finally classified suicide successfully. The belief is that the theorists before were wrong; we are the best and have found the truth. They attribute great authority to a reductionist manual.

And a further point on this issue: Good classification systems require more than discussing facts or evidence; it also requires that we make decisions based on our culture and values (Zachar & Kendler, 2010). However, these are issues beyond the scope of this book; it would need a whole volume itself, even for the forensic investigator. Shneidman (1985) and Meehl (1993) have both cautioned us to adopt the ethic of being cautious—don't jump to conclusions and don't put things in a nutshell.

HOW CAN WE BE MORE VALID?

One approach to validation, introduced by Paul Meehl in the 1950s, is called "construct validation" (Cronbach & Meehl, 1955). This method is based on the rigor of empiricism (Ayer, 1931/1959; Carnap, 1931/1959). Construct validation is a development of that philosophy. People like A. J. Ayer, espoused strict operationalism. That is, operationalists believe that abstract or open concepts had to be explicitly defined in terms of observable data. The methodology had to be empirically explicit (100%) and replicable (100%). For example, water freezes at 0° Celsius. Paul Meehl's genius lay in questioning the absolute commitment to operationalism. (Is that possible with suicide?). It is not that we should throw out Ayer or Carnap's operationalism; rather, it has to be developed for complex open concepts, such as intrapsychic, intention, and suicide. As we have learned more about associations and patterns to suicide, such as drawn up by Edwin Shneidman, we discovered that unbearable pain is associated with other elements such as depression or vulnerability, and for that matter to the interpersonal realm. Suicide and any construction must be explicitly defined, said Meehl (1978, 1986, 1990) by observable events, but implicitly defined in terms of other constructs. (Shneidman did this clinically in the field of suicidology.) Beyond the observable, there are theoretical constructs, such as "unbearable pain." In Meehl's evolved empiricism, pain is construed realistically, not instrumentalistically—in the practical, it is not simply, "Please fill out this suicide questionnaire"or "Give me some bodily fluids."

Ayer and Carnap would argue that a theoretical term like *unbearable pain* is a verbal label to what is being measured (Zachar & Kendler, 2010). For Meehl, it is more. Take Peter Zachar and Kenneth Kendler's example of "depression"—one can simply insert "unbearable pain" for every instance of "depression." They write,

> The goal is to use the measure to infer observable consequences; for Meehl the primary objective of scientific interest is the latent variable called "depression," and our measure is considered to be a fallible indicator of that latent construct. Different measures of depression are conceptualized to be assessing the same thing, but each one is at best a partial measure. Observable evidence is used to triangulate on the construct and better understand its full nature.
>
> Applied to psychiatric classification, the diagnostic criteria for mood disorders are also fallible indicators. Each indicator samples only a part of the domain of depression, and they all work better together to represent the whole domain. These indicators can be assessed for diagnostic validity, but the construct of depression cannot be reduced to its indicators (Zachar & Kendler, 2010, p. 138).

Although some characteristics or elements in suicide may be considered poor criteria, say vulnerable ego or mental constriction, because they are muddled, they are essential. One cannot be a literalist; it is all too complex.

The construct validation approach is an evolution of empiricism, notably of the operationalists. It is a revision. Zachar and Kendler (2010) write,

> One of the things the revised empiricism focused on was laws (Feigl, 1970; Hempel, 1966). Laws describe patterns or regularities in nature that must occur. Knowing about the regularities allows one to predict what will occur, and also to explain why events did occur.
>
> An example of a law is "All copper conducts electricity." If the law is valid, then whenever presented with an individual piece of copper, we know that it has to conduct electricity. This law-like or "nomological" approach to science would seek to confer on "Bill will respond to treatment X because he has schizophrenia" the same degree of certainty that we attribute to statements such as "This metal will conduct electricity because it is copper." Conducting electricity and responding to treatment X would be lawful consequences of the physical nature of copper and schizophrenia.
>
> In this tradition, a theory is considered to be an interconnected network of theoretical terms and observations. Laws and hypotheses relate observations to theoretical terms. Laws also relate theoretical terms to each other. The whole edifice is called a "nomological" network. (p. 139)

For example, on our topic, written expressions, such as in a suicide note, might be associated to theoretical constructs such as unbearable pain, aggression, and helplessness-hopelessness, which are then associated to an even more abstract open concept, namely, suicidality or suicidal risk. Can we find our laws? I believe that we can. Only through careful research can we find some of the similarities or patterns, or what Edwin Shneidman called "commonalities." We can then use the constructs to understand a case and even predict imminent risk. For example, we might predict imminent risk if, for example, a soldier wrote in his note, "It will always be this way. The sergeant will never change. He will never accept that I'm gay. There is nothing I can do except kill the sergeant and myself."

It is all about verification, finding evidence that supports a theory or schema—the various associations or patterns (Cronbach & Meehl, 1955). Of course, there are different kinds of validity, such as predictive and concurrent, which are important. In addition, there are further strategies for testing theories in a logical empirical way (see Cronbach & Meehl, 1955, and Meehl, 1986).

One further point: Meehl (1986, 1990) thinks that the relationship between observation/evidence and a theory is complicated. And this has implications for not only understanding and predicting suicide, but also controlling it. There will always be alternative constructions, thus, it may be wise to start with different points of view on our topic.

How have different and diverse psychological theories come into being? Traditionally, the main classifications have been a product of clinical experience (Menninger, 1963; Shneidman, 1985). Some respected clinicians and scholars, such as Karl Menninger, Sigmund Freud, Aaron Beck, and Edwin Shneidman, have developed theories of suicide. Until recently, suicidological taxonomies were based solely on clinical observation—this was true of Freud, Menninger and Shneidman—but not all, such as Beck's. This is not to say that, for example, Freud's ideas are not useful, only that they need to be put to the test. Verification, within Meehl's method (1978, 1986, 1990, 1993), needs to be undertaken. This will result in a better evidence-based theory and thus, a better means of investigating a death (NASH).

Clinically based concepts such as Shneidman's psychache, that of unbearable psychological pain, were sometimes based on years of observations. Dr. Shneidman is a superb clinician, but he was not a quantitative researcher. Shneidman did not have a mathematical mind, nor did Freud (Leenaars, 2010b). Edwin Shneidman's genius lay in clinically laying bare the very qualities that a clinician would see, hear, and deduce among suicidal people. His observations and categories mirrored what he said that he inferred from the suicidal patients. Yet despite the understanding, it might have led future suicidologists away from pursuing more useful empirical schemas.

Presenting suicidal patients similarities or common factors is useful, and I believe that making them empirical has an even greater advantage. Of course, 50 years ago, Shneidman did not have the advantage of the abilities of today's computers; in fact, although he owned one, he never used it as a computer, only as a typewriter. Computers have made a huge difference. Empirical approaches today can "combine cases in more subtle ways than a clinician's; combinations of features too complex to grasp intuitively may yield better classifications than simple combinations" (Andreason & Grove, 1982, p. 45).

Either you are an empiricist or not! And what is best for your investigation?

There have been rapid developments in mathematical techniques; we can analyze and synthesize vast bodies of data, say for example, thousands of suicide notes. There is a growing body of methods. Millon (2010) writes,

> This growing and diverse body of quantitative methods can be put to many uses, of which only a small number are relevant to the goal of taxonomic construction. Some statistical techniques relate to the validation of existent nosologies (e.g., discriminant analysis) rather than to their creation. Among those used for taxonomic development, some focus on clinical attributes as their basic units, whereas patients themselves are the point of attention for others (Grove & Tellegen, 1991). For example, factor analysis condenses initially diverse sets of clinical attributes and organizes them into potential syndromic taxa. Cluster analysis, by contrast, is most suitable for sorting patient similarities into personological taxa. (Millon, 2010, p. 166)

I have strongly argued for almost four decades that cluster analysis is most suitable for discerning suicide commonalities. Of course, questions remain. Do our cluster algorithms mirror the natural structure of suicidality? Are they better than the traditional clinical categories? Is the evidence that we have more accurate and replicable? Is it useful in our predictions? Do they have applicability and implications for police or investigators? If so, what are they?

Clinicians, of course, have been lukewarm to empirical classifications. Like Shneidman, they have been skeptical about the value of clustering. Shneidman, in fact, wondered if it helped at all (Leenaars, 1999a).

Allow me to quote Theodore Millon (2010) again—a scholarly clinician whom I had the pleasure of meeting years ago:

> In the early stages of knowledge, the categories of a classification rely invariably on observed similarities among phenomena (Tversky, 1977). As knowledge advances, overt similarities are discovered to be an insufficient, if not false, basis for cohering categories and imbuing them with scientific meaning (Smith & Medin, 1981). As Hempel (1965) and Quine (1977) have pointed out, theory provides the glue that holds a classification together and gives it both its scientific and its clinical relevance. In Hempel's (1965) discussion of classificatory concepts, he wrote that the development of a scientific discipline may often be said to proceed from an initial "natural history" stage . . . to subsequent more and more "theoretical" stages. . . . The vocabulary required in the early stages of this development will be largely observational. . . . The shift toward theoretical systematization is marked by the introduction of new, "theoretical" terms . . . more or less removed from the level of directly observable things and events.
>
> These terms have a distinct meaning and function only in the context of a corresponding theory. (pp. 139–140)

As Hempel (1965) stated, mature sciences progress from an observationally based stage to one that is characterized by abstract concepts and theoretical systemizations. (Millon, 2010, p. 167)

I hope to meet Hempel's challenge (I first read Hempel's book as a graduate student and have never underestimated his influence on my science).

A theoretically anchored taxonomy or schema allows one to generate greater insight, and thus, better investigation. One cannot be free of theory. Those who claim to have eschewed theory are naïve. Probably unknowingly, they have given primacy to direct observation, a test score, or a biological anomaly. No one today defends strict operationalism (well, maybe a few).

Allow me one more question and to quote Theodore Millon (2010) once more:

> What distinguishes a true theoretically-based taxonomy from one that merely provides an explanatory summary of known observations and inferences? Essentially, the answer lies in its power to generate new attributes, relations, or taxa—that is, ones other than those used to construct it. This generative power is what Hempel (1961) termed the "systematic import" (p. 6) of a scientific classification. (p. 168)

We will allow you to judge the theoretically-based taxonomy to be presented. Does it help you understand? Do you know better why a person kills himself? Does it help you in your search?

AN EVIDENCE-BASED THEORY OF SUICIDE

Theory must begin with definition. Thus, again, let us offer the formal definition of suicide by Shneidman (1985), "Currently in the Western world, suicide is a conscious act of self-induced annihilation, best understood as a multidimensional malaise in a needful individual who defines an issue for which suicide is perceived as the best solution (p. 203).

Suicide is not simply a psychopathological entity in the DSM-IV (American Psychiatric Association, 1994) or DSM-5 (American Psychiatric Association, 2014). (It is actually only cited twice as a behavior; once under Depression and once under Borderline Personality Disorders.) We do not agree with those who point to an external stress as the sole cause of suicide. We also do not agree that it is only pain. We tend to place the emphasis on the multideterminant nature of suicide. Suicide is intrapsychic. It is stress and pain, but not simply the stress or even the pain, but the person's inability to cope with the event or pain. The issue of any schema about human personality is one that makes an individual an individual (Murray, 1938). It should be the study of the whole organism, not only the stress or pain. People do not simply commit suicide because of pain but because it's unbearable; they are mentally constricted; they have a mental/emotional disorder; they cannot cope and so on.

However, from a psychological view, suicide is not only intrapsychic, it is also interpersonal (or stated differently, it is beyond the individual level in the ecological model, it is also relationship(s), community, societal). The suicidal individual is not only depressed, mentally constricted and so on, but he or she is also cut off from loved ones, ideals and/or even the community. The suicidal person is estranged. People live in a world (a society). Individuals are interwoven; the suicidal person, painfully so. We disagree with those who point to only some intrapsychic aspects such as depression, or primitive narcissism to explain suicide. Suicide occurs in a person *and* between people (or some other ideal; e.g., being loved by someone, being healthy). This is not a Descartesian dichotomy; it is rather a dynamic interactional system. Yet the intrapsychic world is figural. Suicide occurs as a solution in a mind. The mentalistic processes are the foreground (such as the pain, depression). This is an important difference. It is in the inner world that a person makes the decision to jump, shoot, and such. It is here that he or she decides, "This is the best solution." To put it simply, no drama, no stage. It is the intersection between the two phenomenologies that is essential to understanding in suicide. It is, for example, not simply loss of a loved one on the stage, but how the person's drama unfolds this very personal, individual stage. Metaphorically speaking, suicide is an intrapsychic drama on an interpersonal stage.

Two concepts, already discussed many times, that have been found to be essential and helpful in understanding the malaise are lethality and perturbation (Shneidman, 1973a & b, 1980, 1985, 1993a). Lethality refers to the probability of a person killing him/herself, and on quantification scales ranges from low to moderate to high. It is a psychological state of mind. Perturbation refers to subjective distress (traumatized, disturbed, agitated, sane-insane), and can also be rated from low to moderate to high. Both concepts are needed to frame the following theory. It is important to note that one can be perturbed and not suicidal. Lethality kills, not perturbation.

What follows is an explication. To begin, suicide can be clinically understood from at least the following templates or patterns (Leenaars, 1988, 1989a & b, 1995,

2004, 2010a, 2013), each will be followed by the specific concepts or protocol sentences under the cluster.

INTRAPSYCHIC DRAMA

I) Unbearable Psychological Pain

The common stimulus in suicide is unbearable (unendurable) psychological pain (Shneidman, 1985, 1993a). The enemy of life is pain. The suicidal person is in a heightened state of perturbation, an intense mental anguish. The author, William Styron (1990), called it, "The howling tempest of the brain." It is the suicide's mind's torture, some of the barrenest of bones. Edwin Shneidman (2004) called it a "psychache." Psychache, Shneidman so wisely and persuasively presents, is highly consistent with Rudofossi's work on "the tragic self-destructive moments of ending one's existence" (Rudofossi, 2007, 2009); the existential pain. It is the pain of feeling pain, the pain of pain (meta-pain). Although, as Menninger (1938) noted, other motives (elements, wishes) are evident, the person primarily wants to flee from pain experienced in a trauma, a catastrophe. The fear is that the trauma, the crisis is bottomless—an eternal suffering. The person may feel any number of emotions such as despair, anguish, being boxed in, rejection, deprivation, forlornness, shame, disgrace, distress, and especially hopelessness and helplessness. It is the emotion of impotence, the feeling of being hopeless-helpless that is so painful for many suicidal people. The situation is unbearable and the person desperately wants a way out of it. The suicide, as Murray (1967) noted, is functional because it abolishes painful tension for the individual. It provides escape from intolerable suffering. Over the years, I learned to understand why people kill themselves? *It hurts that much.* Suicide is escape.

The specific protocol sentences (concepts) in the cluster are

1. Suicide has adjustive value and is functional because it stops painful tension and provides relief from intolerable psychological pain.
2. In suicide, the psychological and/or environmental traumas among many other factors may include incurable disease, threat of senility, fear of becoming hopelessly dependent, feelings of inadequacy, humiliation. Although the solution of suicide is not caused by one thing or motive, suicide is a flight from these specters.
3. In the suicidal drama, certain emotional states are present, including pitiful forlornness, emotional deprivation, distress and/or grief.
4. The person appears to have arrived at the end of an interest to endure and sees suicide as a solution for some urgent problem(s), and/or injustices of life.
5. There is a conflict between life's demands for adaptation and the person's inability or unwillingness to meet the challenge.
6. The person is in a state of heightened disturbance (perturbation) and feels boxed in, harassed, especially hopeless and helpless.

II) Cognitive Constriction

The common cognitive state in suicide is mental constriction (Shneidman, 1985). Constriction, that is, rigidity in thinking, narrowing of focus, tunnel vision, concreteness, and such, is the major component of the cognitive state in suicide. The person is figuratively "intoxicated" or "drugged" by the constriction; the intoxication can be seen in emotions, logic, and perception. The suicidal person exhibits at the moment before his/her death only permutations and combinations of a trauma (e.g., harassed at work, military scandal, a TBI, and rejection by spouse). The suicidal mind is in a special state of relatively fixed purpose and of relative constriction. In the face of the painful trauma, *a* possible solution becomes *the* solution. This constriction is one of the most dangerous aspects of the suicidal mind. (We highlight this more below.)

The specific protocol sentences (concepts) in the cluster are

7. The person reports a history of trauma (e.g., poor health, rejection by a significant other, a competitive spouse).
8. Figuratively speaking, the person appears to be "intoxicated" by overpowering emotions. Concomitantly, there is a constricted logic and perception.
9. There is poverty of thought, exhibited by focusing only on permutations and combinations of grief and grief-provoking topics.

III) Indirect Expressions

Ambivalence, complications, redirected aggression, unconscious implications, and related indirect expressions (or phenomena) are often evident in suicide. The suicidal person is ambivalent; being at least of two or more minds. There are complications, concomitant contradictory feelings, attitudes, and/or thrusts, often toward a person (or other ideal) and even toward life. There is dissembling or masking (see dissembling below). Not only is it love and hate but it may also be a conflict between survival and unbearable pain. The person experiences humility, submission, devotion, subordination, flagellation and sometimes even masochism. Yet there is much more. What the person is conscious of is only a fragment of the suicidal mind (Freud, 1917/1974a). There are more reasons to the act than the suicidal person is consciously aware of when making the final decision (Freud, 1917/1974a, 1917/1974b; Leenaars, 1988, 1993). The driving force may well be unconscious process.

The specific protocol sentences (concepts) in the cluster are

10. The person reports ambivalence; for example, complications, concomitant contradictory feelings, attitudes and/or thrusts.
11. The person's aggression has been turned inwards; for example, humility, submission and devotion, subordination, flagellation, masochism are evident.
12. Unconscious dynamics can be concluded. There are likely more reasons to the suicide than the person is consciously aware of.

IV) Inability to Adjust/Psychopathology

People with all types of pains, problems, and such, are at risk for suicide. Psychological autopsy studies suggest that 40% to 90% of people who kill themselves have some symptoms of psychopathology and/or problems in adjustment (Hawton & van Heeringen, 2000). It has been claimed that as high as 60% appear to be related to mood disorders. Although the majority of suicides may, thus, fit best into mood nosological classifications (e.g., depressive disorders, bipolar disorders [manic-depressive disorders], adjustment disorder with mixed anxiety and depressed mood), other emotional/mental disorders have been identified. For example, anxiety disorders (posttraumatic stress disorder [PTSD], is, for example, especially prevalent in police, soldiers and veterans), schizophrenic disorders (especially paranoid type), panic disorders, borderline personality disorders, and antisocial personality disorders have been related to suicides (Sullivan, 1962, 1964; Leenaars, 1988). Anxiety may well be an equally important pain, next to depression (Fawcett, 1997). Schizophrenics have a very high rate (about 5%, not the often cited 10%) (Palmer, Pankratz, & Bostwick, 2005). Yet there are other disorders not specified that may result in risk. From the psychological autopsy data it is learned that many may have no disorder identifiable in DSM-5 (or some other classification scheme, such as ICD). The person may be simply paralyzed by pain that life, a future, and the like are colorless and unattractive.

Depression, in its varieties, is, however, the most frequent disorder; but it must be understood by any reader that not all suicidal people are depressed and that not all depressed people are suicidal. It is often cited that 15% of people who develop depression ultimately kill themselves. Bostwick (2000) has, however, clearly demonstrated in a meta-analysis of the research that this is a myth. It may well, in fact, be as low as 2%. It is important to remember that suicidal people experience unbearable pain, not always depression, and even if they do experience depression, the critical stimulus is the "unbearable" nature of the depression (or in some other mood). Suicidal people see themselves as in unendurable pain and unable to adjust. His/her state of mind is, however, incompatible with accurate discernment of what is going on. Having the belief that they are too weak to overcome difficulties, these people reject everything except death—they do not survive life's difficulties.

The specific protocol sentences (concepts) in the cluster are

13. The person considers him/herself too weak to overcome personal difficulties and therefore rejects everything, wanting to escape painful life events.
14. Although the person passionately argues that there is no justification for living on, the person's state of mind is incompatible with an accurate assessment/perception of what is going on.
15. The (suicidal) person (S) exhibits a serious disorder in adjustment
    a) S's reports are consistent with a manic-depressive disorder such as the down-phase; for example, all-embracing negative statements, severe mood disturbances causing marked impairment.
    b) S's reports are consistent with schizophrenia; for example, delusional thought, paranoid ideation.

    c) S's reports are consistent with anxiety disorder (such as obsessive-compulsive, posttraumatic stress); for example, feeling of losing control; recurrent and persistent thoughts, impulses, or images.

    d) S's reports are consistent with antisocial personality (or conduct) disorder; for example, deceitfulness, conning others.

    e) S's reports are consistent with borderline personality disorder; for example, frantic efforts to avoid real or imagined abandonment, unstable relationships.

    f) S's reports are consistent with depression; for example, depressed mood, diminished interest, insomnia.

    g) S's reports are consistent with a disorder not otherwise specified. S is so paralyzed by pain that life, future, and such, are colorless and unattractive.

V) Ego (Vulnerable Ego)

The ego with its enormous complexity (Murray, 1938) is an essential factor in the suicidal scenario. The OED defines ego as "The part of the mind that reacts to reality and has a sense of individuality." Ego strength is a protective factor against suicide. The biological perspective has equally argued this conclusion. Van Praag (1997) has, for example, clearly documented a biological aspect to suicidal people, such as increased susceptibility to stressors, labile anxiety, and aggression regulation. Suicidal people frequently exhibit a relative weakness in their capacity to develop constructive tendencies and to overcome their personal difficulties (Zilboorg, 1936). The person's ego has likely been weakened by a steady toll of traumatic life events (e.g., loss, rejection, abuse, sickness, transfer to a perceived lesser job ["a promotion"]). This implies that a history of traumatic disruptions—pain—placed the person at risk for suicide; it likely mentally and/or emotionally handicapped the person's ability to develop mechanisms (or ego functions) to cope. There is, to put it in one simple word, vulnerability. There is a lack of resilience. A weakened ego correlates positively with suicide risk.

The specific protocol sentences (concepts) in the cluster are

    16. There is a relative weakness in the person's capacity for developing constructive tendencies (e.g., attachment, love).

    17. There are unresolved problems ("a complex" or weakened ego) in the individual; for example, symptoms or ideas that are discordant, unassimilated, and/or antagonistic.

    18. The person reports that the suicide is related to a harsh conscience; for example, a fulfillment of punishment (or self-punishment).

INTERPERSONAL STAGE

VI) Interpersonal Relations

The suicidal person has problems in establishing or maintaining relationships (with a person[s] or with another ideal[s]). There frequently is a disturbed, unbearable

Table 1. A Partial List of Murray's Psychological Needs

Abasement. To submit passively to external force; accept injury, criticism, punishment; to surrender; become resigned to fate; blame or belittle self.

Achievement. To accomplish something difficult; master, manipulate, organize physical objects, human beings or ideas; to overcome; to excel oneself.

Affiliation. To enjoyably cooperate or reciprocate with an allied other; to please and win affection; to adhere or remain loyal to a friend or group.

Aggression. To overcome opposition forcefully; to fight; to attack or injure another; to oppose forcefully or punish other.

Autonomy. To get free, shake off restraint; break out of social confinement; avoid or quit activities of domineering authorities; be independent and free.

Counteraction. To make up for failure by restriving; overcome weakness or repress fear; to maintain self-respect and pride on a high level; overcome.

Defendance. To defend or vindicate the self against assault, criticism, blame; conceal or justify a misdeed, failure or humiliation.

Deference. To admire and support a superior; praise, honor or eulogize; yield eagerly to influence of another; emulate an exemplar.

Dominance. To control other humans; influence or direct others by command, suggestion or persuasion; or to dissuade, restrain or prohibit others.

Exhibition. To make an impression; be seen and heard; to excite, amaze, fascinate, entertain, shock, intrigue, amuse or entice others.

Harmavoidance. To avoid pain, physical injury, illness and death; escape from a dangerous situation; to take precautionary measures.

Infavoidance. To avoid humiliation; avoid or quit conditions that lead to scorn, derision, indifference or embarrassment.

Inviolacy. To protect the self; remain separate; maintain distance; to resist others' intrusion on one's own psychological space; isolated.

Nurturance. To gratify the needs of another person, especially one who is weaker; to feed, help, support, console, protect, comfort; to nurture.

Order. To put things or ideas in order; to achieve arrangement, balance, organization, tidiness and precision among things and ideas.

Play. To act for "fun." To enjoy relaxation of stress; to laugh and make jokes; to seek pleasurable activities for their own sake.

Rejection. To exclude, abandon, expel, separate oneself or remain indifferent to a negatively seen person; to snub or jilt another.

Sentience. To seek and enjoy sensuous experience; to give an important place to creature comforts and satisfaction of the senses—taste, touch.

Succorance. To have one's needs gratified by the sympathetic aid of another; be supported, sustained, guided, consoled, taken care of; protected.

Understanding. To ask questions; be interested in theory; speculate, analyze, generalize; to want to know the answers.

---

interpersonal situation (the stage). A calamity prevailed; one of the most common is a relationship (marital) break-up. A positive development in those same disturbed relationships may have been seen as the only possible way to go on living, but such development was seen as not forthcoming. The person's psychological needs are frustrated. Suicide appears to be related to an unsatisfied or frustrated attachment need, although other needs, often more intrapsychic, may be equally evident, for example, achievement, autonomy, dominance, honor. Suicide is committed because of thwarted or unfulfilled needs—needs that are often frustrated interpersonally. The possible needs that are frustrated or blocked are expansive. Table 1 (on previous page) presents a partial list of needs, adopted from Henry A. Murray's *Explorations in Personality* (1938).

What were the needs of the person who died by suicide?

The specific protocol sentences (concepts) in the cluster are

19. The person's problem(s) appears to be determined by the individual's history and the present interpersonal situation.
20. The person reports being weakened and/or defeated by unresolved problems in the interpersonal field (or some other ideal such as health, perfection).
21. The person's suicide appears related to unsatisfied or frustrated needs; for example, attachment, perfection, achievement, autonomy, control.
22. The person's frustration in the interpersonal field is exceedingly stressful and persisting to a traumatic degree.
23. A positive development in the disturbed relationship was seen as the only possible way to go on living, but such development was seen as not forthcoming.
24. The person's relationships (attachments) were too unhealthy and/or too intimate (regressive, "primitive"), keeping him/her under constant strain of stimulation and frustration.

VII) Rejection-Aggression

Wilhelm Stekel first documented the rejection-aggression hypothesis at the famous 1910 meeting of the Psychoanalytic Society in Freud's home in Vienna (Friedman, 1910/1967). Adler, Jung, Freud, Sullivan, and Zilboorg have all expounded variations of this hypothesis. Loss is central to suicide; it is, in fact, often a rejection that is experienced as abandonment. It is an unbearable narcissistic injury. This injury is part of a traumatic event that leads to pain and in some, self-directed aggression. In the first controlled study of suicide notes, Shneidman and Farberow (1957) reported, for example, that both hate directed toward others and self-blame are evident in notes. The suicidal person is deeply ambivalent and, within the context of this ambivalence, suicide may become the turning back upon oneself of murderous impulses (wishes, needs) that had previously been directed against a traumatic event, most frequently someone who had rejected that individual. Biological research in the field has demonstrated a neurobiological link between aggression and suicide. Despite a minimizing of this fact by some (e.g., Shneidman, 1985), aggression, whether other or self-directed, has for example, an association to serotonin dysfunction (Asberg et al., 1976). Freud's hypothesis appears to have a biological basis, within the biopsychosocial view of suicide. Aggression is, in fact, a common emotional state in suicide. Suicide may be veiled aggression—it may be murder in the 180th degree (Shneidman, 1985).

The specific protocol sentences (concepts) in the cluster are

25. The person reports a traumatic event or hurt or injury (e.g., unmet love, a failing marriage, disgust with one's work).
26. The person, whose personality (ego) is not adequately developed (weakened), appears to have suffered a narcissistic injury.
27. The person is preoccupied with an event or injury, namely, a person who has been lost or rejecting (i.e., abandonment).
28. The person feels quite ambivalent, that is, both affectionate and hostile toward the same (lost or rejecting) person.
29. The person reports feelings and/or ideas of aggression and vengefulness toward him/herself, although the person appears to be actually angry at someone else.
30. The person turns upon the self murderous impulses that had previously been directed against someone else.
31. Although maybe not reported directly, the person may have calculated the self-destructiveness to have a negative effect on someone else (e.g., a lost or rejecting person).
32. The person's self-destructiveness appears to be an act of aggression, attack, and/or revenge toward someone else who has hurt or injured him/her.

VIII) Identification-Egression

Freud (1917/1974a, 1920/1974, 1921/1974) hypothesized that intense identification with a lost or rejecting person or, as Zilboorg (1936) showed, with any lost ideal (e.g., health, promotion, employment, gun ownership) is crucial in understanding the suicidal person. Identification is defined as an attachment (bond), based upon an important emotional tie with another person (object) (Freud, 1920/1974) or any ideal. If this emotional need is not met, the suicidal person experiences a deep pain (discomfort). There is an intense desperation and the person wants to egress, that is, to escape. Something must be done to stop the anguish. The suicidal person wants to leave, to exit, to get out, to get away, to be gone, to be elsewhere—not to be, to be dead. Suicide becomes the only solution and the person plunges into the abyss. *Suicide is escape.*

The specific protocol sentences (concepts) in the cluster are

33. The person reports in some direct or indirect fashion an identification (i.e., attachment) with a lost or rejecting person (or with any lost ideal [e.g., health, freedom, employment, all A's]).

34. An unwillingness to accept the pain of losing an ideal (e.g., abandonment, sickness, old age), allows the person to choose, even seek to escape from life and accept death.

35. The person wants to egress (i.e., to escape, to depart, to flee, to be gone), to relieve the unbearable psychological pain.

In concluding, the theory outlined is only one point of view. Yet the elements have utility in understanding suicide and thus, forensic investigation. We need to know what we are investigating. Indeed, to begin to address the question, "Why do people kill themselves?" or more specifically, "Why did the person die by suicide?" we need a psychology of suicide. We must answer the question, What are the important common psychological dimensions of suicide? rather than, What kind of people die by suicide? The question is critical, for these common dimensions (or "sameness") are what suicide is. (We discussed this early on, "What is science?") Not necessarily the universal but certainly the most frequent or common characteristics provide us with a meaningful conceptualization and classification of suicide. The concept is not new; Plato attributes the first theory of a universal or common in the flux (mess) of everything to the pre-Socratic philosopher, Heraclitus (around 500 BC). He taught, "You can't step twice in the same river." All is flux (All things are in becoming/process). Heraclitus also taught, however, that, "In the same river, we both step, and do not step, we are and we are not". He was trying to classify and understand the underlying coherence (common) of things. Heraclitus called it, "*Logos*." To understand a thing, like a death, we may follow Heraclitus's guidance, "Therefore one must follow . . . that which is common." Heraclitus was a true investigator, a sage for our field (see Freeman, 1971; Kirk & Raven, 1971).

RESEARCH ON THEORY:
AN EMPIRICALLY-BASED UNDERSTANDING

Understanding the act of suicide and motives behind suicide behavior seems extremely important worldwide (WHO, 2002), and in order to do so empirically, many researchers from around the world have used different methods. Shneidman and Farberow (1957), Maris (1981), and others have suggested the following avenues: national mortality statistics, retrospective psychological investigations (often called psychological autopsies), the study of nonfatal suicide attempts, and the analysis of documents (such as suicide notes). All of them have their limitations and there are problems in obtaining them in many countries, including in subpopulations such as police and soldiers. Yet each of these methods has been shown to extend our understanding of suicide and suicidal behavior (Hawton & van Heeringen, 2000; Leenaars, De Leo, Diekstra et al., 1997). We will next examine the theory in the *prime facia* evidence in cases of suicide, suicide notes (Leenaars, 1999b).

Early research (e.g., de Boismont, 1856; Wolff, 1931) on suicide notes largely used an anecdotal approach that incorporated descriptive information (Frederick, 1969). Subsequent methods, using Frederick's (1969) scheme for methods of analysis have used content analysis, classification analysis, and theoretical-conceptual analysis. Each of these approaches has had utility, although Frederick suggested that simple content analysis has limitations (e.g., see Ogilvie, Stone, & Shneidman, 1969; they noted that the word "love" occurs frequently in suicide notes, see also Henken, 1976; Jacobs, 1971; Osgood & Walker, 1959; Wager, 1960). Traditional classification schemes use data such as age, sex, marital status, educational level, employment status, and mental disorder (e.g., see Ho, Yip, Chiu, & Halliday, 1998). Ho and his colleagues (1998) developed the most widely used classification scheme; they studied suicides notes in Hong Kong. Ho's scheme is largely based on forensic data that are gathered at postmortem investigation. They found that suicide notes written by young people were longer and richer in emotions than those written by older people. A similar classification scheme has been used in the United States (Callahan & Davis, 2009), India (Girdhar, Leenaars, Dogra, Leenaars, & Kumar, 2004), Mexico (Chavez, Paramo-Castello, Leenaars, & Leenaars, 2006), Japan (Kubawara, Shioiri, Nishimura, Nushida, Ueno, Akazawa, & Someya, 2006), and Turkey (Demirel, Akar, Sayin, Candansayar, & Leenaars, 2008). However, as Girdhar and her team (2004) noted, there are limitations in these studies. The data are not entirely consistent, and differences in collection occur between researchers in different countries. There are also limitations in the generalizability the findings. For example, unlike Ho et al.'s (1998) findings, Demirel and the team from Turkey (2008) found the notes from the elderly longer. For a further example, Girdhar's team (2004) from India found that many notes involved a specific instruction, mostly for care of the family; physical/psychological illness was the most frequently mentioned difficulty; whereas Chavez and her group (2006) from Mexico found little written about life's difficulties and few specific instructions. Callahan and Davis (2006) noted only that note writers lived alone more often. Furthermore, a comparison of note writers with non–note writers has failed to find consistent results (Ho et al., 1998; Girdhar et al., 2004). Differences of demographic features like age and sex are also inconsistent (Chavez et al., 2006; Foster, 2003; Ho et al., 1998). *The main finding to date is that suicide note writers are essentially similar to suicides who did not leave notes.* The studies have also supported the value of the data that one can validly study suicide by studying suicide notes, and the notion that suicide is complex (Ho et al., 1998; Leenaars, 1988; Shneidman & Farberow, 1957), warranting, among other things, more in-depth study of suicide notes.

Only a very few studies have utilized a theoretical-conceptual analysis (Frederick, 1969), despite the assertion in the first formal study of suicide notes (Shneidman & Farberow, 1957) and in ongoing discussion (Diamond, More, Hawkins, & Soucar, 1995; Millon, 2010) that such an approach offers much promise. To address this lack, over 40 years ago, the author applied a logical, empirical analysis to suicide notes. The method permits a theoretical analysis of suicide notes, augments the effectiveness of controls, provides construct validation, and allows us to develop some theoretical insight into the vexing problem of suicide that may have cross-cultural application.

The method has been previously described in detail (Leenaars, 1988, 2004; Leenaars & Balance, 1984). It treats suicide notes as an archival source. This source is subjected to the scrutiny of control hypotheses, following an *ex post facto* research design (Kerlinger, 1964). The major problem with the current type of research is the lack of control over extraneous variables, and the large number of potentially important antecedent variables; thus, the danger of misinterpreting relationships. Kerlinger (1964) suggested that these problems could be largely overcome by explicitly formulating not just a single hypothesis, but several "control" hypotheses as well. This would call for suicide protocol, such as notes to be recast in different theoretical contexts (hypotheses, theories, models) for which lines of evidence of each of these positions can then be pursued in the data. Carnap's (1931/1959) logical and empirical procedures can be utilized for such investigations. To date, the theories of 10 suicidologists, as noted earlier, have been investigated: Alfred Adler, Ludwig Binswanger, Sigmund Freud, Carl Gustav Jung, Karl A. Menninger, George Kelly, Henry A. Murray, Edwin S. Shneidman, Harry Stack Sullivan, and Gregory Zilboorg. In order to test the formulations, Carnap's positivistic procedure calls for the translating of theoretical formulations into observable (specific) protocol sentences (Ayer, 1959), within the context of construct validation approach (Millon, 2010).

To summarize from the world's largest array of empirical studies on suicide notes (e.g., age, sex, method used, nation) of the theories of the 10 suicidologists, a number of theoretical propositions/implications (or protocol sentences) have been identified to be observable in various samples of notes, the very words of a suicidal person. In the model, Leenaars isolated 100 protocol sentences or concepts from each of the ten theorists (10 for each theorist) and reduced them to 35 sentences; 23 protocol sentences were found to be highly predictive (described) for the content of suicide notes (i.e., one standard deviation above the mean of observations), and 17 protocol sentences significantly discriminated genuine suicide notes from simulated notes (i.e., control data) (with 5 sentences being both) (Leenaars, 1989b; Leenaars & Balance, 1984). Thus, there was not only construct validation, but also predictive and discriminative validity. One unique finding of these studies is that there are a few significant age differences in the suicide notes, but not sex (Leenaars, 2004; Leenaars, de Wilde, Wenckstern, & Kral, 2001). Using cluster analysis, the protocols were reduced to the eight clusters discussed previously, classified into five intrapsychic and three interpersonal aspects: a) unbearable pain, b) cognitive constriction, c) indirect expressions, d) inability to adjust (psychopathology), e) ego (vulnerability), f) interpersonal relationships, g) rejection-aggression, and h) identification-egression (Leenaars, 1996, 2004; Leenaars et al., 2001). Further, from a series of studies, Leenaars (1988, 1996) proposed a metaframe to organize the clusters into intrapsychic and interpersonal elements. Suicide can be, as discussed, seen as an intrapsychic drama on an interpersonal stage. Suicide can, thus, be theoretically understood from the proposed theory (templates, constructs, and frames), outlined earlier in detail. There is, without a doubt, evidence for the theory, having great utility not only for research, but also for DSI.

Table 2 presents the actual protocol sentences within each cluster, presented as a Thematic Guide for Suicide Prediction, TGSP. To apply, the TGSP to each of the suicide notes presented earlier, we present the actual scores. (The reader may wish to score the suicide notes with the TGSP):

1. Adolf Hitler's note:
   1, 2, 3, 4, 6, 7, 9, 12, 13, 15g, 17, 19, 20, 21, 23, 25, 26, 27, 29, 30, 31, 32, 33, 34, 35.
2. Kurt Cobain's note:
   1, 2, 3, 4, 5, 6, 7, 8, 9, 10, 11, 12, 13, 14, 15f, 16, 17, 18, 19, 20, 21, 22, 23, 24, 25, 26, 27, 28, 33, 34, 35.
3. Bill, the 21-year-old soldier's note:
   1, 2, 3, 4, 5, 6, 7, 9, 13, 14, 15f, 16, 19, 20, 21, 22, 24, 25, 33, 34, 35.
4. Joe Smith's homicide-suicide note:
   1, 2, 3, 4, 6, 7, 8, 9, 11, 12, 13, 14, 15g, 17, 20, 21, 22, 25, 26, 27, 29, 30, 31, 32, 33, 34, 35.
5. The police officer's note to the Sergeant:
   1, 2, 3, 6, 7, 8, 9, 12, 27, 29, 30, 31, 32, 35.

Of course, some notes are banal. The poet Sylvia Plath's note read, "Please call Dr. Horder." What does it say?

Independent research on suicide notes (O'Connor, Sheeby, & O'Connor, 1999), investigation of suicidal Internet writing (Barak & Miran, 2005), and biographical studies of suicides (Lester, 1994) have supported the utility of the approach to notes, or any narrative analysis, adding construct validity. Barak and Miran (2005) found that unbearable pain, cognitive constriction and problematic interpersonal relationships were especially evident in writings on the Internet about suicide; Lester (1994) found evidence of all aspects of Leenaars' model in the biographies of people that died by suicide. In-depth studies of interjudge reliability (for example, O'Connor et al., 1999) and over four decades of study by the author and colleagues show that, indeed, the percentage of interjudge agreement has been satisfactory (> 85%; see Shaughnessy, Zechmeister, & Zechmeister, 2000). In our reliability (or credibility) method, we type out each interview, note, personal document, and the like so that more than one rater can score the text. In this way, we "double rate" everything, making sure that an investigator does not get a distorted opinion. This (i.e., consultation) is standard to avoid bias in sound forensic work. Reliability and validity have also been established in different countries.

International studies are not only rare in the study of suicide notes, but suicide in general. There are only a few studies, for example, on suicide notes from different countries. It is well known that Canada has a higher rate of suicide than the United States (Leenaars & Lester, 1994), and Leenaars (1992) examined 56 suicide notes from Canada and the United States whose writers were matched for age and sex (this was the first cross-cultural study of suicide notes). None of the intrapsychic or interpersonal aspects differed. Subsequently, studies from Germany (Leenaars, Lester, Wenckstern, & Heim, 1994), United Kingdom (O'Connor & Leenaars, 2004) Hungary (Leenaars, Fekete, Wenckstern, & Osvath, 1998), Russia (Leenaars, Lester, Lopatin, Schustov, & Wenckstern, 2002), Australia (Leenaars, Haines, Wenckstern, Williams, & Lester, 2003), India (Leenaars, Girdhar, Dogra Wenckstern, & Leenaars., 2010), Mexico (Chavez-Hernandez, Leenaars, Chavez-de Sanchez, & Leenaars, 2009), Turkey (Leenaars, Sayin, et al., 2010), and Lithuania (Leenaars,

Table 2. Thematic Guide for Suicide Prediction

Antoon A. Leenaars, Ph.D., C.Psych.

I. PATIENT DATA   Date: _____

Name _____ Age _____ Sex _____

Date of Birth _____ Marital Status _____ Divorced _____

Education Status _____ _____
                       (years)   (degrees)

Current Employment _____

II. SUICIDAL EXPERIENCE

1) Has the patient ever seriously contemplated suicide? (If yes, note particulars)

_____

2) Has the patient ever attempted suicide? (If yes, note particulars)

_____

3) Does the patient know anyone who attempted suicide? (If yes, indicate family, acquaintance, etc.)

_____

4) Does the patient know anyone who committed suicide? (If yes, indicate family, acquaintance, etc.)

_____

III. REFERRAL DATA

1) Purpose _____

2) What is the referral question? _____

_____

3) What is the presenting problem(s)? _____

_____

_____

Table 2. (Cont'd.)

IV. INTERVIEW SITUATION

1) Observations _____

_____

_____

2) Other procedures (e.g., tests, interviews) _____

_____

V. INTERPRETATIONS

1) Perturbation rating:	Low	Medium	High
scale equivalent	1 2 3	4 5 6	7 8 9
2) Lethality rating:	Low	Medium	High
scale equivalent	1 2 3	4 5 6	7 8 9

3) Guide summary:

scores: I - 1, 2, 3, 4, 5, 6;   II - 7, 8, 9;   III - 10, 11, 12;
IV - 13, 14, 15;   V - 16, 17, 18;   VI - 19, 20, 21, 22, 23, 24;
VII - 25, 26 , 27, 28, 29, 30, 31, 32;   VIII - 33, 34, 35

Conclusions: _____

_____

_____

_____

_____

_____

VI. REMARKS

_____

_____

_____

_____

_____

_____

_____

_____

_____

_____

_____

_____

_____

_____

_____

_____

Include on back any other relevant data.

Table 2. (Cont'd.)

INTRAPSYCHIC	Circle One

I - Unbearable Psychological Pain

1) Suicide has adjustive value and is functional because it stops painful tension and provides relief from intolerable psychological pain. (P) — Yes No

2) In suicide, the psychological and/or environmental traumas among many other factors may include: incurable disease, threat of senility, fear of becoming hopelessly dependent, feelings of inadequacy, humiliation. Although the solution of suicide is not caused by one thing, or motive, suicide is a flight from these specters. (P & D) — Yes No

3) In the suicidal drama, certain emotional states are present, including pitiful forlornness, emotional deprivation, distress and/or grief. (P & D) — Yes No

4) The suicidal person (S) appears to have arrived at the end of an interest to endure and sees suicide as a solution for some urgent problem(s), and/or injustices of life. (P) — Yes No

5) There is a conflict between life's demands for adaptation and the S's inability or unwillingness to meet the challenge. (P) — Yes No

6) S is in a state of heightened disturbance (perturbation) and feels boxed in, harassed, especially hopeless and helpless. (P) — Yes No

II - Cognitive Constriction

7) S reports a history of trauma (e.g., poor health, rejection by significant other, a competitive spouse). (P & D) — Yes No

8) Figuratively speaking, S appears to be "intoxicated" by overpowering emotions. Concomitantly, there is a constricted logic and perception. (D) — Yes No

9) There is poverty of thought, exhibited by focusing only on permutations and combinations of grief and grief-provoking topics. (D) — Yes No

III - Indirect Expressions

10) S reports ambivalence; e.g., complications, concomitant contradictory feelings, attitudes, and/or thrusts. (P & D) — Yes No

11) S's aggression has been turned inwards; for example, humility, submission and devotion, subordination. flagellation, masochism, are evident. (P) — Yes No

12) Unconscious dynamics can be concluded. There are likely more reasons to the suicide than the person is consciously aware. (D) — Yes No

Table 2. (Cont'd.)

	Circle One

IV - Inability to Adjust

13) S considers him/herself too weak to overcome personal diffi-   Yes   No
culties and, therefore, rejects everything, wanting to escape
painful life events. (P)

14) Although S passionately argues that there is no justification for   Yes   No
living on, S's state of mind is incompatible with an accurate
assessment/perception of what is going on. (P)

15) S exhibits a serious disorder in adjustment. (P)

   a) S's reports are consistent with a manic-depressive disorder   Yes   No
such as the down-phase; e.g., all-embracing negative
statements, severe mood disturbances causing marked
impairment.

   b) S's reports are consistent with schizophrenia; e.g., delusional   Yes   No
thought, paranoid ideation.

   c) S's reports are consistent with anxiety disorder (such as   Yes   No
obsessive-compulsive, posttraumatic stress); e.g., feeling of
losing control; recurrent and persistent thoughts, impulses,
or images.

   d) S's reports are consistent with antisocial personality (or   Yes   No
conduct) disorder; e.g., deceitfulness, conning others.

   e) S's reports are consistent with borderline personality disorder;   Yes   No
e.g., frantic efforts to avoid real or imagined abandonment,
unstable relationships.

   f) S's reports are consistent with depression; e.g., depressed   Yes   No
mood, diminished interest, insomnia.

   g) S's reports are consistent with a disorder not otherwise   Yes   No
specified. S is so paralyzed by pain that life, future, etc. is
colorless and unattractive.

V - Ego

16) There is a relative weakness in S's capacity for developing   Yes   No
constructive tendencies (e.g., attachment, love). (D)

17) There are unresolved problems ("a complex" or weakened ego)   Yes   No
in the individual; e.g., symptoms or ideas that are discordant,
unassimilated, and/or antagonistic. (P)

18) S reports that the suicide is related to a harsh conscience; i.e., a   Yes   No
fulfillment of punishment (or self-punishment). (D)

Table 2. (Cont'd.)

INTERPERSONAL	Circle One

VI - Interpersonal Relations

19) S's problem(s) appears to be determined by the individual's history and the present interpersonal situation. (P) — Yes No

20) S reports being weakened and/or defeated by unresolved problems in the interpersonal field (or some other ideal such as health, perfection). (P) — Yes No

21) S's suicide appears related to unsatisfied or frustrated needs; e.g., attachment, perfection, achievement, autonomy, control. (P) — Yes No

22) S's frustration in the interpersonal field is exceedingly stressful and persisting to a traumatic degree. (P) — Yes No

23) A positive development in the disturbed relationship was seen as the only possible way to go on living, but such development was seen as not forthcoming. (P) — Yes No

24) S's relationships (attachments) were too unhealthy and/or too intimate (regressive, "primitive"), keeping him/her under constant strain of stimulation and frustration. (D) — Yes No

VII - Rejection - Aggression

25) S reports a traumatic event or hurt or injury (e.g., unmet love, a failing marriage, disgust with one's work). (P) — Yes No

26) S, whose personality (ego) is not adequately developed (weakened), appears to have suffered a narcissistic injury. (P & D) — Yes No

27) S is preoccupied with an event or injury, namely a person who has been lost or rejecting (i.e., abandment). (D) — Yes No

28) S feels quite ambivalent, i.e., both affectionate and hostile toward the same (lost or rejecting) person. (D) — Yes No

29) S reports feelings and/or ideas of aggression and vengefulness toward him/herself although S appears to be actually angry at someone else. (D) — Yes No

30) S turns upon the self, murderous impulses that had previously been directed against someone else. (D) — Yes No

31) Although maybe not reported directly, S may have calculated the self-destructiveness to have a negative effect on someone else (e.g., a lost or rejecting person). (P) — Yes No

32) S's self-destructiveness appears to be an act of aggression, attack, and/or revenge toward someone else who has hurt or injured him/her. (P) — Yes No

Table 2. (Cont'd.)

	Circle One
VIII - Identification - Egression	
33) S reports in some direct or indirect fashion an identification (i.e., attachment) with a lost or rejecting person (or with any lost ideal [e.g., health, freedom, employment, all A's]). (D)	Yes No
34) An unwillingness to accept the pain of losing an ideal (e.g., abandonment, sickness, old age), allows S to choose, even seek to escape from life and accept death. (D)	Yes No
35) S wants to egress (i.e., to escape, to depart, to flee, to be gone), to relieve the unbearable psychological pain. (P)	Yes No

Gailiene, Wenckstern, Leenaars, L., Trofimova, Petravičiūtė, & Park, 2014) supported this observation. A few differences, however, were observed in some people: some cultural/social groups (e.g., India and Turkey) showed more indirect expressions, such as unconscious processes, ambivalence, and dissembling, and Lithuanian notes were more extreme in all aspects. There are differences by age; younger people will probably show some significant differences from the older group (see below). Yet the theory has been empirically applicable to all people. Thus, the model has significant cross-cultural or social application; be that as it may, questions remain. Does it apply to the case at hand?

The history of suicidology (psychiatry, psychology, criminology, sociology, and so on) gives us the ideas, concepts, formulations, and so on, and science (nomothetic investigation) gives us the observable "valid" ones. This is the best of all possible psychologies, an empirically supported one. The theory outlined is an attempt to do that. It has a great deal of construct validity. There are few such theories in suicidology. It provides an answer to the question posed; it presents some common elements to answer, some forensic unknowns.

These elements, common to suicide, highlight that suicide is not only due to external "stress" or pain or even unattachment. The common consistency in suicide is, in fact, lifelong adjustment patterns (Shneidman, 1985). Suicidal people have experienced a steady toll of life events; that is, threat, stress, failure, loss and challenge—or in one word, pain—that has undermined their ability to cope. Suicide has a history.

Hopefully, the synthesis presented here will provide a useful clinical and forensic perspective for many on the question, "What is the mode of death?" and "Why did the person die by suicide?" and maybe also the question, "How do we prevent such events in the future with suicidal people?"

Of course, we do not know whether the theory applies to all suicides. Suicide bombers, homicides-suicides, suicide martyrs, altruistic suicides, for example, may differ (Leenaars & Wenckstern, 2004). Today we have Islamic extremists who, cognitively constricted to the point of being delusional, in the glory of Allah, kill "infidels" and themselves—a homicide-suicide. There are many different kinds of homicide-suicides. Not so long ago, we had the Korean and Vietnamese monks who burned themselves for democratic freedom and independence of American tyranny. There is a long history, the Christian martyrs being one example. Yet we do not know whether these suicides and homicides-suicides are the same or different. We published the first study in the world on the writings of suicide martyrs. Leenaars, Park, Collins, Wenckstern, and Leenaars (2010) examined 33 letters of "altruistic suicides" and compared them blindly to a matched sample of the more "common" suicides (J. S. Mill's methods of difference and of agreement or similarity.) This study began to answer some key questions for your investigation: Are suicide martyrs the same and/or different than suicide? What intrapsychic elements are critical for predicting a to-be martyr to kill him/herself? To kill you? Are interpersonal protocols relevant? What elements? Is ambivalence salient? There are many unique insights offered by the personal documents (e.g., martyrs' last letters, Internet writings) of suicide bombers. There are increasing questions for the police and forensic investigator.

Finally, on the topic of the suicide martyr (bomber/terrorist), Maltsberger (2001) insightfully speculated,

> One day a messianic leader, inflamed with malignant narcissistic fury, will become so intoxicated with the desire for revenge and destruction of his enemies that he will no longer be deterred by any self-preservative instinct or compassion for the welfare of his own people. Herman Melville imagined such a leader in Captain Ahab, who so nursed his grievance against Moby Dick, the white whale that bit off his leg, that he destroyed himself and his entire crew in his quest for revenge. (p. 145)

Is the terrorist who died by suicide a Captain Ahab? Did he/she have grandiose fury? Or was he/she "altruistic?"

SEX DIFFERENCES

The basic sex difference in suicide is that males kill themselves more than females (although this is not so in China [Pritchard, 1996]). In contrast, females attempt suicide more often than males. This sex difference has been found in almost all nations (Lester, 1988, 1992b). The male-female ratio of suicide has remained fairly stable over time. The generally accepted male-female ratio of completed suicides is three or four males to one female, but there is great variation around the world.

Explanations in the literature (Leenaars, 1988) have varied. Females use different and less lethal methods (drugs vs. shooting). Individuals with severe emotional disturbances (psychiatric disorders) have higher rates of suicide, and men are more likely to be diagnosed with such disorders. There are also alternative social expectations for men and women in trauma such that males act more catastrophically. Yet Shneidman (1985) has argued that genotypic similarities may be more prevalent than differences. Indeed, the author's research (Leenaars, 1988) on suicide notes of males and females confirms this. Pain is pain. Frustrated needs are frustrated needs.

Constriction is constriction. Maybe there are phenotypic differences (e.g., method, diagnostic label) in suicide but not genotypic ones across sex. Could the high rates of completed suicide in males be more influenced by gender roles than psychological factors? Is this relevant to your case?

Tomlinson-Keasey, Warren, and Elliot (1986), in their study of gifted female suicides, came to the same conclusion as our study of suicide notes. They found that the markers (e.g., emotional disturbance, a history of problems) of suicide were the same in both sexes. Others (e.g., Canetto, 1994; Canetto & Lester, 1995) have cited such factors as socioeconomic disadvantage, unemployment, domestic (intimate partner) violence and a history of suicidal behavior among friends and family as relevant to the suicides of women. Such factors have also been observed in the suicides of men (Lester, 1988, 1992b; Tomlinson-Keasey et al., 1986). The area is, however, plagued by stereotypes (Canetto, 1994). For example, the division of women's suicides as irrational and men's as rational is not supported in the data (Leenaars, 1988, 2004). Reflections on this topic for investigators are most relevant (Lester, 1988a).

AGE: A DEVELOPMENTAL VIEW

Shneidman and Farberow (1957), in the first empirical studies of suicide notes indicated that psychological aspects of suicide vary with age. However, too few studies have examined the obvious clinical critical element; for example, very few studies on suicide notes have examined this variable. The research (Bjerg, 1967; Darbonne, 1969; Lester & Hummel, 1980; Lester & Reeve, 1982; Tuckman, Kleiner, & Lavell, 1959), however, consistently supported Shneidman and Farberow's claim. Despite great similarities, there are differences in suicide across the life span.

A problem with the studies of suicide and age is that various researchers have divided their age samples differently, resulting in some difficulties in direct comparison among studies. Leenaars (1988), in the hope of bringing some clarity to the area, proposed a schema that was not only based on extensive research on adult development (Colarusso & Nemiroff, 1981; Kimmel, 1974) but also on Erikson's theoretical model on the stages of such development (Erikson, 1963, 1968), with the understanding that overlap between these groups, as well as even more varied classification within these groups, is possible. It is critical, however, to understand that, from a developmental view, age is not a mere demographic variable; it is a genotypic view. The groups with Erikson's characteristics and proposed age range (with the proviso that no developmental age can be strictly reduced to chronological age) are as follows:

1. Adolescence (Erikson's stage, identity vs. identity confusion; chronological age, 12 to 18).
2. Young Adulthood (Erikson's stage, intimacy vs. isolation; chronological age, 18 to 25).
3. Middle Adulthood (Erikson's stage, generativity vs. stagnation; chronological age, 25 to 55).

    4. Late Adulthood (Erikson's stage, integrity vs. despair; chronological age, 55 and over).

Leenaars (1989b, 1991) studied 60 suicide notes, representing the specific adult age ranges and found that there were more similarities than differences on the psychological dimensions across the adult life span; however, differences were noted About the intrapsychic drama, we learned that people in young and middle adulthood are more indirect and ambivalent in their suicide (indirect expression). Or the con-converse, people in late adulthood are more direct, showing less redirected aggression, complications, and unconscious implications. Older adults are perhaps less confused about their suicide, having a stronger ongoing wish to die. They mask less.

Age Differences

Young adulthood is a discrete timeline in development (Frager & Fadiman, 1984; Kimmel, 1974). It has its unique biological, psychological, cultural, and sociological issues. I tentatively support the position in limiting this timeline from 18 to 25, although some say to 30 (Kimmel, 1974; Neugarten, Moore, & Lowe, 1965). Of course, no developmental period can be rigidly defined chronologically, and at best the 18 to 25 range approximates what can only be defined developmentally, that is, some people mature earlier, others later than the mean. Allow me to reflect a bit more on the topic, largely because young adults are at high risk for suicide and show some anomalies.

Adolescence is a stage marked by the development of a sense of identity. The young adult continues to develop this sense of identity, evolving a finer and more discrete sense of who he/she is in relation to others. Not distinct from this process, the demand to master the challenge of intimacy emerges as the central issue of young adulthood. Erik Erikson (1963, 1980) was one of the first to pioneer work on intimacy (intimacy vs. isolation) in young adulthood, noting that one must have a sense of who one is before one can appreciate the uniqueness of another. Although the capacity to relate to others emerges earlier, "the individual does not become capable of a fully intimate relationship until the identity crisis is fairly well resolved" (Kimmel, 1974, p. 23). Often, before such development, the individual can only avoid genuine closeness or engage in narcissistic relationships. As Frager and Fadiman (1984) note, "Without a sense of intimacy and commitment, one may become isolated and be unable to sustain intimate relationships. If one's sense of identity is weak and threatened by intimacy, the individual may turn away from or attack whatever encroaches" (p. 152). I would add, even oneself! Dissembling, self-deceiving, dissociating, splitting, and/or shattering of identity consolidation result in psychache. By young adulthood, the dissociation process has weakened the ego and altered the ability to adjust. Dr. Dan Rudofossi (2009) writes, "Dissociation may entail behavioral, lingual, memory, and neurological substrates that effect emotional and cognitive processes. In my conceptualization, that intensity may become more like character features, or identity modes" (p. 65). The walls thicken. This is what Erikson meant by identity confusion. Among young adults, the suicidal mode can become a permanent identity.

Research regarding any psychological area of young adulthood is scarce. Studies on suicide in this group are even scarcer. Even the volumes on suicide that are apparently directed to include this age group (e.g., Klerman, 1986) disappoint us, for they only take note of our lack of knowledge about this group of individuals. Insights are often generated from general developmental issues, but we do not find specific information about suicide (see Levinson, 1986). Often young adults are classed together with adolescents, a taxonomic maneuver both theoretically and empirically unsound. There have been exceptions to the overlapping taxonomy in the field (e.g., Leenaars, 1989a & b; 1991; Lomas & Lester, 2011; Rickgarn, 1994); however, clearer definitions are needed in the research of young adults, which needs to be integrated into life-span perspectives (Leenaars, 1991).

In 1988, I received the American Association of Suicidology (AAS) prestigious Edwin Shneidman Award. My presentation addressed the lack; my Shneidman lecture was entitled, "Are Young Adult Suicides Psychologically Different from Those of Other Adults?" Based on the analysis of hundreds of suicide notes across the adult life span, there are enormous commonalities or patterns. Yet a life-span developmental perspective (Leenaars, 1991) is still essential. In an expanded study across the life-span, including teens, we came to the same conclusion (Leenaars, de Wilde, et al., 2001). There were differences, however. This is an issue of more or less, not presence or absence. Young adults' notes significantly more often reflected the probable presence of the inability to adjust or psychopathology. More often than during any other age group we can discern a mental disorder associated with a very vulnerable ego. This likely suggests that young adults' suicides may have a high relation to the crystallization of psychopathology, imbalance, or whatever you want to call it, at this age.

Psychopathology, of course, can be seen across the life span, but it also may be most relevant to people in this age group. Thus, the investigator on a young adult case is cautioned about using current research, needing to be clear and distinct about age, cultural issues, and more in their study. We can, however, tentatively conclude that the proposed theory is applicable across the adult life span. These are the commonalities or similarities. The specific difference, however, may reflect age-specific stressors or concerns that may be important in understanding suicide. Specific differences across the adult life-span, of course, are an issue of more or less, not presence or absence (Leenaars, 1988a).

And a footnote on time: We found that suicide notes from the 1940s and 1950s do not differ from suicide notes from the 1980s and 1990s (Leenaars, 1988). The method of suicide also makes no difference (Leenaars, 1990). The commonalities (*Logos*) are the same.

A NOTE ON THE COGNITIVE STYLE

The best known faulty syllogism may well be "All men are immortal; Socrates is a man; Therefore Socrates is immortal."

The above syllogism is valid, but it is also faulty because it begins with a first premise that is false. All men are not immortal. It is a false universal inductive generalization. It is basic to realize that a valid syllogism can have a false conclusion. This can happen if one or more of the premises are false (Kahane, 1973). And in the suicidal person, the first premise (sometimes called core beliefs) is not only false, but also lethal.

Edwin Shneidman (Leenaars, 1993, 1999a) has been keenly interested in making explicit the latent logical (cognitive) components of everyday thought. He realized how useful it is to examine the cognitive styles exhibited in each suicidal person. For example, in a terse but insightful paper, "On 'Therefore I Must Kill Myself'" (Shneidman, 1999), he shows how vitally important it is for a clinician to understand the patient's idiosyncratic logical style—and then not agree with that patient's major premise when the premise is the keystone to the patient's lethal (suicidal) syllogistic conclusion. Thus, this would be most important for an investigator to understand. For example, "People who have committed a certain sin ought to be dead; I am a person who has committed that sin; therefore, I ought to be dead." For another example, "Soldiers who are rejected by the commander ought to be dead; I am a soldier who has been rejected; therefore, I ought to be dead." For another example, "People who kill ought to be dead. I am a police officer who killed; therefore, I ought to be dead." The homicidal mind is often the same. "People who disgrace me ought to be dead; I am a person who has been disgraced by the president; Therefore, he ought to be dead." This means that investigators need to know the suicidal person's mind. Therefore you have to know what suicide is. Further if you do, you will know that the cognition, the major premise, "People who cannot live up the demands of the professor ought to be dead," or some other lethal premise (or core belief) is a suicidal clue. With the student, you can see the concluding distorted thinking: "I got a B+; therefore, I ought to be dead,"

I, akin to Shneidman (1999), think that the logic of the suicidal person is wrong. It all depends on the word "therefore." It is perhaps the most important word in life and, it seems, death. When we invoke the word *therefore*, we have come to a decision or resolution. Therefore, it is the pivotal word in logic, specifically, syllogisms. Shneidman (1999) writes,

> We all know that there are bridge-words between thought and action. Words like "might," "ought," "should," "must"—which convey *various* amounts of psychological *push*. The point is that *not all "therefores" are psychologically identical*, or to put it another way: not all equal signs are equally equal. Thus the word "therefore" cannot be taken for granted as a word which means "always" or "under all circumstances" as in the syllogism about Socrates. In *that* example, Socrates is *always* mortal, but that example simply illustrates the confinements of traditional Aristotelian syllogisms. (p. 74)

Yet there is an even more important fact, the mind does much more than simply logic. The sinner is an example. The sinner makes the classical error; the major premise is false. All humans are not immortal. And all people who have committed a certain sin ought not to be dead. What were the person's cognitions, premises, beliefs, and such, who died by suicide?

Once you know what suicide is, we believe that it is easy to conclude the following: The suicidal person, at the moment of taking his/her life, is figuratively intoxicated with his/her overpowering emotions and constricted logic. Are these suicidal people "rational?"

Cognitive constriction is an essential element of the suicidal mind (Neuringer, 1976). It is imperative that the reader be reminded that the suicidal person defines the trauma. A trauma is a perception, not a thing in itself. An educational example of Shneidman's is the man who always wanted the perfect car. He saved his money and bought a Ferrari. Then the car got a scratch; his response was to write a suicide note, stating, "There is nothing to live for," and therefore shot himself. For almost all, the scratch appears, to use a popular expression, to be small stuff, but not for him. His belief was "People with a scratch on a Ferrari ought to be dead." His logic can be symbolized by the following: "People with a scratch on a Ferrari ought to be dead; I am a person who has a scratch on his Ferrari; Therefore, I ought to be dead."

Another Shneidman example is the elderly woman who killed herself after her canary died. Her cognition was, "People with a dead canary ought to be dead." She had her "therefore." Thus, we must remember that trauma for both these individuals—and all suicidal people—was/is a perception, not "objective reality." They are so blinded. They had their major premise and the trauma; he about a scratch on a car and she about a dead pet. What was the suicide's trauma(s)? It is, however, so much more. It is not only simply about sinning or having a scratch on a car or suffering from a TBI. It is not only simply about getting a B+ or a dead pet. It is not simply about losing a loved one. ("People rejected by Mary ought to be dead.")

Figuratively speaking, the suicidal person is "intoxicated" by overpowering emotions. Concomitantly, there is a constricted logic and perception. Although the person defines the trauma (situation), one cannot buy into the overpowering emotions and constricted logic presented by the individual, even in a retrospective investigation, a psychological autopsy or police investigation. Yet many do so after events like suicide.

One of the basics of a suicidal mind is the following: There is poverty of thought, exhibited by focusing only on permutations and combinations of grief and grief-provoking topics. A common premise is that something is either black or white. Something is either "A or non-A." To presume that the suicidal individual either wants to kill him/herself or not is an extremely limited point of view, even if the person generates *only* such permutations and combinations in his or her premises. It is not necessary to require a view of the world as "A or not A," (e.g., "health or no health," "canary or no canary") that is, a view (or belief) of the world exhibiting only permutations and combinations of one content. The individual may only think of grief-provoking content, but he/she can also have other fantasies or cognitions. To suggest such an "A aor not A" world is a limited and harsh view of life, one that neither the suicidal person nor we have to accept. Thus, the task is to really understand the first premise or core belief; and therefore, the "therefore," Why the suicide? We must not be limited by what any suicidal person says, writes, communicates, believes, and so on. We in fact need to not buy into the suicidal person's beliefs/cognitions in our case study; some of them may well be intentioned to mask the truth, reality, and so on.

Theory, explicit and implicit, like that presented, plays a key role in understanding any behavior (and for suicidal behavior, it is essential) (Leenaars, 2004). It is only through theory that we will sort out the booming buzzing confusion (mess) of suicide experience. We do not have to accept the mess. Perception is in the eye of the beholder (Kuhn, 1962). Yet do we accept the theory of the soldier suffering from mild cognitive disorder from a TBI? The abandoned person? The man with the scratched Ferrari? The student who received a B+? The government official who committed a crime and was jailed? Thus, it would be wise to reflect on the dead person's conclusion, his/her "therefore." We think many of us can be relatively sure—no, absolutely sure—that at least the scratch on the Ferrari is not cause to therefore kill oneself. It is also not cause to therefore kill someone else too, say the chief who demoted you. However, the dead person did—and that is a huge red flag—*it is suicide!*

DISSEMBLING: CLUES TO SUICIDE RECONSIDERED

"Suicide happens without warning." This is a myth that Shneidman challenged (see earlier discussion, Suicide Facts and Myths). He stated that the fact was "Studies reveal that the suicidal person gives many clues and warnings regarding suicidal intentions." Another fact, according to Shneidman, was "Of 10 persons who kill themselves, 8 have given definite warnings of their suicidal intentions." However, is "Suicide happens without warning" really a fable? People, in fact, today believe that "Suicide happens without warning" is a myth (Leenaars et al., 1988). Be that as it may, for the DSI examiner, the concern is if 8 out of 10 people give warnings, what about the other two? Forensic specialists are more concerned about this group; that is, the dead person who dissembled. Goldblatt (1992) and Litman (1994) have separately noted that a small but noted percentage of completed suicides are seen as having left no clues. A minority of these people are most perplexing to even the most veteran forensic suicidologist. How do we understand and classify their death (Leenaars, 1997)? This is the forensic unmapped.

The classical case, albeit a literary one, is Edwin Arlington Robinson's "Richard Cory" (1953). The poem describes Richard Cory as a "gentleman from sole to crown." He was "human," "rich," "favored," "schooled," and, in fact, people "thought that he was everything." Then, as the poem ends, Richard Cory, unexpectedly puts a "bullet through his head." Here is Robinson's classical poem, one that many of us read in English class in high school:

> Richard Cory
> Whenever Richard Cory went down town,
> We people on the pavement looked at him:
> He was a gentleman from sole to crown,
> Clean favored, and imperially slim.
>   And he was always quietly arrayed,
> Andy he was always human when he talked;

But still he fluttered pulses when he said,
"Good-morning," and he glittered when he walked.
    And he was rich—yes, richer than a king—
And admirably schooled in every grace:
In fine, we thought that he was everything
To make us wish that we were in his place.
    So on we worked, and waited for the light,
And went without the meat, and cursed the bread;
And Richard Cory, one calm summer night,
Went home and put a bullet through his head.

That suicide happened without warning. The Richard Cory-type of person is, in fact, a person who many of us experience in our police and/or forensic career. The fact is that over 80% of the people who killed themselves did leave clues. The other 20% result in the unknown, with the Richard Cory-type being even more infrequent, but perhaps not as few as some believe. This is often true, in fact, in equivocal deaths. A much publicized Canadian case illustrates this point: Acting Inspector Kelly Johnson, from the London Police Service, on June 7, 2007, killed Superintendent Dave Lucio, and then herself with her service gun. She was a highly regarded officer, who managed to hide her spiraling (dissembling) depression from her police-trained family, chief of police, fellow officers, medical doctor, counselor, and so on. Nobody knew who she was. She was discussed on the front page of Canada's national newspapers over and over, and in every other media (Leenaars, 2010a). She was what we call a Richard Cory-type of suicide. I investigated the case; I will present the public report in the next chapter. We need to understand the Richard Cory-type person better. As you will learn, the psychological autopsy is a roadmap to understanding the Richard Cory type. It solves our unknown; it did in the Kelly Johnson case.

In the 1990s, Shneidman (1994) had reconsidered his perspective on clues to suicide. He asked "How it is that some people who are on the verge of suicide . . . can hide or mask their secretly held intentions?" Shneidman suggests that many clues are veiled, clouded, and guarded, some even misleading. He argues that there are individuals who live secret lives. These people do not communicate. They often lie. These people do not process and/or mediate the stimuli in the usual way, having a defensive intent, conscious and/or unconscious, to avoid the situation. There are walls, or barriers. Often these walls reflect a basic coping style, with conscious and unconscious elements in the process (Leenaars & Lester, 1996). This is pervasive in equivocal cases. Shneidman calls it *dissembling*.

To dissemble means to conceal one's motives. It is to disguise or conceal one's feelings, intention, or even suicide risk. These people wear "masks." It is a masking. The story that they tell is that they *do not* tell their story; indeed, they themselves may be unaware of the dissembling or masking. There may be self-deception. There was, as you will read later, with Kelly Johnson. There is frequently an enduring personality pattern. It is an enduring pattern of inner experience and behavior, and the American culture may reinforce it. For example, from an early age, they lie about everything, both omissions and commissions. The behavior often deviates markedly from the expectations of family, friends, and even of one's culture or the culture of a group (or subculture), such as being an officer (or is it?). Often, unconscious processes are involved. Kurt Cobain dissembled; he stated in his note that he is, "faking it and pretending as if I'm having 100% fun." Most investigators encounter such people, not only suicidal people. Their stories are invalid; sometimes they even intentionally produce or feign a behavior (or symptom).

Of course, secrets are universal; people keep secrets. This is very true in homicide. You don't send a note to your victim the day before stating, "I'm going to kill you tomorrow." Suicidal people are often no different. People intent on lethal violence often dissemble; it is at the core of their intention. As you will read in Chapter 2, David Lucio never expected Kelly to kill him, and he was a smart street cop! No one expected it.

It is probably true that secrets must be kept in life—some may be life saving. Yet there are several types of secrets that have varying effects on wellness. Berg-Cross (2000) offered the following list: supportive, protective, manipulative, and avoidant. It is probably true that supportive and protective secrets are often positive and may even have healing value (Everson & Camp, 2011). They may well be essential even in our investigations. Yet the manipulative and avoidant secret—the Richard Cory types—are a source of anxiety, PTSD, depression, suicide risk, and homicide risk. They are deadly. They are *never* helpful in the wellness sense (Everson & Camp, 2011; Imber-Black, 1993). Lethal secrets fall into the latter two categories. They are one of the most lethal, if not the most lethal, aspects of the scenario in suicide. It is dissembling that kills so many, and the American system/culture reinforces the deaths, that is, stigma. Of course, this is not intentionally so, but reinforcing nonetheless. It all too often creates needless deaths. Again, this is why the study of equivocal deaths can be so perplexing, the un*known.*

To intentionally get ahead of my later chapters: Psychologist and lawyer Jack Kitaeff (2007) offers an excellent overview on dissembling, malingering, lying and junk science in the courtroom. It is a must read for any DSI investigator and forensic psychiatrist and psychologist.

CONCLUDING REMARKS

People in general have considerable difficulty appreciating significant characteristics of suicidal individuals. Most fortunately, a host of suicidologists have given us a rich history of theory for understanding suicide. These suicidologists point out that the suicidal history is understandable, and thus we can find the unmapped. There are answers if we have a method to do so. We don't have to conclude "undetermined." Having said that, there will always be some that remain unknown. It is, however, a fact: Most deaths can be unequivocally solved!

The main conclusion is that there may be more commonalities (agreement or sameness) in suicide than differences. By virtue of our human quality, whether male or female, whether from China or not, whether young or not, greater similarities than differences are to be expected in all suicidal events (Shneidman, 1991). Maybe there are classifications, patterns, common constructs, commonalities, or whatever we wish to call it. We presented an array of evidence-based commonalities. Despite clear and distinct commonalities, each individual must still be, however, understood and investigated idiosyncratically (uniquely), even if dissembling.

We need to continue to develop multidimensional models (Goffman, 1974; Kuhn, 1962) to understand suicide; and the suicide of that individual, whether Adolf Hitler or Kelly Johnson, that can be researched and, most importantly, can be classified. We need to be evidence based. What empirically supported roadmaps can be made that are effective with that deceased person? We need to be person centered (or oriented)—what kind of person that person is (or was). This is true for police officers, forensic clinicians, pathologists, suicidologists, and the like—all who work at death investigation. The goal of our book is simple: to help you investigate the death, whether suicide, homicide, homicide-suicide, accident, or whatever. Your question, like mine, is What methods can we use?

A final sign post:

In Herman Melville's (who was an equally troubled soul) monumental study of people's anguish and suicide, *Moby Dick*, Chapter 36, "The Quarter Deck," Captain Ahab speaks:

> Hark ye yet again—the little lower layer. All visible objects, man, are but as pasteboard masks. But in each event—in the living act, the undoubted deed—there, some unknown but still reasoning thing puts forth the mouldings of its features from behind the unreasoning mask. If man will strike, strike through the mask! How can the prisoner reach outside except by thrusting through the wall.

We—police, forensic specialists, and so on—must understand and reach through the suicidal mask to find the forensic unknown, to find the barren bones of the mind's pain.

CHAPTER 2

The Many Faces of Death: Homicide, Homicide-Suicide, Self-Harm, and Accidents

The forensic specialist or officer needs to understand more than suicide; he/she needs to understand the many faces of violence and death. Suicide is violence. Homicide is violence. Suicide is self-directed violence. Homicide is other-directed violence. They are lethal violence. Suicide, homicide, homicide-suicide, and other violence have probably always been part of the human experience. (Why?) In this chapter, we will look into homicide, but also other forms of violence, especially self-directed ones. We will look into accidental deaths (some are intentional), and self-harm. I will begin, however, with other-directed violence: homicide.

SUICIDE AND HOMICIDE

"What is homicide?" is an age old question (Allen, 1980; Henry & Short, 1954; Stevenson & Cox, 2008; Unnithan, Huff-Corzine, Corzine, & Whitt, 1994; WHO, 2002). Death is superordinate to homicide. Like suicide, homicide is one category of the four universally recognized modes of death—what Edwin Shneidman (1985) called the NASH categories of death: natural, accident, suicide, and homicide. There are different types of homicides, and homicide can be unintentional, such as accidental homicide. Homicide, defined by intention, is murder. Murder is the intentional use of physical force or power, threatened or actual, against another person or community that results in death (WHO, 2002). Again, like in suicide, intentionality is central. This type of homicide is chosen on purpose. Although there is a problem in clear definition, in Chapter 1, we defined suicide as follows: "Currently in the Western world, suicide is a conscious act of self-induced annihilation, best understood as a multidimensional malaise in a needful individual who defines an issue for which the suicide is perceived as the best solution" (Shneidman, 1985, p. 203).

If that is so, we can define intentional homicide as follows: Currently in the Western world, *intentional* homicide is a conscious act of other-induced annihilation, best understood as a multi-dimensional malaise in a needful individual who defines an issue for which the homicide is perceived as the best solution.

Of course, the definition has complexities. Like in discussions on suicide, a question that can be asked is, When is homicide a conscious intentional act of other-directed cessation? These issues are beyond the scope here, and we advise the reader to look at WHO (2002) and a host of other good available books for discussion on the topic.

It is estimated that almost two million people die by violence each year. Almost half of these are suicides and one third are homicides. No single factor or event, as you have learned, explains why so many people die by suicide. It is the same with homicide. Suicide, homicide, and the like are the result of an interplay of individual, relationship, social, cultural, and environmental factors. This is, as you read, called the ecological model.

Thus, a number of questions on our current topic of suicide and homicide arise: Is suicide the same as homicide? Or is it different? Similar and different? What about homicide? How is it similar and different? Are there commonalities? What about homicide-suicide? Are there shared factors? And what about the other many faces of violence?

According to the WHO (2002), "While some risk factors may be unique to particular types of violence, the various types of violence more commonly share a number of risk factors" (pp. 13–14). There are associations between suicide and several other types of violence, especially homicide, in fact (Alan, 1980, 1983; Malmquist, 1996; Stevenson & Cox, 2008; WHO, 2002). They are associated in multifaceted ways and by implication, because violence is a multifaceted problem with biological, psychological, social, and environmental factors, it needs to be confronted on several different levels at once. The ecological model guides us. And on one more point, from the model's implications, violence, like death, has patterns or commonalities, and thus is capable of being investigated (WHO, 2002, 2006). It is not random. It is not like white things. However, to do so, a comprehensive approach is needed to answer forensic undiscovered: Is it suicide? Homicide? Accidental? An order: One should not shoot into the dark for our investigations!

The question, thus, can be posed: Are suicide and homicide related? If so, how are they associated? How can we understand homicide and suicide in our forensic cases?

The public typically distinguishes between homicide and suicide. They are seen as fundamentally different. Indeed, health professionals, police, coroners, politicians, the media, and so on distinguish between them. Many investigators do. Yet there is a different way, as we are already hinting at, to understand the behaviors. Homicide and suicide may be more similar than often believed. There may be commonalities (or common factors).

In the Western world, suicide and homicide were not always seen as different. Early Christian thought made no distinction. St. Augustine categorically saw suicide and homicide as the same; like homicide, suicide violated the commandment, "Thou shalt not kill." Only God had power over man's life and death. Homicide and suicide were greater sins than any other. This was not only true only for Christians but also for many other religions; for example, Muslims, Hindus, and Buddhists. These views continue today. Suicide, in the Western world, in fact, is a relatively new term, probably dating from the 1600's. Before that, the words used were self-killing or self-murder. The classical and current German term is in keeping with this tradition: *Selbstmord* or self-murder.

In science in the 1800s, Enrico Morselli (1882) and Enrico Ferri (1917) saw homicide-suicide as having the same underlying principle. This position was criticized by the well-known sociologist Emile Durkheim (1897/1951). Sigmund Freud (1924/1974), however, held the same view as Ferri and Morselli. Freud saw suicide as homicide turned inward on the self. Freud noted,

> Just as the suicidal person may be attempting to kill an introjected ambivalently regarded other, the murderer may be killing an object of projection; the other, then is one in whom one sees one's own badness. The close linking of suicide and murder is seen in the mechanism of seeking to be killed, to be punished for one's own transgressions particularly for one's own murderous feelings. (as cited in Allen, 1980, pp. 86–88)

Of course, many other scientists hold to Freud's or Ferri's view. Yet, it was probably Andrew Henry and James Short (1954) who constructed the best-known theoretical explanation of the relationship between homicide and suicide (Unnithan et al., 1994). Of course, there are differences between homicide and suicide, but there is much to be gained by following Henry and Short. Despite accepting unique differences, both general and specific, we need a unifying model, a best fit possible (not perfect) at this time. Unnithan et al. (1994) stated the basic argument as

> that although there are disagreements between homicide and suicide, there is much to be gained from revitalizing the theory developed by Henry and Short. Specifically, there are numerous issues related to lethal violence that can be better addressed—and, in some cases, understood—by working from an integrated model that emphasizes the similarities between self-directed and other-directed violence. . . . We are not, however, advocating a cessation of research that views homicide and suicide as distinct behaviors. Depending on the topic of investigation, this approach may be entirely appropriate and reasonable. Our contention is that for many research questions related to human violence, the goal of explanation will be better served by a theoretical model that explicitly takes into account the connections between homicide and suicide. (p. 5)

For our forensic case, I agree! It helps to solve the "mysteries" better.

Suicide is self-induced annihilation. To understand suicide, as we have stated, it is useful to understand related topics of violence, especially homicide. In fact, as I have argued, suicide and homicide can be seen as interwoven expressions of the same stream, called the *stream analogy* of violence. Both can be conceptualized as a lethal response to experience of trauma and the frustration of needs (e.g., honor, attachment), differing only in the direction in which the response is expressed.

The stream analogy of lethal violence is not new to this century. In the 1800s two Italian scholars, Enrico Ferri (1917) and Enrico Morselli (1882) were best known for the idea. Many did not agree, nor today. Emile Durkheim (1897/1951) espoused that "suicide sometimes co-exists with homicide, sometimes they are mutually exclusive" (p. 355). In science, Copernicus was not the only great scientist silenced. For approximately a century, Durkheim's view dominated sociology and forensic study; Sigmund Freud in psychology, however, held to a view consistent with the stream analogy. In 1954, Henry and Short resurrected the view.

Historically, Ferri (1917) and Morselli (1882) noted that different societies (or nations) had different rates of suicide and homicide and raised an important question. Why do persons in some social groups kill themselves more while other groups commit murders more? For example, why do Americans kill others more and themselves less compared to Canadians (Leenaars & Lester, 1994)? Given their close geographic and cultural proximity, that fact is worth remembering. (There are many other differences in suicide and homicide in those two nations.) Thus, do not assume, around the world, that a suicide is a suicide or that a homicide is a homicide (Leenaars, 2007). There are different views or core beliefs and thus different conclusions on the *unmapped.*

Unnithan et al. (1994), following Henry and Short (1954), suggest that there is a stream of available destructiveness in a society (or culture). Ferri (1917) called this production. They propose that this can be measured by what they call lethal violence rate (LVR). LVR measures the size of the stream of violence—LVR = suicide (S) + homicide (H). The direction of the stream, as Ferri called it, can be measured, on the other hand, by the suicide-murder ratio, SHR. SHR gauges the proportion of the total, which is expressed as suicide rather than homicide—SHR = $S/(S + H)$.

Unnithan et al. (1994) suggest that these two measures allow one to understand the specific lethal violence in groups. From an integrated model, they write, "At the individual level, both forms of lethal violence result from a combination of negative life events (frustration, stress) with attributional styles that locate blame either in the self (suicide) or in others (homicide)" (p. 94).

Prediction is based, they argue, on attribution. Attribution is a product of situational and cultural factors. The American culture would highly add to attribution. Ferri (1917) and Morselli (1882) had espoused biological factors (degeneration, impotence or decay of the organism), whereas Unnithan et al. (1994), like Henry and Short (1954), present a more social meaning view, and where Freud presented a more individual view (see ecological model).

Of course, this view is not without criticism. After Durkheim, Jack Douglas (1967) was most critical and influential. He wrote, "It is not possible to explain specific types of social events such as suicide in terms of abstract social meaning" (p. 339). Moreover, Douglas maintained that the data on which statistical studies are based are inherently biased. Be that as it may, it is a well-established fact that we need multiple sources to understand violence, for example, personal documents, third-party interviews, research on attempters (of suicide and homicide), and mortality statistics, something that we should do in all forensic cases, in fact. There should be no single technique (or assessment); one must be multimodal in technique and approach in all cases of death (Leenaars, 2004). *Regrettably, many do; not wise!*

The importance of this model is that the stream analogy of violence resurfaces for us to understand suicide, which is something that allows us to better understand annihilation, whether homicide or suicide or, for that matter, homicide-suicide. On a footnote, it can be asked whether this is true for males and females. The answer appears to be, yes (Johnson & Hotton, 2003; Leenaars, 2004). On one further footnote, we highly encourage the reader, as already stated, to consult some classic texts on homicide. Space limits us here. At least we recommend Nancy Allen's *Homicide* (1980; a person the author has consulted with on the topic on a number of occasions).

To conclude, a question raised by David Lester (1987b) on homicide and suicide was, "Are they polar opposites?" As we have seen from an ecological view, murder is violence and suicide is violence. They are intentional acts of aggression. Suicide is the human act of self-inflicted, self-intentional cessation. Homicide is the human act of other-inflicted, other-intentional cessation. Can homicide and suicide then be opposite behaviors? Scientifically, this is a difficult question as there have been few studies that have compared suicides and homicides (Lester, Perdue, & Broockhart, 1974).

Several types of suicidal and homicidal behaviors exist that appear to transcend the simple dichotomy. Homicide-suicide is the obvious one; and, as will be discussed below, it is not uncommon for murderers to commit suicide after murdering their victim (Allen, 1980, 1983; Lester, 1987b). Yet many such as Palermo, Smith, Jentzen, Henry, Konicek, Peterson, et al. (1997) equally argue for homicide-suicide to be seen as separate from homicide. I agree. There are several possible reasons for some killers killing themselves after the homicide, and we share below the insights from those studies. In fact, Lester (1987b) has concluded,

> All murderers are not alike. Megargee (1966) has distinguished between the overcontrolled murderer (who is calm, peaceable, and unaggressive much of the time, but who explodes occasionally into dramatically violent behavior) and the undercontrolled murderer (who is continually assaultive to the least frustration or insult). Clearly, these two kinds of murders handle their aggressive impulses very differently. Similarly, suicidal people differ. Some are chronically suicidal, making repeated suicide attempts before, in some cases, eventually killing themselves. Others who kill themselves have no history of prior suicidal behavior (Lester & Beck, 1976). These two types of suicidal individuals may be appropriately characterized as undercontrolled and overcontrolled, respectively. Identification of types of murderers and suicides may eventually lead to a better understanding of which factors (intrapsychic, interpersonal, and situational) lead some individuals to direct their aggression outwards while others turn aggression against themselves. (p. 59)

Next, I want to discuss homicide-suicide in more detail.

HOMICIDE-SUICIDE

Suicide is a multidetermined event. Homicide is a multidetermined event. Thus, it follows that homicide followed by suicide is also not determined by one factor. We cannot here provide all of the literature, but allow us a few signposts for your roadmap. We begin with a direct quote by Nancy Allen (1980), a world expert on homicide and a lifelong friend of Edwin Shneidman. She writes,

West (1966) has pointed out that murder-suicide offenders are a far less deviant group than the sample of ordinary murderers. The majority of murder-suicide cases are married and live in a conventional family setting, free from criminal associations. The killings are most likely to be of the spouse or child.

The perpetrator commits suicide out of despair rather than hostility. She or he has excessive frustration and enormous guilt because of a greater degree of social consciousness. Selkin's (1976) study revealed that a homicide-suicide usually symbolizes the stark failure of a family's attempt to live together productively. There is evidence of a long-term malignant situation, with either a history of interpersonal discord or a history of life-threatening disease, or both. The perpetrator's attitude toward the victim is marked by ambivalence—jealous rage versus affection so strong the perpetrator removes himself or herself from the murder through suicide.

Freud (1924) noted, "Just as the suicidal person may be attempting to kill an introjected ambivalently regarded other, the murderer may be killing an object of projection; the other, then is one in whom one sees one's own badness. The close linking of suicide and murder is seen in the mechanism of seeing to be killed, to be punished for one's own transgressions particularly for one's own murderous feelings."

In Narioch's (1973) study of homicide in California, it was reported that 10 percent of the perpetrators of homicide commit suicide. This was not found to be the case in the sample this investigator studied. Murder followed by suicide occurred in five percent of the cases studied. Two of these cases will be discussed below. These are cases where the suicidal individual had been disturbed by his or her life situation. Both couples were married and living in what appeared to be a conventional family setting as law-abiding citizens. (pp. 86–87)

The early theorists on homicide-suicide were West (1966), Wolfgang (1958), and Allen (1980, 1983) (see Harper & Voigt, 2007). Allen (1983), for example, studied 104 homicide-suicides in Los Angeles during 1970–1979. The rate of homicide-suicides was 2% of all homicides and suicides. However, Wells (1966) reported a rate of 33% of all homicides and Wolfgang (1958) reported a rate of 4% of all homicides (One has to read carefully; the comparative groups are not always the same). There are further findings of note in Allen's Los Angeles study: 93% of the offenders were male; 80% of the victims were female. (As an unusual tangent, in the West (1966) study, 40% of the offenders were female. That is high.) The majority (71%) of the killers were husbands/boyfriends of the victim (2% of the women murdered their children, a subgroup of homicide-suicides. Not all homicide-suicides are the same.) In all, 20% of the victims (4 males and 7 females) and 21% of the offenders (16 males and 1 female) were intoxicated (having a blood alcohol level of 0.1% or higher). Traces of alcohol were found in 29% of the tested victims and 34% of the total offenders; 50% of the victims and murderers had been drinking. Therefore, once more, alcohol increases risk, not only for suicide but also homicide and homicide-suicide (Allen, 1980) (and, I would add accidental deaths too). It can be explosive.

Suicide notes were left by 14% (15 people) of the homicide-suicides. We provided an example in Chapter 1, and here we cite another example:

Dear Mary
You made it impossible to live with you, and there is no way that I can live
without you. I'd rather be dead. I loved you more than life.
     George

This note is prototypical.

Despair appears to be primary. The pain is unbearable. This appears to be more
evident than hostility. There is such traumatization, rage, excessive frustration, and
enormous guilt (Allen, 1983). Milroy (1998), however, suggested that after the
murder, remorse is a minor reason for the suicide. He asked, "Is it then revenge?"
Our read is that may be true, but also it is escape. Indeed, not all homicide-suicides
are alike. In one group, there is a history of interpersonal discord, domestic violence,
and frequently jealous rage. However, in another group, namely, the older or
terminally ill, there is an overwhelming sense of incapacitating, painful illness.
In another group, often women, there is a history of severe depression, and, facing
their death, they also kill their children. (Of late, we have also seen mass murder-
suicide, like what we saw on 9/11). Regardless of whether there are one or two or
more groups, Allen (1983) concluded that "All (is) quite different from what is
usually implied by the phrase, homicide-followed by-suicide."

Steven Stack (1997), a friend and prolific sociologist, has provided the best
presentation on the known research on homicide-suicide, and I encourage a read of
his study. Stack provides a long list of correlations: frustrated personal relationships,
ambivalence, jealousy and morbid jealousy, separation, depression, helplessness,
and guilt—an endless list of factors. The similarities between these observations and
the ones that we made earlier on suicide are striking. There may well be a stream of
violence. Homicide-suicide and suicide are not polar opposites. They are highly
correlated, but also they may be less correlated with homicide. Homicide-suicide
is more a suicide than a homicide (see Leenaars, 2010a, for details). Thus, allow
me to go into more detail regarding Stack's important study.

In 1997, Stack studied the records of all homicides in the murder files of the
Chicago Police Department from 1965 to 1990. Stack attempted to correct previous
methodological problems by having at least a homicide comparison group.
Regrettably, he did not have a suicide comparison group, something commented on
by David Fishbain (see below). In the archives, Stack found 267 homicide-suicides.
Stack, in his analysis, controlled for sociodemographic variables (possible confounders). For the killers, these variables were male, age, and Caucasian race. For
the victims, female, age, and Caucasian race. Statistical procedures, simple bivariate
analyses, multivariate and logistic regression analyses, were undertaken representing
a sound array of comprehensive statistical techniques.

The incidence of homicide-suicides to homicides in Chicago was 1.65%, low by
worldwide standards. Stack (1997) concluded,

> The structural relationship that increases the odds of homicide-suicide the most is
> that of ex-spouse/lover. For ex-spouses/lovers, the risk of homicide-suicide
> is 12.68 times higher than in nonintimate homicides. In these cases, the bond that
> once held a couple together is officially broken. The loss is final; it is no longer

just threatened or simply coming in the future. For persons very dependent on the old bond, this loss of their love object can be unbearable. For some ex-spouses/lovers jealousy intensifies after the breakup as they perceive that their former love object is involved with new partners, persons who have taken their place in love.

As anticipated, the current girlfriends or boyfriends of killers are at less risk (6.11 time higher odds of homicide-suicide) than spouses and ex-lovers. Here the bonds are not quite as intense and so the loss of support is not as great. Further, since the couple was not living together, it is less likely that a killer would feel that "I can't live without you" relative to someone he or she is already living with or once did live with under the same roof. (pp. 447-448)

In relation to our previous discussion on Unnithan et al.'s (1994) work on homicide and suicide, Stack (1997) stated,

This study has some implications for hypothesis formation in the general area of homicide-suicide. Unnithan et al. (1994) have proposed a "stream analogy", wherein the choice between homicide and suicide depends on attributional concerns. Persons and groups faced with frustration will choose suicide to the extent that they attribute the cause of their problem to themselves and to the extent that they are depressed and feel helpless. Other groups and individuals will opt for homicide if they tend to attribute the cause of their problem to others and to the extent that they feel angry as opposed to depressed. Drawing on a dozen qualitative studies on homicide-suicide, this study contends that the principal source of frustration in homicide-suicide is a frustrated, chaotic, intimate relationship marked by jealousy and ambivalence. These relationships are marked by a feeling that one cannot live with the other person but cannot live without them either. A separation or threatened separation arouses anger and depression at the same time. The act of homicides overcomes a sense of helplessness. However, the associated depression and guilt over the loss of one's love object result in suicide. Perhaps homicide-suicide can be best thought of as containing both attribution styles discussed by Unnithan et al. (1994). (pp. 448–449)

Stack's observations are worth remembering in our investigations (he is today's leading sociologist studying suicide).

Probably the best Canadian study on the topic is by Jacques Buteau, Alain Lesage, and Margaret Kiely (1993), who studied homicide-suicide in Quebec from 1988 to 1990. Buteau and his team examined 39 consecutive cases of homicide-suicide. Sociodemographic data, circumstances surrounding the event, and clinical data were recorded. Yet they noted limitations to the data and called for psychological autopsies. One important homicide-suicide, the case of 14 victims of the mass murder-suicide at the Polytech in Montreal in 1987, had a large impact on the data. These events make a difference. The victims of Columbine would be another extreme example. The thousands of victims of 9/11 make a huge difference. These mass homicides-suicide(s) are different, but also the same.

Buteau and his team (1993) further concluded that coroner's files, police reports, and so on, lack rich psychological data. The necessary, unequivocal, evidence is "scarce." This scarcity makes it difficult to offer insightful conclusions. For example, it does not allow us to isolate psychopathology, such as the hypothesis of a high incidence of borderline personality disorder. To date, the research is not sufficient, surely not sufficient enough to answer the question in our retrospective investigation. They state, "Psychological Autopsies, well known in suicide studies, is the method of choice." The need for psychological autopsies is well recognized (Palermo et al., 1997). I agree.

Fishbain (1994) has, however, also criticized Buteau and his team, namely, for the lack of utilization of proper control comparison groups. Fishbain noted that from his research, presented below, homicide-suicides are more like suicides. This is true about female homicide-suicides. Despite this, the tendency to only compare to homicide continues. This gives us more unknowns. This is not to say that it is not useful, only that it is lacking. The empirical data call for a comparison to a suicide group or a homicide group and suicide group, but not only to a homicide group. The knowledge from only erroneous comparisons is constricting. Fishbain, Rao, and Aldrich (1985) demonstrated this fact. Thus, caution is in order even in the best studies. They have limits, especially for our day-to-day work.

There is one unequivocal fact: intimate partner homicide (and thus, homicide in general) and homicide followed by suicide, have different characteristics/factors and probably distinct etiologies. A few differences are the predominance of female victims, the predominance of intimate partner victims, older age of perpetrator, and use of firearm. Lund and Smorodinsky (2001) present a study that examined homicide between intimate partners in California to determine whether homicide followed by suicide differs in important ways from those without a suicide outcome. They studied the homicide files of the State of California during 1996. They found that out of 186 homicides committed by intimate partners, 181 were heterosexual intimate partner relationships, and 40% (N = 74) committed suicide subsequent to the homicide. All offenders were male. The main conclusion was, indeed, that there are more significant differences in the characteristics of victims-perpetrators and circumstances of intimate partner homicides and intimate partner homicide followed by suicides. Unequivocally, they are two distinct groups. Lund and Smorodinsky confirmed the markers (red flags) for the homicide-suicide group: the predominance of males, dysfunctional relations, uses of guns, and so on. Indeed, one of the significant predictors is the use of firearms is that it is likely that the perpetrator intended to commit both homicide and suicide by gun to ensure the lethality. Yet, once more, these researchers call for more in-depth study.

Suicide as aggression turned inward has been presented; it is a well-accepted fact. However, the intense role of aggression in homicide-suicide appears to be equally critical, but also not well known. As one homicide-suicide perpetrator said, "If I can't have you, no one can." This is common, aberrant thinking; a lethal major premise (core belief). It easily follows, "I can't have you. Therefore, no one will. I'll kill you."

We would be remiss if we did not highlight the importance of intimate partner violence in homicide-suicide. It is present in almost all cases (Bossarte, Simon, & Barker, 2007). It may well not be universal, but at least common. Of course, domestic murder-suicide is the ultimate example of domestic violence. The fact that it is almost always a male phenomenon needs to be better understood. Why is it that men, in particular, are so determined not to allow their partners to leave? Why would the male offender feel jealousy and hatred to such extent that they would rather kill the one they love and die themselves than to accept that their partner no longer wishes to be part of their lives? Like others, Barnes (2007) suggests that these are urgent women's issues. Barnes suggests power/control is central. She offers a feminist perspective and "argued that the patriarchal nature of our society provides the fertile context for the individual to kill a loved one and then commit suicide" (p. 10). If so, we need to look to the ecological model for effective, comprehensive investigation.

The discussion to this point begets a core question: What about female homicide-suicide offenders? Regrettably, there is only one study; yet it is probably one of the best-designed studies of the topic, a study by David Fishbain and his team (1985). We will, in concluding this section on homicide-suicide, examine their study in detail. Maybe it will allow us to better understand homicide-suicide in females like Kelly Johnson.

Making the now-obvious observation, female homicide-suicide perpetrators are rare and unusual (Fishbain et al., 1985). The percentage of female to all homicide-suicides has been low. Further, given that homicide-suicides are more like suicides, there had been no study until Fishbain on the very topic. Fishbain and his team (1985) examined the case files of the Dade County Medical Examiners Department from 1957 to 1981. Inclusion in the homicide-suicide group was determined by the principles of medicolegal death (coroner) investigations, albeit they have limits. Control groups were selected; female homicide victims in homicide-suicides were compared to female homicide perpetrators in homicide-suicides and to female individual suicides. Thus, there are three groups. The information reviewed was as follows: death certificate, report of the police officer investigating the deaths, medical examiner's autopsy report, toxicology report, suicide note if written, newspaper clippings, hospital records if patient lived for a while after the homicide or suicide, and previous hospital records if available. All available chart information was reviewed for all three-victim groups. The task was a very large undertaking, but also most helpful, including for us in our NASH investigations.

Some 133 homicide-suicides were identified. Of these homicide-suicides, females were the perpetrators in only 10 cases. The percentage, thus, was 7.5%. Significant differences were found between the groups; yet the female homicide-suicide perpetrators were more like female individual suicides than female homicide-suicide victims. The following were the results.

The following items were determined to be significantly different between female homicide-suicide perpetrators and female homicide-suicide victims: type of residence, living with whom, object of homicide, type of discovery, weekend deaths, presence of suicide note, and recent history of depression.

The following items were determined to be significantly different between female homicide-suicide perpetrators and female individual suicides: type of residence, living with whom, and recent history of depression.

There are a great number of relevant facts. The great majority of homicides involved family members or acquaintances; this is even more so for murder-suicide. It is largely a dyadic event. There is a strong attachment (identification). "Typically," stated Fishbain et al., "because of the strong affection of the victim, the murder perpetrator did not want to go on living without him or her and committed suicide" (1985, p. 1152). After the homicide, suicide becomes escape. Female perpetrators were much less likely to live with the spouse or acquaintance than female homicide-suicide victims. The object of the homicide, compared to male perpetrators, was much more likely to be a lover or ex-lover. There was an extreme and probably dysfunctional intimacy providing a primary source of attachment; once this is lost, jealous rage may occur (Selkin, 2005). Often the discovery of the homicide-suicide was not a surprise to survivors; yet in female homicide-suicide perpetrators it was almost always not anticipated. No one knew or predicted it. Few people expected the tragedy; no one knew who the perpetrator was. There is deep isolation. Is masking/dissembling more common in female homicide-suicide perpetrators?

Compared to data on male homicide-suicide offenders, female homicide-suicide perpetrators are less impulsive and more planned the murder. For example, they more often leave a suicide note. These women's murders are not impulsive, but are manipulative and very highly planned. There is a need for a high degree of preplanning, in fact. There is a great deal of dissembling or masking. It is often a response to trauma, such as chronic domestic (intimate partner) violence. Fishbain and his team (1985) allow us to see many of these women differently. Alcohol abuse, although present, was not discriminative. It did occur frequently, however. The weapon was usually a gun, but also it does not discriminate. Of course, availability of means is always critical in our investigations.

On one more important point, the female murderers in homicide followed by suicide often saw themselves as acting in self-defense, but the suicide followed nevertheless. It is likely that despite trauma, such as domestic violence or loss, the female perpetrators felt remorse or guilt. Suicide becomes an escape. Female perpetrators often had abusive, unstable relationships. They sometimes killed their partner while being beaten, sometimes in self-defense, but not always. The murder was sometimes victim precipitated. Of course, the question arises, is this true in a specific case? It was not in the Kelly Johnson case, discussed below, for example, except *the* domestic violence, that is, the murder of David Lucio by Kelly Johnson.

Female homicide offenders frequently suffer from mental disorder (psycho-pathology), notably affective disorders and alcoholism. Personality disorders are evident. However, female homicide-suicide perpetrators differ. Female homicide-suicide perpetrators more often suffer from depression. Thus, the female homicide-suicide offenders are different in important ways from female homicide perpetrators and female homicide-suicide victims. Furthermore, Fishbain et al. (1985) show that they are more like female individual suicides. There are, in fact, very few statistical differences. Thus, Fishbain et al. concluded that female homicide-suicide can be best understood as types of suicide, not as homicides. I highly agree (Leenaars, 2010a).

Mental disorder (psychopathology) is a striking similarity between suicide and homicide-suicide. Female individual suicides are most likely to have a history of depression than female homicide-suicide perpetrators, who in turn are more likely to have a history of depression than female homicide-suicide victims. The percentages are as follows: 92% versus 40% versus 2%, respectively. Suicide and psychopathology, or an inability to adjust, are intimately related. The same is true for homicide-suicides. Psychopathology is a risk factor not only in suicide.

A final fact: suicide of a loved one has often been considered a suicide risk factor. This appears to be true for homicide-suicide as well (Perdue & Brookhart, 1974). There may be a contagion.

The main conclusion from this sole study on female homicide-suicide is that they are most like suicides. To conclude, homicide-suicide is an extension of suicide (Leenaars, 2010a; Marzuk, Tardiff, & Hirsch, 1992; Milroy, 1998).

HOMICIDE-SUICIDE POLICE CASE:
DAVID LUCIO AND KELLY JOHNSON

Kelly Johnson killed David Lucio; she then killed herself. It was a homicide-suicide. I investigated the case and present the public forensic report below. An obvious question: why present a case before your method, the psychological autopsy (PA)? Is this not like putting the cart before the horse? Why present the David Lucio-Kelly Johnson case now?

The answer: Because it is not a PA report; it is a public report vetted by the London Police Services (LPS). An excellent psychological autopsy report is presented later by Dr. Jerome Motto. Edwin Shneidman would call it a forensic investigation. It is not a PA. What is meant by a PA report is all very different from that report.

By way of history, I was asked by LPS to chair an independent forensic committee to undertake a retrospective investigation of the homicide-suicide, a front-page event, covered by the media in Canada and the world. Dr. Peter Collins, my co-investigator, is a forensic psychiatrist and investigator with the Ontario Provincial Police (OPP). There was a third member who investigated the possible domestic violence in that case (There was no violence except Kelly's, of course). I undertook a PA; I reviewed the documents, suicide e-mails, and such, and undertook other PA interviews with many informants. I even went back to her kindergarten friend. It was extensive; Drs. Leenaars and Collins submitted a 254-page detailed PA report; a 65-page summary PA report, and a 26-page executive summary report, the anticipated public PA report. The LPS vetted a new police report, the one presented below. The report is factual; yet it is not a PA report. Dr. Shneidman would have given me an F (a failing grade). I do not mean to suggest that it has no value, only that it is not a PA report. It is a different roadmap. It is a common forensic/police one. It does give us some markers in the backwaters of despair. Later you will read about real PA enquiries and reports. They will uncover some of the real deeper barren bones of the suicide's mind. I present *res ipsa loquitor*:

**Report to the
London Police Service and London Community on the Deaths
of David Lucio and Kelly Johnson**

**Authors:
Antoon A. Leenaars, Ph.D., C.Psych., CPQ Windsor, Ontario
Peter Collins, M.C.A., M.D., F.R.C.P(C) Ontario Provincial Police &
University of Toronto
Deborah Sinclair, MSW, RSW Toronto, Ontario**

**Prepared for: Chief Murray Faulkner
London Police Service**

May 20, 2008

Overview of Committee Mandate

Opening Statement: *The committee wishes to express sincere condolences to the family and friends of David Lucio, to the family and friends of Kelly Johnson, and to the police officers and staff of the London Police Service. We also thank them for their cooperation, not only to understand the tragic events, but also for their input into the recommendations. We also recognize the profound effect that the tragedy has had on the London community.*

David Lucio died by homicide on the June 7th, 2007. Kelly Johnson died by suicide following the homicide of David Lucio on the June 7th, 2007. They had been police officers of the London Police Service. Chief Murray Faulkner, LPS, on June 11th, 2007, released the following report to the public:

> "As a result of a case conference and extensive investigation involving members of the Regional Coroners Office, the Pathologist and the London Police Service, the Coroner has determined that retired Superintendent David Lucio died as a result of sustaining a single gunshot wound. The investigative findings indicate that the passenger of the vehicle, Acting Inspector Kelly Johnson, fired the gunshot that killed David Lucio prior to taking her own life with a single gunshot. As a result this tragic incident has been determined to be a murder/suicide."

The London Police Service, as part of its response, established a committee, with Dr. Antoon A. Leenaars, Dr. Peter Collins, and Ms. Deborah Sinclair, to investigate and examine this tragic murder/suicide. The background of the committee members is summarized in Appendix A of this report. On July 9th, 2007, Chief Murray Faulkner requested an examination of the following:

- "The extent to which the murder/suicide was predictable and preventable.

- What safeguards could be in place to reduce the risk of future incidents?"

A psychological autopsy was conducted as part of this review. A psychological autopsy involves an analysis of available data and evidence, such as personal documents, reports, electronic mail, and third-party interviews to understand the reasons and dynamics underlying a tragedy. In this matter the psychological autopsy was developed in the context of David Lucio's and Kelly Johnson's lives and addressed the fundamental questions, "Why did the homicide-suicide happen?" and "What can we do to prevent a similar occurrence?"

Throughout our investigation, the committee has taken its responsibilities very seriously and acted diligently with the charge of not only understanding the tragedy but also for making recommendations that will hopefully save lives in the future with regard to suicide and homicide-suicide at the London Police Service or other police services who may face similar circumstances.

Homicide-suicide is a complex and multi-determined event. People are naturally perplexed, stressed, confused and overwhelmed when they are confronted by a homicide-suicide. These thoughts and feelings are especially true in the tragic David Lucio/Kelly Johnson homicide-suicide, both well-known and respected senior police officers. Understandably, homicide-suicide, given its complexity, is most difficult to understand. It is a rare event and even more rare to have the perpetrator a woman. There is in fact, only one study on female perpetrators of homicide-suicide. In a recent U.S. study, 95% of the perpetrators in a homicide-suicide were men who acted most often in the context of family and intimate relationships.

There were a number of contributing factors in the Lucio/Johnson homicide-suicide: emotional disturbance, historical stressors (diagnosis of her mother's illness), stress (the loss/rejection of David Lucio that probably resulted in unbearable distress and anxiety), alcohol abuse, and the availability of a firearm. There are common aspects of homicide-suicide, such as domestic violence, that were not evident in this case. There was no evidence of domestic violence between David Lucio and Kelly Johnson.

Kelly Johnson was unable to adjust to her life's demands. At the time before her death, she was "desperate". She had not been eating or sleeping, was experiencing "panics", was drinking alcohol often, was depressed and was not coping well. She appears to have had both generalized anxiety and separation anxiety. She was observed to be depressed and "emotional" at times, but also masked or hid her emotions, thoughts and intentions. Kelly Johnson was observed to be a capable friend and employee and there were no clues to suicide or homicide-suicide. No profes-sional involved with Kelly Johnson, her friends, family or colleagues had any foresight of the lethal circumstances and impending tragedy.

A main conclusion is that at the time of her death, Kelly Johnson possessed the characteristics and dynamics more like a person who died by suicide than a female perpetrator of homicide. Kelly Johnson's death was a suicide; one must adopt that point of view to understand her. She had the following intrapsychic characteristics of suicide: unbearable psychological pain, cognitive constriction (or narrow thinking), indirect expressions (or ambivalence), emotional disturbance, and a feeling of being vulnerable. She had the following interpersonal characteristics: problematic relationships, rejection-aggression and the wish to escape. In too many Canadians, suicide becomes the only solution, and in a very small group, homicide-suicide becomes the best solution. These terms are defined in Appendix B of this report. She also had some of the markers for intimate partner homicide-suicide, such as frustrated personal relationships, ambivalence, jealousy, separation, depression, helplessness, and guilt. However many aspects of Kelly Johnson and these circumstances were rare and unique and made any prediction difficult. Suicide among police, in Canada, occurs but is less than in the general population. The incidences of suicide in policing is higher in other countries.

Although there is little research on homicide-suicide, among police there appears to have a higher occurrence than in the general population. We hope our report and recommendations are a step towards a better understanding of these complex issues.

EXECUTIVE SUMMARY

During the summer of 2004 David Lucio and Kelly Johnson were both married to their long-term spouses. It was during this summer that Kelly Johnson's mother was diagnosed with cancer. This diagnosis was devastating for Kelly Johnson as she and her mother were very close. Shortly after this diagnosis Kelly Johnson and David Lucio began an intimate extramarital relationship. This relationship continued until June 2007 and led to the dissolution of both marriages. During this time a number of other significant events occurred, which had a traumatic effect on Kelly Johnson. In December of 2005 Kelly Johnson's mother succumbed to her illness and passed away. Her pet of fifteen years also passed away, and she also dealt with on-going relationship issues as she and David Lucio parted ways so that she could attempt reconciliation with her husband. This attempt was short lived as David Lucio and Kelly Johnson continued their relationship during this reconciliation.

During this time Kelly Johnson had sought professional counseling, first through the London Employee Assistance Consortium, and then with a private counselor. In the weeks preceding June 7th, 2007, a number of things occurred to create additional stress for her. Kelly Johnson's ex-husband was retiring from his position as Inspector of the Professional Standards Branch, which meant Kelly Johnson would no longer have ready access to him at work. To complicate matters Kelly Johnson was being promoted to the rank of Inspector and was taking over for her ex-husband in Professional Standards as his retirement facilitated her promotion.

At the same time David Lucio's daughter, who worked outside the country, was in London for two weeks. David Lucio and his estranged wife spent time with their daughter as a family, which meant David Lucio was less available to Kelly Johnson. The Lucio's re-connected during this time and decided to give their marriage another chance. David Lucio told friends that he was ending his relationship with Kelly Johnson after his daughter left to return to work. There is no doubt that the relationship between David Lucio and Kelly Johnson ended on Monday June 4th, although some may argue about who ended the relationship. It is clear that on June 5th and 6th Kelly Johnson was in a very fragile state. She was highly perturbed and was not eating or sleeping. Close friends were concerned about her. Upon analysis after the tragedy, her electronic mail reflected emotionality, narrow thinking and other indicators of suicidal ideation.

On June 6th Kelly Johnson went to David Lucio's residence for the evening and sent an electronic mail to David Lucio from his own computer (David Lucio was not at his residence when the electronic mail was sent). The electronic mail was very desperate in nature, requesting that David Lucio and Kelly Johnson reconcile under whatever terms David Lucio would find acceptable. This electronic mail was opened by David Lucio at 9:50 PM and no one knows what occurred between this time and just prior to midnight when Kelly Johnson had David Lucio drive her to the London Police Service Headquarters where she retrieved her service pistol and subsequently shot David Lucio and then herself.

The Independent Review Committee is of the view that these deaths were neither predictable nor preventable by the London Police Service or other individuals associated with David Lucio and Kelly Johnson. These findings are based on the following facts.

1. Kelly Johnson was seen by a mental health professional just prior to the tragedy and that professional did not document Kelly Johnson to be at risk for suicide or homicide. Although she attended appointments, with professionals, overall it appears that she was non-compliant with treatment. The non-compliance reference is in relation to the fact that she was attending counseling but perhaps not discussing the depth of her problems, as well as, being prescribed medication, but concerned about the side effects and did not follow through with the prescribed treatment.

2. Kelly Johnson had been seen by her family doctor, who diagnosed her as having an adjustment disorder relating to her mother's illness. She was also perceived to be depressed but was not viewed as being a threat to herself or others. She was also seen by the London Police Service employee assistance plan, London Employee Assistance Consortium counsellor who did not deem her a risk to herself or others in prior years.

3. David Lucio was a highly skilled retired senior police officer and apparently did not suspect anything on June 7th, 2007, in spite of the recent relationship break up. He was aware of Kelly Johnson's distress about the break up. He also spent the evening with her and drove her to the police station enroute to her residence. Clearly he did not suspect that she would be picking up her service pistol.

4. Kelly Johnson received ongoing positive evaluations from supervisors and peers and had just been promoted to Acting Inspector of the Professional Standards Branch. There were no warning signs in the workplace of a pending tragedy.

Although this tragedy was neither predictable nor preventable in our opinion, there are a number of issues that Kelly Johnson was dealing with which have only come to light with the benefit of hindsight and access to critical information from professionals, friends, family, colleagues, and most importantly, information gleaned from the psychological autopsy. The psychological autopsy that reviewed all the information after the tragedy concluded she was suicidal. These issues were identified and followed by recommendations, which flow from the facts of this tragedy.

RECOMMENDATIONS

These recommendations flow from the findings of the Review Committee. The recommendations are based on the facts as we understand them. One of the major reflections in our review is in the area of mental health and the stigma surrounding mental health, which in many cases leads to barriers to seeking help. Police officers are no different from society at large in facing problems in regards to mental health. Police are not exempt from being perpetrators and potential victims of domestic violence. The Review Committee believes that prevention is the best intervention and education is the best tool to achieve this outcome. The Review Committee supports education and initiatives through training opportunities, which would reduce barriers to seeking help.

1. The London Police Service should continue to be committed to the mental health and well being of all its members. The London Police Service could explore an expansion of services by innovative models such as the Psychological Services Section in some larger police services (e.g., Calgary Police Service). The mandate of this section could include being a support to members experiencing emotional difficulties through early intervention. The London Police Service could consider hiring a Police Psychologist to manage the section. We recommend that a committee be established to determine the framework for such a section, realizing that the London Police Service may not have the need for a full time psychologist or the resources to fund a full time section based on the model of larger police services.

2. The London Police Service should continue to build liaisons with the London Employee Assistance Consortium and other community services, to help prevent, intervene and address aftermaths of suicide and other traumatic events.

3. The London Police Service should continue to support ready access to psychological, medical and empirically based interventions. Furthermore, the London Police Service should prepare a list of senior counselors in the community with experience in dealing with police officers. This list should be re-compiled on an on-going basis and be readily available to officers to compliment the existing employee assistance plan.

4. On the recommendation of the committee, the London Police Service has already implemented a more comprehensive psychological assessment for recruiting, the Minnesota Multiphasic Personality Inventory-2 (MMPI-2), with inclusion of the revised clinical scales. The latter scales are most effective in screening a wide array of risks. Furthermore, the committee recommends that additional re-assessment be undertaken at the promotional level and when members are transferred to higher stress areas such as Emergency Response Section, Drug Units, Cyber Crime Units, Forensic Identification and fatal motor vehicle collision investigations.

5. The committee recognizes the London Police Service document, "Handling of Firearms"; it clearly articulates the safe storage, discharge, handling and transportation of firearms. Kelly Johnson's behaviour was a clear violation of this procedure. We do not advocate further gun controls measures. We recommend that London Police Service continue to remove access to firearms for officers who are off duty due to a stress related illness or mental disturbance. Policies should be developed to determine if and when officers should have access to firearms upon their return to work.

   Notwithstanding our review, it is important to note another police officer homicide-suicide in Eastern Ontario in 2004. Upon review, the Chief Coroner suggested supervised control of issue firearms when officers are off duty. While police services have not found this policy change to be a feasible and practical solution to date, the Lucio-Johnson tragedy affords the London Police Service and other police services the opportunity to re-examine this issue. The costs and practical implications of such a new policy may make this recommendation difficult to implement but we feel that a study together with other organizations such as the Ontario Association of Chiefs of Police may be helpful to thoroughly address the issue. As with all policies regarding weapons, it is necessary to weigh the practical, physical, and financial implications of undertaking changes for such a large police service against the obvious likelihood that supervised control might have altered the outcome of this particular tragedy.

6. The London Police Service should develop a clear policy on conflict of interest; regulations and procedures need to be developed and implemented. We recommend that the London Police Service develop a committee to establish such regulations and procedures including a clear personnel policy regarding conflict of interest involving related members. These should not restrict officers' rights, but also London Police Service's policies need to eliminate any actual or potential conflict of interest in the workplace, which may arise from a working relationship between immediate family members and/or intimate partners.

7. The London Police Service should develop new initiatives to deal with vicarious trauma and stress management for police personnel. There needs to be greater awareness and recognition to the unique demands facing female police officers in a male dominated police profession.

8. Postvention refers to those interventions after the tragic event has occurred and deals with the traumatic after-effects. In this case, these effects refer not only to family, friends and fellow officers, but the entire London community. We recommend that the London Police Service, together with community experts, develop comprehensive efforts for postvention in response to this tragedy.

9. We recommend that for those individuals who would like to gain a better understanding of suicide, and homicide-suicide review the selected readings that were used to form the basis of this report be made available to any person who wishes to review them. These could be kept in hard- copy form in

the London Police Service library and made accessible via an Internet link. We believe that it is important to ensure ongoing education for all police personnel and their families on domestic violence, suicide, mental health issues, substance abuse, health and wellness and the aspects unique to police culture including strengths and stressors.

The following website is recommended: http://www.suicideinfo.ca

Request topic: homicide-suicide

APPENDIX:
Glossary of Terms

Access to Firearms:

Access to firearms greatly increases the lethality in suicidal persons.

Cognitive Constriction (or Narrow Thinking):

Tunnel vision, or rigid thinking, is common and one of the deadliest aspects of the suicidal state. The individual sees suicide as the one and only solution for their current difficulties. They think everything is hopeless and things will never be better.

Domestic Violence:

Refers to any behaviour within an intimate relationship that causes physical, psychological or sexual harm to those in the relationship.

Emotional Disturbance (or Psychopathology):

About 60-90% of suicidal people have a psychiatric disorder, the most common being depression or psychosis.

Indirect Expression (or Ambivalence):

The suicidal person is deeply ambivalent about living or dying.

Interpersonal Relations (Problem Relationships):

The suicidal person often feels alone and cut off from others. They have experienced conflict and rejection from others.

Intrapsychic:

Existing or taking place within the mind or psyche.

Rejection/Aggression:

An experience of loss or rejection (for example, spouse leaving, fired from job, ill health, death of a fellow officer) is often a trigger for suicide. Research suggests that those who react with anger or aggression may be more at risk for suicide. Suicide is an act of self-directed violence; homicide-suicide is an act of other-directed violence and self-directed violence.

Unbearable psychological pain:

The common trigger for suicide is unbearable pain, a deep anguish, in which the person feels hopeless and helpless.

One update: The LPS has implemented all of the recommendations.

A most important question that arises, including for DSI is, On a continuum, when does a discrete event of suicide, such as that of Robin Williams, become a relationship one, from suicide pacts, ranging from co-equal involvement, such as lovers, to one of pressure and coercion, such as the author Arthur Koestler and his wife, to unwilling victim and a perpetrator as in Dave Lucio and Kelly Johnson, or even mass murder-suicide bombers/terrorists, such as 9/11?

ACCIDENTAL DEATHS

The NASH categorization (natural, accident, suicide and homicide), according to which deaths in most nations are classified, obscures many of the psychological dimensions of death. As I discussed before, it treats death merely as a biological event and fails to address issues of intention and subintention (Shneidman, 1985). Moreover, it suggests that the categories in NASH are distinct, when in fact there may be considerable overlap in modes of death. For example, some deaths categorized as accidental may in fact be suicidally motivated. The automobile is a lethal weapon (or potentially a lethal weapon).

Probably the best known classical book on accidents and suicide is Norman Tabachnik's *Accident or Suicide* (1973). Dr. Tabachnik was often considered the fourth "horseman" within the troika of Drs. Shneidman, Litman, and Farberow. He was the accident expert. Like the first step in our topic, I hereby copy verbatim Dr. Tabachnik's definition of accident:

> *Accident* may be associated with a number of values and thus have several meanings and definitions. We must try to make our particular understanding of it explicit.
>
> There are three components to the type of accident we concern ourselves with in this book. We shall list them as follows:
>
> 1. *An accident is an event associated with a significant personal or social loss.* There are many events called *accidents* which do not result in loss. An accidental slip of the tongue may not even produce embarrassment. An accidental meeting with a friend may bring about pleasure, etc. However, we are interested in those accidents following which a person or group of persons experience that something important—life, well-being or property—has been taken from them.
> 2. *An accident involves a transfer of physical (or chemical, or thermal, or electrical) energy between two separate reservoirs of energy.* This uncomfortably technical statement tells in specific terms how the loss occurs. What

it means is that people and inanimate objects can be damaged or destroyed when something without much resilience hits them with great force or when something very hot or highly charged with electrical energy comes into contact with them.

3. *An accident is unplanned and mostly unanticipated.* Although there are "reasons" why accidents happen, they are not completely or at all known to the victims.

   This general attribute must obviously be modified, however, if some accidents are suicides. In such cases, the event would *seem to be unplanned and unanticipated to the outside observer.* (If this observer would believe the event to be a suicide attempt, he would call it that and not an "accident.") However, research would establish that the victim knew very well what would happen. In this case, we would have a suicide masquerading as an accident. (pp. xi–xii)

An accident, thus, is also a multidimensional event; it too, is not simple (Tabachnik, 1967, 1973). We are here most interested in *suicide by car.*

Freud (1901/1974), Menninger (1938), Shneidman (1963, 1985), Murray (1967), and others have speculated that there is a vast array of subintentional deaths that occur beyond intentional suicides. Alcoholism, drug addiction, mismanagement of physical disease, car accidents, self-harm, and many other behaviors can be seen in this light. Farberow (1980) edited an insightful volume on the topic, *The Many Faces of Suicide*, providing an array of studies on subintentional death. How can we study the faces of violence, whether intentional and/or subintentional. Can we show associations? Causes? What do we know?

Sigmund Freud (1930/1974) speculated that such phenomena can be studied, not only at an individual level, but also at a social level. He argued, for example, that civilization and its discontents can be measured in the level of self-destruction present in a society. Subsequent views, such as those by Farberow (1980), support Freud's opinion. This would be expected because social mortality data are based on the population of individual cases, and if the individual cases are misleading so are the aggregate data. (Nomothetic data are based on individual cases, not vice versa.) Of course, we do not suggest that social analysis can do real justice to the psychological analysis of subintentional deaths. Regrettably, the split between the individual approach and nomothetic approach is pervasive in suicidology today, with both sides calling the other's perspective "useless," "trivial," and so on. The truth is suicidology needs both approaches to advance as a science. This is at the heart of my approach and, I believe, a sound roadmap. We need both!

Farberow, Freud, Menninger, Shneidman, and others have, therefore, concluded that self-destructive behaviors, that is, suicide and its many forms, originate from psychological and social/cultural forces, that is, our ecological model holds. In order to understand the act of suicide and its substitutes, it has been shown to be useful to relate the behavior to other kinds of violence, especially homicide (Freud, 1917/1974a; Henry & Short, 1954; Leenaars & Lester, 1996; Unnithan et al., 1994). Suicide, homicide, alcohol abuse deaths, and so on, are seen as interwoven. Can we prove it?

Leenaars and Lester (1998) explored three correlates of suicide, namely, homicide, one form of accidental death (motor vehicle accidents), and one form of natural death (cirrhosis of the liver caused by alcohol abuse) that is sometimes assumed to be a subintentional death (Farberow, 1980). The question raised is whether the NASH classification obscures the complexities of suicide at a societal level. Specifically this question will be addressed through a study of the mortality data of Canada.

Durkheim (1897/1951) is probably the best-known theorist on suicide at the sociological level. He theorized that social integration—the degree to which people in a society are bound together in social networks—is associated with the self-destructive behavior of suicide, and research has indicated that measures of social integration (such as marriage, divorce, and birth rates) may be associated with suicide rates (Leenaars, Yang, & Lester, 1993). Other research has suggested an association between unemployment and suicide (Leenaars et al., 1993; Platt, 1984).

The primary question of Leenaars and Lester's (1998) study was the following: Are the social correlates of various kinds of death the same or different? Data were obtained for Canada for the period 1960 to 1985. The results showed that suicide, homicide, and death caused by alcohol are alike, but also that *not* all accidents were, only some. These results, therefore, suggest that the impact of social integration on society may apply to self-destructive behaviors other than suicide, consistent with our hypothesis. The results raised questions whether motor vehicle accidents, sometimes identified as a possible subintentional death (Farberow, 1980), can be grouped together with self-destructive behavior at a social (nomothetic) level. The answer is that it depends. Not all accidents are so. MacDonald (1964) reported a disproportionate representation of former psychiatric patients in accidents. He also noted a striking feature was that half the patients made the attempt very impulsively following an argument with a lover, marital partner, or less commonly with a neighbor or superior at work. Each individual case must be evaluated separately, as it has been shown that occasional motor vehicle accidents may, in fact, be subintentional deaths (Farberow, 1980). The most likely are single-car accidents, especially if there was substance abuse.

On a different note: Can the NASH categories be distinguished from one another as is frequently assumed? Do they blur the complexities involved in determining cause of death? Do they obscure our understanding of not only the rates of suicide but also complex social circumstances of death, and thus, bias our investigation? Death by automobile offers special opportunity for concealment of suicide and homicide. There may be dissembling. It would conceal humiliation or disappointment, for example. The extent of deliberate death on the highway is not known. It is not like putting a gun to your head, yet it is just as lethal. Imajo (1983), for example, reported on five suicides by motor vehicle drivers; however, he concluded that there was a concerning problem in the method of investigation of suspected cases. He asked, How can we determine the mode accurately? What evidence exists that certain accidents represent direct and conscious suicide or suicide attempts? "The very presence of some accident-like suicides would support the possibility that there might be many other accidents which are quite similar to the 'suicidal ones'" (Tabachnik, 1973, p. 14). Of course, some such accidents may differ in the degree of conscious intention of a desire to kill oneself. Some may differ in degree of conscious awareness—there can be, like suicide, self-deception, not only deception. To traverse through these deaths, like Shneidman and Tabachnik, I believe that the PA is the best tool.

Pompili, Girardi, Tatarelli, and Tatarelli (2006) addressed the issue of a possible link between single-car-accident drivers and suicidal intent. They selected 30 single-car-accident drivers who had been admitted to emergency departments and then hospitalized for an average period of 10 days. They matched these patients with a control group of drivers who had never had a car accident. Results showed that single-car-accident drivers were not exposed to a higher overall suicidal risk, though they reported fewer reasons for living. They expressed tiredness of being alive. These patients had experienced more traumas too. Pompili et al. (2006) concluded that, although suicide risk was low in the patients, they were engaged in looking for a solution to their problems in which the accident played a role in such a process. In fact, there are associations to constricted logic and cognitions. An example of core beliefs of suicidal individuals is "I need to escape. An accident is a solution." Connolly, Cullen, and McTigue (1995) reported the same conclusion on a constricted solution becoming the only available, acceptable, and best solution. *It is the only solution.* Some may even be like a Russian roulette fantasy: "I left it up to fate" (Tabachnik, 1973). Thus, for example, are the single-road traffic deaths of the deceased, accidents, or actually suicides? There are many faces of suicide.

There are some further excellent studies from Norway, maybe the best. Thoresen and Mehlum (2006) investigated 43 suicides and 41 fatal accidents in Norwegian soldiers/peacekeepers (1978 to 1995). They undertook a psychological autopsy. The groups differed. Mental health problems were the most important risk factor for suicide. Living alone and the breakup of a love relationship were especially more evident in the suicide group, even when controlling for psychopathology. PTSD was especially high in the suicides. This was, however, not evident in Thoresen and Mehlum's accidental deaths, keeping in mind these were not single-car accidents. The individual (case control) study is reflected in my social (aggregate) level (Leenaars & Lester, 1998) study. The aggregate, of course, should reflect the individual cases.

Thoresen and Mehlum (2004), examined risk factors for more specific types of fatal accidents and suicides, asking, Is there an overlap? It is commonly believed that there is an increased risk of fatal accidents and that such accidental deaths may be related to mental health problems. Thoresen and Mehlum conducted a study to investigate fatal accidents in Norwegian former peacekeepers. Unlike their previous studies, looking at all accidents, they looked at a subgroup of alcohol-related fatal accidents; a PA was undertaken (e.g., military records, police reports, interviews). Thoresen and Mehlum examined 17 cases of alcohol-related fatal accidents compared with 28 cases of other accidents and 43 cases of suicide. Thoresen and Mehlum appeared to confirm Freud's belief. They found that, "the alcohol-related fatal accidents were found to share many common features with the suicide group, such as depression, alcohol and substance abuse, and various social problems, and were also found to differ significantly from the other fatal accidents" (p. 990). These facts may make a great deal of difference in our classification of mode of death.

Farberow (1980) coined the term *indirect self-destructive behavior* for the many faces of suicide. Freud (1901/1974) called it "unconscious" suicidal dynamics. Shneidman (1985) proposed the term *subintentioned death*. Thoresen and Mehlum, in their unique study, in fact, showed the existence of the many faces of violence. They speculated that alcohol abuse, drug ingestion, excessive smoking, and self-harm are various forms of risk taking. Tabachnik (1973) had already pointed out the central role of alcohol in accidents that are suicides, but also accidents in general. Thus, the question for investigators is how many accidental deaths are, in reality, hidden suicides. Secrecy is prevalent. A small sub-group of motor vehicle accidents and drug-related deaths may be labeled a face of suicide (and thus, violence). This should make a difference in answering the unknown. A sub-group of fatal accident, namely, alcohol-related cases, is so. In the Thoresen and Mehlum study (2004), alcohol-related accidents resembled suicides. They are suicides in many ways. I also believe that some could be homicides. We need to target all self-destruction and other-destruction in our conclusion!

Tabachnik (1973) asks some prototypical practical questions about the driver of the automobile in an accident. He writes,

> One would have to consider his knowledge of the characteristics of the vehicle, his knowledge of the roadways, traffic patterns, and other characteristics of the path which he traverses, his physical health and, last but not least, a number of psychological attributes. Here one would ask: How alert is the driver? Does he have a characteristic driving pattern (cautious or impulsive)? Is he able to be flexible in terms of his response to shifts in traffic and possible hazards? And finally, does he have suicidal or self-destructive trends? (Tabachnik, 1973, p. xiv)

It is these self-violent facts that we shall have to consider in our DSI investigations. Was it an accident, or suicide? It may also be homicide-suicide, of course. One has to know the person—the driver—to really know if it was an accident, intentional, subintentional, or unintentional. To answer such questions, the best available technique is the PA, I believe. I will illustrate, by way of a suicide note in a case, in a later chapter.

SELF-HARM

Norman Farberow (1980), among many other scientists, raised awareness of the problem of self-harm or sometimes called self-mutilation. Farberow noted that there was an interest or curiosity about self-destructive behavior of our fellow man. He thought that some people's behaviors were motivated by what we would consider to be irrational. Albeit being taboo to study for centuries, Farberow thought it was essential that the secrecy be made visible (a common belief by now). He asked, Why do people inflict or harm themselves? Why defeat themselves? Why would a diabetic stop taking insulin? Why would a person endlessly cut him/herself? There are many behaviors that contain a high potential for serious physical injury and for serious damage. Yet there is no intention to be dead; well at least, often. Self-injurious behaviors or self-harm behaviors with no intentional cessation are not suicidal behaviors per se. These are behaviors that involve deliberate self-harm with no intent to die. However, it is also obvious that these people are more like suicidal people than more indirect self-destructive behavior in some ways; yet in others they are not. They lack intent to be dead. (That is a critical criterion, as you have read, in suicide.) The self-harm has special meanings, often excitement and pleasure (Farberow, 1980).

> While self-mutilation takes many forms and may be inflicted on many parts of the body, the most familiar form is wrist-cutting, in which the act of cutting often serves the significant purpose of helping the person to regain contact with reality and to come out of a depersonalized state. Blood is often involved with a special significance, a kind of visible evidence of a sacrificial act which the person must carry out, perhaps to expedite some overwhelming guilt. (Farberow, 1980, pp. 9–10)

Beyond guilt, shame, and disgrace, for examples, would be other motivators.

Farberow (1980) goes on to note that the pain experienced in the cutting becomes important too, as indicative of the need to transfer psychological pain to physical pain. Sometimes the physical pain numbs the deeper psychological pain—the unbearable pain of pain; the same motivation as for suicide. (There are commonalities.) Physical pain is more acceptable and maybe manageable; cutters may be more tolerated. It may well be potentially suicidal, however. It is similar but not identical with a true suicidal condition (Shneidman, 1985). Both are inimical behaviors. Kreitman, Philip, Greer, and Bagley (1969) suggested the word *parasuicide* for the behavior, in fact. I will, however, keep to the more common term here (see Chapter 3). Of course, there is great overlap between the two—suicide and parasuicide. People who have a history of self-harm do kill themselves sometimes. However, not all people who are at risk of self-harm kill themselves. Only some do. It is a risk factor, and this may be a clue in your investigation.

In Farberow's book (1980), Simpson presents a few insights; here are the words of a self-cutter:

> This time I slashed my wrist. I crushed a burnt-out light bulb and saved the piece of glass. But razor blades are better. I cut parallel lines across my arm, avoiding old scars. I watched myself cutting, not feeling a thing, as if it wasn't really my own arm. My head was full of images of blood and glass glittered and gleamed. The blood creeping stickily across my skin felt good and real. The blood is me. The cuts are neater than my handwriting. They're not too deep—just deep enough. I'm in control, in an odd way, just when I'd been getting out of control. I'm really alive again, when I'd been feeling so dead. I told them I flushed all the glass down the toilet. I lied. I've got the best bits hidden away. For next time. (p. 257)

There are abundant studies on self-harm in the general population. There is, however, an exceptional study about the topic regarding armed forces personnel that I wish to present. Hawton, Harris, Casey, Simkin, Harrison, Bray, and Blatchev (2009), present a unique study wherein they investigated the characteristics of armed forces personnel in the UK, presenting to a general hospital following self-harm. They compared these individuals with matched controls in the general population who had self-harmed.

The method called for investigation of armed forces personnel presenting to hospital between 1989 and 2003 following self-harm. They found that 166 armed forces personnel presented with self-harm (184 episodes) during the study period; 72.3% (120) were male. Almost two thirds (62.7%) were young, under 25 years of age. Females in particular tended to be young, with nearly three quarters (73.9%) being in the 16–24 years age group. Common problems were relationship problems (62.0%), employment problems (43.9%), and alcohol abuse (40.5%). Fewer armed forces personnel than controls had evidence of current or past psychiatric disorders (psychopathology). Fewer soldiers had treatment or a prior history of self-harm. Their suicidal intent was judged to be lower (males only). Of 64 people in the armed forces who presented during the first nine years of the study period, 6 had died by probable suicide (9.38%). Hawton et al. (2009) concluded that self-harm by soldiers in the UK may often be a response to interpersonal and employment problems. Alcohol abuse was often implicated. Of course, alcoholism itself is a risk factor in suicide among armed forces.

Methods of self-harm varied:

> Four out of five (80.1%) of the self-harm episodes by the armed forces per-
> sonnel involved self-poisoning alone. More than three-quarters of these involved
> non-opiate analgesics (77.3%, 116/150). The next most frequently used groups
> of drugs were minor tranquillizers and sedatives (9.3%, 14/150), followed by
> antidepressants (7.3%, 11/150). Nearly a third of the overdoses involved a
> range of other prescribed drugs (31.3%, 47/150). These included substances
> such as non-steroidal anti-inflammatory drugs and antibiotics. (p. 268)

Self-cutting was also a frequent method, and may be more prevalent in the United States than the UK samples.

There were diverse traumas reported. The most common type of problem was a relationship with a partner (62.0%). Next was employment problems (43.9%). The work-related problems were common military ones. "The most common type of employment problem concerned specific difficulties relating to the individual's job within the Forces. Including the job being stressful, disliking the job, the job being boring and repetitive, and failure to progress or be promoted" (Hawton et al., 2009, p. 269). Relationship issues with fellow soldiers within the forces were another source of difficulty. At the time of self-harm, more armed forces personnel were facing problems concerning a relationship with a partner and employment. Although self-harm is also more common in females in the general population, female soldiers were overrepresented in the self-harm population.

Alcohol abuse was common. Disciplinary problems occurred in 16 (11.5%) individuals. These were mostly related to military disciplinary issues, although in other cases consequences of civilian offenses (e.g., being convicted). Incarceration was a trauma. Shame and disgrace again seemed implicated.

Stigma was clearly evident. Hawton et al. (2009) note that, "Minimisation of symptoms due to perceived stigma may have influenced these findings" (p. 271). There "may be a sizeable problem of self-harm in the armed forces that does not come to clinical attention" (p. 271). Once more, secrecy is a risk factor. Be that as it may,

Hawton et al. "suggest that self-harm by armed forces personnel is often used as a means of communicating distress related to current personal circumstances" (p. 271). This is what Farberow had suggested is "a cry for help." All of this is so relevant to answer our unmapped.

CONCLUDING QUESTIONS

In a highly recommended book, *The Many Faces of Suicide* (1980), Dr. Norman Farberow asked some important questions. I hope that they "will resonate to some commonalities."

1. Why did the person stop taking his insulin today when he knew he had to take it regularly to stay well or even stay alive?
2. Why did the person go on an eating binge of all his forbidden foods when the doctor told him over and over how important it was that he observe a strict diet if he wanted the hemadialysis to work?
3. Most people know what drugs and alcohol can do if you become addicted. Why did the person abuse a substance?
4. Why does a person overly pop his prescription medication, Oxycontin, when they're known to be completely irrational and might make him violent enough to injure or kill someone? Him or herself?
5. Why does the alcoholic deliberately stop attending AA knowing that it is a trigger for another binge, which he knows from bitter experience of the pain and depression that follow?
6. Why did the person, while intoxicated, drive so fast, and through the treacherous mountain terrain?

We must keep all faces of violence and death in mind. The road that we need to travel forces us to traverse through multitudinous bones.

PART TWO

Methods

How do we study suicide? What methods can we use in uncovering the forensic unmapped? What will assist in developing a roadmap for digging up the barren facts/evidence of a death? What idiographic (individual) approach can we use? A core belief in science and policing is that the idiographic or case study approach allows us to do the main business of death investigation—the intense study of the human person and thus the understanding of his/her mode of death and most important, why.

The first chapter in this section, Chapter 3, looks at the nomothetic and idiographic approaches. The nomothetic approach is well documented and ingrained in forensic psychology; the idiographic less so. Thus, this chapter examines the idiographic approach in more detail. A main problem in the use of case histories is the one that is the ubiquitous issue of psychology itself: The mind-body problem or admissibility of intrapsychic accounts as opposed to objective report. This chapter spells out an idiographic approach; after all, in forensics, we have no choice. We are interested in that person's death. I appeal to authority—the International Academy of Research (IASR), Gordon Allport, and Edwin Shneidman, to name a few.

Chapter 4 spells out the psychological autopsy (PA). The PA is the work of Dr. Edwin Shneidman, my mentor. Shneidman's key papers, according to his own decision (Leenaars, 1999a) on the psychological autopsy are "The Psychological Autopsy" (1977), which will be presented in verbatim detail; a paper on what a PA is, "Comment: The Psychological Autopsy" (1994), actually a very terse statement on what a PA is not; and Shneidman's favorite case paper, "An Example of an Equivocal Death Clarified in a Court of Law" (1993b), an example of a PA. I will present this chapter essentially as Shneidman taught, *res ipsa loquitor*.

Chapter 5, "A Conversation With Edwin S. Shneidman on Suicide and the PA," presents some very personal discussions that I have had with Dr. Edwin Shneidman that he wanted recorded. The material has been used before in the interstitial material for my edited book, *Lives and Deaths: Selections of the Works of Edwin S. Shneidman* (1999a). However, I present here for the first time verbatim our conversations on suicide, death, NASH, and the PA. The conversations offer one more different angle to develop your expertise in DSI. Our conversations were recorded at his home in Los Angeles, sitting under a birch tree in his backyard. They are what I learned from Dr. Shneidman on the very topic of this book.

The next three chapters examine some core issues in the PA today. Chapter 6, "Problems With the PA," examines the various criticisms made of the PA and offers some ways to correct the methodological problems. The main debate today is how is a mental disorder determined? Chapter 7, "How Many Informants Are Needed?" looks at the common practice of interviewing one or two informants, resulting in limited insight into the psychological bones and thus potential bias. Chapter 8, "Benefits for Informants," offers some research findings that informants find the PA process to be positive, likened to meaning making, gaining new insights, and hope to help others. Overall, this part shows, as already established in the 1950s, that the PA can be a most helpful guide to uncovering a suicide.

CHAPTER 3
The Nomothetic and Idiographic Approaches

From the first day that I found a copy of Shneidman and Farberow's book, *Clues to Suicide* (1957), suicide notes have been a focus of mine in studying the suicidal mind. I was an undergraduate student at the time at the most rewarding educational institution that I ever attended, Brock University in St. Catharines, Ontario. The book was not on my courses, but I noted it and started reading it in the university bookstore. I was absolutely fascinated with the collection of suicide notes in the back of the book; however, I never imagined that that discovery would be the defining moment of my suicidological career. Why would a young student assume that the famous Dr. Shneidman would become his mentor, and not only he, but also his wife, would call him "son"? From that day, I never looked back.

In Dr. Shneidman's own reflections, he does not know whether suicide was looking for him or he was looking for suicide. Part of his motivation on a day in 1949, when he discovered hundreds of "genuine suicide notes" in the vaults of the Los Angeles Coroner's Office, was that he was restless and looking for some niche in psychology. In religion, we talk about epiphanies and epiphany moments. That the notes were "genuine" was an epiphanic moment for Shneidman. He had an autonomic reaction with the feeling, without verbalizing, that it was important to say "genuine" suicide note. Within a couple months of saying "genuine" and then "simulated" and then eliciting notes, and then calling Norman Farberow (I am honored to say, also a lifetime friend of mine), he was beginning a career and a discipline. He said, "Oh boy," suicide notes, "the golden road to the unconscious of suicide," and suicidology began. Decades later, I had the same "Oh boy" in the stacks of Brock's bookstore, while reading a sample of those very notes.

Suicide is a human malaise and suicide notes are the penultimate act, giving a voice to this despair. Suicide notes, of course, are only one type of case study document. If I may quote my friend Shneidman (1980), in *Voices of Death*, wrote that such "documents contain special revelations of the human mind and that there is much one can learn from them." Suicide notes allow us to learn about a person, to advance the nomothetic and idiographic approaches in science, and to aid in the aims of science in general—understanding, prediction, and control. It is in forensics, *prima facie*. It allows us to investigate the barren bones.

A CORE BELIEF STATED BEFORE
THE PRESENTATION

A core belief: The idiographic or case study approach allows us to do the main business of psychology: the intensive study of the human person, and thus, the deceased person. Case study, through personal documents, biography, and so on, allows us to understand the suicidal mind better (Shneidman, 1996). Like Windelband (1904) noted at the turn of the last century, my core belief is that we need idiographic and nomothetic pathways in science and thus, in forensic study.

CONSULTATIONS FOR RESEARCH IN SUICIDOLOGY

Science means research. Research generates the accepted knowledge in a particular scientific community, herein suicidology. There is no other substitute for sounder knowledge. Current research in suicidology, however, needs development. Let us begin with the question in this volume: How do we certify a death as a suicide? What is a suicide? Are there guidelines for psychological autopsies (often referred to as PAs)? Are there operational criteria?

To begin to answer this critical question: I was once asked to chair an international group of experts on that very question. I had the opportunity to lead a task force of the International Academy for Suicide Research (IASR) on the very topic (although the complete report extends beyond the topic—the focus is on future direction for study in suicide). I will here quote what was stated (the complete text was published in *Archives of Suicide Research* (1997, Vol. 3, pp. 139–151; Leenaars, De Leo, Diekstra, Goldney, Kelleher, Lester, & Nordstrom, 1997). I cannot write it any better than on that occasion; the researchers assissting me were the who's who in the field: Diego M. D. De Leo, Rene F. W. Diekstra, Robert D. Goldney, Michael J. Kelleher, David Lester, and Peter Nordstrom. One could have wanted no better group; I am indebted to each of them. As a final word, it should be understood that these recommendations are not exhaustive and obviously call for revision as our field develops rapidly.

Thus, I quote verbatim:

1. There is no substitute for theory in research. There is no data without interpretation. Our view holds that research, whether quantitative or qualitative, should not be atheoretical. Explicit or implicit, theory plays a role; whether solving a specific problem, testing an existing theory, developing new theories or expanding existing ones. One problem is that frequently the theory used or implied is not stated. That is problematic because it is only theory that allows us to sort out the "booming buzzing mess of experience" (Wm. James). Another problem, related to the previous one, is that research in suicidology over the last two to three decades is rarely designed to test hypotheses derived from theory. Most theoretical statements have been formulated "ad hoc" or "after the fact" i.e., after data were collected and had to be interpreted in one way or another. Consequently, the robustness of theories have not been tested and significant theoretical development virtually non-existent of late. . . .

3. A major division in suicidology research is between qualitative and quantitative research. There is a great gulf, for example, between quantitative research reports based on hundreds of subjects and descriptive reports from therapists of interesting patients whom they have encountered. Typically, these reports are authored by different suicidologists, between whom there is little communication, though, of course, there have been attempts to integrate the two (e.g., Leenaars & Lester, 1996). We see this position as akin to the need to encourage the scientists-practitioner perspective in clinical practise of psychiatry and psychology. . . .

4. Related to this, another problem that is a ubiquitous issue in research on people is the admissibility of introspective accounts as opposed to objective reports. This resonates to Windelband's (1904) division of two possible approaches to knowledge, the nomothetic and the idiographic. The tabular, statistical, arithmetical, demographic, nomothetic approach deals with generalization, whereas the idiographic approach involves the intense study of an individual—the clinical methods, history, biography. In this latter approach personal documents—such as suicide notes—are often utilized (Leenaars, 1988). Both approaches should be utilized in the science of suicidology. . . .

6. Shneidman (1985) has argued that definitions in the field are the most important direction for progress. This recommendation should be followed. We offer the following prolegomena.

A. Definitions. Suicide today is defined differently depending on the purpose of the definition—medical, legal, administrative, etc. In most countries reporting to the World Health Organization (WHO), suicide is defined as one of four possible modes of death. An acronym for the four modes of death is NASH: natural, accidental, suicidal, and homicidal. This fourfold classification of all deaths has its problems. Its major deficiency is that it treats the human being in a Cartesian fashion. It obscures the individual's motivations, intentions and much more, never mind the degree of these characteristics. . . .

Yet, it is essential that matters relating to suicide be operationally defined in order to facilitate comparisons and to measure efficacy of interventions both intra-nationally and internationally. Even if we simply divided suicide into (a) suicide and (b) nonfatal suicidal behavior (or simply, suicidal behavior), obscurity would occur. Nonfatal suicidal behavior would encompass suicidal ideas and suicidal acts, yet here issues of nomenclature are rife.

Clustering of suicidal ideation amongst suicidal behavior has and may continue to create confusion. Ideas are separate from actions, which is equivalent to saying that ideation *per se* does not imply any consequent behavior. Obviously, defining in a simple, clinically sounding way nonfatal suicidal behavior (or just suicidal behavior) is a much more complicated issue.

Suicidal ideas, for example, may themselves be divided into those signifying that life is not worth living and those signifying that death is preferable. The hierarchy of ideas is further extended by active consideration of methods, including the where, the when, the how, and the consequences. There is a further step in the hierarchy if the methods and attendant circumstances are both practical and accessible. Such a hierarchical model of suicidal ideas should not presuppose that the individual moves up or down the hierarchy in a linear manner, but the clear definition of where his/her ideas rest on such a continuum would clarify comparisons. To begin such clarification, a major international project is needed to clearly define terms, concepts, and such.

Efforts to begin to address these issues have promised hope, yet to date there is no accepted nomenclature. The word *parasuicide* is a good example. Parasuicide, first introduced by Kreitman et al. (1969), is typically defined (see Kerkhof, Schmidtke, Billi-Brahe, De Leo, & Lonnquist, 1994) as

> An act with non-fatal outcome, in which an individual deliberately initiates a non-habitual behavior that, without intervention from others, will cause self-harm, or deliberately ingests a substance in excess of the prescribed or generally recognized therapeutic dosage, and which is aimed at the realizing change which the subject desired via the actual or expected physical consequences.

The definition includes numerous self-harm acts including suicide attempts. Yet both the words *parasuicide* and *suicide attempt* lack specificity. What are we referring to by the terms? For example, in parasuicide as defined, a person who fortuitously survives an attempt by a shotgun is clustered with a person who mismanages his/her prescription pills. Even at the front lines of suicide prevention, these events mean different things. Simply defining something does not make it useful. According to the majority of the authors of this paper, parasuicide, in fact, has not helped in our steps forward, and we recommend dropping the use of the word.

The minority report, however, sees a value in the term *parasuicide*, both at an individual level and an international one. First, words imply meaning. Consider the term *attempted suicide*; if we call a certain behavior an attempted suicide, then we imply an attempt to bring about a fatal outcome, but then hastily add we truly mean that always or most of the time not. Then we are already in a terminological mess. Second, terms have social and emotional meaning; for example, if we say that an adolescent girl, who after a quarrel with a boyfriend swallows a limited number of benzodiazepines of low lethal potentiality, made an attempted suicide; then attached to the label are far-reaching consequences (Diekstra & van der Loo, 1978). The term *attempted suicide*, according to this minority view, is more a prescription than a description (Diekstra, 1997). Parasuicide is offered as a more objective term, concluding that it is in no way a matter of indifference what term is used. Clinicians, policymakers, and such are affected by the words. The terms, in fact, that we use in the field and disseminate have important individual, social, and political implications.

The term *parasuicide* may also be useful at an international level in cross-cultural studies (to avoid confusion in determination of suicidal intention). This is one of the key values seen in the term *parasuicide* by the investigators in the WHO/EURO Multicentre Study on Parasuicide. It allowed various countries in Europe to study nonfatal suicide acts without addressing the various meanings that different cultures apply to such behavior. The problem, however, with a term like *parasuicide* is that it encompasses such a broad range of behaviors that it may easily become a nondiscriminative and therefore nonsignificant category itself.

To begin to address these issues and to develop a basic nomenclature, we propose some basics that are consistent with other independent endeavors (Rosenberg, Davidson, Smith, Berman, Ganter, Gay, et al., 1988). At the very minimum, the following should be considered: defining suicidal acts, definition of circumstances, definition of medical lethality and definition of intent. These aspects will be addressed briefly below. . . .

B. Defining suicidal acts. Suicidal acts should be operationally defined. Such definitions must include clear-cut descriptions of methods and medical lethality. The WHO now gives a list of methods which should form the basis of future comparisons. Assessment of lethality includes not only methods but also attendant circumstances. Before such assessments are made, it is therefore necessary to operationalize the circumstances.

C. Definition of circumstances. Such definition must include whether the person was alone at the time and secondly, whether he was likely to remain alone until the methods had had, or had ceased to have an effect. If in the presence of others or likely to be discovered by others a judgment would have to be made as to whether these others would prevent the act, allow the process to continue without intervention or facilitate the process.

D. Definition of medical lethality. After method and attendant circumstances have been defined, then gradation of medical lethality is allowed. Medical lethality refers to the degree that a method causes or is sufficient to cause death. The assumption is that acts of high lethality are failed suicides and acts of low lethality have other personal or social meanings. Suicidal behavior is taken to exclude other high risk behaviors, e.g., cliff climbing, car speeding and alcohol and substance misuse.

E. Definition of intent. There should be a distinction between medical lethality and suicidal intent. Intent is defined as to have suicide or deliberate self-killing as one's purpose. Intent includes issues such as "definition of circumstance." Evidence of intent to die rather than knowledge that death will follow should be the basis for the definition. It may well be that how intent is handled is the most important aspect of the definitions. Formal suicide intent scales may be of assistance; however, a recent review of such scales for specific use with adolescence (with application across the lifespan) by the National Institute of Mental Health (NIMH) of the United States concluded that *few, if any, are useful* (Garrison, Lewinsohn, Marsteller, Langhinrichsen, & Lann, 1991). Yet, the NIMH group did isolate two intent scales that had sound empirical support. They are as follows: 1) Beck Suicide Intent Scale (BSIB) (Beck, Beck, & Kovacs, 1975; Steer & Beck, 1988), and 2) Lethality of Suicide Attempt Rating Scale (LSARS) (Smith et al., 1984). All this is not meant to suggest that other scales may not be useful, only that there are abundant reliability and validity issues in measuring intent. Being innovative and using items from other questionnaires can be undertaken with caution. For example, the much-used General Health

Questionnaire (GHQ) in the 28-item version has 4 questions related to suicidal thoughts, with differing responses depending on degrees of suicidal ideation. This can be used to give a basic suicide ideation score (Goldney, Winefield, Tiggemann, Winefield, & Smith, 1989). There are literally scores of papers that use the GHQ and which could be reanalyzed to examine the degree of suicidal ideation with whatever else is being researched. Again, however, there are questions about reliability and validity that the NIMH group found lacking in all simple tests. And of course one needs the caveat that one can not necessarily assume that such persons definitely represent the future suicides.. . .

10. Suicidology needs to generate new avenues of study. We would suggest at least the following:

A. The psychological (or psychiatric) autopsy suicide research approach is a promising avenue to enhance our understanding of suicide, although there are clear limitations with research on third party interviews that is too infrequently noted. . . .

I agree. Thus, I appeal to authority and in suicidology, at least in the research, there is no greater authority than IASR. I am aware that from a logic perspective, appeal to authority may be a fallacious argument, however. I do so anyway.

OPERATIONAL CRITERIA FOR THE DETERMINATION OF SUICIDE

Each year death certificates are filled out by thousands of different certifiers. On each death certificate the manner of death must be indicated as either "natural," "accident," "suicide," "homicide," or "could not be determined." These are the NASH categories. There are many factors that affect valid and reliable certification of suicide. The determination of suicide requires establishing that the death was both self-inflicted and intentional. Intentionality is central (Litman, 1984; see also Chapter 1). It would be a truism to state that establishing intentionality is the most difficult task that is inherent in the determination of suicide. Many certifiers lack explicit understanding of suicide and clear distinct criteria for assessing suicidal intent. Without specified criteria, certifiers might seek and collect a narrow range of evidence concerning intent. They jump into the dark—jumping to conclusions and many more cognitive distortions. All-or-nothing thinking is equally often present. There is cognitive constriction, and thus, the certifier's mind is no different from the suicidal mind—blind!

There are of course many sound reflections on our central topic, so I will once more appeal to authorities; Rosenberg et al.'s article, "Operational Criteria for the Determination of Suicide," in the *Journal of Forensic Sciences* in 1988. It is excellent, perhaps the best. They begin with noting that suicide is self-inflicted intentional death.

On self-inflicted death, Rosenberg et al. (1988) write, "There is evidence that death was self-inflicted. This may be determined by pathological (autopsy), toxicological, investigatory, and psychological evidence, and statements of the decedent or witnesses" (p. 1448). The determination of self-inflicted is often easier than that of intent. Intention is, however, core. On intent, Rosenberg and his team note,

> There is evidence (explicit, implicit, or both) that at the time of injury the decedent intended to kill himself or herself or wished to die and that the decedent understood the probable consequences of his or her actions.

1. Explicit verbal or nonverbal expression of intent to kill self.
2. Implicit or indirect evidence of intent to die, such as
   - preparations for death inappropriate to or unexpected in the context of the decedent's life,
   - expression of farewell or the desire to die or an acknowledgment of impending death,
   - expression of hopelessness,
   - expression of great emotional or physical pain or distress,
   - effort to procure or learn about means of death or to rehearse fatal behavior,
   - precautions to avoid rescue,
   - evidence that decedent recognized high potential lethality of means of death,
   - previous suicide attempt,
   - previous suicide threat,
   - stressful events or significant losses (actual or threatened), or
   - serious depression or mental disorder. (p. 1448)

Intention, as I have discussed before, is central to the criteria of suicide in NASH. Whether or not the decedent intended to kill himself or herself is usually difficult to determine (Litman, 1984). Intention requires that the decedent knew or had in mind that a specific act would probably result in death. Rosenberg et al. (1988) offer further reflections on specific criteria on intention, and offer some explanations and examples. Here are a few examples:

1. Preparations for death inappropriate to or unexpected in the context of the decedent's life.
2. Expression of farewell or the desire to die or an acknowledgment of impending death.
   Examples: "I won't be here to be kicked around anymore"; . . . "Have a good life."

On applications, they argue:

> These criteria are meant to aid decision makers in exercising their judgment, not to replace judgment with a mathematical formula for decision making . . .
> Absolute certainty is not the goal in certifying deaths. With respect to suicide deaths in particular, no decision maker will ever be certain of the decedent's intent because the decedent is unavailable for questioning and because almost everyone who contemplates suicide has some degree of ambivalence . . .
> Rather than absolute certainty, a "yes" or "no" decision is needed representing the decision maker's best judgment after collecting and reviewing all the evidence. (p. 1451)

And, I would argue, following Shneidman, Litman, and IASR, that the PA is the best tool available.

WHAT IS THE IDIOGRAPHIC APPROACH?

Suicide is complex; this, as we saw in Chapter 1, within that context, there is a need for multidisciplinary perspectives. In our investigations, how do we study suicide? What raw data can we legitimately use? After all, unlike most other areas of forensic investigation regarding complicated human acts, we cannot ask questions of the dead suicidal person. We cannot ask, "Why did you kill yourself?" This forces us to look elsewhere. Yet you do not need to stab in the dark. Shneidman and Farberow (1957), Maris (1981), and Leenaars (1988) suggested the following alternatives: statistics, third-party interviews, the study of nonfatal suicide attempters and documents (including personal documents). All of these have their limitations. Statistics reflect by themselves only numbers and are, at best, only a fraction of the true figures. (It is the nomothetic story.) Third-party interviews, often called psychological autopsy (PA) studies, can only provide a point of view that is not the suicide's (It is the survivor's story.) Nonfatal attempters are different from completers. (It is the attempter's story.) Documents may provide, to use Maris's word (1981), only a snapshot of an event that requires a full-length movie. (It is, however, the deceased's story.)

Of course, there is the problem of obtaining any of these data, statistics, interviews, reports by attempters, and personal documents. Maris (1981) has discussed at length some of these problems; he states, "One of the major problems in understanding self-destructive behaviors is that the data base for such potential explanations is conspicuously absent." However, such a formulation or core belief should not deter us in our study of suicide. Rather, it should make us, as Shneidman (1980) suggested, rethink the problem (and the specific problems with each source of data) anew (i.e., cognitive problem solving). In the study of death, homicide, and suicide, there may be no single datum or forensic evidence. The issue of *the* data base does not only exist in suicidology, it is ubiquitous in science. In science, data are samples; some areas of science have greater accessibility to data, whereas others have less (e.g., astronomy). Equally, as in all science, all sources of data in suicidology have limitations; yet, equally they have strengths. For example, personal documents may have limitations such as providing only a snapshot; but sometimes they provide a vignette of sufficient length so that some essential essences of the entire movie can be reasonably inferred. Examples of such documents are case histories, psychological test results, death certificates, suicide notes, and a host of others, as will be seen in the Terman-Shneidman case of Natalie that I will discuss later. It allows us to tell the story of the person who died by suicide.

THE PROBLEM IN STUDYING CASE HISTORIES

A problem in the use of case documents is the one that is the ubiquitous issue of psychology itself: the mind-body problem or the admissibility of introspective accounts as opposed to objective reports. This resonates to Windelband's (1904) division of two possible approaches to knowledge between the nomothetic and the idiographic. The tabular, statistical, arithmetic, demographic nomothetic approach deals with generalizations, whereas the idiographic approach, which largely uses qualitative analysis, but as my studies of suicide notes show, not only, involves the intense study of individuals via clinical methods, history, biography. In this latter approach, personal documents are frequently utilized—personal documents such as letters, logs, e-mails, memoirs, diaries, autobiographies and suicide notes. Before addressing the topic at hand, let us explore the views on the idiographic approach in more detail; the other (the nomothetic approach) is well ingrained in suicidology, psychology, and science in general.

Allport (1942, 1962) has provided us with a classical statement on the advantages of an idiographic approach. Allport (1962) notes that psychology is "committed to increasing man's understanding of man," humans in general and humans in the particular. What concerns psychology deeply is individual human personality. John Stuart Mill proposed that we make distinctions about the general and the individual in science, both being critical for science's development, although some scientists—and that includes suicidologists—object strongly to the study of individual cases. What a constricted core belief!

Allport (1962) provides the following:

> Suppose we take John, a lad of 12 years, and suppose his family background is poor; his father was a criminal; his mother rejected him; his neighborhood is marginal. Suppose that 70 percent of the boys having a similar background become criminals. Does this mean that John himself has a 70 percent chance of delinquency? (p. 411)

Allport answers "Not at all. John is a unique being."

Allport (1962) noted that the real concern about the idiographic and nomothetic is developing methods that are more rich, flexible, and precise, that "do justice to the fascinating individuality" of each individual. This is what we need in the study of suicide today if we are ever going to answer the forensic unknowns.

Runyan (1982a, 1982b, 1983) has outlined a detailed defense for idiographic approaches. The criticisms of idiographic studies and Runyan's defenses are as follows:

1. It is difficult to generalize from them. Defense: Psychology is not only concerned with the general.
2. There is no such thing as a unique trait or element. Defense: A concept can be created to describe an individual; it can be later applied to others.
3. It is useful for generating hypotheses, not for testing them. Defense: There are not only general laws but also unique. Equally, there are not only general methods but also single case methods.
4. It is impossible to conduct an idiographic study of every individual. Defense: Indeed one cannot study all, but one can study individuals of particular interest.
5. It is not science. Defense: It is clearly untenable that science is not concerned with particulars (e.g., a comet, a star, a volcano, a whale, or a human).
6. There are no adequate methods. Defense: There are, indeed, adequate methods.

SOME CONCLUSIONS ABOUT PERSONAL
DOCUMENTS

Allport (1942) has noted that personal documents have a significant place in psychiatric/psychological research. Although Allport cites some shortcomings in the use of personal documents in psychological science—unrepresentativeness of sample, self-deception, blindness to motives, and errors of memory—he makes a clear case for the use of personal documents, citing the following: learning about the person, advancing both nomothetic and idiographic research, and aiding in the aims of science—understanding, prediction, and control. One is here reminded of Maslow's view (1966) that much of scientific psychology is "mechanistic and ahuman." Most psychologists only know the controlled quantitative experiment, and many actually believe that this is the *only* golden road to the truth. But, according to Maslow (1966), and Shneidman (1980), if we want to know the person, then we have to be more open minded. The experiment (such as used in statistical studies, third-party interviews, and studies of attempters) has an important place, but so do other methods (and questions). Maslow (1966) has noted, for example, that we can use subjective reports in psychology as well as "covert communications, paintings, dreams, stories, gestures, etc.—which we can interpret." Personal documents provide this invaluable source of data. As an interesting footnote to his trailblazing work, Allport (1942) wrote about diaries, memoirs, logs, letters, and autobiographies, but it did not occur to his capacious mind to think of perhaps the most personal documents of all: suicide notes.

I am not defensive about the use of personal documents or pleading for their occasional admissibility in suicidology and psychology in general. On the contrary, I emphasize their special virtues and their special power in doing the main business of forensic psychology—the intensive study of the person.

Furthermore, the use of case documents does not mean that the essential method of science, Mill's (1992/1984) method of difference, has to be abandoned, as comparison between genuine and simulated suicide notes clearly illustrates (see Chapter 1). I believe that personal documents provide a unique place in forensic science where maximum relevance can be mated with acceptable precision. There are not many marriages like that in psychology.

Before I proceed, I want to comment a little further on suicide notes. Suicide notes are the ultrapersonal documents. They are the unsolicited productions of the suicidal person, usually written minutes before the suicidal death. They are an invaluable starting point for comprehending the suicidal mind and for understanding the special features of the people who actually commit suicide and what they share in common with the rest of us who have only been drawn to imagine it. Suicide notes are a way through the looking glass to suicide, although unlike Alice, we will not find "beautiful things" there, but unbearable pain—psychache (Shneidman, 1985, 1993a).

There are the perpetual questions. How representative are suicide notes? To what extent can one generalize from the note writers to those who do not leave a note? Regarding the latter, it seems that approximately 12% to about 40% of people who commit suicide leave notes. Erwin Stengel provided the best answers to these questions, I believe, in *Suicide and Attempted Suicide* (1964) when he stated,

> Whether the writers of suicide notes differ in their attitudes from those who leave no notes behind it is impossible to say. Possibly, they differ from the majority only in being good correspondents. At any rate, the results of the analysis of suicide notes are in keeping with the observation . . . common to most suicidal acts. (pp. 44–45)

I believe that research on suicide notes has been useful and can be made more so, even though suicide notes by themselves do not give a complete account of the suicidal mind—and no data will. Like any other data in a case study, the notes must be put in the context of people's lives (Shneidman, 1980). This is the very aim of this book. Even more important, the notes and other personal documents must be put in context of broad theoretical models—theory—about suicide and personality functioning in general (Leenaars, 1988).

A common criticism is that documents, such as suicide notes, letters, and case histories, are open to different beliefs or theories. Runyan (1982a), for example, had noted that "it is claimed that Freud's case studies suffer from the critical flaw of being open to many interpretations." It is true that the studies of most people's lives are open to any number of theoretical templates. Gergen (1977) has argued that the events of people's lives allow the investigator freedom to support his or her formulations. I would agree that such misuse is possible, not only in the application of personal documents but, we would add, in any form of research. Statistics too can be manipulated by one's formulations, as the studies on gun control show. Runyan (1982a) suggests that to avoid this misuse, one must "critically evaluate alternative explanations and interpretations." This has been one of Shneidman's (1980, 1985) richest contributions—his willingness to sow and harvest different points of view. Indeed, being open to different points of view constitutes the very richness of personal documents rather than some experiment that is preplanned to address one's favorite theory. Ultimately, however, the truth is that as humans, we cannot but make formulations about things (Husserl, 1907/1973). Of course, this is the age-old battle of what science should really be.

A related issue (although discussed earlier, it needs to be repeated) is that theory should not play any role in research. This view holds that research, whether quantitative or qualitative, should be atheoretical. However, I believe that theory, explicit and implicit, plays some role in research, whether solving a specific problem, testing an existing theory, developing new theories, or expanding existing theories, and thus by implication, our forensic study. The problem is that frequently the theory is not stated. Regrettably, much of the research to date on suicide, including suicide notes, is atheoretical. Yet it is only theory, as W. James and I earlier suggested, that we could sort out the "booming buzzing mess of experience."

As a source of data, suicide notes are not uncontroversial themselves regarding the utility of such documents. Some see suicide notes as the key to unlocking the mysteries of suicidal phenomena, or the looking glass to suicide. The barren bones are discovered. Others believe that suicide notes, unlike other personal documents, can never be illuminating. Suicide notes are no looking glass at all; indeed, suicide notes are written by the very person, who because of his/her constriction, "knows" least why he/she is doing it. Shneidman's point of view (1985), at this time, is that these notes may not be bountiful, but they are rarely banal. Like other documents, suicide notes can, indeed, have a great deal of meaning if, as suggested by Shneidman (1980); they are put within the context of the details of that person's life. Furthermore, if put in the context of different formulations or theories of suicide and personality functioning in general, I believe that documents can allow us to understand our deceased better. It is all about construct validation (Cronbach & Meehl, 1955; Meehl, 1986, 1990; Millon, 2010; Zachar & Kendler, 2010). I believe suicide notes and other documents can provide us with important evidence not only for idiographic use but also nomothetic use. My core belief is that documents give us the philosopher's gold in our forensic digs. It is the *aurum philosophorum*, the philosopher's gold. It is like a golden star. It illuminates all the roads to the psychological barren bones.

AN IDIOGRAPHIC ILLUSTRATION

To illustrate the value of suicide notes and personal documents in the idiographic approach, the following case, a subject in the Terman study of the gifted, will be presented. The intent is to highlight the qualitative value of understanding a person, something that because of the efforts of Dr. Terman, is possible. The actual documents were collected by Dr. Shneidman during his studies of suicide in the gifted. Subsequently, Dr. Shneidman loaned me the file, having a number of discussions about the same. To begin, here is part of what one reads on the death certificate:

> On arrival, contacted Deputy Smith, who directed writer to the bathroom where victim was observed lying on the floor, head resting on a pillow, toward the north, feet pointed toward the south. Victim was dressed in a green housecoat; was cold to the touch, rigor mortis having started to set in. On the pillow it was noted there was a stain, caused by purge from victim's mouth. Photographs of the scene were taken.
>
> Deputy Smith turned over to the undersigned a small bottle with the label bearing "prescription No. XXX, Dr. Joe, Mrs. Natalie _____, one capsule at bedtime, dated ____ ____; Sam's pharmacy, telephone 000-0000, _____, _____." This bottle was empty. Also a small plastic container was received from Deputy Smith, with label inside the cover reading, No. XXXX, one tablet 4 times daily, regularly, Mrs. Natalie _____, Jane's pharmacy _____, telephone 000-0000, Dr. Ed; this contained had 30 white tablets," _____ printed on one side a d a line on the other side. Also at this time, notes, reading as follow, were turned over to the writer, by Deputy Smith.

"Natalie," a 39-year-old woman, had killed herself. What is instructional about this case in suicidology is that in addition to her suicide notes, there exist over 100 separate documents. They include the following: early school records, teacher's notes to her parents, physicians' reports, school evaluations, college records, several psychological tests, numerous questionnaires that she had completed, dozens of letters, and miscellaneous personal documents. These personal documents and other records provide us with the associations that are lacking in suicide notes. They allow us to get a clearer glimpse of her life. A full account of the case has been presented by Shneidman (1980, 1996).

Let me begin with Natalie's five suicide notes cited verbatim(with the actual protocol sentences of the TGSP in the right hand column):

*   *   *

1. To her adult friend:
   Rosalyn - Get Eastern Steel Co. - Tell them and they will find Bob right away. Papa is at his business. Betty is at the Smiths - Would you ask Helene to keep her until her Daddy comes - so she won't know until he comes for her. You have been so good - I love you - Please keep in touch with Betty - Natalie.

2. To her eldest daughter:
   Betty, go over to Rosalyn's right away - Get in touch with Papa.   3, 8, 9

3. To her ex-husband, from whom she was recently divorced:
   Bob, - I'm making all kinds of mistakes with our girls - They have to have a leader and everyday the job seems more enormous - You couldn't have been a better Daddy to Nancy and they do love you - Nancy misses you so and she doesn't know what's the matter - I know you've built a whole new life for yourself but make room for the girls and keep them with you - Take them where you go - It's only for just a few years -   1, 2, 3, 4, 5,
   Betty is almost ready to stand on her own two feet - But   6, 7, 8, 9, 10,
   Nancy needs you desperately. Nancy needs help - She   11, 12, 13,
   really thinks you didn't love her - and she's got to be   15f, 17, 18,
   made to do her part for her own self-respect - Nancy   19, 20, 21
   hasn't been hurt much yet - but ah! the future if they   22, 23, 25,
   keep on the way I've been going lately - Barbara   26, 27, 28,
   sounds warm and friendly and relaxed and I pray to   29, 31, 32,
   God she will understand just a little and be good to my   33, 34, 35
   girls - they need two happy people - not a sick mixed-up mother - There will be a little money to help with extras - It had better go that way than for more pills and more doctor bills - I wish to God it had been different but be happy - but please - stay by your girls - And just one thing - be kind to Papa (her step-father] - He's done everything he could to try to help me - He loves the girls dearly and it's right that they should see him often - Natalie

Bob - this afternoon Betty and Nancy had such a horrible fight it scares me. Do you suppose Gladys and Orville would take Betty for this school year? She should be away from Nancy for a little while - in a calm atmosphere.

> 3, 4, 5, 6, 7, 8, 10, 13, 19, 20, 21, 25, 28, 31, 35

4. To her step-father:

Papa - no one could have been more kind or generous than you have been to me - I know you couldn't understand this - and forgive me - The lawyer had copy of my will - Everything equal - the few personal things I have of value - the bracelet to Nancy and my wedding ring to Betty - But I would like Betty to have Nana's diamond - have them appraised and give Betty and Nancy each half of the diamonds in the band. Please have somebody come in and clean - Have Bob take the girls away immediately - I don't want them to have to stay around - You're so good Papa dear -

> 1, 2, 3, 4, 6, 8, 9, 11

5. To her two children:

My dearest ones - You two have been the most wonderful things in my life - Try to forgive me for what I've done - your father would be so much better for you. It will be harder for you for awhile - but so much easier in the long run - I'm getting you all mixed up - Respect and love are almost the same - Remember that - and the most important thing is to respect yourself - The only way you can do that is by doing your share and learning to stand on your own two feet - Betty try to remember the happy times - and be good to Nancy. Promise me you will look after your sister's welfare - I love you very much - but I can't face what the future will bring.

> 1, 2, 3, 4, 5, 6, 7, 8, 9, 10, 11, 12, 13, 15g, 17, 18, 20, 25, 34, 35

From a qualitative view, in her notes Natalie seems pushed, weary, harried, and beaten by life. Her personal documents clearly give evidence of trauma; even her everyday life was described as too "enormous." She noted that life was too painful. She wanted immediate relief. She wanted to depart. To her children she wrote, "I can't face what the future will bring." For her, suicide had adjustive value. It provided relief from intolerable suffering.

> 2, 7, 8, 13, 34, 35
>
> 1, 5, 13, 15f, 17, 25, 26

Natalie's step-father had reported the following to the police:

. . . that approximately two weeks ago, victim told him that she was going to commit suicide. He said

> 1, 2, 3, 4, 5,

he talked her out of the notion at that time, and did not figure she would make any further attempt on her life. He further said Victim had been in ill health since her divorce and had been treated by a psychologist, address unknown; also that the victim had filed a will which is currently in the possession of her attorney.

6, 7, 20, 21, 25, 27, 34, 35

To put the situation into the appropriate historical context (something that a suicide note does not provide but may be essential in understanding the suicidal person), the following brief synopsis of Natalie's life is provided from the documents: Natalie's birth and early years were noted as normal. When Natalie was six, her mother wrote to a friend; "I have tried to use a lot of common sense and have answered every question to the best of my ability because she is an understanding child and will listen to reason. I have not had to stimulate a desire to learn because she always wanted to know everything her older playmates knew and she would try to learn voluntarily." She had a brother, who was 8 years older than she. Later she would say about him that "he could never make a living."

When Natalie was six years old, in the first grade, she was given the Stanford-Binet Intelligence Test, scoring in the extremely superior category (IQ of 153). Curiously, one of the few items that she missed on the test was this one: "Yesterday the police found the body of a girl cut into 18 pieces. They believe that she killed herself. What is foolish about that?" Her nonprophetic answer was "She wouldn't kill herself."

A very important event occurred in Natalie's life when she was seven: her father deserted the family. It is noteworthy that Natalie became quite irritable after the desertion. Later in her life, she noted, with obvious sadness, that "My father never came to see me except once."

7

3, 21, 24, 33

A characteristic of Natalie's that is worth remarking about that started to develop at this time was her irritability, a psychache (Shneidman, 1993). It would be a marker to her personality. Her personal documents from the very beginning - with an hiatus during most of her teen years - until her death are full of references to this characteristic. Before the age of seven, Natalie's family doctor described her as nervous. Records, notably after her father's desertion are replete with words like "somewhat irritable," "very irritable," and "mental characteristic is irritability." School records, except in high school, concurred. The psychologist who administered Natalie the IQ test at age six noted that she fatigued quickly. Natalie's mother in the early years denied the problem. There were numerous medical tests, all reporting that there was no physical basis for the irritability.

6, 15c, 21, 22, 23, 25, 33 15f

A few years after the father's desertion, Natalie's mother remarried, a marriage that had a very positive influence on Natalie and her family.

When Natalie was thirteen, her stepfather was described as "devoted," encouraging Natalie at home, school, and elsewhere. It is, in fact, noteworthy that after Natalie's death, her children lived with her stepfather.

The records of her childhood are interesting. Natalie's mother saw Natalie at this time as understanding, competent and having a stimulating desire to learn. Her mother also saw her as egotistical and vain, which was in sharp contrast to teachers' reports. At school, Natalie was seen as decidedly modest. By age ten, her mother noted that Natalie had overcome these problems.

At age twelve there were several items of interest. She suffered from numerous headaches and had prescription eye glasses but she 7, 17 still reported troubled eyestrain. She was a straight-A student (in the seventh grade) and indicated that she wanted to go to college. A hearing loss had been diagnosed earlier. It was now assessed and found to have increased, and she was somewhat sensitive about it; she would not admit this difficulty to any of her teachers. One teacher reported that although Natalie was extremely bright, she "shrinks from opportunities for leadership." During these years, school records are, however, generally positive. Natalie was described as well liked, as having many friends and as belonging to many clubs. At this time, Natalie wanted to be a dancer; however, this vocational choice was 5, 21, 25, 26, stopped by her parents. For Natalie, this was quite painful and became 33, 34 a dream never realized.

She finished high school and went on to college for 3 years but did not graduate. At the age of twenty-five, having been, in her own 7, 11, 15a, words, "an unsuccessful secretary," her "ultimate goal [was to] be a 17, 21, 25, successful homemaker." She married and in the next 2 years lived in 26 five different cities due to frequent moves related to her husband's employment. Understandably, she wrote that "it is hard to develop interests in any one place and then have to leave them." She hoped to settle down. She became pregnant almost immediately after getting 19, 21 married. Natalie's life revolved around her husband, seeing her husband as having a profound influence on her life. The frequent 22, 24 moves, however, became seen, especially in the later years of the 33 marriage as, an irritating factor. Her own aspirations were neglected; 21 she wrote: "I feel that I haven't made the most of my opportunities."

There are a number of other letters about her relations over the years. Here are a few excerpts.

> My marriage is my career. Being a housewife and a mother . . . but I married because I wasn't a success in my career . . . and all my friends were getting married - I'm not a good housekeeper - but I genuinely like homemaking - cooking - sewing - etc., and I would rather do it than anything else I know of. 5, 20

> Neither my husband and I were prepared for marriage. Just being married, moving around and taking care of my little girls have been as much as I can do.

Although she adds in the same letter that her husband and herself [10, 28] are "quite compatible."

Natalie's twenties were marked by irritability. She herself often remarked about her constant irritability. She wrote, "I let small things [22, 29] upset me." Elsewhere she wrote, "fatigue is my biggest problem." [3, 5, 6, 15c/f]

There is a gap in the records for 5 years. By age thirty she had two [17, 21, 25] children and reported a "great tendency to worry and extreme [1, 2, 3, 6, 7, 14,] nervousness." Her marriage was not peaceful. Her husband was [15f, 17, 20, 22,] drinking rather heavily. In her letters, there are frequent remarks [24, 25, 27, 29,] like "my husband drinks" and "after being very drunk." There was a [32, 33, 34, 35] dramatic change in her own physical and psychological state, her psychache. She reported that she was "too tired even to wash the windows."

Her irritability became quite painful in her thirties. She wrote, "Great tendency to worry and extreme nervousness." She describes [1, 3, 4, 5, 6, 8,] herself as "chronically worn out and tired." She was well aware that [10, 15f, 21, 35] there was no physical basis, recognizing "that I had neurotic tendencies." Often the pain was overpowering (unbearable?). She longed for relief, a solution. She wrote, "In my heart I've never doubted that I can be a happy - relaxed - useful [7] human being." The relief never came.

In the later years of her life, it was especially the strain with her [19, 20, 21, 22] husband that was unsatisfying and frustrating. Here is part of a letter she sent to Dr. Terman, written when she was about thirty-five:

> . . . Until I was 25 I didn't know there were such things as problems in this world, but since then with the exception of my two lovely children and my perfect relationship with my mother, I've had just one struggle after another, made one blunder after another. My husband and I bicker constantly. I've wanted to divorce him a thousand times and still I know that is not the solution. We were both raised in broken homes and we both love our children too much. He comes home drunk at night far too often. He can't afford it. He refuses to look at the bills and says "Why haven't you saved money?" I have no one to talk to. I feel like I'm cornered. . . . My mother's youngest brother and my nearest neighbor both committed suicide in one month (about a year before).

[1, 2, 3, 5, 6, 7, 8, 10, 11, 12, 13, 15c, 17, 19, 20, 21, 22, 25, 26, 27, 28, 29, 30, 31, 32, 33, 34, 35]

Natalie's children were very important to her at these times; yet, 21, 24
even here there was a strain. Here is a letter regarding her relation to
her children:

10, 11, 15f,
21

> Our little ones are nice, but the eldest still bites her
> fingernails and fights constantly with her younger
> sister. She is the result of my selfishness. . . . Well,
> I've poured out my heart and I'm a little ashamed. In
> my heart I've never doubted that I can be a happy,
> relaxed, useful human being, but it's taking such a
> long time to get there.

33

Her children were, a critical attachment; yet, she worried about
them in her marriage. Often she was critical of herself as a mother. 7, 11
For example, she wrote: "A successful woman has happy, 21, 29
well-adjusted children." 2, 4, 7, 10, 28

When Natalie was thirty-nine, she and her husband separated
because of "his violent temper, his selfishness and his drinking."19
Yet, the separation was like their marriage, painfully ambivalent.
Both stayed in the marriage for the children. They separated
followed by a reconciliation after one month, only to separate again. 10, 22, 28
Natalie stated during the reconciliation that she was determined to 17, 23, 25
make her marriage work. In a letter to Dr. Terman, she wrote:

> Three months ago I asked my husband for a divorce
> and told him I definitely didn't love him anymore
> because of his violent temper, selfishness, and
> drinking. He wouldn't cooperate in giving me an
> uncontested divorce. He was going to try to disprove
> my points and ask for partial custody of the children.
> I was awarded $300 a month to support the children.
> After three months of being alone I began to realize
> something that is so obvious it seems ridiculous. In
> spite of everything - he was the father of my children,
> a good Daddy, and I needed him desperately - I had
> always felt that I was a little better than he and that
> with my own small properties I'd be much better off
> without him. This wrong attitude of mine undoubtedly
> caused a lot of the temper, etc. My step-father, who
> had little use for my husband was living with us the
> year before our separation and I was constantly in
> a stew to keep them both happy. But my loyalty
> should go to my husband. I'm not saying our problems
> are solved - but two people fighting against instead
> of for one another can never be successful.

7, 8, 10, 11, 16,
17, 18, 19, 20,
21, 22, 24, 25,
26, 27, 28, 29,
33

It would appear that her life with her husband was in many ways a 2, 10, 18
recapitulation of her attachment to her father, strikingly ambivalent
and painful.

Nine months after the above letter she was divorced. Four months [1, 2, 7,] after the divorce was final (and he had already remarried), she was [3, 4, 6, 8, 9,] dead. At the end, Natalie was frantic to achieve a satisfying relation, [15c, 16, 17,] "the feeling of childhood love." This love was expressed in one of [19, 20, 21,] her suicide notes to her stepfather, "You're so good Papa dear." But [22, 23, 24,] to her own father there was no note. Shneidman (1980) summarized [8, 12, 21, 23,] the relationships thus: [24, 25]

> In her suicide she reenacted her own earlier life drama [1, 2, 3, 4, 5,]
> - the yearning for her parents to be together - and in [6, 7, 8, 9,]
> this misdirected symbolic sacrifice, instead of giving [10, 11, 12,]
> her children a (seemingly) united home, she, in the [13, 14, 15f,]
> most traumatic way possible, deprived them of their [16, 17, 18]
> own mother. Her aspirations - to be her father's [19, 20, 21,]
> favorite, to be accepted and not abandoned, to care for [22, 23, 25,]
> and not reject her own children (as she had been [27, 28, 29,]
> rejected and not cared for), to be symbolically [30, 31, 32,]
> reunited with her father in a happy home, to sacrifice [33, 34, 35]
> herself so that some of the problems of her children
> might be solved - were no better realized in her death
> than they were in her life. (p. 66)

[1, 6, 8,]
As can be gleaned from Natalie's suicide notes and her personal [9] documents, Natalie was figuratively overcome by her pain, an unbearable pain. Her notes are full of permutations and [9, 10, 28,] combinations of grief-provoking content (despite the ever-present [15g, 16] thrust of ambivalence). She believed that her life was hard, futile. She was occupied with the following: "I can't face what the future [18] brings." She said that she was "making all kinds of mistakes." She clearly believed, with flawless logic from her perspective, that once she was dead it would be "so much easier" for her children, her [1, 3, 8, 9, 14] ex-husband, herself - everybody. She almost stated the following prototypical sentences in the documents: "Everyone will be much better off when I'm dead. Everything will be much better when I'm dead." She would sacrifice everything for love. [1, 16]

One can conclude that Natalie's pain was deep. Natalie's history, as revealed through personal documents, attests to the fact that she [1, 2, 5, 6] had difficulties developing constructive and loving attachments. She had suffered defeat which, at the time of her death, she felt she could [13] not overcome. The active withdrawal by key significant others - notably the desertion of her father and likely the death of her mother, a few years earlier, the divorce from her husband, plunged Natalie into despair, grief, hopelessness, and helplessness. She was not able [2, 19, 21,] to go on; she described herself as "a sick mixed-up mother." Indeed, [6, 8, 22, 25, 27] her notes suggest that she was figuratively "drugged" by [1, 8, 18] overpowering emotions and constricted perceptions. Her history was full of these "mix-up" states, which one of her doctors described as "neurotic tendencies." These symptoms had developed out of childhood experiences. Life, in fact, she said, "seems so enormous." [15c, 15f]

In her mid-thirties, a medical doctor had noted that Natalie was on "the verge of a nervous breakdown." She went to see a therapist. [7, 15c, 15f] About this treatment, she wrote, "my tension symptoms are so [7, 25] chronic and severe that they must have their origin in my childhood." [24] Regrettably the therapist's notes were not in her Terman file. Did [25, 27] Natalie gain some insight into the rejection by her father? The [10] attachment to her mother? Her husband failed to support her in her treatment, seeing Natalie's problem as exaggerated and therapy as [10, 21] "plain silly."

She was often strikingly ambivalent about treatment. At one time, she wrote:

> I feel now that a psychologist is the last thing in the world I need to see. Now I am just capable of furnishing (earning) part of our monthly needs and being a wise mother to my girls. [1, 2, 6, 8, 15f]

She saw herself as hopeless and helpless, not knowing "the [6, 8, 9] rudiments of daily living." Life was painful, noting that "the slightest response is a strain." One can conclude that at some time her pain, [1, 3, 5, 6, 7,] psychache became unbearable. Suicide became the only solution. [9, 13, 14, 17,]

In the end, Natalie appeared to have been so preoccupied with her [25, 27, 35] trauma that she was unaware of how to adjust and she chose, cessation. We would here follow Shneidman's belief that: Each individual tends to die as he or she has lived, especially as he or she has previously reacted in periods of threat, stress, failure, challenge, shock and loss. Natalie's history, as shown through the looking glass[7] of personal documents, was so important in her conscious choice of death. Drs. Terman and Shneidman have provided us with a rich source of personal documents.

*   *   *

CONCLUDING REMARK

The idiographic approach allows us to do the main business of psychology and forensic psychological investigation: the intensive study of the human person. Natalie, through her personal documents, allows us to understand the suicidal mind better (Shneidman, 1996). The truth is, as Allport, Shneidman, and many suicidologists have stated, we need to fully understand the suicidal person to be able to determine his or her intent. This is the task of DSI. I think that there are no better solutions. Is it any wonder that so many death cases are not wisely investigated and certified? We therefore need the psychological autopsy.

CHAPTER 4

The Psychological Autopsy

The psychological autopsy (PA) is the work of my mentor, Dr. Edwin Shneidman (see my 1999 edited volume of his edited works, *Lives and Deaths* (1999a). All quotes are from my edited volume; it is Ed's story). Shneidman's key papers, according to his decision (Leenaars, 1999a), on the psychological autopsy are: "The Psychological Autopsy" (1977); "Comment: The Psychological Autopsy" (1994), a one pager for *American Psychologist*; and Shneidman's paper "An example Example of an Equivocal Death Clarified in a Court of Law" (1993b), an example of a psychological autopsy. I will present this chapter essentially as my master taught, *res ipsa loquitor*. Although I will first make a brief comment how the psychological autopsy came to be, I will let Ed speak for himself.

There was an important man in Shneidman's life, Theodore J. Curphey. He, a Canadian, was the first MD in Los Angeles County to be the coroner. He knew from his life, as a pathologist, as a certifying officer, that many deaths are equivocal as to mode. In those cases, you know what the person died of, but you do not know how to identify that death as suicide or accident or homicide. These were cases that depend on the decedent's intention. It was the person's intention vis-à-vis the death that is core to mode. He had heard of Edwin Shneidman, Robert Litman (the psychiatrist of the trio, a friend), and Norman Farberow (also a dear friend), and called the three of them and they became deputy coroners and went to the scene of the death where they gently interviewed a number of key survivors, and reported back to Dr. Curphey. Shneidman simply labeled this clinical-scientific investigating procedure one day, as a psychological autopsy. He writes,

> The main function of the psychological autopsy is to clarify an equivocal death and to arrive at the correct or accurate mode of that death. In essence, the psychological autopsy is nothing less than a thorough retrospective investigation of the intention of the decedent—that is, the decedent's intention relating to his being dead—where the information is obtained by interviewing individuals who knew the decedent's actions, behavior, and character well enough to report on them. (Leenaars, 1999a, p. 388)

THE PSYCHOLOGICAL AUTOPSY

The paper, "The Psychological Autopsy" (1977; see Leenaars, 1999a) provides, according to Dr. Shneidman's opinion, his best paper on the topic. It is an overview of the psychological autopsy (PA) procedure. Here are his words:

It is probably best to begin by defining a psychological autopsy and its purposes, then to discuss some related theoretical background and ways of actually performing psychological autopsies. The words psychological autopsy themselves tell us that the procedure has to do with clarifying the nature of a death and that it focuses on the psychological aspects of the death . . . ideas, important to understanding the psychological autopsy, need to be discussed. The first is what I have called the NASH classification of deaths.

From the beginning . . . the certification and recordkeeping relating to deaths have implied that there are four modes of death. It needs to be said right away that the four modes of death have to be distinguished from many causes of death listed in the current International Classification of Diseases and Causes of Death (World Health Organization 1957, National Center for Health Statistics 1967). The four modes of death are natural, accidental, suicide, and homicide; the initial letters of each make up the acronym NASH. Thus, to speak of the NASH classification of death is to refer to these four traditional modes in which death is currently reported. Contemporary death certificates have a category which reads "Accident, suicide, homicide, or undetermined"; if none of these is checked, then a "natural" mode of death, as occurs in most cases is implied.

It should be apparent that the cause of death stated on the certificate does not necessarily carry with it information as to the specific mode of death. For example, asphyxiation due to drowning in a swimming pool does not automatically communicate whether the decedent struggled and drowned (accident), entered the pool with the intention of drowning himself (suicide), or was held under water until he was drowned (homicide).

Historical Background

In 1662 John Graunt, a London tradesman, published a small book of observations in the bills of mortality that was to have great social and medical significance. By this time the weekly bills were consolidated at the end of each year, and a general bill for the year was published. Graunt separated the various bits of information contained in these annual bills and organized them into tables. When the available data on deaths were believed accurate, Graunt then focused on individual causes of death. He next turned to the subject of population estimations. Finally he constructed a mortality table, the first attempt to organize data in this manner. Of greatest significance was his success in demonstrating the regularities that can be found in medical and social phenomena when one is dealing with large numbers. Thus, John Graunt demonstrated how the bills of mortality could be used to the advantage of both the physician and government (Kargon, 1963). . . .

From the time of John Graunt and his mortality tables in the seventeenth century . . . the classification of causes of death has constantly been broadening in scope, the changes are characterized primarily by attempts to reflect additions to knowledge, particularly those contributed by the new professions as they have developed—anesthesiology, pathology, bacteriology, immunology, and advances in obstetrics, surgery, and most recently, the behavioral sciences. . . .

Purpose of the Psychological Autopsy

As long as deaths are classified solely in terms of the four NASH categories, it is immediately apparent that some deaths will, so to speak, fall between the cracks, and our familiar problem of equivocal death will continue to place obstacles in our path to understanding human beings and their dying. Many of these obstacles can be cleared away by reconstructing, primarily through interviews with the survivors, the role that the deceased played in hastening or effecting his own death. This procedure is called "psychological autopsy," and initially its main purpose was to clarify situations in which the mode of death was not immediately clear.

The origin of the psychological autopsy grew out of the frustration of the Los Angeles County Chief Medical Examiner-Coroner, Theodore J. Curphey, M.D., at the time of the reorganization of that office in 1958. . . . As a result he asked the Los Angeles Suicide Prevention Center to assist him in a joint study of those equivocal cases, and it was this effort—a multidisciplinary approach involving behavioral scientists—which let to my coining the term "psychological autopsy." . . .

At present there are at least three distinct questions that the psychological autopsy can help to answer:

1. *Why did the individual do it?* When the mode of death is, by all reasonable measures, clear and unequivocal—suicide, for example—the psychological autopsy can serve to account for the reasons for the act or to discover what led to it . . .
2. *How did the individual die, and when-that is, why at that particular time?* When a death, usually a natural death, is protracted, the individual dying gradually over a period of time, the psychological autopsy helps to illumine the sociopsychological reasons why he died at that time . . .
3. *What is the most probable mode of death?* This was the question to which the psychological autopsy was initially addressed. When cause of death can be clearly established but mode of death is equivocal, the purpose of the psychological autopsy is to establish the mode of death with as great a degree of accuracy as possible.

Conducting the Psychological Autopsy

How is a psychological autopsy performed? Talking to some key persons— spouse, lover, parent, grown child, friend, colleague, physician, supervisor, and co-worker—who knew the decedent, does it. The talking to is done gently, a mixture of conversation, interview, emotional support, general questions, and a good deal of listening. I always telephone and then go out to the home. After rapport is established, a good general opening question might be: "Please tell me, what was he (she) like?" Sometimes clothes and material possessions are looked at, photographs shown, and even diaries and correspondence shared. (On one occasion, the widow showed me her late husband's suicide note—which she had hidden from the police!—rather changing the equivocal nature of the death.)

In general, I do not have a fixed outline in mind while conducting a psychological autopsy, but inasmuch as outlines have been requested from time to time, one is presented below with the dual cautions that it should not be followed slavishly and that the investigator should be ever mindful that he may be asking questions that are very painful to people in an obvious grief-laden situation. The person who conducts a psychological autopsy should participate, as far as he is genuinely able, in the anguish of the bereaved person and should always do his work with the mental health of the survivors in mind.

Here, then, are some categories that might be included in a psychological autopsy (Shneidman, 1977):

1. Information identifying victim (name, age, address, marital status, religious practices, occupation, and other details)
2. Details of the death (including the cause or method and other pertinent details)
3. Brief outline of victim's history (siblings, marriage, medical illness, medical treatment, psychotherapy, suicide attempts)
4. Death history of victim's family (suicides, cancer, other fatal illnesses, ages of death, and other details)
5. Description of the personality and life-style of the victim
6. Victim's typical patterns of reaction to stress, emotional upsets, and periods of disequilibrium
7. Any recent—from last few days to last twelve months—upsets, pressures, tensions, or anticipations of trouble
8. Role of alcohol or drugs in (a) overall life-style of victim, and (b) his death. *(I [AL] would add questions, especially for police and soldiers, about guns and weapons)*
9. Nature of victim's interpersonal relationships (including those with physicians)
10. Fantasies, dreams, thoughts, premonitions, or fear of victim relating to death, accident, or suicide
11. Changes in the victim before death (of habits, hobbies, eating, sexual patterns, and other life routines)
12. Information relating to the "life side" of victim (up-swings, successes, plans)
13. Assessment of intention, that is, role of the victim in his own demise
14. Rating of lethality
15. Reaction of informants to victim's death
16. Comments, special features, and so on.

In conducting the interviews during a psychological autopsy, it is often best to ask open-ended questions that permit the respondent to associate to relevant details without being made painfully aware of the specific interests of the questioner. As an example: I might be very interested in knowing whether or not there was a change (specifically, a recent sharp decline) in the decedent's eating habits. Rather than ask directly, "Did his appetite drop recently?" a question almost calculated to elicit a defensive response, I have asked a more general question such as, "Did he have any favourite foods?" Obviously, my interest is not to learn what foods he preferred. Not atypically, the respondent will tell me what the decedent's favourite foods were and then go on to talk about recent changes in his eating habits—"Nothing I fixed for him seemed to please him"—and even proceed to relate other recent changes, such as changing patterns in social or sexual or recreational habits, changes which diagnostically would seem to be related to a dysphoric person, not inconsistent with a suicidal or subintentioned death.

Function of the Psychological Autopsy

The retrospective analysis of deaths not only serves to increase the accuracy of certification (which is in the best interests of the overall mental health concerns of the community), but also has the heuristic function of providing the serious investigator with clues that he may then use to assess lethal intent in living persons.

Shneidman offered some clear and distinct suggestions for the conceptual improvement of the death certificate; he states,

The current NASH classification of death grew out of a seventeenth century way of thinking about man (as a biological vessel who was subject to whims of fate) and tended to leave man himself out of his own death. Twentieth century psychology and psychiatry have attempted to put man—conscious and unconscious—back into his own life, including the way in which he dies. The NASH classification of modes of death is not only apsychological but it tends to emphasize relatively unimportant details. . . . (Leenaars, 1999a, pp. 387–410)

This is quite a task. Dr. Shneidman's wisdom here is not an endnote, but a prolegomena. There is a treasure trove of writings (see Leenaars, 2004). Before I proceed there is one very terse, but most important comment needed in answering, "What is a PA?" Keeping J. S. Mill in mind, "How is the PA different from other retrospective death investigations?" I will next present some of Dr. Shneidman's core beliefs.

COMMENT ON THE PSYCHOLOGICAL AUTOPSY

Dr. Shneidman thought that there were different legitimate approaches of retro-spective death investigations. He clarified this point often and presented his standard comment in "Comment: The Psychological Autopsy" (1994; see Leenaars, 1999a). It is a one pager for *American Psychologist* that says that the psychological autopsy for Shneidman is about intention. There are different kinds of procedures; some are not psychological autopsies. This did not mean that they had no value, only that these studies were a different method to understand an event. There are many legitimated means; they simply are different (and often each can provide a perspective on the death). For example, if you do a ballistic test and take blood samples and so on, that is not a psychological autopsy, that is a forensic autopsy or a clinical autopsy. If you look at bullet markings, blood type, and DNA profiling, that is not intention (Raina, Dogra, Leenaars, Yadov, Bhera, Lalwani, & Leenaars , 2011). The psychological autopsy is about the person's intention vis-à-vis the death.

Dr. Shneidman identified minimally four kinds of death investigations: the medical autopsy, the forensic investigation, the statistical or demographic report, and the psychological autopsy (The Kelly Johnson report would be a forensic investigation, not a PA report). I next present verbatim his brief description of the other three types of death-follow-up procedure:

1. **Autopsy**. The autopsy involves inspection and partial dissection of a dead body to learn the cause of death, the nature and extent of disease, and where possible, the mode of death. It is an examination by a physician-pathologist (and ancillary personnel). It is objective; it reports the facts—the weight of the brain, alcohol content of the blood, appearance of the liver, and so forth. The pathologist acts as an amicus curiae, specifically as a friend to the state, reporting the findings concerning a particular dead person for public and archival record . . .

2. **Forensic investigation**. The forensic investigation relates to the physical evidence surrounding the death. It may include a plethora of relevant details: windows open, doors locked, trajectory of bullets, powder marks, finger-prints, handwriting analyses, personal documents (suicide notes, threatening letters, cashed checks, etc.). Although these facts can be centrally relevant in either criminal or civil cases and need to be done as thoroughly as possible, a report of forensic details is, of course, not an autopsy at all—and certainly not a psychological autopsy—but an investigation. . . .

3. **Statistical or demographic reports**. If one is interested in, for example, the prevention of suicide, then it is obvious that knowledge of past patterns of behavior of individuals who have committed suicide can be a useful tool. These patterns might be called prodromal indices or premonitory signs. They make up the now well-known "clues to suicide" (Shneidman & Farberow, 1957). What may not be so obvious is that the statistical truths about a large number of committed suicides do not necessarily tell us anything about any particular case. The frequent error in this field is to confuse statistics with individual events and then to argue that because this individual does (or does not) have certain desiderata characteristics of a group, suicide must have (or must not have) occurred. Statistics are made up of individual cases; an individual case is not controlled by statistics. To argue from statistics to an individual case is a tyro's error. One must be on the alert for this kind of reverse reasoning. In any event, the citation of statistical and demographic data, even when cogent and sensible, is clearly not a psychological autopsy. . . . (Leenaars, 1999a, pp. 411–412)

What is meant by a psychological autopsy (PA) is all very different from these procedures. The clarification of the mode (NASH) of some deaths devolves on the intention of the decedent in relation to the death. Suicide, as we read in Chapter 1, is an intentioned death. The PA was devised to clarify what the mode of death was, why the individual did it, and when the person did it (Curphey, 1961; Leenaars, 1999a, 2004; Litman, Curphey, Shneidman, Farberow, & Tabachnick, 1963; Shneidman, 1969, 1973a & b, 1977, 1985, 1993a & b). A psychological autopsy is an objective procedure that seeks to make a reasonable determination of what was in the mind of the decedent vis-à-vis his or her own death. It does this by looking at the history of the decedent, the lifestyle, the intrapsychic and interpersonal characteristics, the cognitive style, the psychopathology, and so on, as discussed in this book in detail. It is at the core of what the Greeks meant by autopsy.

It legitimately conducts interviews (with a variety of people who knew the decedent) and examines personal documents (suicide notes, diaries, and letters) and other materials (including the autopsy and police reports) that are relevant to the psychological assessment of the dead individual's role in the death." (Leenaars, 1999a, p. 414)

All of this is evidence gathering. Of course, as Ed often reminded me over the hundreds of hours of discussions, the results of a PA cannot be stated with certainty.

One additional thought: We are talking about equivocal cases! This is important because some police educators advocate not getting caught up in the details. They advocate the use of William of Occam's approach; make it simple. If you have a number of hypotheses, choose the easiest hypothesis. That works easily in unequivocal cases, not the equivocal cases of suicide or accident or homicide or natural (the NASH question). Yet it is not a mystery. To quote the famous reflection, "If you hear the sound of hoof beats approaching, look for yourself to see if it is a horse, or a zebra" (or maybe even an elephant on that very rare occasion). *It is about the individual!*

I will next discuss the value of documents in the PA, the best practice (tool) to dress down a psychological anomaly.

PERSONAL DOCUMENTS

Suicide notes, as discussed in Chapter 3, are not the only valuable personal document. Indeed, there is a host of personal documents worthy of psychological digs—diaries, poems, letters, biographies, psychological reports, medical files, police records, newspaper reports, and so on. The possible list of documents is endless. To be more inclusive, however, it may include the following: auto-biographies, medical records, mental health records, psychological reports, police records, school records, legal records, criminal records, suicide notes, poems, suicidal diaries, e-mails, social media reports, *Google* searches, autopsy reports (such as toxicology report, if available); indeed, an endless list. A most fascinating kind of personal document left by suicides is the suicide diary. A suicidal diary is a suicide note with a history. It meets the following criteria: It is a lengthy, literate document kept over a fairly long period of time, often years; the diarist writes explicitly about suicide, including his or her suicidal thoughts, impulses, reflections, and resistances—and the diarist commits suicide. The suicidal diarist is but one subgroup of people who keep a book about their life. Rosenblatt (1983) notes that diaries "allow one to see . . . clearly day-to-day changes, long-term trends, and the effects of specific events." A diary is a document about how life is lived. Most of us are curious about diaries as we are about suicide notes. To cite a diarist, Evelyn Waugh, "The routine of their day properly recorded is always interesting." The personality of its keeper is richly found within a diary—a document not only of events but the very writer him/herself.

Why do people write such a document? Mallon (1984) cites Virginia Woolf, who later drowned herself, reflecting on her diary, "I wonder why I do it . . . . Partly I, think, from my old sense of the race of time 'Time's winged chariot hurrying near.' Does it say it?" Anais Nin notes that the diary is a personal document, an exploration, a growth, a meaningful personal relationship and much more. Both Mallon (1984) and Rosenblatt (1983) point out that there is a large variety of diaries that are written for various reasons—all diarists wanting to write "it" down on pages, like the writer of the suicide note. Both the diary and the suicide note are rich personal documents left by their writers, something they wanted to communicate to themselves and, almost always, to specific and/or unknown others.

Diaries, like suicide notes, sometimes show us the wretchedness and unbearable pain as it unfolds day to day for the keeper. Franz Kafka, as he worked on *The Castle* and *The Trial,* contemplated and wrote about suicide in his diary. Kafka's writings, in fact, are piercing insights into the unbearable suicidal pain. In the *Trial*, we read about Mr. K, who each morning rises to the same routine; the landlady has his breakfast ready, always an egg. One morning, there is no egg; there is no landlady. He waits, and the police arrive, arresting him. He asks, "What have I done?" He is led to jail at the court. There he waits, becoming ever more anxious, depressed, and forlorn. One day, he is led to the judges in a dreamlike courtroom, and he asks his question again. The head judge says, "You know what you did"; his anxiety becomes unendurable. The judges pronounce a verdict, "Guilty," and Mr. K. is led away. Detached, he is led to his death! Other diarists write about their own suicide attempts. Mallon, for example, cites Lee Harvey Oswald, who attempted suicide and later wrote, "I decide to end it. Soak wrist in cold water to numb the pain, then slash my left wrist. . . . I watch my life whirl away." Some diaries are about extremely inimical life-styles, such as *Go Ask Alice,* a diary by a 15-year-old runaway girl who finally died of a drug overdose. A few diarists write about their death, a fascinating example is the Arthur Inman diaries, probably now the most studied suicide diary (Aaron, 1985; Leenaars & Maltsberger, 1994). There are some 50 references in his diary to death and suicide. He is known to have had three serious suicide episodes, and his suicide at age 68. Here are a few raw passages, taken from Aaron (1985):

> Not growing in stature, I was painfully aware of how offsized for my age I looked and how artificial and sissy I seemed. . . . It stamped me as outside my class, a scorned thing to myself and to others, a blasted tree. I felt then a failure, a person confined within himself (p. 98; 1913, age 17).
>
> As I watched the receding campus through the rear window of a shaky old station cab, I felt very small, very tired, very lonely. If I could have foreseen ahead, I would have killed myself. Or would I have? (pp. 130–131; reflecting back to 1915, when he was 19; written in 1923, age 28).

Exactly what is life worth to me? I hate life with a consuming and virulent hatred. I have always hated life, yet have never sought immediate and self-inflicted death for the very reason, I suspect, that to kill oneself were so vastly easy. But now I am weary. Under certain circumstances I feel I would take my own life and end all this (p. 272; April 1925, age 30).

I lay awake at night and thought. I concluded, although not decisively enough to please me, that were my back to fall to pieces in an agonizing way, I would kill myself (p. 464; December 1931, age 36).

I wish I were not so terrified of the inexorable vengeance of a cruel God meted out to those who take their own lives, of ill luck that would cause me to mangle myself if I attempted suicide (p. 633; June, 1935, age 40).

I don't wonder I tried to bump myself off. This noise is almost unendurable to me. Less than three hours sleep last night. Am inside out with wildness this morning. . . . Almost anything at this juncture seems preferable to being kept awake from two to eight in the mornings, thus becoming conscious of a daytime noise I otherwise might forget. . . . It would be good to vanish from all consciousness forever. I wish I were dead. . . . The whole affair, save for the hospital part, was no worse than a bad illness. I shouldn't be afraid to try it again one day, should I? (p. 1047; December 1941, age 46).

I'm a fool and a fool and a fool, and I could shed tears that are long and pendant gray rain exuding from the heart of a sentimental idiot. I'm sad. I'm no good. I'm only as good (drunk me) as those who love me—love me for myself. Who is myself? A "pile of shit" as Pearl says. More than that—I think. I am honesty and no false estimation. Into this world; into and out of it. A shithead with good intentions—me. I want to be good, to be helpful, to be a person devoted to helping others. Am I? Who knows? I am solitary, popish, frightened Artie. That's me (p. 1563; 1956, age 61).

Jumping out of my skin with nervousness from the nearer and nearer demolition, motors racing, walls falling (the ball is being used), the building shaking and creaking. . . . With every building demolished, new electric lights and signs are let free to shine into my sitting room where it is so bright I have to shield my eyes with something to raise the window opened at night. As soon as the buildings opposite my bedroom are down, God knows what shafts of light will shine in on my walls past the curtain I tie out at night to get air. I feel a Medieval baron in his besieged keep, forces and weapons constricting ever tighter around his security. It may be I'll survive this, but then again I may not, now that D-day is here, to survive within the limits of my disposable defenses. My truest weapons are designed by ingenuity. They are indeed my final weapons. Until tested, who can know their temper? (p. 1596; March 1963, age 67).

There are few such documents available. Mallon (1984) provides a detailed account of suicide diaries—of Sylvia Plath, Dora Carrington, and others—all worthy of intense study. David Lester in 2004 published a book on a suicide diary, called *Katie's Diary*. It expresses so many of the suicidal protocols, as discussed in Chapter 2. One does not, in fact, have to read far—she says it almost all in the very first entry.

Katie writes,

I am so depressed and suicidal. My body feels restless and tired. I don't know who to turn to for help. I don't want to bother anyone with my battle. I've been acting out in all sorts of ways. I just feel like crying. I presume that all has to do with the fact that I love Mark so deeply. I think he cares for me but, however, I don't know if it's true love for him. It definitely is for me. I really want to marry him so badly. I don't care if he reads my journal at all. I am just so stressed out. I haven't done any of my work. I have a hard time getting along with people. I really hate my body. I really hate my life where it is, with everything I am. I decided to start exercising today. I need to do it every day. I leave all my life's frustrations there out on the track.

God give me strength. Help me today. I feel so unbelievably lonely and battered. (Unpublished manuscript, not numbered)

Of course, there are a wide array of insightful documents, beyond diaries, notes, and poems. A most insightful account of the suicidal mind; much because of its literary style, is the exegesis by William Styron, in his book, *Darkness Visible* (1990). It is an autobiography. He writes, "For some time now I have sensed in my work a growing psychosis that is doubtless a reflection of the psychotic strain tainting my life." William Styron is no stranger to writing; he is a most respected author. He is author of *Lie Down in Darkness, The Long March, Set This House on Fire, The Confessions of Nat Turner, Sophie's Choice,* and *This Quiet Dust*—books which themselves give expression to the desolation of melancholia and suicide. He has been awarded numerous awards, including the Prix Mandial Cinco del Duca, which itself played a special significance in William Styron's own suicidal malaise. It is his literary skill that makes this document rich. One can learn much from his success at painfully making darkness more visible. After his survival in balancing the life and death scale, William Styron advises those who suffer depression: "Chin up." He quickly adds that although this is "tantamount to insult" that "one can nearly always be saved." This is necessary advice to a suicidal person.

THE SUICIDAL POEM

A related document—and in many ways a personal one—is the poem. Poems have always been seen as a looking glass, being open like the diary and suicide note to understanding the human mind. This is especially true about the poems left by suicides, although, of course, they are likely written to be more public than the note but not more public than many diaries. There is a host of poets who killed themselves, including John Berryman, Hart Crane, Cesare Pavese, Anne Sexton, Sara Teasdale and, of course, Sylvia Plath (Leenaars, 2004; Lester, 1993). These poets' lives, as evident in their poems, diaries, and other documents, were full of pain, despair, and suicidal behavior.

Cesare Pavese is an illustrative example of the poet's inimical life; his life was characterlogically suicidal (Shneidman, 1982b). Pavese's childhood was, by his own words, a desolate existence (Pavese, 1961; Shneidman, 1982b). His father died when Pavese was age 6 and his mother was described as "spun steel, harsh and austere." He was haunted by pain all his life. Even in adolescence, he wrote about suicide ("You should know that I am thinking about suicide.") He did so deeply in his life and at the age of 42 on August 27, 1950, committed suicide. His writings are reflective of his pain, as one can read in the last words in his diary:

18th August
The things most feared in secret always happens. . . .
All it takes is a little courage. . . .
It seemed easy when I thought of it. Weak women have done it. It takes humility, not pride.
All this is sickening.
Not words. An act. I won't write any more.

Anne Sexton's life was equally marked by suicide. Lester (1993) lists the following attempts: 1949, November 1956, May 1957, November 1961, July 1966, August 1970, September 1973 (two), Winter 1973–1974 (two), February 1974, Spring 1974, and eventually killing herself with car exhaust in 1975. Dorothy Parker, a well-known American poet, writer, critic and satirist, was suicidal for years, although she never killed herself (Keats, 1970). Once, she wrote these most revealing lines:

If wild my breast and sore my pride,
I bask in dreams of suicide;
If cool my heart and high my head,
I think, "How lucky are the dead."

Of course, the poetry and writing of these poets are often projective of their unbearable pain. Cesare Pavese, for example, once wrote that he fought the pain "every day, every hour, against inertia, dejection, and fear." He and the others in the end chose death, leaving their poetry as documents to their suicidal mind. And like diaries, biographies, and suicide notes, they are open to analysis by placing them in the context of broad theoretical formulations about suicide and personality functioning in general. This was the very aim of my theory. It will allow us to understand the person's self-directed violence better. Of course, there are many other personal documents that can be used for case histories; I could have, for example, illustrated the topic at hand with letters or social media records. However, I have here illustrated the value with the diary, notes, and poems, and will use other documents in my cases. The belief: Documents contain special revelations to why the person died by suicide. They allow us to stab in the light for evidence to support our determination of the mode and conclusions.

SOME OTHER BOOKS ON THE
PSYCHOLOGICAL AUTOPSY

It would be accurate to state that there have been few books published on the psychological autopsy. Dr. Shneidman published one book on the topic. In 2004, he published an edited book, entitled *Autopsy of a Suicidal Mind.* It is Shneidman's last publication on the psychological autopsy. The book is, however, more; it is also on case consultation, a part of the PAs at the very beginning. Dr. Shneidman asked some friends to offer opinions on a case—Arthur, a 33-year-old Caucasian male physician and attorney, who died by suicide—they included some of who is who in the field: Robert Litman, Jerome Motto, Norman Farberow, John Maltsberger, Ron Maris, and Avery Weisman. One could want no better consultants on the PA. The book is insightful, and I will address some of Dr. Shneidman's reflections later.

On the PA, Dr. Shneidman first published a paper in 1963 with Litman, Curphey, Farberow, and Tabachnick entitled, "Investigation of Equivocal Deaths," in the *Journal of the American Medical Association* (JAMA, 184, 924–929). In 1977, he published his best paper on the topic by his own declaration, entitled, "The Psychological Autopsy," published in L. Gottschalk et al. (Ed.), *Guide to the Investigation and Reporting of Drug Abuse Deaths*. It is in the public domain and is reproduced in my 1999 edited book, *Lives and deaths: Selections from the works of Edwin S. Shneidman*. A second favorite article, actually one-page, which is also reproduced in my edited volume, was entitled, "Comment: The Psychological Autopsy," presented multiple times and originally published in *American Psychologist*. Dr. Shneidman here attempts to distinguish the psychological autopsy from other forensic reports, as often the forensic investigation is assumed to be a PA. I demonstrate the differences in this book. Probably Dr. Shneidman's best case example is also in my edited book and illustrated next in this volume; it was entitled "An Example of Equivocal Death Clarified in a Court of Law," published first in his own 1993 book, *Suicide as Psychache*. It is the best idiographic example, according to himself, of his published work on the PA.

There have been, to the best of my knowledge, a few other books published on the topic. In 1968, Avery Weisman published the book, *The Psychological Autopsy: A Study of the Terminal Phase of Life*. It offers an investigation into the psychological aspects of the death of older people. Dr. Weisman published a second book in 1974 entitled, *The Realization of Death: A Guide to the Psychological Autopsy*. It studies the same topic, offering some insights into death, with special focus on attitudes toward death. Dr. Shneidman wrote the foreword to the book, and stated that Dr. Weisman's work on the PA is very similar to his own. In 1981, Eli Robins published, *The Final Months: A Study of the Lives of 134 Persons Who Committed Suicide*. Shneidman would not call this study a PA; it is a psychometric (nomothetic) study of 134 suicides that took place in St. Louis between May 1956 and May 1957. It offers some insights into diagnosis, not the psychology of suicide. There is an additional book, self-published by James Selkin (1987), *The Psychological Autopsy in the Courtroom: Contributions of the Social Sciences to Resolving Issues Surrounding Equivocal Death*. It offers some psychoanalytic views on evidence and serving as an expert witness in the U.S. courtroom. Dr. Selkin in 2005 published some of the same notions in the book, *Suicide and the Law: Cases, Theories and Strategies for Prevention*. He offers four cases, concluding that at times the PA cannot determine if the person died by suicide or by accident (a margin of error). Of course, it is true that some cases will remain undetermined. Yet the PA approach, as shown already in the 1950s, does allow us to credibly certify most undetermined cases. Nothing is absolute, Dr. Shneidman often stated. The PA, however, offers us utility. Therefore it is easy to conclude that there was a need for my new book on the psychological autopsy, illustrated with idiographic enquiries that might be like a guide for understanding the PA for mental health and public safety professionals. I hope it does that.

I will next illustrate the PA, Dr. Shneidman's favorite case.

THE PSYCHOLOGICAL AUTOPSY TO MILITARY COURT

Shneidman's paper "An Example of an Equivocal Death Clarified in a Court of Law" (1993b, see Leenaars, 1999b) is an example of a military psychological autopsy. This one was done in the adversarial setting of a court of law, specifically an Army court martial. Everything except a few names is verbatim. The bare facts were that an Army officer was charged with the murder of his wife and faced a lifetime sentence in Leavenworth federal prison. The prosecution claimed that it was a homicide, citing that his wife had died in the nude and, after the testimony of some so-called expert, that since suicides do not occur in the nude, therefore it was homicide. The defense for which Shneidman was an expert witness, believed his death was a suicide, and that the officer had been wrongly accused. It is instructive to read the various experts different opinions, to take in Jerome Motto's model report, and to note Shneidman's testimony on the state as he holds ground on behalf of the accused. Next, I present some excerpts from Shneidman's testimony (a true window to Shneidman's mind). This chapter is an illustration of the principle of *res ipsa loquitur*: "The facts speak for themselves."

The Charge

I shall begin by reproducing a local newspaper account.

CAPTAIN CHARGED IN DEATH

ARMYVILLE, Sept. 22-A five-man court-martial panel was seated Wednesday in the trial of an army officer who was accused of slaying his wife in their Armyville apartment last July.

Capt. Joseph P. Campbell, 33, is charged with premeditated murder in the shooting death of Peggy Scott-Campbell on July 12. The 30-year-old woman was killed by a single blast from a 12-gauge pump shotgun.

The case, being heard before Judge (Col.) George D. Maris, is expected to last two weeks and involve dozens of witnesses and a trip to Los Angeles to hear testimony from an expert on suicide.

In his opening statement, Dan R. Hyatt, a civilian attorney who is representing Campbell, said he would prove that Scott-Campbell had suicidal tendencies. Also representing Campbell is Maj. James Purdich.

Prosecuting attorney Maj. Stanley Bates told the panel that the Campbells, who had been married about five years, were having marital problems and had discussed separation and divorce only hours before the shooting.

Bates said he would represent evidence to show that following the argument, Scott-Campbell went to a nearby pizzeria where she was well known. She stayed late, he said, to help with the dishes. She left for home, but returned a few minutes later, telling the owner she had too much to drink. She asked that a cab be summoned to take her back to the couple's apartment.

Bates said he would introduce evidence that would indicate that Campbell beat her after she returned home and cut her five times with a knife. Bates told the court that Campbell later retrieved a shotgun from the bedroom, took her into the bathroom near the living room, and shot her in the chest.

Campbell woke up a neighbor and told him his wife had shot herself, Bates told the court.

In his opening statement, Hyatt said Scott-Campbell had made several prior suicide attempts. On the night she died, Campbell had awakened to find her in the bathroom shower stall cutting her abdomen with a knife. His shotgun was sitting nearby, Hyatt said.

He said that when Campbell attempted to move the shotgun she grabbed the barrel with her right hand and pulled it toward her. The gun discharged.

Hyatt challenged the prosecution to prove that Campbell beat his wife. No witnesses, he said, ever saw Campbell strike his wife, although the bruises noted in the autopsy of the 130-pound woman could not be accounted for, he said.

Hyatt termed the cuts on Scott-Campbell's body as "hesitation marks" and said a doctor would testify that such marks are often inflicted by suicide-prone people.

"Why should he (Campbell) shoot his wife intentionally when she was trying to commit suicide?" Hyatt asked during his opening remarks.

Prosecutors told the court that the case would be based on circumstantial evidence from investigators and forensic experts.

In summary, the events were as follows: Peggy Scott-Campbell, age 30, is dead as a result of a shotgun wound to her chest. Her husband, Army Capt. Joseph P. Campbell, age 33, asserts that the gun was accidentally discharged as he sought to take it from his wife who was in the process of attempting suicide by cutting herself in the abdomen (while seated in the shower of their apartment bathroom). The government charges that, following a domestic quarrel, he willfully murdered his wife by deliberately shooting her and then cutting her abdomen to make the event appear like a suicide attempt. He is being tried by a court-martial.

The Issues

To either the ordinary observer or the trained investigator, the nature or mode of a death is usually self-evident. Each falls into one of the four modes: natural, accidental, suicide, or homicide (NASH). In some cases, however, the mode of death is not so clear; it is equivocal. Then what usually occurs is . . . a psychological investigation that focuses on the decedent's intentions vis-à-vis his or her own death.

The main function of a psychological autopsy is . . . to clarify the mode of death in cases where the mode appears unclear.

Putting the human drama aside, what we have in this case is a psychological enigma within a legal context.

Pretrial Report of Military Special Investigator

What follows in this section is a paraphrased and excerpted presentation of the "Report of Consultation in the Matter of Peggy Scott-Campbell (deceased) dependent wife of Capt. Joseph Campbell.". The report was written by Perry N. Olds, a special agent of the Army Office of Special Investigation (below are a few publicly available sections):

1. **Introduction**. This report was prepared for the Criminal Investigation division to better understand the deceased's manner of death. The key issue is whether she was attempting suicide or whether she died from homicide. . . .

4. **The Crime Scene**. The criminal investigation agents reported the crime scene as "a real mess." In the bedroom the agents observed what they believed to be bloodstains on the pillows, on the bedspread, on the fitted (bottom) sheet, and on the wall next to the bed. They also reported some damp washcloths with blood on the floor. In addition, they reported finding a trail of blood from the bedroom into the bathroom, and what they called "drag bloodstains" from the bedroom to the living room. They reported finding blood in places where Campbell denied having been subsequent to his contact with his wife's blood.

5. **The Autopsy**. An autopsy of the deceased was conducted by a forensic pathologist. He reported a number of findings, including a contact shotgun wound, which would indicate that the barrel was against her skin. The direction of fire was approximately level. On her lower abdomen there were four stab wounds. One of the cuts had numerous pricks around it. These the autopsy surgeon indicated might have been caused by "taunting" (tentative cuts on the body before a deep cut is made). In addition, there were multiple bruises on the extremities and the back of her head. He identified sixty bruised areas, with a majority being less than four hours old at the time of her death. There was a bruise on her chin. He also noted scars on both wrists and in each elbow. He reported her blood alcohol level was .10—actually it turned out to be .17—and no other drugs in her body. "The manner of death was ruled homicide." . . .

10. **Deceased's Nudity at the Time of Her Death**. At the time of her death she was nude. What was the significance of this point? A review of 150-plus female active-duty and dependent suicides revealed no one in which the person was nude at the time of her death. "Her reported nudity at the time she was reported to be attempting suicide is thus highly unusual and correspondingly improbable." . . .

1. **Summary**. It is my professional opinion that Captain Joseph Campbell shot deceased with the shotgun and attempted to conceal the true facts of the event by staging the scene he subsequently reported."

/ signed /
Perry N. Olds
Special Agent
Office of Special Investigations
U.S. Army

REPORT OF PSYCHIATRIC CONSULTANT
FOR THE DEFENSE

Besides Shneidman, the Defense had contacted another great giant in the field, Jerry Motto (a friend of Ed's and mine). I present the verbatim report, which is in the public domain. Dr. Shneidman once told me that it was the best prototype of a forensic report in the field. I agree.

Consultation Report

The problem at hand is the determination of the mode of death of Peggy Scott-Campbell. The question addressed is whether her death on July 23, 1990 was an accident in the course of thwarting her suicide attempt, or whether other issues played a role.

In order to form the basis for answering the question at hand, four preliminary questions are addressed: (1) Was Peggy Scott-Campbell the kind of person who would resort to suicide under adverse circumstances; (2) Was she being subjected to significant emotional stress at the time of her death; (3) Was there a precipitating event or circumstance that could reasonably have provoked a suicidal act at the time of her death; and (4) Would Captain Campbell's character and behavior pattern be consistent with either premeditated or impulsive homicide?

1. **Was she vulnerable to suicidal impulses or behavior?** The record is very consistent as regards the emotional vulnerability of Mrs. Scott-Campbell. Her medical record indicates an ongoing affective disturbance since early adolescence. In 1984 she complained of severe dysphoria, anger with episodic aggressiveness, and suicidal thoughts. She was diagnosed at that time as suffering from a major depressive disorder with borderline personality traits. The recommendation that she have a psychiatric evaluation and follow-up treatment with anti-depressive medication was not implemented. Nor was the recommendation that she be seen for psychiatric and psychological treatment.

Mrs. Scott-Campbell is said to have exhibited outspoken suicidal behavior on at least four occasions. . . . . These events are given varying dates by different informants, but the episodes themselves appear to be discrete and separate experiences. Some were related by Mrs. Scott-Campbell to confidants, and others are noted in Army medical records.

In addition to specific suicidal behaviors, there is virtual unanimity among those who knew her best that she was moody, emotionally volatile, prone to act impulsively and violently, and moved to intense feeling states by seemingly minor issues. The most provocative of these issues were apparently feelings of being criticized, ignored, or in some own description (on tape) of the altercations with her friend Marlene, and the episode in which she is said to have kicked in the bathroom door after Capt. Campbell retreated there to escape her angry outburst.

2. **Was she under significant emotional stress?** Mrs. Scott-Campbell made no secret of her discontent with army life, with "not fitting in" with the separations entailed or with other army wives, or with the "homebody" nature of her husband, leading to repeated consideration of divorce. Her persistently heavy drinking underscored her inability to find a stable adjustment; at the same time she apparently felt guilty about her behavior. She was heard to repeat "I'm sorry-I'm sorry" when in an intoxicated state. She confided that Captain Campbell treated her well and that she wanted to reward him with a party. Though emotionally very immature, she was intelligent enough to know that sooner or later her repeated drunkenness and violent outbursts would catch up with her-that it was only a matter of time, and that time might be getting short. For a person with intense rejection sensitivity, the threat

of being abandoned would constitute an ever-increasing emotional pressure in addition to her underlying insecurity and dissatisfaction with her life.

3. **Was there a precipitating event?** A recurrent theme in the available data regarding Mrs. Scott-Campbell's behavior is the sequence of (1) argument, (2) withdrawal by Captain Campbell, (3) drinking by Peggy Scott-Campbell, (4) guilt, depression, and contrition on the part of Mrs. Scott-Campbell. In one such previous sequence, Mrs. Scott-Campbell came home from a bar, told Captain Campbell she was going to cut her wrist, and when he tried to calm her down. She hit him with a chair. On the night of her death, this sequence seems to have been repeated. . . . . Whatever the facts were, they went beyond the usual pattern of returning from a drinking episode feeling depressed, and calling someone to talk, or even making suicidal threats. Mrs. Scott-Campbell was unable to get Captain Campbell to respond to her that night, even to placate her, and combined with the progressive dissatisfaction of her life and the depression and guilt she was prone to express after drinking, this experience of "being ignored" could easily have triggered a characteristic violent act. In this instance the act was directed at herself, but her disorganization and ambivalence created only preparation for a lethal act (loaded gun, cutting abdomen).

4. **Would his character be consistent with homicide?** Any effort to determine the likelihood of a given behavior by a given individual must take into account that person's behavioral history, as well as the characterological elements that contribute to that history. In short, the best predictor of behavior is past behavior.

In Captain Campbell's case, those who knew him on a day-to-day basis could hardly be more consistent in their impressions; "loving and supportive," "good natured," "least prone to violence," "Violence is not in him. He is not capable of violence," "Absolutely no way he could have done anything to hurt Peggy," and the like.

While it appears to be sophisticated to be skeptical of such unequivocal statements, it is difficult to document contradictory evidence. Mrs. Scott-Campbell's multiple bruises are only a mild example of what one sees in chronic heavy drinkers, as falls and bumping into objects are so common. Even cracked ribs, severe facial bruises, and head trauma are not uncommon. She stated that some bruises on her arm were from his trying to stop her from swinging a broken glass at him. In short, Captain Campbell's apparent need to be protective of his wife under the most provocative conditions, and to reflect this demeanor toward the rest of the world as well, is a virtually unanimous perception, and the record gives us nothing substantial to question it.

Comment on Report of Investigator Olds

Investigator Olds recapitulates the events surrounding Mrs. Scott-Campbell's background and death, and then asks whether she would have been "sufficiently depressed to become suicidal." The question is irrelevant. The nature of her pathology is not depressive but characterological. This is familiar to persons engaged in the field of suicide prevention, although lay persons and even some professionals continue to consider suicide a function of depression rather than psychological pain.

Investigator Olds' subsequent three questions are based on epidemiological comparisons that are interesting but likewise irrelevant. Though some of the numbers can be challenged, the most important issue in this analysis is that such issues as nudity, methods used, and the nature and extent of injury are unique to each individual. The degree of ambivalence, clarity of cognitive functioning, how organized and obsessive the individual is, his or her state of turmoil and agitation, and so forth are the determination of behavior. What another or a thousand others have done plays no essential role in understanding a given individual's behavior. In the present instance, an intoxicated, frustrated, angry, disorganized individual is involved. Trying to create a scientific aura by judging how common a given pattern appears is simply sophistry.

In short, I believe Investigator Olds' data are interesting, as is his discussion, but they are of no significance whatever in the individual instance under consideration. Thus, an opinion based on such considerations is little more than speculations and fertile imagination.

Summary and Conclusions

In summary, Mrs. Scott-Campbell was a person with a lifelong emotional vulnerability, manifested by extreme of reactivity, a very low threshold for psychic pain, and limited behavioral control. She required a great deal of emotional support and in its absence had repeatedly demonstrated a pattern of self-destructive behavior. In suicide prevention language, she would be regarded as "chronically suicidal," implying that even at her best level of functioning she was vulnerable to becoming suicidal in adverse circumstances, especially if a perceived rejection was involved.

Captain Campbell demonstrated an inexplicable ability, perhaps a need, to protect and nurture this emotionally vulnerable young woman. The record is replete with observations documenting his consistency in this regard. No evidence is available of traits that would contradict this.

The circumstances surrounding Mrs. Scott-Campbell's death are entirely consistent with her patterns of behavior and with Captain Campbell's efforts to protect her from her own lack of control. I find nothing in the record to indicate otherwise, and regard undocumented hypotheses to the contrary as speculative. Though the documented record can mislead us, I felt that it provides a better basis for sound judgment than hypotheses without documented support.

> Jerome A Motto, M.D.
> Professor of Psychiatry
> University of California, San Francisco

EXCERPTS FROM DR. EDWIN SHNEIDMAN'S TESTIMONY, WITH COMMENTS

The following is an excerpt of my responses to questions from Mr. Dan Hyatt, counsel for the defense.

Hyatt: The army investigator, Mr. Olds, has testified earlier in this case. He offered an opinion that it was unusual to see two instrumentalities when either attempting or committing suicide. Do you have an opinion with respect to that statement?

ESS: Yes, in a picayune way he is right. But in an overall way he is howlingly wrong. I'll tell you about each of those if I may.

Hyatt: Please.

ESS: Suicide itself, fortunately, is an event of infrequent occurrence. So that you can make tabulations of methods and all sorts of things. A lot of events are infrequent, but if the incontrovertible evidence is that the person has done it, then you can't say that the person has not done it simply because it is infrequent. Using two methods is much more infrequent than using one. That's true. But then to argue from that to this particular case is a tyro's error. It's a mistake that freshmen, undergraduates in my Death and Suicide course at UCLA make of going from statistics to an individual case. Statistics are an interesting background for a case but they don't tell you about that case. Here we are talking about this case.

Hyatt: Mr. Olds also testified that he thought it was very rare based on his study of Army personnel and their dependents, his data base, that it was very rare to find a dependent female to commit suicide or attempt to commit suicide in the nude. Do you have an opinion about that?

ESS: Yes. Well, I would say to him, "That's true. That's absolutely true. But you're really not seriously making an argument that that has a bearing on this case, are you?" And if he said, "Yes," my already low opinion of him would drop precipitously.

Hyatt: What value do you see of statistical information such as that offered by Mr. Olds in determining the cause of death?

ESS: In a particular case?

Hyatt: Yes.

ESS: None. It's background material.

Hyatt: Is the utilization of statistics in the manner testified by Mr. Olds a scientifically acceptable method, or is that data reasonably relied upon by other experts in your field as a means of drawing conclusion?

ESS: If your question is, is it a scientifically credited method the way he has done it, the answer is no.

Hyatt: And why would that be?

ESS: The technical response is that in these matters, in suicidology, the confusion of statistical-demographic-epidemiological-numerical data with the etiology or outcome of any particular individual case, to make a judgment about that individual case on the basis of statistics is a methodological error.

Hyatt: Why is it a methodological error?

ESS: Because it has things backwards. It isn't that the statistics generate the case; it is that the cases taken in long series or large numbers generate the statistics. To say that it is rare is not to say that it did not occur.

Hyatt: What do you say when you hear that Peggy Campbell was nude on the evening of her death?

ESS: I would say, "Gee whiz, isn't that unusual." But then to argue as he did that it couldn't be suicide on that account is a howler. It boggles the mind. Where did his logic go?

Hyatt: And would you have the same opinion as to the use of two instrumentalities?

ESS: Yes, sure. What is persuasive is the whole history of her lifetime (Leenaars, 1999a, pp. 433–434)

NEWSPAPER ACCOUNT OF THE VERDICT

Captain Acquitted in Trial

ARMYVILLE, Oct, 1- An officer charged with the shotgun slaying of his wife last July was found innocent Friday by a five-man court-martial panel.

CONCLUDING THOUGHT

In keeping with the mode of this chapter, I will add no more except to state the belief: Like Dr. Shneidman, I think that the PA, with special use of documents, is the best possible way (and probable, for that matter) to answer the question: Why did the person kill himself? It uncovers the barren bones. It thaws the hidden motive (the "why") in suicide. It provides closure for the unrequited mystery.

CHAPTER 5

A Conversation With Edwin S. Shneidman on Suicide and the PA

On June 27 and 28, 1996, I interviewed and audio taped Edwin Shneidman under his birch tree at his Kingsland Street house in Los Angeles. Dr. Shneidman wanted his story told. I used the recordings for the interstitial material for my edited volume of his selected works, *Lives and Deaths: Selections from the Works of Edwin S. Shneidman* (1999a). Later I used the tapes to construct two articles on Dr. Shneidman after his death (dob: 05-13-1918; dod: 05-15-2009) (Leenaars, 2010b, 2010c). Yet the bulk of the material has never been published. It seems fitting on this occasion to present some verbatim transcripts of our discussions. It is what I learned about the topics that may interest the reader of the current volume. It is one final way to show the barren bones of the suicidal mind's despair. Does it do it?

DEFINITION

Leenaars: Dr. Shneidman, you have always been keenly interested in definition, as you called it, an *a priori* step in the road to understanding suicide.

Shneidman: Here, almost 80 years old, I don't know whether suicide was looking for me or I was looking for suicide. But that was part of my motivation on that day in 1949, I believe. Part of what was in my head was that I was restless and looking for some niche in psychology or someplace in which to have a career. I remember saying then—I said many times—that I was tired of paddling around in the backwaters of schizophrenia. And I don't mean the schizophrenic disease, I mean the schizophrenic concept. So that we talk about in religion about epiphanies and epiphany moments. That they were genuine was an epiphanic moment for me. I really mean it. I had— My hairs on the back of my neck, stood. I had an autonomic reaction with the feeling without verbalizing that this was important to say "genuine" suicide note. So, within a couple months of saying genuine and then simulated and then eliciting notes, and then calling Norman Farberow, and then doing thematic analyses (I'd done the book in 1951 which was two to three years later), but I had the book in mind, and certainly I'd done the MAPS test and I was aware of thematic materials and so on. And I said, "Oh boy, suicide notes, the golden road to the unconscious of suicide." And I felt that I was on to something. And there was another man in my life, let me see. I'll start with the present, with Antoon, and I've mentioned Ginger [Joseph Gingerelli] and I've mentioned Harry [Murray], and I've mentioned Yolly West, and there was a colonel in the army, and I'm now thinking of Hal Hildreth. . . . they gave him a job at an NIMH without really serious responsibilities. So he had to find causes, and he found the cause of homosexuality and suicide and I think battered children, or whatever. Two or three causes, and promoted them. He got people to write grant proposals in these areas. Evelyn [Hooker], for example, in her area, and me in mine. So he and NIMH gave me a grant for $5,000. But three years later I was the PI of a grant for $1,600,000. I'm talking about serendipity and all these coins. . . .

So the canniness and the way in which I've planned the career that's been attributed to me is sheer hokum. You can't arrange these events, do things and so on. On the other hand, I've contributed to my own career by staying with the main topic, which is suicide and attempting to explicate it. A wonderful magical professor at UCLA named Charles E. Rebert, there's a Rebert Hall now, and he was then Dean Rebert, professor of philosophy and logic. He put on the board one day the simplest thing in the world. He was talking about something he put Roman I and Roman II and then he put the capital A and capital B and C and then he put Arabic I and Arabic II III and then he put lowercase. And I didn't know the word then, but I saw on the blackboard an explication. It's a little different from the definition. A little different from an explanation. And what I've tried to do in my career is to explicate the word, suicide. That is this outline which is essentially a Roman thing. It's not a taxonomy. It's an explication. Taxonomy is different. But a taxonomy, part of a taxonomy, is this explication. Tell me about this dolphin. Well it's animal kingdom. It is in the phylum of chordata. It's in the subphylum of vertebrates, vertebrata. It's in the class of mammalia. It's in this and then you have this particular dolphin that lives in the estuary of the River Planta in South America. Boom.

What about this butterfly? Well it's insecta, and there's nothing, there's no etcetera. That's the model. It's a 19th century model. I'm a 19th century thinker. I don't like—I'm not cathected to Kraeplin but I'm cathected to Linnaeus. Which is so that it is a very simple science and if they don't exist, I make one up.

I say disregarding all of biology and genetics, that it is essentially psychological pain. I know that it is not entirely so, and maybe not centrally so, but that's what I can investigate and explicate. And the explication—I looked and looked and there are Murray's needs. So potentially there are 20 kinds of suicides, but not in actuality. They're probably a half dozen. So I put together what I know. I'm a great person at maximizing my limitations. That's really true. I have an education which is pretty good. My high school, there was this principal and so on and she divided the people very unfairly and I lucked out and got four years of Latin and four years of math and four years of science. My physics teacher was an ROTC instructor. He was a Westpoint graduate and he was qualified to teach high school physics. And there he was in his uniform and I had nothing to do with ROTC, but I had very qualified people. And the Latin teacher was devoted to a single lady that was, he taught Latin to these kids. She made us mildly interested in Latin history and so on. So when I went to Harvard at that status, I found out that they conjugated the verbs the same way. And if you knew them, you knew them. And if you'd read a novel and knew it, you could talk about Madame Bovary. And if they mentioned a book you didn't know, you had to say you hadn't read it. Very simple. But I make the most of what I know. And occasionally I extend it by some neologisms.

So, you begin with definition and theory, and if it's pain then I talk about perturbation and lethality. . . .

And the concept of psychological autopsy, that comes later. What other neologisms, postvention, suicidology. I like to play with words. I have minimal, almost zero mathematical skills. I can add and divide and so on. But I'm not, I got through high school math but I was not gifted at it. It didn't come intuitively. And I have a nonmathematical brain. I have a verbal brain. My grandson has a mathematical brain. He can look at a blackboard of all sorts of symbols and just know intuitively and read it. I would have to labor through it and I couldn't get by the second line. But I can read words. And I like 18th century essays and so on. I like the swing of it; it has a sort of Baroque swing. . . .

PSYCHOLOGICAL AUTOPSY

Leenaars: Can you tell me about the psychological autopsy?

Shneidman: The psychological autopsy is another man in my life. A benign, dear man. Theodore Curphey, a real English gentleman. He was Canadian. And he was an MD, the first in Los Angeles County to be the coroner. They were political jobs before. And a scholar and he understood immediately that some—no, I didn't tell him, he told me, he knew, not immediately, he knew from his life as a pathologist as a certifying officer that many deaths are equivocal as to mode. You know what the person died of, but you don't know how to identify that death as suicide or accident. And it was in the mind, it was a psychological thing of the person's intention vis-á-vis the death. So actually he said he heard me and then called the three of us [with Robert Litman and Norm Farberow] in and we did these interviews. We had a name tag. We were deputy coroners. We did these interviews and then we presented our findings to him and I simply labeled it one day as a psychological autopsy. And then what's in print and Bob [Litman] wrote it, a paper for *JAMA* and the word, it's a common word now. I don't know if it's in OED. I should look it up. And if it's attributed to me, I don't know. But I know I made it up.

Leenaars: You wrote a paper on the PA in the American Psychological Association's *American Psychologist*. I know you've said the same thing many times before, such as AAS [American Association of Suicidology] conferences, but can you tell me about this paper?

Shneidman: The comment is a one pager for *American Psychologist* that says that there are different kinds of procedures and some are not psychological autopsies. If you do the ballistic test and blood samples and so on, that's not a psychological autopsy. That's a forensic autopsy. Or a clinical autopsy. But if you look at bullet markings and blood, that's not intention. And I also indicate that it's [PAs] been oversold and I have in mind here specifically, a guy I like, named, he's in a town in

Massachusetts, and he's a member of AAS. And he edited the book called the *Harvard View of Suicide*.

Leenaars: Douglas Jacobs.

Shneidman: Yes, Douglas Jacobs. And he went down to Florida and said I know exactly what was in this girls mind, and so on. Remember that.

Leenaars: Oh, absolutely.

Shneidman: He made a circus out of a concept. So it can be overdone.

Leenaars: Third-party retrospective interviews are also now used by some researchers for testing third-party informants to obtain a DSM mental diagnosis of the diseased. That is now also called a PA. This is also not the original meaning.

Shneidman: Yes. The fact is I have—But you can't have the copyright on a concept.

Leenaars: I understand.

Shneidman: You can't patent it. You can't say, look you're misusing my word.

DEATH AND NASH

Leenaars: Dr. Shneidman, we have been talking about suicide, but can you tell us something about death?

Shneidman: Well, my notion of suicide is that it can't have a full definition without evoking the word death. That is, I don't think it is comparable to "I think I'll go to sleep" or "I think I'll disappear" or "I'll just move out of the city" or "I think I'll do something." It's that I cannot stand this pain and I want the cessation that death will give me. Now it doesn't matter whether you believe in heaven, hell, none of these things; whether you're theistic or atheistic, but the concept of ending it all—the "it" is life. And stopping the painful flow of consciousness, a phrase from William James used by Henry Murray, is an integral part of understanding suicide and preventing it. What you're preventing is not the person's ingesting or cutting, you're preventing the person being a corpse in the coroner's office. So the prevention has to do with death and the doing of the act involves a thought of death.

Now the dichotomy in the NASH categories [natural, accident, suicide, and homicide] was in death with either intention or unintention. So the S category, suicide, was intentioned death and all the others were unintentioned. That's what that category implies or assumes philosophically, psychologically.

And Harry [Murray] pointed out to me at a luncheon at Yamashiro's, which is a Japanese hotel and restaurant and only a couple hundred feet away from Hollywood Boulevard—you'd climb this hill to the magic castle up to Yamashiro's. And we were sitting seated there in the terrace and I was taking notes, very naughtily on a napkin—it was the only thing I had. I didn't want to stop his flow and ask someone for some paper, and I wrote on a cloth napkin with a pen I had and took a note. And at that luncheon, I made up the word *subintentioned death*. Harry made up other phrases like, *comparable to death*, *as good as dead*, *socially dead*, and he talked all around subdeaths, etcetera. I simply said intentioned, unintentioned, and in the middle, so to speak, subintentioned. There are all sorts of ways in which you could hasten the day, the date, or the hour of your death by imprudence, stupidity, hostility, disregard for medical regimen, risk taking, and so on. Then there are all sorts of questions which are immediately asked: Is smoking the huh huh? Is motorcycle huh, huh? and so on. And the answer is, it depends. I think if you have emphysema and you're end-stage lung cancer and have to sneak out in your gown to get you're a little Chesterfield, I think there's more than just happens.

I'm impressed . . . with Evelyn [Hooker], who absolutely could not stop smoking and spent thousands of dollars with this conditioning thing, and this behavior mod, and she had special trainers and so on and one day she was hospitalized for her back or her knee or her—didn't matter. It was irrelevant. I mean, it was not related to her smoking, but there was no smoking. Absolutely none. There were oxygen tanks and so on. She was there two or three weeks and came out not smoking. And I'm making a point, it's a point of conation, which is the psychology of *intention*.

Now, I'd like to say . . . I suffered from that the last couple of months. I'd lie in bed and there were things I wanted to do, needed to do, ought to do, plan to do, really wanted to do. And I couldn't connect the will to the first movement of my life. So there's a lot to subintention. You see it in patterns of life. And you can see it in the Terman lives. It has to do with—you read it in the case histories and I think you read it in the nuances of the case histories. But I don't want to say that people are star-crossed and doomed, otherwise I couldn't believe in the interventions of psychotherapy.

Leenaars: Can you say something more about intention?

Shneidman: So that "Orientations toward death," which also has a psychological autopsy of Ahab at the end, was a theoretical paper of mine. I don't want to say major, in which I said that along with natural, accident, suicide, homicide, the NASH categories, every death can be intentioned, subintentioned, unintentioned. I sort of did a little experiment with a coroner in Muren County who helped me with this and a lot of subintentioned deaths. And that's my sort of philosophic conceptual piece about the kinds of deaths, and I've noted this in myself hundreds of hours of introspection in the last couple of months.

FINAL THOUGHTS, DREAMS, AND REFLECTIONS

Leenaars: Any final thoughts, dreams, or reflections?

Shneidman: The final thoughts and reflections are in a book about suicide, but they're an address to me that I have to find the courage and the stability and the maturity to die well. I talk a good game, but there have been times in the last couple of months when I haven't been able to sustain it. I've just fallen apart and Jeanne [Shneidman's wife] knows about it. I shared some of it with some of the kids, but I came close to being a kind of basket case, and I have to understand I can go totally blind and live, or I could be totally incapacitated, not be able to walk and live. I don't want to be like certain people I know. I am thinking of an aunt of mine, and an old female friend of mine, who I won't mention by name, who are less than noble in their whining and carrying on—"Oh my elbow hurts" and so on. I, until my eye happened and my sciatic nerve got pinched, I hurt every day. I lived with back pain and this I've had vicissitudes and illnesses, I mean that's what happens. And Harry [Murray] never complained. I would like not to complain, but I don't think I can keep up to that, but that chapter ("Final Thoughts and Reflections." In Leenaars. (1999a), *Lives and Deaths: Selections from the Works of Edwin S. Shneidman*, ch. 36, pp. 511–517]) is about those reflections. It's a very personal chapter. . . .

I know, our needs, human needs, for love are insatiable. And not omnipresent. Freud is reputed to have said *Liebe und Arbeit*. Love and work. But I think there's a deeper profundity to that which he probably understood. For me, work is a substitute for love. That's totally misunderstood when I say it. I don't mean it's a substitute for love. I mean it's in lieu of love, which then becomes forgotten and irrelevant. That is, if you use a psychoanalytic term *cathexis*, when I write, I don't mean when I type up a table of contents, but when I'm composing (if I may say that at the word processor), when we write this essay and it's going to be read or given in '97 for Harry, I'm not thinking about Jeanne or my kids or anybody, not even about Harry. (Yes, I am.) Not thinking about the word, I'm thinking about the English language, about producing sentences, thinking, and so on. That is love and work.

And so love and work for me, those are somewhat discrete and separated categories of my life. When I loved I'm not working and when I work I'm not sentimental or loving. I've a great cathexis to the language and I listen carefully, especially with patients; unfortunately, not at home. And so, when I said to myself, "Oh these are genuine suicide notes," assuming that the noun is a compound noun, suicide note was one word. The adjective is terribly important. Usually people say, "Oh, those are suicide notes." But if you listen to yourself saying genuine, then another voice in you, the didactic scientific voice, might very well say, "Well, the converse of genuine is simulated, fake, elicited." And can I elicit some notes and get simulated notes and compare them, and once you have that thought, you're off and running in a scientific suicidology because you're invoking the method of difference. But I've never worked out the role of self and the role of luck in a life. Now, when I said genuine and simulated and took steps to illicit documents and count words in a blind study, that was self-actualization. I did that. I did that. That is my self and my ego played a part in then creating or promoting a career. But most of it has been something in which I not only didn't do but wouldn't have dared to plan and wouldn't think to plan. And I'm willing to give that credit that Pasteur gave to himself: Chance and the prepared mind. But even their mind—mine was prepared by parents and mentors and teachers. I doubt I would have stumbled across the Mills Method if I hadn't gone to a university. I don't mean to UCLA. I could have learned that at Columbia or Harvard or Princeton or Michigan, but you need to learn it or to be guided toward it. So that Bertrand Russell said that if he had his life to live over he'd gratefully jump at the chance to do so. And I think he meant by that that even though he was orphaned when he was about 2 years old, and had some storms in his life, that's not the point. I think he meant by that that he'd been a pretty lucky fellow. And even to be born with his capacious brains, that's luck too, considering his father died of syphilis. All of which is true.

WHAT I KNOW

To conclude what I have learned from Dr. Shneidman, let me finish with his final words; the last signs for our roadmap to his chapter, "Final Thoughts and Reflections." Once more he reflected on Herman Melville, his favorite author, and without a doubt, his favorite book was *Moby Dick*. Dr. Shneidman offered the following endnote:

> Moody, stricken Melville expressed his lament and his psychological insights, at age 29:
>
> Cold, bitter cold as December and bleak as its blasts, seemed the world then to me; there is no misanthrope like a boy disappointed; and such as I with the warm soul of me flogged out by adversity. . . . Talk not of the bitterness of middle-age and after life; a boy can feel all that, and much more, when upon his young soul the mildew has fallen; and the fruit, which with others is only blasted after ripeness, with him is nipped in the first blossom and bud. And never again can such blights be made good; they strike in too deep, and leave such a scar that the air of Paradise might not erase it.

That uncovers the barren bones of a mind's *pain*, I know.

CHAPTER 6

Problems With the PA

Of course, from the very beginning, it was known that the PA had problems. Originally, Shneidman's PA was designed to assist medical examiners and coroners in classifying deaths that were equivocal; the deaths were ambiguous or undetermined. As you read in Chapter 4, the method was designed to clarify the mode of death. Shneidman, Litman, and Farberow would examine the psychological details—factors surrounding the death and the deceased. The team examined the official records, including medical autopsy, police reports, personal documents (such as suicide notes, diaries); yet the main procedure was talking to some key person—spouse, lover, parents, grown child, friend, an endless list. However, there was never one or two people interviewed; it was a large array of people who knew the decedent (see Chapter 4). Shneidman believed that the questioning should be detailed (and lines of inquiry pursued), only as they bear or clarify the mode of death. Of course, Shneidman, Litman, and Farberow were highly trained interviewers (and they trained other clinicians, like me). Of course, the whole process depended on having established rapport with the respondent. This was key.

SOME FURTHER REFLECTIONS
OF SHNEIDMAN

Of course, the PA did not stop with the interviews. In my 1999 volume (Leenaars, 1999a), Shneidman outlines the next steps:

> The results of these interviewing procedures are then discussed with the chief medical examiner or coroner. Because it is his responsibility to indicate (or amend) the mode of death, all available psychological information should be included in the total data at his disposal. Since a sizable percentage of deaths are equivocal as to mode precisely because these psychological factors are unknown, medical examiners and coroners throughout the country are robbing themselves of important information when they fail to employ the special skills of the behavioral scientists in case of equivocal deaths. The skills of behavioral scientists should be employed in the same way as the skills of biochemists, toxicologists, microscopists, and other physical scientists. The time has long since passed when we could enjoy the luxury of disregarding the basic teachings of twentieth century psychodynamic psychologist and psychiatry. Certification

procedures (and the death certificates on which they are recorded) should reflect the role of the decedent in his own demise, and in equivocal cases this cannot be done without a psychological autopsy.

The retrospective analysis of deaths not only serves to increase the accuracy of certification (which is in the best interests of the overall mental health concerns of the community), but also has the heuristic function of providing the serious investigator with clues that he may then use to assess lethal intent in living persons. (Leenaars, 1999a, p. 401)

It would seem obvious that the whole process is complex, not simple. You could not, for example, speak to one person alone. Some deaths, of course, could not be classified; some remain undetermined. There is a margin of error. The purpose was all to eliminate the error and to reflect on our understanding of intent—the issue of conation: Was it suicide? Accident? Or homicide? The OED defines conation as, "The desire to perform an action. Voluntary action. Volition."

On causes, modes, and intent, Shneidman (Leenaars, 1999a) writes,

In summary, the following points may be emphasized:

Causes. The classification of causes of death has been rather well worked out and is consistent with contemporary knowledge. There is currently an international classification which has wide acceptance.

Modes. The modes of death have not been stated explicitly and have not been too well understood. In general, four currently implied modes of death—natural, accidental, suicidal, and homicidal—suffer from the important deficiency of viewing man as a vessel of the fates and omitting entirely his role in his own demise.

Intent. The addition of the dimension of lethal intention serves to modernize the death certificate, just as in the past, advances have been made from the teaching of bacteriology, surgery, anesthesiology, immunology, and so forth. The time is now long overdue for the introduction of the psychodynamics of death into the death certificate. The addition of a single item on imputed lethal intent (High, Medium, Low, Absent) would provide an appropriate reflection of the psychological state of the subject and begin, at last, to reflect the teachings of twentieth century psychology. In this way we might again permit the certification of death to reflect accurately our best current understanding of man. (Leenaars, 1999a, p. 409)

The study of the PA was idiographic, a single case. It was never nomothetic. It was doing the real thing—forensics—which probably concerns the reader of this volume deeply. It was psychological DSI. Of course, the individual study was not without controversy. Selkin (2005) noted that some cases could not be classified; the case remained "undetermined." That is true; there are always cold cases.

CRITICAL ISSUES IN PA STUDIES

Somewhere along the way, the PA became the primary approach in studying risk factors. As you read in Chapter 4, Dr. Shneidman would not call these studies PAs. Be that as it may, in suicidology today (at least the nomothetic study), the PA is regarded as the most direct, reliable and valid method. It is espoused (Cavanagh,

Carson, Sharpe, & Lawrie, 2003; Kelly & Mann, 1996), that the PA is the best general, authoritative way to study the relationship between particular antecedents and suicide. Almost always, mental disorders, especially mood disorders, are found to be the most strongly associated variable with suicide. A causal link is accepted; it is espoused that the barren bones are now fact. All suicides are caused simply by mental disorders (Cavanagh et al., 2003; Isacsson & Rich, 2003).

Although the first responders and forensic specialists who are entrenched in their particular roadmap may not be interested in the nomothetic, I believe it is best that they are aware of the issue and generally knowledgeable. Not only in that way but also others I differ from Shneidman. He saw little value in tabular, arithmetical study, especially in regard to death certification. I think he was wrong about that. One needs to know the problem of a technique, specific and general. I will here not detail each PA study; there are a number of good reviews (see Hjelmeland, Dieserud, Dyregrov, et al., 2012; in that paper, with my colleagues, I spell out the specific studies).

In the nomothetic study, the PA is associated with a number of methodological issues; there have been abundant reviews (Pouliot & De Leo, 2006). Many disappoint us (e.g., Cavanagh et al., 2003; Conner, Beautrais, Brent, et al., 2011). However, there are a number of insightful reviews (Conner, Beautrais, Brent, et al., 2012; Hjelmeland et al., 2012; Pouliot & De Leo, 2006). There are problems. Hjelmeland, Dieserud, Dyregrov, Knizek, & Leenaars (2012) are of the following opinion: "The severe problems indicated in the PA studies have not received the attention they deserve" (p. 607). This statement is about current studies, not Shneidman's procedures. The current studies need to be scrutinized. Hjelmeland and her team ask, Are PA's methodologically flawed?

I believe that the best review of the critical issues in the nomothetic studies is authored by Louise Pouliot and Diego De Leo (2006). I highly encourage a read in the interested officers or forensic experts, as well as my own with Heidi Hjelmeland's team (2012). I here summarize the issues and offer some solutions.

Pouliot and De Leo (2006) note that the PA approach has offered an opportunity to provide people with a great deal of information on suicide, such as psychiatric disorder/mental illness, childhood histories, life events, protective factors, and the like. Yet there are inconsistencies in their findings due to four problems. They state,

> (1) the type of paradigm under which PA studies have been undertaken till now; (2) the absence of standard protocols; (3) the introduction of method-ological artifacts in the procedures; and (4) the lack of specific training guidelines for interviews. (p. 492)

To ascertain the results, Pouliot and De Leo (2006) used a systematic review, a computerized database (PubMed) search, augmented by screening previous publications for reference lists. A systematic literature review is a standard in the field (Leenaars, 2013).

On the first critical issue, unlike Shneidman's intent, most PA studies used a single paradigm of medicine. According to the medical model, all suicides are the result of a mental illness, "a consequence of biological based alterations of the brain."

The brain is an organ; it is in the anatomy book. It is, from this view, no different than a kidney disease. People in the medical model believe the mental illness fact because they prefer to believe it is true, or rather they know it is true; thus, the end of all investigation. Yet a fact: most mentally ill patients do not commit suicide. Does it, thus, help us to understand our forensic unknown? It would mean, no mental illness, not a suicide. If the person had a diagnosis of mental illness, it is a suicide. All death investigations are simple, just find a mental disorder. The truth is, as discussed in detail, "suicide is a multi-causal phenomenon." Pouliot and De Leo (2006) are, thus, espousing the ecological model; those models look beyond mental illness.

Second, researchers have been quite labile in the measurement of mental illness. The large majority of instruments are ill-defined. First and most important, as I will discuss in more detail below (see Hjelmeland et al., 2012), many of the instruments used have not been adapted and validated for administration to informants, proxies.

The measurement of life events has been diverse, often developed by the researcher him/herself, or existing instruments have been used that were not designed to be used by proxies. Shneidman, of course, would never use a test, a measure, and so on. The original PA used the interviewing technique, not administration of a test—Can you fill out this questionnaire, and can you give me a sample of your body fluids, is now standard in the PA. (Really!) Pouliot and De Leo (2006) concluded something different than Shneidman, however; they note the lack of equivalence of the instruments is the problem, not presence or absence of their use. Shneidman would not use them; yet we may use a guide like the TGSP to organize our observations and informants' reports; that is all very different than giving proxies tests, MRIs, blood tests, and the like. I agree here with Shneidman.

Third, Pouliot and De Leo (2006) found a further problem, "The lack of systematic control in the type of informants and their number in research designs are two major weaknesses in many PA studies" (p. 499). There are differences between and within studies; the variability in informants, such as spouses, parents, coworkers, siblings, adult children, general practitioners, psychiatrists, friends, and numbers results in issues in reliability and comparability. Nothing is the same!

Pouliot and De Leo (2006) noted bias related to informants; for example, their emotional/mental state; age, gender, degree of closeness, and the like; attitudes toward suicide; recollections of the deceased, memory, and such. The characteristics of the interviewers are also suspect. It is well established that people react to the psychological and social characteristics of the interviewer (e.g., police vs. psychiatrist). There are questions about the training of the interviewers; often this is not listed in the PA. It is quite easy to ascertain the training of Shneidman, Litman, and Farberow, the very reason that Curphey chose them. On a further overall observation, "results revealed that experienced clinicians outperformed lay interviewers in inter-rater reliability and specificity of diagnosis assigned to patients" (Pouliot & De Leo, 2006, p. 501). This has also been shown in distinguishing genuine suicide notes from fake (suicidal) ones too. On one final point: Interviewers, whether in PA or forensic investigations or police inquiries, can introduce error, systematic or otherwise, in the data. This impacts the results.

The range of interviewers has been huge—1 to 245! Nothing more is needed to be said about this problem, and among officers.

Noticeable variations are observed in time intervals between the time of the death and the time that the survivor was interviewed. Between studies, it has ranged from 7 days to 8 years; within studies, the range has been one month to several years. The confounding potentials are obvious regarding factors such as memory and meaning making, to name two.

Nomothetic studies often use control groups, what are called case-control studies. As one would predict, research has used different variables (e.g., psychological disorder, age, geographic region) to match cases. Thus, garbage in, garbage out.

Pouliot and De Leo (2006) note a "pervasiveness" of methodological shortcomings and ask, How can we fix the problems? They argue for more standardization; Shneidman would say we already have the standard. Hjelmeland and her team (2012) argue for fewer controls, and allowing the informants to tell their story. Would any police officer give an informant a guideline or what to say, who to ask, or such? Do we let the survivor tell the facts, or do we study what facts they tell us. Think policing or the PA.

THE NEXT GENERATION OF PA STUDIES

Conner, Beautrais, Brent, Carwell, Phillips and Schneider published two papers, entitled, "The Next Generation of Psychological Autopsy Studies" part one on interview content (2011), and part two on interview procedures (2012). The first (2011) is about ways to improve collecting data on mental disorders; that paper is seriously flawed and offers little insight to us. The second, however, on interview procedures (2012) makes some helpful statements. Much of the review echoes Pouliot and De Leo (2006), however.

Conner et al. (2012) note the need to keep time intervals somewhat consistent, although flexibility will always be necessary, such as due to delays in determining cause of death (e.g., by coroner, medical examiner). They state (and I agree), "In general, there is agreement that the most important consideration in deciding on timing is the need to strike a right balance between allowing for acute bereavement and avoiding unacceptable degree of memory decay and reconstruction" (p. 87). From the view of the participant, it is well established that soon is more satisfying than later, but how soon? Indeed, as you will read in more detail in Chapter 8, informants are often satisfied in participating in a PA. Of course, there is no study on timing of interview to determine the actual impact. There is no evidence-based conclusion. Most PA experts recommend waiting 2 to 6 months, although the reason for the PA itself may affect that recommendation. If the reason is determining the mode of death, this may be too long. We should let our case guide us, not fabricated beliefs of psychologists and psychiatrists.

Conner and his team (2012) also note the issue of which potential proxy informant(s) to interview. Regrettably, many PA's, and so do Conner et al., recommend only one primary informant, allowing additional interviews only in selected cases. This is simply wrong! Some have gone too far as to be able to deter-mine the "best" proxy. Is there a "best" informant possible in death investigation? How do you determine before the investigation, a person's "knowledge," "cooperative," and "unbiased," whatever? Perhaps some of the researchers, such as Shaffer, Perlin, Schmidt, and Himelfarb (1972), who espouse the "best," have crystal balls. I do not.

Informants were typically chosen by virtue of the relationship to the decedent. It was never one or two (see Chapter 4). Yet rightfully, Conner and his team note that in retrospective investigation, one needs to expect some selective recollection, selective forgetting, unawareness of facts, deception, and so on. It is human. Furthermore, for example, relying on parents alone in the suicide of an adolescent is likely problematic; often parents are not aware of key aspects. Friends give a different story, with less guilt, defensiveness and other reactions (Conner et al., 2012). There are a host of factors, as noted by Pouliot and De Leo (2006), that may be important; for example, age, gender, education, and the relationship between informants and the person who died by suicide. Thus, it is best to decide before starting the PA who and how many informants to interview, but not select Shaffer et al.'s (1972) "best." Of course, Conner et al. (2012) note that all biases cannot be eliminated; one more reason for many informants.

Conner et al. (2012) discuss a most important topic, not discussed before, that is, integrating interview data with records. They write,

> Interview data are the primary source of information in PA studies but need not be the only source. In particular, records may provide vital complementary information, such as where to identify at-risk individuals prior to suicide (e.g., primary care), whether certain treatments or settings are found to be helpful, and how to best align treatment and preventive services for at-risk individuals. Indeed, historical records from a variety of sources may constitute an efficient and effective means by which to place data obtained by proxy informant inter-views into a larger and more informative context. Using such data, however, poses an entirely new set of challenges—which records to choose, how they might be obtained, and approaches to extracting and managing the data, including their integration with information from other sources in a method-ologically sound manner—and what to do when these supplementary data are only available for some of the cases and controls. (p. 94)

There is no question, the personal documents are essential—the investigator's gold. There are questions, such as choice of records. Accessing medical records may be difficult (although very useful; see Chapter 9). There are issues in release of information; who decides? There are privacy rules. Conner and his team (2012) also stated, "Provider and system in which they work may resist release of records owing to concerns about legal liability" (p. 96). Another issue is extracting and managing data; in nomothetic studies, we should use the same scientific rigor as for interviews. In our idiographic cases, we need to manage data with some forensic or policy rights that we must honor, by duty, with any investigation. I learned that in one investigation, the interviewer demanded the cellphone of the deceased, yet the bereaved mother could not part with the pictures of her son. They took it anyway.

She howled months later (sanctuary/system trauma). In one military death investigation, the military threatened the parents of a deceased soldier with prison if they did not cooperate. What are some of us becoming?

A further records issue is asymmetry of data; yet again this is always true in each death case. Nothing is absolutely uniform, the same. As noted in Chapter 1, we need our theory to sort out the mess. There will be asymmetry.

Conner and his team also added interview considerations, most of which we discussed earlier. However, one important observation is worth repeating: *Enhanced ability of empathic responding.*

PA: METHODOLOGICALLY FLAWED?

As you have read, over the years, a number of issues inherent in PA studies have been discussed. Regardless of their imperfection, it is also a truism that PA studies have contributed significantly to our current knowledge of suicide, both the general and the specific. Yet further reflection is necessary. Shneidman would want nothing less.

As I am obviously biased; an article by Heidi Hjelmeland, Gudrun Dieserud, Kari Dyregrov, Bitte Knizek and Antoon Leenaars (hence, the bias), examined the major flaw in most PAs (not Shneidman's PA)—how psychiatric diagnoses are assigned to the deceased in PA studies (2012). Although there are accepted methods to do so, ideographically (see Chapters 9 and 12), the current method, such as espoused by Conner et al. (2011) undermines the reliability and validity of diagnoses assigned in PA studies. Earlier, I reflected on Pouliot and De Leo's (2006) scrutiny.

The instruments used in the process of diagnosis are unknown or nonstandardized. The truth is that measures used today in PAs were never designed for retrospective investigation. Often, researchers are vague. Yet a few studies have used standardized instruments and *a priori* claimed the diagnoses obtained are reliable and valid. All is well. We can credibly diagnose. We can rest easy and collect our Nobel Prize. We have been so wise.

Kelly and Mann (1996) are often cited as the basis for the claim that we can perfectly diagnose a deceased person. They claimed to have clearly shown that in almost all cases, we can be absolutely sure. However, let us examine the study, following Hjelmeland and our team (2012).

Kelly and Mann (1996) studied 13 suicides (rather meager, only 13!); all 13 had psychiatric treatment before their suicide. They contacted the treating psychiatrist and obtained the diagnoses set by clinicians that "in most cases" treated the person just before the suicide. They had a control; they used the same method with 19 controls who died from other than suicidal causes. Thus, Kelly and Mann had a diagnosis before interviewing one to four (mainly two) first degree relatives. One criterion of inclusion was that the relative knew the diagnosis. Not surprisingly, there was high agreement in the diagnosis "found" in the PA study and the treating clinician's diagnosis. Kelly and Mann claimed that they have uncovered the psychiatric illness in their study. Therefore, it was argued that the psychiatric illness caused the suicide. All was proven. Of note, this study is often used as the basis for the claim that the validity of diagnosis found in the PA studies is "evidence-based." It is all genetic, after all. What do you think?

If you examine Cavanagh et al.'s (2003) comprehensive review of PA studies, you will read that PAs are considered to be valid in determining a diagnosis by referring to Kelly and Mann (1996). Cavanagh and his team concluded, "Our results are consistent with the strong positive evidence for the role of mental illness disorder throughout the suicide literature" (2003, p. 401). Hjelmeland and our team concluded, "Their argument seems a bit tautological" (p. 612). Maybe the problem is that all the studies use the same problematic methodology. Hjelmeland et al. (2012), then, go on to scrutinize the PA studies in more detail. I will follow our words in that article.

Hjelmeland et al. (2012) state, "If the responses from informants are unreliable, inter-rater reliability is worthless. The important issue then is whether the questions in standardized diagnostic instruments are possible to answer reliably by anyone else than the person being diagnosed" (p. 612). That is obvious. As Pouliot and De Leo (2006) already indicated, if instruments used are not validated for use with proxies, they are useless. Hjelmeland and our team (2012) go on to offer examples from instruments often used; I provide a few:

> In the last month, did you lose interest or pleasure in things you usually enjoyed?
> Did you feel tired or without energy almost every day?
> Have you been feeling guilty about things you have done or not done?

Can an informant know the answers? Only the decedent can answer these questions. Shneidman, in fact, never intended such questions to be asked.

A further question: How do you distinguish between disorder and comorbidity? How do you sort that all out from informants answering a questionnaire? This is futile. It would be unequivocal that proxies simply cannot answer many questions included in standardized diagnostic instruments reliably. A case is overstated. Further, Zhang, Conwell, Zhou, and Jiang (2004) found that informants sometimes might exaggerate symptoms of psychiatric disorder to justify the suicide. There are further motivations to do so. Indeed, "it is difficult or even impossible to know when there might be an overestimation and when there might be an underestimation of psychiatric diagnoses in PA studies" (Hjelmeland et al., 2012, p. 617). Lanny Berman (2006) made a worthwhile remark to remember: "If I hold to a belief that one has to be mentally disordered to die by suicide, I am more likely to see and report symptoms that fit my belief" (p. 3). Francis Bacon, the philosopher, would agree. He said, "People believe what they prefer to be true."

Next, there are differences in the rates of the different types of psychiatric disorders in different PA studies. Which is correct? This is due to such enormous differences in method, samples, age, gender, geographic region, hospital vs. rural setting; an endless list.

It is, thus, easy to conclude that not only unreliable standardized tools, never designed to be used by informants, are useless in our forensic idiographic enquiries.

They are, however, also useless from a nomothetic point of view. To answer the questions raised in this subsection, Hjelmeland and our team concluded,

> Yes, as a tool to assign psychiatric diagnoses to dead people by interviewing proxies, PA studies are methodologically flawed. It is simply impossible to assign a reliable diagnosis of mental disorder to someone by interviewing someone else. PA studies can therefore not serve as an evidence based for the claim that most people who die by suicide are mentally ill. (2012, p. 621)

One of the challenges for me on this point is resisting the inclination to repeat oneself ad nauseam. Perhaps I am even overly defensive. Yet there has been gross dehumanism and reductionism in our fields; that is a marriage that makes me fearful. It is simply not good science or policing. Officer, know what you do; if you don't, the judge in the courtroom will. This is totally in line with the original purpose of the PA method (see Chapter 4).

A FEW FURTHER NOT-HELPFUL REVIEWS

The systematic review of nomothetic PA studies by Cavanagh et al. (2003) is often cited by researchers who believe it is true that suicide is most strongly associated with only mental disorders. The researchers who use standardized questionnaires with proxies cite it always; it says what they believe. Case closed!

Allow me a few of Cavanagh et al.'s (2003) conclusions:

> Is our finding of a strong and consistent association between mental disorder and suicide reliable? First, the psychological autopsy technique is regarded as valid in determining accurate diagnosis and in systematically measuring other variables post-mortem (Kelly & Mann, 1996). Secondly, our results are consistent with the strong positive evidence for the role of mental disorder throughout the suicide literature. (p. 401)

Conner et al., in their 2011 article, unlike their 2012 review, offer little new. However, they do state,

> Most of the instruments employed were originally designed to obtain information from a living subject, so the administration of these instruments needs to be revised to obtain the information from proxy informants and there needs to be independent assessment of the validity of this indirect method of generating a diagnosis. (p. 595)

Therefore, they agree with our conclusions; yet they go on in a sophist style, yes—but do it anyway. Would any sane forensic investigator? Again, imagine doing police or forensic work this way.

THEREFORE

From the beginning, Edwin S. Shneidman took his identification as a clinical psychologist seriously and believed that the main endpoint or goal of the clinical enterprise is understanding a needful person. Further, he believed that psychological assessment is fundamental to the foundation—"at the heart"—of psychological redress. He had a rather critical view of reductionism. In fact, Shneidman always held a reasonable or unreasonable, supercilious view of Emile Kraepelin. Kraepelin is seen as the end of human understanding and, by extension, the *DSM* and its various revisions are seen as the end to wisdom. On this point, he likes to quote his mentor, Henry Murray: "Never denigrate a fellow human being in fewer than 2,000 words."

Gavin and Rogers (2006), from their review of many of the current PA studies, concluded,

> It seems likely then, that those undertaking psychological autopsies are doing no more (or less) than using their imaginations to "construct" plausible, common-sense theories about why people kill themselves. Thus, as Blum and McHugh (1971) comment in their essay relating to how motives come to be ascribed to certain behavior:
>
>> He killed himself because he was depressed, or he left the party because he was bored—both are observers' ways of saying that killing oneself is a method of *doing* depression, or that prematurely leaving the party is a way of *doing* boredom (p. 107; emphasis added). (p. 139)

There is an old story about pink elephants that addresses the issue at hand: Atran (2010) tells the story as follows:

> A woman was standing at a bus stop, wildly flailing her umbrella. A curious onlooker approached and asked, "Why do you keep waving your umbrella about?"
> The woman replied with some annoyance that such an idiotic question should be asked of her: "Why, to keep the pink elephants away, of course."
>
> "But, my dear lady," the onlooker protested, "there are no pink elephants around."
> The woman, exasperated, retorted, "Precisely, because I keep them away."
> (p. 266)

The pink elephants fallacy is an example of cognitive distortion. It is the simplest of all reductionistic thinking. It is mental constriction, no different from the suicidal mind. It is a logical fallacy. It is circular reasoning. It is tautological.

We are told by many of the researchers on the PA that mental disorders cause suicide. They state, We studied it in the psychological autopsy. We showed in the questionnaire that the informant (singular) filled out that there was a mental disorder. Therefore, mental disorder causes suicide. Shneidman, Litman, Farberow, Hjelmeland, Dieserud, and I would add, "But, my dear researchers, there is no evidence in your PA studies of mental disorders." The answers Mann, Shaffer, Cavanagh, Conner and many more provide, "Precisely, because we believe it, it is, therefore, true. There are 'pink' mental disorders."

To make it simple, if you want to measure a temperature, it is better to use a thermometer than a barometer. Every cop knows that; it seems not some researchers.

CHAPTER 7

How Many Informants are Needed?

"One sees what one can best see oneself" (Jung, 1971, p. 9). This fact is often called the *personal equation*. (The pink elephant [pink mental disorder] is a good example). Thus, it follows that it is an issue in the use of informants in NASH investigations. John Graunt and Edwin Shneidman were aware of that fact. It has been a concern in death studies since well before the 1600s, in fact. Our question and the answer may well be as old as humankind.

Shneidman (Leenaars, 1999a) stated, and I repeat, that a PA "is done by talking to some key persons—spouse, lover, parent, grown child, friend, colleague, physician, supervisor, co-worker—who knew the decedent" (p. 399). Shneidman, Litman, and Farberow never talked to only one person. Yet, as you read in Chapter 6, somehow this has become a common practice—a fatal flaw!

HOW MANY INFORMANTS AND PROBLEMS

Of course, every PA is unique. Shneidman and the early team agreed that many informants were needed. Shneidman often mentioned to me that we need at least four or five minimum. Yet there is no agreed-upon appropriate number of people to interview in much of the current literature (Snider, Hane, & Berman, 2006). Most quantitative PA studies have asked only the next of kin to be informants. For example, in research on adolescent suicide, it has been typically the parents who were interviewed, and sometimes a sibling and/or friends were added, but only rarely. For another example, in adult suicide, the spouse or other close family member is interviewed. Some researchers have argued that only the "best" person needs to be seen; we addressed that issue earlier. Despite that issue, some researchers still argue that "only a few interviews of highly observant and knowledgeable reporters" are needed. Yet the question remains. Hawton, Appleby, Platt, Foster, Cooper, Malmberg, & Simkin, (1998) have reported that, for our teen example, friends often know more than parents about substance abuse, interpersonal problems, and/or suicidal risk. Thus, Hjelmeland et al. (2012) concluded, "different informants can contribute with different information and this makes it crucial to know 'who' we are interviewing in terms of intimacy of the relationship between informant and the deceased" (p. 618). Knowledge varies considerably from one informant to the next. No one has all of the elephant—the well-known story of the three blind men and the elephant (more elephant stories). They are asked to say what the elephant is. One has the trunk; one has the side; and one a leg. Each "best" informant is asked to tell his/her story. Personally, I hope in your enquiries you never have just the back end.

There are further problems in many nomothetic studies. Few studies discern the importance of the characteristics of the relationship between deceased and informant. Many cite one or two observers; yet it is important to discern who. The closeness is either not or poorly defined. Further, it is often unclear if more than one informant is used, if the people were seen alone or together; whether people discussed the information; how disagreements were reconciled; how concurrence was achieved; and so on. We do not know. The mental state of the informant is also never stated; if that person was depressed or grief-stricken, of course, the information would be colored by what the informant sees. There is an endless list. Hjelmeland and her team (2012) note that researchers simply state that the true version of the deceased's story is determined "by a 'best estimate,' based on all available data." Can you imagine reporting that to your commander, never mind a judge in court?

The solution and thus a standardized procedure: *Interview many informants*.

Snider et al. (2006) put the dilemma nicely. Thus, in a nutshell,

> As the number of persons interviewed increased, however, the problem of deciding what information is and is not valid or skewed increases. A larger number of friends and family of the decedent interviewed often cause an over-representation of opinions regarding the decedent. A standard for validating informant information needs to be proposed. Relying on consensual validation by two or more observers, however, would exclude potentially vital information known only by a single observer. (p. 514)

THE IMPORTANCE OF MANY INFORMANTS IN PA STUDIES

I have had the good fortune of being an international expert on a PA study. Under the capable leadership of Gudrun Dieserud, our team also included Kari Dyregrov, Heidi Hjelmeland, and, from time to time, other researchers. The study was part of an ongoing PA study of nonclinical suicides at the Norwegian Institute of Public Health, Oslo, Norway. A criterion in the study was that the deceased had no previous history of suicide attempts or treatment in mental health care. I actually had a memorandum of understanding with the Norwegian Institute of Public Health, Division of Mental Health. My title was Senior Advisor; I travelled to and from Norway from 2006 to 2013. They were exciting years. Aside from the numerous peer-reviewed scientific publications, this book, next to my decades of study with Dr. Shneidman, reflects my work in Norway. I am most grateful to each of my Norwegian colleagues.

I will next present our PA method, a reflection of Ed's teachings, outlining procedures, sample, interview, and ethical issues.

METHOD

Procedure

Based on death certificates and forensic reports, chief municipal medical officers in all municipalities of the seven counties with the highest suicide rates in Norway in 2003 were asked to identify suitable cases of suicide. Data were collected in 2007–2009. The chief municipal medical officers provided the name of the general practitioner (GP) of the deceased and asked the GPs to ensure the exclusion of cases with a history of suicide attempts and/or treatment in mental health services and to identify the name and address of next of kin. Based on this information, the chief municipal medical officer sent a letter to the next of kin. The letter provided information pertaining to the project and requested the return of a consent form to the project leader. After written consent was received, the interviewer contacted the next of kin by telephone and arranged a time and place for the interview. The informants were asked to provide suicide notes if available. After the interviews were completed, the informants were asked to provide names and addresses of other knowledgeable informants (the snowball method). The project leader sent a letter requesting them to participate, and the interviewer called them after a written consent was received. The procedure of recruitment was repeated until at least five informants (in one case four) had been included in each case. When the researchers used the snowball method, they used key informants (mostly parents or partners of the deceased) to recruit other informants who had known the deceased in various contexts and in different epochs of life. These would be central persons high in the "grief hierarchy," persons who had been close to the deceased. Recruitment was stopped when no new information seemed to be presented or the informants did not have suggestions of further relevant informants.

Sample

The sample consisted of five (four in one case) to nine (in one case) key informants from each of 20 suicide victims. Altogether, 120 individuals close to the deceased were interviewed. In the present study, we have focused both on the number of informants and their relation to the deceased. In most cases there were five informants (40%), followed by six (25%), seven (15%), and eight (10%), whereas two deceased (10%) were represented by four or nine informants. The informants included spouses/(ex-)partners (n = 15); (step-)parents (n = 25), grown-up children (n = 7), siblings (n = 19), in-laws (n = 5), aunts/uncles (n = 2), cousins (n = 2), close friends (n = 37), (ex-)girl-/boyfriends (n = 2). In addition, one neighbor and five close work colleagues were interviewed. Fifty-five (46%) of the informants were women, and 65 (54%) were men, ranging between 18 and 82 years of age (M = 36).

The age of the deceased ranged from 18 to 62 years (M = 36), and the female/male ratio was 4/16. The methods of the suicides were hanging/strangling (12), shooting (6), CO-poisoning (1), and drowning (1). Regarding employment, 11 were employees (two on sick leave), four were students, two were company owners, one had quit the job voluntarily, one was unemployed but planning studies, and one was on disability pension. Nine of the deceased were married/cohabitant, three were living by themselves after having experienced recent break up of love relationships, one was divorced several years before the suicide, five were single without a girlfriend/boyfriend, and two were living by themselves but were in love relationships.

Interviews

All interviews were conducted by three researchers/clinicians with extensive experience and knowledge in the field of suicidology as well as in-depth interviewing of suicide bereaved individuals (Gudrun Dieserud, Kari Dyregrov, and another colleague, Mette Lyberg Rasmussen). All the suicides took place in the time period 2007–2009, and in all except one case, the interviews were conducted between 6 and 18 months after the suicide (M = 8.7). In one case, the interviews took place 24–27 months after the death. Each interview lasted approximately 2.5 hours (range 1.5–3 hours). Most of the interviews were conducted in the homes of the bereaved, and some in the researchers' offices or hotels, depending on the preferences of the informants. They were audiotaped and transcribed verbatim. Brief notes about immediate impressions were written by the researchers after each interview. In order to strengthen the interrater reliability of the transcriptions, a coding system for paralinguistic expressions (e.g., pauses, laughter, crying) was used by two trained transcribers. All transcripts were controlled by the interviewers.

The interview consisted of a combination of a narrative part and follow-up questions. The narrative started with the opening question: "What are your thoughts on the circumstances that led to the suicide of X?" The informants were asked to talk freely about their own perceptions. Thus, this initial part of the interview was primarily governed by the informants, where the informants told about their own experiences of the deceased in their own words. After the narrative part of the interview, the interviewer asked pertinent follow-up questions, based on a "empirical" theme guide developed by Shneidman and his fellow deputy coroners, 60 plus years ago (as outlined in Chapter 4). Topics, as you have learned, covered by Shneidman included details of the death, personal and family history of the deceased, personality and lifestyle, emotional patterns, interpersonal issues, any significant changes in the deceased's life in the years preceding death, substance use, and their strengths and successes. Toward the end of the interviews, the informants were asked whether there was anything further that they wanted to tell us.

After the interviews, a debriefing session was held to ensure that no informant was left in distress. Arrangement for follow-up was made when needed (one informant asked for professional assistance related to family conflicts and in two other cases names of professionals were given in case some other persons in the families would want to see someone).

Ethical Issues

The project was conducted in accordance with the the Declaration of Helsinki (2008), as well as research experiences with vulnerable individuals (Dyregrov, 2004). The project was approved by the Data Inspectorate and the Norwegian Regional Committee for Medical Research Ethics South. Informants had the right to withdraw at any time from the study. Identifying information about the deceased and the informants have been altered in the publication process in order to protect anonymity. The purpose and the procedure of the study was repeated to informants when they were contacted by telephone and prior to commencing the interview.

MANY INFORMANTS

Dieserud, Leenaars, and Dyregrov (2015) undertook a study on the issue at hand, "The importance of many informants in PA studies." I here present our findings, but first a few more opening thoughts.

I have already discussed problems with informants, not only in PAs, of course, but also in all our informant-based investigations. Not only may the memory of informants be unreliable, but close ones may actively be denying any role in the suicidal process (Lester, 2004). It is important to secure information from many informants and to include informants who position themselves in different ways to the deceased. This may be crucial in getting the kind of information we need to be able to understand significant barren bones behind suicides. Based on the assumption that suicide is an act of communication, the narratives of the informants are expected to reflect the stories behind, and to offer an uncovering of the suicide process as possible. To achieve this goal, as I have argued, several informants are needed to give their specific input. For the closest relatives, for example, the narratives of the suicides may be so influenced by shameful feelings that they are looking outside of the family to find explanations (blaming work, colleagues, lovers, spouses). This may be particularly true for parents of deceased adolescents. Parents' narratives may therefore be influenced by a need to restore both their own and their child's moral reputation (Owens, Lambert, Lloyd, & Donovan, 2008). In particular, the closest informants may downplay information that reveals family conflicts and puts themselves in a shameful position regarding the mental pain of the deceased. Stigma may be a central factor in this process.

As Shneidman taught, our understanding of suicide may be highly enriched by interviewing several informants around each case. Rather than limiting, diverse points of view add to the richness of our inquest, not distract from our observations. By exposing the divergent views that may come to the fore when interviewing several individuals who knew the deceased better, the aim of our study was to demonstrate the difference between relying on one or two close informants and the gathering of information from multiple informants. It allows the story to be told and better uncovered.

WHAT WERE THE FINDINGS?

Dieserud et al. (2015) spell out the method and analysis in detail. I here focus on our results. We were, of course, searching for patterns or commonalities in the reasons given by informants. We did a thematic (theoretical) analysis. Three superordinate themes, we believe, emerged from the interviews. In the opinion of the close bereaved, reasons for the suicides were due to (a) reasons other than mental illness. These reasons were predominantly grouped as (b) long-standing problems; and (c) problematic relationships. We will first present some variations along demography and then elaborate on the content of each theme. Of course, a basic belief of phenomenology (Husserl, 1907/1973) is that there is only one's observation of reality, not objective reality. Observations are subjective. Thus, different positions to the deceased were related to different narratives when asked to give their personal opinions or explanations on the circumstances that led to the suicide. To avoid issues of confidentiality, we offer only some excerpts of the informants.

Variations Along Demography

The most obvious variations connected to demography were the diverse reasons given to why the suicide had happened. There seemed to be obvious differences, depending on the deceased (young vs. old), and the relationship to the deceased. Of the 11 mothers of the young deceased, eight (73%) saw the reason as trouble in a love relationship. However, the problems in the partner relationships were divergent: partner mental health, broken heart, conflicts. The single most frequent reason in the problematic relationship was loss/rejection. The three other reasons were mental health problems of the deceased, such as occasionally too much alcohol, or anxiety.

Of the fathers of the young deceased (N = 11), seven (64%) stated the main reason as problematic love relationships, although at times there were additional explanations provided, such as parents' divorce and occasionally too much alcohol (partying). Two stated too much alcohol prior to the suicide as the primary reason. Other reasons were mental health problems, such as depression (one informant in one case) and perfectionism.

Spouses/ex-spouses of older deceased (N = 8) offered very different explanations. The most frequent reason (N = 5, 63%) was familial, whether historical (such as divorce), and/or current (relational problems). The other three informants saw the reason related to system problems, such as the health system (N = 2, 18%), or work (N = 1, 13%). Often, the informant offered additional explanations, such as health problems (N = 3, 37.5%). Other reasons given were economic problems (N = 2, 18%) and alcoholism (N = 1, 13%). Out of the eight cases, all informants offered long-term reasons, not acute, like within the younger deceased cases. There was one case with no spouse; the reason offered by a family member was long-term family-of-origin problems.

The mother or father of the older deceased (N = 2) offered long-term problems in the family-of-origin as the main reason, namely, problematic relationship with parent(s).

Explanations given from siblings/cousins/uncles and aunts/partners/friends differed and were often very different from parents or spouses. Together, there were 86 informants outside of parental figure/spouse. The reasons for the suicide were much more varied. Twenty-three (27%) of the informants saw the reason as problematic relationship (N = 9) with a partner (spouse) or parent. Other reasons were long-term problems, such as divorce of parents, physical illness, economic problems, occasional alcohol problems, bad conscience, low self-esteem, mental health problems, self-destructive behavior, system problems (especially noted were health system), work-related, perfectionism, and many more. Often more than one reason was pointed out. Long-term problems were offered in all but three cases (85%). Three informants saw no specific reason; one simply stated, "Just ordinary problems."

Three themes emerged as central to why people kill themselves. The most frequent explanations were long-standing problems and problematic relationships. Thus, there are many more reasons than mental illness; indeed, long-standing problems and problematic relationships, as would be predicted in my theoretical model (see Chapter 1), were more salient.

Reasons Other Than Mental Illness

It would be a truism to state that almost all, if not all, survivors of the suicides searched for a meaning of the suicide. Yet what is also obvious from the interview content is that people give different meanings or reasons. Often the focus was finding some other person or system responsible for the suicide. In particular, for parents of young suicides, the reason was given as partner relationship problems (e.g., spouse, boy/girlfriend). Despite the PA literature's focus to date, rarely did the informant assign the blame to the person's mental health problems.

One person, who saw the reason as the lack of support from the health and social system, stated, "For me, his suicide is a result of not getting his disability pension; they did not believe him." Yet the majority was person related; one stated, "Something in the relationship between X and his father was definitely not good. . . . It was a very cold relationship." Others stated, "The parents did not get along"; "The parents got divorced"; "He quarreled a lot at work"; "I think that he just gave up because of the family situation"; "The problems started the day he got married"; "His spouse rejected him"; "His love relationship was lost . . . The break-up"; "His temper was sometimes too explosive"; "He had been drinking a lot"; and "He was always anxious." Importantly, the transcripts also do not reflect the same explanations—even within the same case. It was also not always a current one; one noted that the deceased had been abused as a child, suggesting, "That could be the reason why." In summary, these nonclinical suicides were not conceptualized as symptoms of mental illness, although some mentioned that the deceased must have been mentally ill, although no one had noticed. Following this, it was striking how the informants were divided in their time perspective when explaining the main reasons for the suicides.

Long-Standing Problems

We will next look into long-term problems. In one case, informants offered "lack of safety and stability in his childhood"; "many broken relationships during childhood"; and "his mother's troubled life" as explanations. In another case, an informant noted "basically it started many years ago . . . people say that there was abuse in the family . . . the deceased must have experienced this." What is of note, when focusing on long-term problems, how striking it was how parents and spouses in 50% of the cases did not mention long-standing problems, such as family-of-origin conflict, but only noted current ones. Not uncommon, it seemed to be part of the family's belief system to avoid looking for reasons inside the family and to look for explanations elsewhere (the outside), such as the spouse. In many cases, the mother or father of young deceased males described the upbringing of the son as "terrific," "good," "privileged," and that "many people loved him." "I was perfect," one parent said, "All was well." However, in the same cases, other informants stated, "He probably missed the stability in his life . . . it was hectic"; "From the outside it looked really cool, but from the inside I believe he had been struggling really hard"; and "There was no love in the family." And, in one case, the informant stated, "A lot is from his childhood, a lot of bad things happened in his childhood that he never dealt with," such as "alcohol," and "violence" (related to parents). In another case, where the family is described by parents as as "wonderful," one informant stated, "He often said he was depressed. . . . He was abused so much by his family." Others stated, "Another fact was family problems, between X and his parents . . . it went on for years"; "The family problems wore him down"; "The family problems were more serious than expressed." Often informants stated that the deceased had not been informative to the parents years ago and/or currently; one stated, "He usually was not very informative towards his family," and "He kept secrets."

Problematic Relationships

The third theme that emerged was problematic relationships, mainly related to spouses/sweethearts. Often in the young deceased, the problem was with love relationships, although it could be with a parent. Loss and rejection were frequently noted. Yet the parent, spouse, girl/boyfriend, often stated, "We had a perfect relationship" (or "wonderful," "good," "the best," and so on), while other informants saw that same relationship as less than perfect; one even stated, "Now she (spouse) managed to kill him." Often in the partner relationship the spouse or ex-spouse (or partner), stated that "There was never a fight," or "We did everything together." Yet other informants, especially after a break-up, noted, "She found another partner," "She got remarried," or "She left him." One spouse noted a "perfect" relationship ("we talked every day . . . we never quarreled"); yet other informants noted alcoholism and violence in the relationship. Almost all the time the parent or spouse saw "no reason in the relationship"; others saw it as the main reason. Indeed, as our descriptive statistics show, it was the most frequent explanation given; not unexpected from the suicidology literature. As one person stated, "This is a relationship of façade. They dissembled. All is perfect on the outside, but it was falling apart . . . he felt rejected by his ex-spouse . . . he lost everything. He had no reason to live." Further, informants often noted that "anger," "shouting," "scream-ing," "abuse," and so on were evident; yet efforts to intervene were not undertaken or refused. One informant who noted the problem stated, "I told him, you must get away from that woman. . . . I guess he did. He committed suicide."

DISCUSSION

Our findings (Dieserud et al., 2015) reveal how informants with different positions to the deceased are telling different stories regarding their understanding of the suicide. Thus, the suggestions of more standardization in the use of semistructured interviews and diagnostic scales for future PA studies (Conner et al., 2011, 2012; Pouliot & De Leo, 2006) would not have captured the understanding of informants who are telling their stories in their own ways. The effect of the personal equation begins in the act of the observation, not merely in explanations. As I opened this chapter, "One sees what one can best see oneself" (Jung, 1971, p. 9). Like Husserl (1973), Jung (1971), and many more, I mistrust the fact of "pure observation" or "objective observation"—a key problem in many PAs, especially if one uses one or two informants. No doubt one sees the reasons for suicide in another person or system (the outside), but the person seeing is the seer and, as our data show, this hampers observation. There are no pure objective facts, only diverse observations, and thus, explanations. Indeed, the human factor is even more evident in the explanation than the observation. This is not strange, only a fact of being human. By the very nature of our humanity, we share a number of commonalities and that includes the unquestionable facts of the personal equation in explanation, namely, of why people kill themselves. It is the informants' point of view, not that of the suicide victims.

As discussed, and since the very early discussions, PA studies have numerous faults (Leenaars, 1999a; Maris, 1981; Shneidman, 1993a). One of the most serious errors, if not the most serious, is the use of only one informant. This is contrary to the very beginning of the efforts of getting deeper insight into the complexity of the suicidal process (Shneidman, 1993a). It will not assist a bright investigator, maybe the bad ones. Gudrun Dieserud et al.'s study (2015), we believe, clearly shows this flaw. There are unquestionably validity and reliability issues with the studies—we here use quantitative terminology. We believe that we have to go back to the PA roots to find a new direction for a paradigm, and we agree, for example, with Pouliot and De Leo's (2006) current methodology that the PAs have serious weaknesses. Regardless of whether we use Shneidman's paradigm or not, many informants must be used in PA studies. Otherwise we will never truly understand the suicide's mind, or answer our NASH question and the why—is that not our intention in forensic science and policing?

Gudrun Dieserud et al.'s findings (2015) demonstrate clearly how proximity of the relationship to the deceased is governing the search for a reason. The closest ones may be too close to see what was going on to make the correct interpretations and take the needed action (Lester, 2004; Owens et al., 2008). Thus, they may in fact be the least knowledgeable individuals to interview in a PA study. Parents of young suicides may be the least informed ones, and yet many PA studies rely on just parents as informants of their grown-up children's suicides (Hjelmeland et al., 2012). Like in the study by Owens and co-workers (2008), our findings clearly demonstrate how parents (and spouses) may actively deny any responsibility for the suicidal crisis, underplay long-standing family conflicts, and look for explanations outside the family.

How should a PA study be undertaken? According to Shneidman (1993a, p. 194), a psychological autopsy is done "by talking to some key persons—spouse, lover, parent, grown child, friend, colleague, physician, supervisor, co-worker—who knew the decedent." Thus, right from the beginning, the PA was meant to include many informants, and taken together, the information could give some understanding of the barren bones for suicide. Suicide, as I noted in Chapter 1, may be metaphorically depicted as "an intrapsychic drama on an interpersonal stage" (see also Leenaars, 1996), and it seems reasonable to listen to many of the players on that stage.

We have to acknowledge the interplay between multiple factors; individual, relationship, community, social, and environmental (the ecological model), and thus, we need many informants, as each informant is only telling his/her story, but together they may provide enough aspects of the suicidal process that we get a more complete picture of the whole story than by interviewing one or two persons only. However, there is no such thing as one truth (explanation) of a suicide. There might be one truth for each individual since what is perceived as true depends on which perspective one is looking at a phenomenon from (Hjelmeland & Knizek, 2010; Husserl, 1907/1973; Jung, 1971). This is the basis of a sound forensic approach to science and policing.

FINAL POINT: YOU

On a point of epistemology, I do not mean to imply in any way that one person's explanations (or even observations) are fact and the other person's is a myth, or that one is objective and the other is subjective. They are just different points of view. This is the personal equation. And I need to add one more point of view in DSI: Yours.

CHAPTER 8

Benefits for Informants

It is chiefly in times of distress (trauma) that our eyes turn with anxious hope to the future for meaning ("What will the future bring?") (Jung, 1957). Years ago Drs. Shneidman and Curphey found that there were benefits to the PA. Shneidman writes,

> And there is still another function that the psychological autopsy serves: In working with the bereaved survivors to elicit data relative to appropriate certification, a skillful and empathic investigator is able to conduct the interviews in such a way that they are of actual therapeutic value to the survivors. A psychological autopsy should never be conducted so that any aspect of it is iatrogenic. Commenting on this important mental health function of the psychological autopsy, Curphey (1961) has stated:
>
> > The members of the death investigation team, because of their special skills, are alert in their interviews with survivors to evidences of extreme guilt, serious depression, and the need for special help in formulating plans for solving specific problems such caring for children whose parents committed suicide. Since we noted this phenomenon, the coroner's office has, in some few cases, referred distraught survivors of suicide victims to members of the team specifically for supportive interviews even when the suicidal mode of death was not in doubt. (p. 116)
>
> This therapeutic work with the survivor-victims of a dire event is called *postvention*. (Leenaars, 1999a, pp. 401-402)

The PA can be meaning making. The process of meaning making may facilitate adjusting to one's loss/pain/grief through a complex reconstruction of the world—a system change. This would be true after suicide, homicide, and accidental deaths. The idea is not new; Heraclitus of Ephesus held the view centuries ago ("War is the father of all") (Freeman, 1971). Jung (1957), Shneidman (1984; Leenaars, 1999a) and many others held the view. Much is associated to the loss, the disruption of the *attachment* ("identification") bond (Bowlby, 1980). As elaborated by Neimeyer (2000, 2001; Neimeyer, Klass, & Dennis, 2014), the meaning-making process is largely intrapsychic, but also interpersonal/relationship, and also within the broader community and social levels (and thus, highly consistent with the ecological model). For example, Leenaars (2009) looked at the different (and same) meanings of death systems and suicide around the world. Like Shneidman (1984; Leenaars, 1999a),

Attig (2010) considers grief to be an individual process; by this, they mean there are no *the* stages and phases. Each individual has to climb out of her/his "dark cave" in a unique way, often the way that she/he previously coped with trauma (lifelong adjustment patterns; see Heraclitus). We each have a history and a future. No different than suicide, all deaths result in the need to take an individual journey to making meaning out of the death. The only choice we have is how!

Maybe the best police ecological model is that of Sergeant Doctor Daniel Rudofossi's (2007, 2009). Rudofossi presents some unique insights into police officers and public safety personnel, if they die by suicide. We are talking about (and in DSI, investigating) our own, which has implications on the personal equation. For example, as we noted in the case of Kelly Johnson, there is a culture of secrecy ("blue walls"), even after a suicide. Rudofossi writes,

> The blue wall of tight-lipped silence among public safety officer's opening or closing can mean the difference between life and death for the officer-patient and all others involved. This blue-wall opening is a choice that can be made by the officer-patient who chose to disclose his own psychache, or hides his feelings of extreme distress, often acting out with tragic consequences (suicide & homicide). (2007, p. 62)

It follows that if a police suicide occurs, you need to understand the death system differently (see also, Leenaars, 2010a; Violanti, 2007); and therefore different meaning making, and how. This is true for every culture (e.g., Chinese, U.S. military). Like Shneidman, Jung, and Neimeyer, Rudofossi makes meaning of death, but within a police system. He calls his theory the Eco-Ethological Existential Model (Rudofossi, 2007, 2009). As a footnote, his work can also be applied to your investigation of the mentally ill person who dies on the street (Rudofossi, 2015).

The PA is an excellent way to make meaning. Humans have a penchant for "Storying" (Neimeyer et al., 2014). The PA is a narrative process. The PA draws on the need of people "to reassert order and significance in a world made disorderly by loss (Nadeau, 1997). Psychologically, narration of personal loss may also serve larger social agendas" (Neimeyer, Klass, & Dennis, 2014, p. 487). It serves us at all levels of the ecological model. There are few such healing processes available for us after loss, if we are motivated and willing to take the risk (Leenaars, 2004). Although some, including Freud (1917/1974a), saw no value in identifications (attachments) to the dead, Bowlby (1980), Jung (1957), Neimeyer (2001), Shneidman (1984), and many others have proven this belief to be false (and maybe even a dissembling). The PA, if done properly in an empathic humane fashion, is one process that helps. This statement is evidence based. PAs heal. People who participate in a PA, as Shneidman noted in the 1950s (Curphey, 1961; Leenaars, 1999a), fare better than those who find no answers to the forever question, "Why did he kill himself?" (see also Neimeyer et al., 2014).

Of course, a question could be asked about why survivors would be motivated to participate in a PA. Our team in Norway—Dyregrov, Dieserud, Straiton, Rasmussen, Hjelmeland, Knizek, and Leenaars (2011)—investigated this very question (I outlined the detail of our method in Chapter 7). What we learned was that the majority of the informants were motivated to participate in the PA study because they believed that this would somehow be a help to themselves and/or others. It is intrapsychic, interpersonal, community, and societal motivation. We identified four categories of motivation: (a) Helping Others, (b) Venting, (c) Insight, and (d) Just Because. The majority of our interviewees were altruistically motivated; they hoped that by taking part they would/could, in understanding suicide better, play a role in helping to prevent suicide. We found that especially close family members were more likely to be motivated by a desire to help. They hoped that the death would have some meaning; often that no one else goes through their pain. Thus, like Shneidman, I believe that there is a meaning making through the PA interviews.

Allow me to be more detailed on this very question.

MEANING MAKING: PAST RESEARCH

Dyregrov, Dieserud, Straiton, et al. (2011) undertook an empirical study of the benefits of the PA. It has been argued, despite the observations already in the 1950s, that the PA will evoke painful memories. It is feared that the interview will provoke feelings and thoughts that are buried and hidden. (It is believed that it is best to be silent. Avoid! Dissemble!) Cook and Bosley (1995) point out that the survivors of the death will find the interview distressing, exhausting, and emotionally difficult. Begley and Quayle (2007) note that the negative effect will be even greater for survivors of suicide who experience confusion, guilt, shame, and stigma. Thus, should we believe this belief, held by many, or should we research the actual or real facts? (What does an officer do in a CSI?) Some would encourage silence! Yet Dyregrov (2004) has shown that harm can be easily minimized; it all depends on the interviewers being skilled, sensitive, and experienced in dealing with the bereaved, whether suicide or not. Surely Shneidman and his team were. Curphey thought so. Are you empathic? The working alliance (attachment) is crucial.

Hawton, Houston, Malmberg, and Simkin (2003), in an excellent study (a standard of Hawton's) found that very few people actually felt distress when involved in a PA investigation. Participants did not feel worse after a 4-week follow-up. The reported benefits from participation have included the following: increased self-awareness (Hutchinson, Wilson, & Wilson, 1994), gaining insight into the death (Asgard & Carlsson-Bergstrom, 1991; Cook & Bosley, 1995), feelings of empowerment (Asgard & Carlsson-Bergstrom, 1991; Hawton et al., 2003), feeling a sense of purpose (Hutchinson et al., 1994), and improved communication (Dyregrov, 2004). As noted by Curphey and Shneidman, Dyregrov (2004) also found a "therapeutic effect." As elaborated by Neimeyer (2000, 2001), the process of meaning making may facilitate coping with grief through a complex reorientation to the world. Gillies and Neimeyer (2006) discuss how significant losses disrupt the coherence of life, calling for active attempts to (a) make sense of the loss, (b) find some sort of "silver lining" or benefit in the experience, and (c) reorganize one's identity as bereaved. Attig, Bowlby, Heraclitus, Jung, Neimeyer, Shneidman, and many others, including me, hold that belief. Yet not only does the participation in a PA help them, often there is a feeling that their participation will help others in the future, and this is another positive aspect commonly voiced by participants (Dyregrov, 2004; Dyregrov, Dieserud, Hjelmeland, et al., 2011). Many survivors want to help, and that includes in your psychological DSI. *That is meaning!*

Therefore, we believe that the PA is most positive for the participant. Yet there are conditions that can affect the process.

WHAT FACTORS MAY INFLUENCE THE EXPERIENCE?

Our Norwegian team noted that closeness and character of the relationship to the deceased may affect the intensity of the grief (Dyregrov, 2004; Middleton, Raphael, Burnett, & Martinek, 1998). For example, a parents' grief may be especially intensive and prolonged. It is possible that this may impact the person's experience in the PA. Gender may be another factor. Men are known to be more avoidant (Kavanaugh & Ayres, 1998). This avoidance may influence the PA, of course. Further, the more violent or brutal method of suicide, the deeper the stress (pain) (Leenaars & Wenckstern, 1991); thus, some informants may find the more violent death more difficult to discuss. It may be more traumatizing; the DSM says so. Of course, there may be further factors; yet this list begins to allow one to think about the factors that may influence the PA experience.

OUR STUDY

After the PA interviews, the informants in our study were asked about his/her experience of participation by the question: "How did you find being interviewed about this?" The Dyregrov, Dieserud, Hjelmeland, et al. paper (2011) described, analyzed, and discussed the answers to this question. Of course, one has to keep in mind that not all investigators are alike; ours were highly trained PhD psychologists with skills in suicidology and the PA. As discussed in Chapter 6, some PA experiences may be quite negative, if not suicidogenic.

Our informants' experiences were classified in one of three ways: (a) overall positive experience, (b) unproblematic experience, and (c) positive and painful experience.

The majority of informants (62%) responded with an overall positive experience. They were unambiguous. The descriptions conveyed included the following: "very good," "it did me good," "good to talk about it," "it was therapy," and so on. They regarded it positively, either because of venting, helping others, and insight. Many felt positive due to having an opportunity to express their thoughts and feelings; for many it was the first opportunity to put their experience into words. They found that the interview eased their stress (pain/grief). They saw a value in understanding the suicide, making sense of the death. Often they employed the skills of the interviewer—the interviewer "knew what she was doing."

Even though everyone labeled the PA experience as therapeutic, many emphasized the benefits of increased insight and understanding of the unacceptable and/or incomprehensible. Some even described an "aha" experience. Most important, and I quote from our team's report,

> The review of the deceased's life following the theme list of Shneidman (1993a) informed them about the enhanced complexities around any suicide. This increased knowledge contributed to the possibility of thinking differently about why the suicide had happened. New insights led to new perspectives, e.g., the importance of the deceased's childhood and upbringing. They recognized that their new insight could contribute positively to the grieving process. (Dyregrov, Dieserud, Hjelmeland, et al., 2011, p. 695)

The positive meaning-making aspects of the PA participation were also associated with "have something positive coming out of the negative." They saw themselves as offering something of value—"They were not just being passive victims." Here is the narrative of one young adult who lost his father to suicide:

> It was completely fine. It felt wonderful . . . I had maybe processed it a bit internally, so it felt wonderful to be through with all my rumination and deliberation. It is probably always going to be there, I am always going to feel that it is unfair. But, I think that it feels okay now. Really lovely! I feel that it is completely fine, and above all, if it can help others in the future. This is the most important—to be able to help others in the same situation as I have been in.

A small group of informants (10%) were quite neutral and impartial: they reported the experience as "unproblematic." Common expressions were "I didn't have difficulties," or "wasn't problematic." We found that more often men than women provided this neutral view.

A total of 24 informants (28%) had categorized what we called a "good-painful" experience during the interview. Unlike the first group, people in this third group were positive but also expressed dissatisfaction prior to or during the interview situation. Some had feared the interview beforehand; most of these often said that it went much better than they expected. Of note, two found the tape recording of the interview a little uncomfortable; one said it was like "feeling monitored." They also felt it was difficult to find the right words.

There were actually very few who felt that they had emotional difficulties during the course of the interview. Our team writes,

> Those who found the interview the most demanding were individuals who had tried to avoid both talking about the suicide, and/or approaching things that reminded them of the deceased. These informants found that the interview made them confront thoughts and feelings and "stirred things up" in such a way that their emotions were triggered. (Dyregrov, Dieserud, Hjelmeland, et al., 2011, p. 698)

However, even these individuals commented that they knew it was good to talk. Some experienced sadness by acknowledging and understanding new and hurtful bones around the deceased's life. It was "good and painful."

A man who had lost his friend of 20 years said,

> It has been difficult, it really has. I have, like, in many ways, put it on the shelf a bit. Not gotten rid of it; I haven't done that, but put it at the back of the drawer—right. But in the wardrobe at work, you know, I have the death announcement taped up. I won't forget it, I don't want to. But . . . well it gnaws away at you, but it isn't anything . . . you still have it lying right at the back of the drawer. You don't pull it forward, unless it is absolutely necessary. So it [the interview] has been hard, so it has. But it has to be, I guess. I guess it eases the stress a little. So . . . it was a more positive experience than a negative. Absolutely!

We explored how the interview experience was related to gender, relationship, method, age of informant, age of deceased, and time between the suicide and the interview. We found no significant differences.

DISCUSSION: DO INFORMANTS BENEFIT?

Most of the suicides were experienced as "out of the blue." This, for me, was no surprise; it is common. This is what I noted, for example, about Kelly Johnson. No one expected her to die by suicide or to kill—except her friend from childhood. Indeed, he knew Kelly best. I have in fact learned that the issue of dissembling, as discussed in Chapter 1, is huge and much larger than the literature reports. A bare fact: There is a mask of suicide.

In our Norwegian study and every PA that I have undertaken for that matter, participants were emotionally affected by the respective suicide. Despite this undeniable fact, the large majority of informants were exclusively positive toward the PA participation, whereas a minority had mixed feelings. Our study confirmed many of the previous benefits for participating in a PA (Dyregrov, 2004; Hawton et al., 2003). Without a doubt, as Shneidman and Curphey discussed in the 1950s, there is meaning reconstruction. The PA is useful. That is an evidence-based fact! Informants in our study found benefits in the PA experience. The positive experience also seemed to facilitate continued attachment with the deceased (Gillies & Neimeyer, 2006; Klass, Silverman, & Nickman, 1996). The PA, indeed, can be a survival tool, helping the bereaved not only make sense of the past but also to transverse to the future (Klass et al., 1996); this is what Jung and Shneidman, and I, advocate.

A question: What makes PA participation painful? Almost all informants who reported pain associated it to avoidance. They had been attempting to deny, inhibit, and/or suppress the feelings, if not the reality; all negative. They had dissembled (or masked) and the interviewers made them face reality. The conversation brought back the loss. Only a small group of (ex)spouses, who experienced pain, associated that pain to feelings of guilt, anger, and grief. It had been simply difficult to divulge. Most had never experienced the feelings before. This was/is negative maybe for the first time, the PA allowed them to express the unacceptable, such as rage at the deceased. However, from a therapeutic perspective (Leenaars, 2004), this is positive, despite being difficult. It is meaning making. Indeed, as Neimeyer (2001) had pointed out, the process of meaning reconstruction may actually lessen the long-term negative consequences of the repressed (masked) bereaved informant. It helps!

ONE FINAL NOMOTHETIC FACT

The fact that the interviewers were experienced researchers and suicidologists was appreciated. Cook and Bosley (1995) and Dyregrov (2004) found that bereaved individuals seek a researcher who is empathic, caring, understanding, gentle, humane, interested, and sincere. It is of interest that these are the very same descriptors that patients report about therapists who are helpful in psychotherapy or counseling (Dyregrov, 2004; Leenaars, 2006). (Dyregrov, Dieserud, Hjelmeland, et al., 2011, pp. 705–706)

Without question, if done empathically, the PA will be appreciated. It heals, not only allowing us to uncover the barren bones of the suicide's mind. It is meaning making for you too!

PART THREE

Idiographic Study

This section presents three specific chapters, all showing the value of the PA in forensic investigation and in the courtroom. John Stuart Mill showed that both the nomothetic (general) and idiographic (unique) are critical in science's development. Dr. Gordon Allport, one of the great American psychologists of the 1900s, provided us with a classical statement on the advantages of both approaches. Forensic psychology is in fact committed to understanding a person in their entirety—the person in general and the person in particular. Like psychologists, what concerns the public safety professional is the individual case; that is true in the mode of death (NASH). The real concern is what is the mode of death, and why, although we are most interested in intent, we are also curious about why at that particular time. This section hopes to lay out the barren bones.

In Chapter 9, I present a PA. It is the death of a real American hero in the Navy, Hospital Corpsman Third Class Chris Purcell. Through the courage of his survivors and his personal documents (e.g., his suicide notes, e-mails), why a person kills himself comes alive. The bare facts of his psychache are uncovered. The PA makes meaning of Chris's life and death. Chapter 10, "Documents in the Courtroom," presents some issues in using documents in the courtroom. It presents the case of Daniel Beckon, a case first categorized as homicide due to a reputable expert's fallacious opinion, which was ruled ultimately as undetermined. It teaches us to be cautious in jumping to conclusions, black and white thinking, and magnification—cognitive distortions easily made in investigating psychological pain. A second case looks at the question, "Is everything reported in a suicide note truthful?" It offers some further cautions. I next present some detail of a study into the myths about suicide notes. Of course, the issues, as the reader will learn, about what is truthful or not can occur with other evidence, such as informants' reports, a reason for using many informants and personal documents. I end the chapter with a car-truck "accident" case; was it an accident or a suicide?

The final chapter in this section, "The PA in the Courtroom," presents an example of a psychological autopsy carried out in an adversarial setting—the courtroom. It presents the barren bones: the interviews with informants, an autobiography, a reported suicide note, some further pretrial documents, and my verbatim testimony. It concludes with examining whether the PA has been accepted under the rules of evidence in the US courts (I also look at the Canadian courts). The admissibility of a PA dates back to 1976 in the courtroom. The science is not seen as new and passes the classical Frye test of "general acceptance" (although it is the Federal Rules of Evidence, not Frye, that provides the standard for admitting expert scientific testimony in a federal trial). We conclude with looking at the Daubert ruling.

CHAPTER 9

A PA: A Barren Bones Investigation

Chris Purcell was born on December 19, 1986, in Keflavik, Iceland. His father, Mike Purcell, and his mother, Helene Purcell, were in the Navy. The Purcell family was a proud decorated military family. Chris joined the Navy in 2005. Thus, before I tell Chris' story, I need to let you know who Mike, Helene, Chris, and the Navy are. I present verbatim as Mike Purcell told me.

Mike Purcell enlisted in the U.S. Navy in 1982 in Great Lakes, Illinois, afterwards graduating from Radioman "A" school in San Diego, California. In his 27 years of Naval service, he and his family were stationed in Naples, Italy; Keflavik, Iceland; Great Lakes, Illinois (three tours); Charlotte, North Carolina; Sasebo, Japan; and San Diego, California. Purcell served as a Radioman (renamed Information System Technician in 1999) overseas in Naples, Keflavik, and Baghdad; in Great Lakes as an instructor; as well as two forward deployed ships and one ship on the West Coast. In addition to serving as a Naval Communicator, he served in various capacities as a Drill Instructor, Drug and Alcohol Program Advisory, Family Advocacy Representative, Fleet Quality Assurance Inspector, and Individual Augmentee Coordinator. He served during 2 wars, on dozens of shipboard deployments, as well as a 6-month tour "boots on ground" in Baghdad, Iraq, as a Communications Watch Officer in the Joint Operation Center in Camp Victory. He has received numerous unit awards and citations, his personal medals include six good conduct medals, five Navy Achievement, one Navy Commendation, and one Joint Commendation. Purcell retired as a Chief Petty Officer in 2009 with 27 years of honorable service.

Helene Purcell enlisted in the U.S. Navy in 1981 in Orlando, Florida, afterwards graduating from Radioman "A" school in San Diego, California. Purcell's first duty station was the Naval Oceanographic Processing Facility in Dam Neck, Virginia, as a communications equipment operator. Her second duty station was the Naval Communications Area Master Station Mediterranean in Naples, Italy, as a communications clerk. Purcell's final duty station was Naval Communications Station in Keflavik, Iceland, where she served as a communications watch supervisor. Purcell was discharged in 1986 with 5 years of honorable service.

Christopher Lee Purcell enlisted in the U.S. Navy in 2005 in Great Lakes, Illinois, afterwards graduating from Hospital Corpsman "A" school. Purcell's first duty station was Naval Health Clinic in Brunswick, Maine. While serving at the health clinic, Purcell was handpicked to serve his commander-in-chief on the emergency medical response team during a presidential visit to the Kennebunkport, Maine, compound. Purcell was posthumously promoted to Hospital Corpsman Petty Officer Third Class in 2008.

They are a proud family; however, like all military families, they had their traumatic events. The worst nightmarish tempest was on January 27, 2008. *Chris died by suicide.*

The mode of death was unequivocally suicide. That is a fact. I will answer the following questions: Why did Chris kill himself? How did Chris die and where; that is, why at that particular time? This does not mean that I will not address a third question, what is the probable mode of death? Yet, in this case, this was already known. This chapter will present Chris Purcell's story; it is a barren bones story.

Shneidman, among others such as Henry A. Murray (the famed Harvard suicidologist), have explicitly supported the intensive study of a unique case. Murray's most important (and his proudest) psychological case (specific) investigation was of the personality of Adolf Hitler; he was an officer with the Office of the Strategic Services (OSS), an intelligence agency of the U.S. federal government. Murray predicted the violence and murders, followed by Hitler's suicide, a homicide(s)-suicide. We present the unique case of one hospital corpsman.

To answer the questions in the case of hospital corpsman Chris Purcell, I will follow the principle of *res ipsa loquitur*. The facts that show the mind's despair— personal documents, suicide notes, psychological autopsy notes, and so on—will be presented verbatim, that show the mind's endless pain.

The data convey the story. I assembled them here as the case unfolded to me, beginning with the suicide of Chris. Next, I present Chris' notes, his suicide chat on MySpace, and the analysis of the last communications. The specific procedure within suicidology that would assist, as you have read, is called the psychological autopsy. In the psychological autopsy (PA), data are obtained—personal documents, reports, e-mails, and third-party interviews. The suicide note is valuable—sometimes essential—within this larger procedure of the PA. It is the person's own story. The note, when placed in the context of that person's life, allows us to tell the story better.

An outline of the PA was provided in an earlier chapter following Shneidman's perspective on the technique. There are standard questions. The data, beyond the note examined, include psychological report, newspaper accounts, medical records, court documents, and other personal documents. In Chris' case, we have his own reflections on life in a Navy family. A most important technique in the psychological autopsy, as you learned, is the third-party interviews. I plan to present abbreviations of the interviews of Helene Purcell, mother; Mike Purcell, father; Kristin Purcell, sister; and Derek Ozawa, friend.

Let me begin with the death.

THE DEATH

There are, of course, almost always different perspectives on a death. Death is a perception. I here present verbatim a court account and some newspaper reports. I am sure the Navy, the Purcells, and so on, may have different views. I begin with the account from Circuit Judges Bauer, Flaum, and Evans, as it is presented in Purcell v. U.S. (2011) (http://www.gpo.gov/fdsys/pkg/USCOURTS-ca7-10-03743/pdf/USCOURTS-ca7-10-03743-0.pdf):

Christopher Lee Purcell ("Purcell") committed suicide in his barracks at the Brunswick Naval Air Station, where he was serving on active duty in the Navy. Navy and Department of Defense ("DOD") personnel were called to the scene after being informed that Purcell planned to kill himself. They arrived at his residence before he attempted suicide, but did not find the gun they were told he had. Later, they permitted Purcell to go to the bathroom accompanied by his friend. Upon entering, he pulled a gun from his waistband and committed suicide by shooting himself in the chest. . . .

Purcell was twenty-one years old and working on active duty in the Navy as a hospital corpsman at the Brunswick Naval Air Station when he committed suicide. The brief submitted by Purcell's father, Michael Purcell, notes that shortly after enlisting, at the age of eighteen, Purcell began experiencing social and emotional problems. It also mentions that the Navy intervened on several occasions by providing substance abuse treatment and mental health care.

On January 27, 2008, someone contacted the base at around 8:30 PM to inform them that Purcell had a gun in his room and was threatening suicide. In response to the call, Junior Corpsman Stephen Lollis told base security that Purcell had a gun and was about to kill himself, and provided Purcell's address. DOD Police Officers Shawn Goding and Matthew Newcomb were among the first local law enforcement officers to arrive at Purcell's apartment, followed by DOD Patrolman Francis Harrigan and Petty Officer First Class David Rodriguez. Each was aware that Purcell had a gun and was suicidal.

Purcell was alive when the investigating officers arrived at his on-base residence. They searched his residence and found evidence indicating that he had a firearm, including an empty gun case and bullets on top of a television stand, but they did not find a weapon, and they never searched Purcell's person.

Rodriguez spoke to Purcell and suggested they go outside to talk. Purcell responded calmly. Outside, Petty Officer First Class Mitchell Tafel approached Rodriguez and stated that they needed to get Purcell into custody to protect him and local law enforcement. Purcell became irate and non-compliant when told he would have to be put in restraints. A struggle with Rodriguez, Tafel, Harrigan, Goding, and Thomas Robinson, also with DOD, ensued. The five eventually subdued Purcell, handcuffed him, and escorted him back to his room. Once upstairs, Tafel permitted Purcell to use the bathroom and instructed Robinson to remove one of Purcell's handcuffs. Purcell went to the bathroom accompanied by his friend, Nathan Mutschler. After entering the bathroom, Purcell pulled his gun from his waistband and committed suicide by shooting himself in the chest.

A NEWSPAPER'S STORY

Steve Mistler (2008) in the newspaper, *Forecaster*, presented the following report:

Navy investigating apparent suicide at BNAS

By Steve Mistler Forecaster staff writer

Published on Friday, Feb 1, 2008 at 5:05 am,

Last updated on Wednesday, Sep 2, 2009 at 12:12 am

BRUNSWICK - The Naval Criminal Investigative Service is reviewing Sunday's apparent suicide by a 21-year-old sailor who was in custody at Brunswick Naval Air Station.

Christopher Purcell, a Navy corpsman, was found dead from a gunshot wound shortly after base personnel responded to a call from Purcell's family and friends warning that he was distraught.

Six security officers arrived at Purcell's apartment at Building 731 on Fitch Avenue sometime before 9:47 p.m. According to Brunswick police, who began the investigation prior to its being taken over by NCIS, Purcell had been detained at his residence by base security.

Police Cmdr. Richard Desjardins said Purcell apparently died of a self-inflicted gunshot wound while he was in the bathroom of his apartment. Desjardins said a base security officer was in the bathroom at the time of the shooting. Desjardins added that a struggle occurred prior to Purcell's death, but it's unclear if the fight occurred in the bathroom or when security arrived.

"The circumstances of the case are now being investigated by NCIS," BNAS spokesman John James said, adding that he couldn't say how long Purcell had been detained or what base security had planned to do with him.

According to police records, Brunswick police received a 9:47 p.m. call from BNAS security after Purcell had shot himself. An emergency medical services team arrived at 9:51 p.m. and attempted life-saving measures. Purcell was pronounced dead shortly thereafter.

The incident raises questions about a recent decision by the Department of Defense to no longer allow base personnel to be deputized and trained by local law enforcement agencies. Prior to October, on-base arrests at BNAS were handled by two DoD detectives who held reserve status in the Brunswick Police Department. Now Brunswick police must be called to the base to enforce Maine laws.

Desjardins said the DoD detectives were not present during Sunday's incident and that Brunswick police were not called to the base until after Purcell shot himself.

James said the six-man security team that detained Purcell included four civilian guards and two masters-at-arms.

It's unclear if Purcell was searched for weapons or restrained by the security detail, a measure police typically take in suicide situations.

"These people can have knives or guns, so our first priority is to control the situation and dictate the pace," Desjardins said, adding that suicidal individuals are typically taken to a medical care facility and held there.

"At that moment, the individual really does want to die," Desjardins said. "But once the emergency is over, they're often thankful that we intervened."

Desjardins said Brunswick police typically handle 200 to 300 protective custody cases yearly.

It wasn't known how Purcell was able to bring a firearm into his living quarters. According to James, BNAS personnel are not allowed to bring privately owned weapons onto base property. He said security personnel are required to check their service weapons, and added that Purcell, who worked at the base's medical clinic, would not have been issued a weapon by the Navy.

Purcell served in the Navy since July 2005 and reported to BNAS in March 2006. James said BNAS was Purcell's first assignment. He had not been deployed overseas.

Purcell, whose immediate family is in Illinois, lived alone in condominium-style housing near the BNAS field house.

An issue: In the case Purcell v. U.S., it was ruled that the military was not responsible. The case was denied. The judges affirmed a decision based on the *Feres* doctrine, which provides that, "the Government is not liable under the [FTCA] for injuries to servicemen where the injuries arise out of or are in the course of activity incidental to service" (Feres v. United States, 340, U.S., 135-146, 1950).

THE AUTOPSY REPORT

Although I will abbreviate the final autopsy report, Mike Purcell provided me with a copy and permission to reproduce the report authored by Major M., Deputy Medical Examiner, dated February 12, 2008.

> Circumstances of Death: This 21-year-old active duty Sailor was, by report, in his housing at Brunswick NAS when he called a friend stating that he was going to kill himself. Authorities were notified and responded to his residence. He was restrained by the Master-of-Arms with handcuffs. At some point, he requested to use the bathroom and one of the handcuffs were undone. A corpsman was helping him steady himself when the corpsman noted that he had a gun. The deceased shot himself in the chest and all resuscitative efforts were unsuccessful. After examination of the scene by NCIS, the body was transported to the Maine State Medical Examiner's facility in Augusta, Maine. Dr. G. signed the manner of death as gunshot wound to the chest and the cause of death as suicide. The body was released to the jurisdiction of the Armed Forces Medical Examiner.
>
> Authorization for Autopsy: Office of the Armed Forces Medical Examiner, IAW 10 USC 1471.
>
> Identification: Positive identification by ante-mortem and post-mortem finger-print and dental comparisons.
>
> CAUSE OF DEATH: Gunshot wound to the chest
>
> MANNER OF DEATH: Suicide.
>
> ### OPINION
> This 21-year-old male, Christopher Lee Purcell, died of a gunshot wound to the chest. The bullet injured the heart, liver, and aorta (major blood vessel). A deformed, jacketed bullet and fragment of jacket were recovered. There was

evidence of close range discharge of a firearm (soot deposition on the skin surrounding the entrance wound and soot deposition and searing of the clothing). The abrasions of the face and small subarachnoid hemorrhage of the brain are consistent with either the history of being restrained or terminal collapse. The contusions of the wrists are consistent with being restrained with handcuffs. The toxicology screen was positive for ethanol in the blood and vitreous fluid. Autopsy findings and investigation are consistent with a self-inflicted injury. The manner of death is suicide.

M.

Maj, USAF, MC

Deputy Medical Examiner

Captain P., Chief Deputy Medical Examiner, undertook a toxicological examination. The report, dated January 31, 2008, reads in part as follows:

VOLATILES: The BLOOD AND VITREOUS FLUID were examined for the presence of ethanol (cutoff of 20 mg/dL), acetaldehyde, acetone, 2-propanol, 1-propanol, t-butanol, 2-butanol, iso-butanol and 1-butanol by headspace gas chromatography. The following volatiles were detected: (concentration(s) in mg/dL)

	Ethanol
BLOOD	140
VITREOUS FLUID	180

DRUGS: The URINE was screen for acetaminophen, amphetamine, anti-depressants, antihistamines, barbiturates, benzodiazepines, cannabinoids, chloroquine, cocaine, dextromethorphan, lidocaine, narcotic analgesics, opiates, phencyclidine, phenothiazines, salicylates, sympathomimetic amines and verapamil by gas chromatography, color test or immunoassay. The following drugs were detected:

None were found.

No mefloquine was detected in the blood at a limit of quantification of 0.01 mg/L using liquid chromatography/mass spectrometry.

P., Ph.D.

CAPT, MSC, USN

Chief Deputy Medical Examiner

Office of the Armed Forces Medical Examiner

A note: The information in the military documents may contain information exempt from mandatory disclosure under the Freedom of Information Act; however, the reports were released to Mike Purcell and he, with informed consent, released them to me to have his son's story told.

PERSONAL DOCUMENTS

Like Allport, Shneidman, and many others, I believe that the best documents are personal ones. I hereby present Chris' very personal documents: an autobiography, suicide notes, and his last chat. I also report here on his psychological assessment at age 14; it seems to fit best among his own documents. I begin with his autobiography at age 14, the beginning of his tempest.

AN AUTOBIOGRAPHY

Chris Purcell
Mr. O.

2-10-00
LA 5-6
Chris Purcell

Mr. O.

2-10-00
LA 5-6

Life Blows

Is change for the good? I would say not. Ever since I moved to Northbrook last March, I have hated it here ever since. Everybody thinks that change is so good, but why? I rather things always just be the same, forever and ever.

I remember the first day I moved to Charlotte. I have faint memories of how long the trip took to get there. I was little and have brief dreams of when we moved to there, but I can recall it well enough. I was constantly moving; always walking around catching other buses that we needed to take in order to get to our cousins. I remember when we finally got to my aunts and uncles house. It was in the middle of winter, and we spent the night at my cousin's house (my mom's sister). I some what have the memory standing there looking at my cousins that I had never really met them that much. We stood there gawking at each other, I remember I was standing behind my dad grasping his leg, just staring for like ten minutes or so. But when I got over all the shyness that was shown on the outside of my face, and showed my smile underneath the shyness, we had a blast, we played so many games and it was so fun!

Then I have memories of when I was older. Behind my cousins house, they were building a highway, and were under constructions, so . . . there was a lot of mud, and my cousins (I had a lot there were 7 kids in their family) and I would go back to the construction site when no one was around. And we would play around there for fun, and we would have so, so, much fun in the winter. They had these little mud puddle, not really little, but HUGE! They would freeze up, so we would take like these huge poles and just toss them into the frozen puddles and watch them crack open. I did some pretty weird things with my cousins, and we had a great time.

I remember one time my two cousins and I were walking and talking and all of sudden my older cousin (James, he's now 16) just dropped, we looked over at him and his leg was in a huge pile of mud, we had to pull him out. My cousin and I were laughing at him, he was mad, but afterwards, he too found it funny. I remember going to my even older cousins (John, he's 18) baseball and basketball games. I remember my cousin would wake me up in the morning and ask if I wanted to go to his games, so then I would wake my mom up and ask her, she would usually say yes, then I would tell my cousin yes and his dad would come and pick me up. After that I would usually end up spending the night and my cousins house for a couple of days.

I remember my uncle real well; he was kind of carefree, last minute decision guy. For example, I remember when the movie "Mortal Kombat" had just came out, and it was like eleven at night and my uncle couldn't sleep so he came downstairs (where my cousin and I were playing or something) and said "do you guys wanna go to a movie or something" and we said "yeah." And we went to see Mortal Kombat and got back at like two in the morning. That was awesome. I remember when it was a Friday morning and my cousins were going to the beach, and they asked if I wanted to come with them. So, I got to skip school that day and go to the beach with them. It was so, so, so FUN! I have great memories of my cousins and I and I hope that I will never lose or forget them.

Then there was my school Piedmont Middle, I loved it there also. It wasn't the richest school or the best, but I loved it. I remember going outside after lunch and playing tackle football then getting in trouble by the other teachers. I remember all my old friends that I had there. When I hear certain songs, I remember Charlotte and everything about it. Even today when I hear songs I have memories of Charlotte. At my old school, it wasn't the best because there were always a lot of fights and threats and stuff like that. But, I still loved it there. I really remember my best friend Chris Spears, I remember going to his house all the time. We would talk about anything and everything. I had the greatest memories of Chris and me.

Then, I remember those dreadful words that my mom said to me, they were "Chris, w . . . were going to be moving sometime". It was around the middle of the school year. And by that I thought that my met maybe in a couple of years. But then we were expecting it sometime in the beginning of next year. Then we were moving in two weeks, and I was like, "You're kidding right"? And my mom said, "no I'm not". And I just sat down to take a breather.

I remember saying goodbye to all of my friends. But, I was telling lies, it wasn't a goodbye at all, it was a badbye. I was saying "see-ya-later" when I would not see most of them for the rest of my life. That last day went by slowly, it all felt like a dream, that last day of school. But, I got to go to my friends for the weekend. I got to go home with him at least. I was saying goodbye to everybody, then I had to go. My friends sister was honking the horn, and I had to go. I remember seeing my friends faces dissolving over the horizon as we drove to his house.

I still had a little while to have fun before I was dragged into hell. I got to spend the week at my friends house. Then we got to go to the Hornets game. We got V.I.P. tickets, so we got to go in the media entrance. So that was pretty cool. We didn't see any basketball players, but we did see scouts for other teams and stuff, and that was pretty cool. I remember playing all week at Chris's house, we rented video games, and we stayed up all night long. Playing video games. Watching videos, and watching T.V.

Them I remember when my parents came and it was time for me to go. I still keep in touch with some of them, but that is not enough for me. Well, what can I do? My mom says were never going to move back to Charlotte. I guess I'll just have to get over it.

I remember my first day here, it was my sister and I, and I remember when I opened the doors to Wood Oaks, I remember seeing the big Wood Oaks banner in the hall to the side of the gym. I remember the smell of Wood Oaks. It smelled pretty good for being opened in 1972. It looked like it was built recently. I remember Mr. Louis showing me around. I was so nervous coming into all these classrooms with all these people I didn't know. I felt like hiding, and going home. I didn't want to be at Wood Oaks, I was totally silent like the first week of class. I didn't do well on any of tests or quizzes. I felt like an outcast. After awhile I started to hate Wood Oaks. And teachers think that I have no friends at all, I have a lot of friends, I just don't like Wood Oaks or most of the people, and I probably never will like it here.

Coming from a school where it was half whites, and half blacks, then coming to Wood Oaks where it's a lot whites, a lot of Asians, and a couple blacks is kind of a big change (I got nothing against them too). And them I remember how many Jewish people there were. (I got nothing against them). I don't think I have ever met a Jewish person in my life until I came to Wood Oaks. I remember thinking that Wood Oaks was going to be just like my old school. But I was way off. I would pinch myself and try to wake up from this hellish nightmare. But, I wouldn't wake up. I remember thinking that this is all just a dream and that one day I would wake up from it all. But, I probably never will. I know that there are things I cant change, I have to change myself. But, I will never change myself. I will always hate it here no matter what anyone says, or no matter what anyone does. I know I don't show it much that I hate it here but I do. Sometimes I feel like I don't care about school, so I will slack off, but that's getting me nowhere, so I try my hardest but sometimes my hardest just ain't good enough. In Charlotte I was getting A's and B's, here I'm getting B's and C's. I just wish everything would change back to normal, the way it used to be.

My dad keeps on saying that it will get better, back to normal, better than it was in Charlotte, but I'm seeing no light at the end of the tunnel. Now, my parents are already talking about moving again in a couple of years to Indiana, where my dad grew up. *IT IS SO BORING THERE.* Well, I guess my life lesson learned is that everything happens for a reason, I just got to find my reason. And I know that life will take me on journeys, places that I don't want to be, things that I don't want to do, but I will have to learn to deal with them. And life will throw a lot of crap at me, but I will have to keep on going on. For me that's hard, but I know I will have to get over it, and go on with my life. I hate Wood Oaks and always will. That's why life totally blows.

PSYCHOLOGICAL REPORT

Chris Purcell's autobiography, written on October 2, 2000, got the attention of his teacher. Chris was in grade 8 at White Oaks Junior High School, Northbrook, Illinois. Chris had moved to this school in March 1999. Mrs. Purcell had reported that Chris was "depressed." Chris was exhibiting a poor self-image and low self-esteem, for example, calling himself "stupid." Teachers were concerned about significant anxiety and depression. There was also a concern about suicide risk. Chris was overheard to have stated to another boy about getting a "stun gun" and shooting himself with it. Mr. Purcell had reported that Chris had spoken about killing himself before when they lived in North Carolina. Chris Purcell was reported to be very upset about the frequent moves, due to being in a Navy family, and the plan to move to Japan. Chris dreaded that fact.

On December 21 and 23, 2000, Chris Purcell, at the age of 14, was seen for a psychoeducational assessment. A report, authored by Dr. N., offers some early insightful observations. The reason for referral was "to address Chris's educational performance and difficulty with work completion." Chris was having academic problems. However, a major concern was that Mrs. Purcell was noted to have stated, "Chris has been 'depressed' since he moved to Northbrook" (February 1999).

The relevant background information indicated that Chris did well in kindergarten and was a "joy to teach." During his early education, Chris received good grades, abundant acceptable scores on standardized tests, and exhibited "excellent" conduct. In sixth grade, he received A's and B's; however, math was problematic (he received an F). In grade 8, we read a different story, and I quote verbatim:

> Chris attends a regular departmentalized eighth grade program at Wood Oaks. His first quarter grades were: B's in applied studies, language arts, and PE; C's in art, reading, social studies, and math; and an F in science. Teachers note that the content of his work fluctuates. Many times Chris will say that he will do his assignments, but then he does not follow through. In language arts and reading he often appears tired, and he becomes angry if pressed about his assignments. In most classes he is not focused. He appears not to care whether he is successful. He will often pull up the hood of his jacket over his head and lay on the desk. Chris requires one on one attention to keep him on task.

Dr. N. saw Chris for an interview. Aside from academic concerns, when Chris was asked, Dr. N. recorded the following problems:

> Although Chris was open about his feelings about school, peers, moving to Japan, and life in general, this openness did not appear to alleviate the emotional pressures he was experiencing or to help him focus on test measures presented in the last two sessions. Because of the presence of depression, with its attendant concentration difficulties and motivational problems, test scores may not reflect Chris' true abilities.
>
> Chris reported adamantly that he is "not good at school." His biggest problem at school is "keeping organized." He forgets to do or misplaces assignments. Wood Oaks is much harder than his other school. He admitted readily to feeling depressed, saying, "Everything is bad, not just school." Chris does not like most of his fellow students, perceiving them to be "stuck up." However, he does enjoy meeting students from Highland Park, whom he perceives as being more diverse, less driven by high academic achievement, and "not so stuck up." Interestingly, despite his academic and behavior problems, Chris appeared to genuinely like all his teachers, with one exception, about whom he feels "neutral because I don't especially like the subject."
>
> The procedures used for the assessment were the following: Interview with Chris; Classroom Observation; Wechsler Intelligence Scale for Children-III (WISC-III); Woodcock Johnson Tests of Cognitive Ability Revised (WJ-R)—selected subtests; Bender Gestalt Test of Visual Motor Integration; Wechsler Individual Achievement Test (WIAT); Test of Written Language-3 (TOWL-3); Achenbach Teacher Report Form (TRF)-1991 version; Achenbach Youth Self Report Form (YSR)-1991 revision; Sentence Completion Test (SCT); and Human Figure Drawings.

The assessment findings were as follows:

Cognitive Abilities

The WISC-III is an individually administered test that provides an estimate of a person's general learning ability. The WISC-III groups an individual's abilities into different clusters, and Dr. N. reported on three global areas: attention and concentration, which measures short term memory; verbal comprehension/reasoning, which measures verbal ability; and visual/perceptual reasoning, which involves the manipulation of concrete materials or processing of visual stimuli/information to solve problems non-verbally.

Based on the WISC-III, Chris earned a Full Scale IQ of 103, which classifies his overall ability as falling in the Average range. The chances are good (95%) that Chris' IQ is somewhere in the range of 97 to 109. His IQ is ranked at the 58th percentile, indicating that he scored higher than 58% of other children of the same age in a standardized sample. Thus, there was no overall intellectual impairment. The findings were deemed, in fact, to be an underestimate of Chris' functioning at that time.

Chris' non-verbal/perceptual skills were better than his verbal skills. The non-verbal/perceptual abilities (Perceptual Organization Index) were in the high average range (POI = 110, 75th percentile), whereas his verbal abilities (Verbal Comprehension Index) were in the average range (VCI = 98; 45th percentile). Such a difference is not significant. The WISC-III includes six Verbal subtests and six Performance subtests. Verbal subtests ranged from 8 on Comprehension to 11 on Information; Performance subtests ranged from 9 on Block Design to 15 on Picture Completion. Such variability is common. Thus, there did not appear to be a specific learning deficit.

The Bender Gestalt is a measure of visual-motor integration functioning; Chris received an average score. His visual-motor recall (redrawing the designs from immediate memory) score was average.

Overall, Chris was seen as "a teenager who is functioning within the average range intellectually." Although strengths were identified, there were no cognitive weaknesses. Chris' measures of attention and concentration, verbal reasoning, and visual reasoning were within expected limits. However, and this is very significant, it was noted that due to Chris' depressed mood, problems were predicted to occur. It was stated, "processing efficiency, focus, and academic follow-through is likely to decrease as the complexity of the task increases because of emotional concerns, in particular, depression." This was predicted, prophetically, to increase without psychological assistance.

Basic Academic Skills

The WIAT is an individually administered test that measures a person's academic functioning. The WIAT assesses reading recognition, reading comprehension, written spelling, and mathematics. Chris' level of academic skills, based on the WIAT, is as follows:

Subtest	Performance Standard Score (Percentile)	Approximate Grade Equivalent
Reading Composite	104 (61st percentile); Average	8
Reading Recognition	102 (55th percentile); Average	8
Reading Comprehension	107 (68th percentile); Average	8
Spelling	107 (68th percentile); Average	8
Mathematics Reasoning	107 (68th percentile); Average	7
Arithmetical Calculation	71 (3rd percentile); Below	4

Thus, Chris achieved at least average, except in arithmetic. It was a significant weakness. Chris was noted to make "errors in regrouping operations and simple addition."

Behavior Functioning

The Achenbach Child Behavior Checklist (1991 version) for ages 6-18 asks people to describe behavior of the child, now or within the past 6 months. The teacher completed the Teacher Report Form (TRF), and Chris completed the Youth Self-Report Form (YSR). The Achenbach checklists are deemed to be one of the best self-report measures available; I agree and use it in my clinical practice for over 20 years. Among the many strengths, it has good construct validity. I will quote verbatim Dr. N's observations:

> Several of Chris' teachers completed the Teacher Report Form, a questionnaire that lists problem behaviors and attitudes that teachers may observe in their students and compares the student's behavior to age and gender peers. Both teachers reported a large number of concerns in several areas. Specifically, they observed a significant number of behaviors found in depressed teenagers: sadness, sulking, tiredness, self-consciousness, apathy, lack of motivation, withdrawal from class activities, inattention, failure to complete work, and poor school work. Teachers also observed that Chris often appears tense and moody and tends to associate with other students who get in trouble. All of Chris' teachers observed that Chris has a very poor self-image as a student. Recently, a teacher overheard Chris talking to another boy about getting a "stun gun" and hitting himself with it. Teachers have seen many instances of Chris' calling himself "retarded" or "stupid." Given positive reports about Chris' behavior in his previous school, his negative behaviors such as swearing, disrespect toward adults, and disturbing other students appear to be "acting out" behaviors in which actions are substituted for unpleasant feeling sates, in particular, depression. On the TRF, teachers reported highly significant levels of anxious/depressed behaviors (>99th percentile) and significant attention problems (98th percentile).
>
> Chris willingly filled out questionnaires and a sentence completion test carefully and elaborated on most of his responses. Chris was administered the student form of the above teacher questionnaire, the Youth Self-Report Form.

Chris reported that he often could not get his mind off his thoughts in order to concentrate on schoolwork. He hates school and wishes that he could attend school in Highland Park. Chris acknowledged disobeying his parents and teachers many times but had shared no insights in these behaviors. He does not want to move to Japan but is preparing for this eventuality by seeking out other teenagers and adults who have lived there and asking them about their experiences.

Chris feels confused, "in a fog," anxious, and fearful most of the time. He has many depressive, self-defeating thoughts such as "nothing will ever work out for me," and believes that he has never done well in school and that is he "retarded." Chris ruminates about "the meaning of life" and is fearful that there is none. He is very disappointed in social relationships, painting a broad picture that "People suck." Chris stated that he feels "terrible," is always tired, has trouble sleeping at night, and hardly ever has fun at school. He does not see a future but only a painful present. He worries about many aches and pains—headaches, stomachaches, and nausea. On the YSR, Chris reported that he sets fires often but would not elaborate on this. Chris denied on questionnaires and in the interview ever having suicidal thoughts or suicide attempts. He dismissed his comment about the stun gun as "just goofing off." Chris' father recalled that Chris had spoken of killing himself when they lived in North Carolina. Mrs. Purcell, however, did not recall this. On the assessment's structured questionnaires, Chris' responses fell in the highly significant range in somatic complaints, withdrawal, attention, and anxiety/depression (YSR). On the Child Depression Inventory, responses indicated perceptions of significant problems in the areas of interpersonal problems and anhedonia, the inability to experience life or specific activities as pleasurable.

Conclusions

Chris, a 14-year-old male, was referred for psychological "assessment because of behavior and academic concerns." The main and final conclusion was: "Chris presented as an extremely depressed, demoralized youngster." Dr. N goes on to state,

> Student, teacher, and parent reports confirm that Chris is suffering from a depressed mood that infiltrates his academic performance. Depressive symptoms include depressed mood, sleep problems, low self-esteem, anhedonia, poor concentration, feelings of hopelessness, and fatigue. At school, depressed mood appears to affect Chris' attention span, ability to concentrate, work production, decision making, organization, motivation, self-confidence, teacher and peer relationships. Some of Chris' behaviors also appear to serve the purpose of expressing anger, hopelessness, and self-reproach. However, Chris maintains a positive view of his teachers and acknowledges his feelings openly, improving the probability of success of interventions.

Thus, Chris was diagnosed with a mood disorder—depression—already at the age of 14. It is probable that he was depressed before that age. Not only was the depression evident, it was deemed that the symptoms caused clinically significant distress or impairment in social, school, and other important areas of functioning. It caused, in fact, in light of no cognitive deficits, significant academic problems.

Chris was deemed to be experiencing trauma, most significantly, the frequent moves due to the Navy life. He was reacting with horror, fear, and helplessness to the next move to Japan. I believe that Chris may well have been suffering from PTSD about age 14. Indeed, I have little doubt of that fact. There was predictable traumatization, not being insane.

Chris was suicidal at age 14. This is unequivocal. Yet we do not know the lethality. Was it medium? High? Chris also exhibited characteristics, already then, of denial, avoidance, and dissembling. I believe that he lied. This was to be an enduring characteristic of his all too short life.

Dr. N, in her report, made some strong recommendations. Dr. N recommended that Chris' emotional and behavioral needs needed to be monitored and responded to in school. She recommended, "counseling within the school setting be considered"; a referral for psychotherapy in the community for Chris "as some of Chris' issues appear to be non-school related"; and a "psychiatric consultation regarding medication should also be considered because of the chronicity of Chris' depression." She specifically noted the need for Chris to be provided "a safe place in which he can express his feelings and begin separating from friends, relatives and his country in an adaptive way." Japan was, she believed, to be traumatizing—it was.

Please note that all conclusions rendered in Dr. N's report are based on clinical assessment and the documentation available at the time. However, based on the psychological report, my belief is the following: Chris, at age 14, was on his road to destruction.

SUICIDE NOTES

Chris Purcell left two suicide notes. I hereby present the notes and an analysis.

Note 1:
Mom, Pop, Kristin, and Blair
I'm so sorry . . .
Laugh as much as you
breathe
and love as long as you live
I love you
    Chris

Note 2:
Suicide Note
Mother, Father, Kristen, and Blair: I'm sorry . . . I don't know what else to say. You all mean so much to me . . . I just can't go on anymore . . . I love you all more than you could ever imagine.

I feel it is only right to state my reasons for what I am about to do. First and foremost, this has nothing to do with anyone or anything. I just no longer have the desire to live. Life bores me. Blame it on whatever you want, the season, depression, alcohol abuse . . . it makes no difference, because in the end it is just me. I've always felt this way. I have suffered in silence most of my life . . . and I don't want to suffer anymore. I could go off on a philosophical tangent but in the end it doesnt matter. I appreciate everyones help and guidance . . . I really do.

I've learned a lot from everyone, people I like, people I loathe . . . it's been an experience. I also want to apologize to anyone I may have caused issues with . . . im not a bad guy . . . im really not . . . I have the purest intentions inside my heart . . . I think they just come out all wrong. I think saying I've felt pretty misunderstood my whole life would be an understatement. I don't expect anyone to understand why I did this . . . I'm sure most will see it as the easy way out . . . me being a coward, etc. I'm not escaping any problem, im not running from anything. I'm saving me from myself. I came from nothingness and I will return to nothingness. This is probably making a pretty shitty suicide note, but I don't care, I'm just trying to convey my reasoning to who ever might care. It is all just meaningless to me . . . wake up . . . work, eat, masturbate, get drunk, pointless conversation . . . rinse and repeat. It's fucking madness.

I'm done with it. I'm not sure what kind of emotion this will ellicit to people I know . . . anger, denial, sadness, guilt . . . but just know that there was absolutely nothing anyone could have done Like I said, this is about no one. It is about me. You can see it however you want . . . this has been the hardest decision of my life but it has also been the most liberating one as well. At only 21 I realize I never will . . . meet the love of my life, hear my favorite song, play the best videogame, have sex . . . hear the best joke, have the best original idea . . . etc . . . I will also never disappoint myself or anyone else, never fail at anything again, never suffer alone, never watch life pass me be, never wonder what the fuck my problem is, never be rejected again, and ultimately . . . never live. Goodbye life, I have lost all interest in you.

THE ANALYSIS OF THE NOTE

Chris' case, given the suicide note (#2), presents a unique opportunity: to postdict a communication as allowing us to answer why and why at that time. The TGSP will be used. In performing my analysis, I first looked at the note before any background information was known and interviews were available. In Chapter 1, I presented the complete text of the protocol sentences: I here use abbreviations (see Chapter 1). The note had the following characteristics of suicide:

INTRAPSYCHIC DRAMA

I - Unbearable Psychological Pain: 1) Suicide as a relief, 2) Suicide as a flight from trauma, 3) Emotional states in suicidal trauma, 4) Loss of interest to endure, 5) Inability to meet life's challenges, 6) State of heightened disturbance.

II - Cognitive Constriction: 7) A history of trauma, 8) Overpowering emotions, 9) Focus only on grief topics

III - Indirect Expressions: 11) Aggression has turned inwards, 12) Unconscious dynamics

IV - Inability to Adjust: 13) Feels weak to overcome difficulties, 14) Incompatible state of mind, 15) Serious disorder in adjustment (f & g)

V - Ego: 16) Weakness in constructive tendencies, 17) A "complex" or weakened ego, 18) Harsh conscience

INTERPERSONAL STAGE

VI - Interpersonal Relations: 19) Problems determined by situations, 20) Weakened by unresolved problems, 21) Frustrated needs (e.g., abasement, autonomy, harmavoidance, infavoidance), 22) Frustration to a traumatic degree, 23) Positive development not forthcoming

VII - Rejection – Aggression: 25) Report of a traumatic event, 26) Narcissistic injury

VIII - Identification – Egression: 33) Identification with person/ideal, 34) Unwillingness to accept life, 35) Suicide as escape.

THE LAST CHAT

On January 27, 2008, Chris had his last chat with a stranger on MySpace. Having removed identifying data, I here present his last chat:

what branch are you in?
navy
thank you for your service
whats this talk about taking yourlofe?
i see no end. nothing but agony of my mind. you know . . . i don't rwant to die i just want ito stop . . . i see no other options.
agony from being overseas?
No . . . it's a very fucking long story . . .
have you talked to a councilor or psychologist, or anymilitary support?
yes i have. Im not supposed to see them until next week . . . I just feel like I cant go on . . . nothigh will ever change . . .
don't' let these people in the chat room ruffle you r feathers
whats bothering you?
i understnad if you don't want to talk about it.
yes they do, a lot of stuff is ruffering my feathers, my whole fucking life has been nohtig but depression. . . . im a 21 year old vigin . . . the best friend of my life doesnt see me the way i see her . . . im just tired of everything . . . im done . . .
but i have been told, God only gives you what you can handle. at times that is very difficult to believe but, its amazing to look back and see what all i have made it thru
first of all change chat rooms or get out of that one
im out
wait
there is NOTHING you can't overcome
do you have an emergency number for your counsilor?
if you don't call 911 and they will take you to the hospital for immediate help and attentoin
i don't help. im done with help. nothing can help me. i just want this suffering to end. the thought of death is comforting

i don't believe that because you are asking for help
you have been asking for help from people in a chat room you don't even know,
you do want help
i want it . . . from people who mean something to me . . . i don't want ot die . . . i
don't know what else to do . . . i have ea loaded gun in my lap right now . . . im so
scared . . . i don't want to live anymore
unload the gun
i am not your family and i don't mean anything to you, but i khnow what its
like to be scared
scared of the unknown
but it will all unvail itself and we become better stronger people
im not even scared of the unknown . . . i embrace it . . . when we die we die . . . im
just so tired of life . . . i cant even describe it . . .
is Kristin your sister?
yeah . . .
why
when was the last time you saw her
in November
thanksgiving?
yeah
were you happy to see her?
yes . . .
i was happy to see all of my family . . .
have you spoken to you mom lately?
within the past week . . . i don't tell her much though..it hurts too much...so i don't
bring anything up . . . she thinks im fine...
i don't know what type of relationship you have with her but trying talking to her.
Its ok to get upset and express hurt
i don't want to talk to much people right now . . . im so lost . . .
did you unload the gun?
fuck no. its sittong my desk
unload it
no
other than Kristin do you have any siblings
yeah, they don't have myspace though. i have a bunch of good friends . . . im just
done . . . im fucking ugly . . . im over i . . . ill never meet anyone worthy . . .
there are SO many people out there to meet, but you will not find them sitting in
front of a tv
have you looked on line or going out to clubs?
i go to clubs onc ein awhile . . . im just fucking ugly . . . im done with it . . . i don't
give a fuck anymore
what about your appearance do you not like?
fucking everything. my face especially. look at my pictures for christ sake
there is nothing wrong with you face, you have two eyes a nose and a mouth
so sorry i don't believe that
fuck you. don't lie to me. i don't give a fuck anymore. i know im ugly jsut tell me
it
you are not ugly
but people can tell you that all day and yopu wont believe it, you wont believe it
until you are ready to

what else about your appearance bothers you?
as if you couldnt see it . . .
my receding hairline, my bags under my eyes. my crooked teeth. my 50 year old
face
what else
im hideous
get some,rest that will take care of the bags, try invisiline for your teeth, shaving
your head to hide you hair line and working out
fuck it. you odnt understand. im done talking.
goodbye
im just trying to show you for the problems you have expressed, there are answers
to
it may take time to heal and change things but it can all work out
hello?
who do you live with?
myself
bye
what do you want to change in your life
don't ever do that again
do what?
don't act stupid
so . . . youre g0oing to stop me?
just goes to show you people do care

ANALYSIS OF THE CHAT

As with the note, I analyzed Chris' conversation. The scoring would be identical to the suicide note except (and this is important), under rejection-aggression, the aggression that was missing in the note is screaming. The protocols are 25) Report of a traumatic event; 26) Narcissistic injury; 27) Preoccupation with person; 28) Ambivalent feelings toward a person; 29) Aggression as self-directed; 32) Revenge toward someone else (see Chapter 1 for complete text/protocols).

Chris, thus, was not only self-destructive but also other-destructive. There is no question that he was angry! Yet, akin to the note, he dissembled; he is explicit; no one is to blame. I believe that is not what Chris believed; yet being a good soldier, he kept secrets.

GOOGLE

Like many of us, Chris Purcell used Google (www.google.com). He Googled in the weeks prior to his dying by suicide, compiled from his laptop computer by his father on June 7, 2008, among others, the following items: how to commit suicide, adjustment disorders, philosophy & suicide, sgli & navy & suicide, sgli & navy, sgli & suicide, .38 hollow caliber, albert camus, albert camus the stranger, effective suicide methods, ptsd symptoms, suicide guide forums, suicide guide, suicide message boards, best suicide scenes, suicide notes, effective suicide, used guns & marine, gun registration state laws, signs of alcoholism, fuck you, van morrison.

MOVIES

Not only notes, emails, chats, diaries, and poems, movies are also a window to a mind; in this case, Chris Purcell's. There is a growing interest in suicide movies. My friend, Steven Stack and his wife, Barbara Bowman (2011) recently published a book on the very topic, *Suicide Movies*. It is the first-ever comprehensive study of film suicide. Stack and Bowman analyze more than 1,500 film studies. They ask, "How is suicide portrayed in the cinema and what does it mean for suicide prevention?"

Without question, Chris' favorite movie was *Donnie Darko*. It is a suicide film. If you want to understand Chris' deeper mind (intention), I think that the movie helps to know Chris better and why he killed himself. *Donnie Darko* is best described as a psychological thriller, a psychological suicide thriller. This 2001 American film was directed by Richard Kelly and starred, among others, Drew Barrymore, James Duval, Jake Gyllenhaal, Jena Malone, and Patrick Swayze.

The main character is a teenager named Donnie Darko. He has a troubled, abusive history and has mental pain and adjustment problems; he sees a psychiatrist, Dr. Lilian Thurman. One day, a demonic-looking rabbit, Frank, appears, draws Donnie out of the house, and hypnotically tells Donnie the world will end. This will occur in 28 days, 6 hours, 42 minutes, and 12 seconds. Then there will be a huge trauma. Donnie shares his vision. Dr. Thurman believes Frank is a hallucination, and Donnie suffers from paranoid schizophrenia. At a Halloween party, Gretchen Ross, Donnie's friend, arrives. It is implied that they had their first sexual encounter. At midnight, Donnie realizes 28 days have passed; he awaits the sixth hour. Therefore, Donnie, Gretchen, and two friends go to see "Grandma Death." They are assaulted by bullies. A car suddenly comes toward Grandma Death; the car avoids Grandma Death, but Gretchen is killed. It is a narcissistic loss. The rabbit appears. There is an overwhelming feeling of pain. This is trauma. A tornado comes. Then, after 6 hours, 42 minutes, and 12 seconds, Donnie kills himself. (I will leave the plot's details a secret.)

A suicide note is a snapshot; this film is a full-length movie. It reveals the unbearable pain and why people kill themselves. Unlike Alice's looking glass, there are not wonderful things in this film. It, in a simple word, is *dark*.

Since I cannot show you the film in a book's printing (today), I will reproduce some important lines. One can analyze the words, no different from a suicide note. Here are some quotes:

> Donnie: How can you do that?
> Frank: I can do anything I want. And so can you.
>
> Jim Cunningham (He is a motivational speaker at school, whom Donnie has murderous impulses toward): You are a fear prisoner. Yes, you are a product of fear.
>
> Gretchen: My mom had to get a restraining order against my stepdad. He has emotional problems.
> Donnie: Oh, I have those too! What kind of emotional problems does your dad have?

196 / THE PSYCHOLOGICAL AUTOPSY

Gretchen: He stabbed my mom four times in the chest.
Donnie: Oh.

Donnie: I made a new friend today.
Dr. Lilian Thurman: Real or imaginary?
Donnie: Imaginary.

Dr. Lilian Thurman: What did Roberta Sparrow (a former teacher at Donnie's school, who is now senile) say to you?
Donnie: She said, "Every living creature on earth dies alone."

Donnie: Frank, when's this gonna stop?
Frank: You should already know that.

Dr. Lilian Thurman: Do you feel alone right now?

Donnie: You're right, actually. I am pretty- I'm, I'm pretty troubled and I'm pretty confused. But I . . . and I'm afraid. Really, really afraid. Really afraid. But I . . . I . . . I think you're the fucking Antichrist.

Gretchen: Some people are just born with tragedy in their blood.

Donnie: [reading poem in class] A storm is coming, Frank says / A storm that will swallow the children / And I will deliver them from the kingdom of pain / I will deliver the children back the their doorsteps/ And send the monsters back to the underground / I'll send them back to a place where no-one else can see them / Except for me / Because I am Donnie Darko.

Dr. Lilian Thurman: What is going to happen?
Donnie: [crying] Frank is gonna kill . . .
Dr. Lilian Thurman: Who is he going to kill? Who is he going to kill, Donnie?
Donnie: [sees Frank] I CAN SEE HIM RIGHT NOW!

One other film, Chris' second favorite film, was *Jacob's Ladder*. It is a psychological PTSD thriller. The main character, Jacob Singer (Tim Robbins) is a U.S. soldier fighting in the Mekong Delta during the Vietnam War. The story begins with helicopters flying overhead. There is a Viet Cong offensive; solders are killed. During the trauma, Jacob is stabbed with a bayonet. The film next chronicles Jacob's life after the battle. There is no lack of traumatic aftershocks—Jacob suffers from lethal PTSD. This movie is a second mirror to Chris' mind. (Did Chris suffer from PTSD?)

Do the movies show it? Do they help uncover the barren bones?

HEALTH RECORD

Chris Purcell's early medical record was unavailable, with the exception of the psychological report at age 14. When he was born in Iceland, his mother was in the Navy. It was a caesarean birth; there were no complications. His medical record as a child and teen are unremarkable. Chris Purcell's records (a banker box full, weighing over 50 lbs.) were made available to me. I hereby summarize Chris' medical records, from the Naval Health Clinic, New England (Newport), beginning March 17, 2006. Before Chris joined the Navy, there is no medical record of treatment. The first important health date available to me was March 17, 2006; Chris had an outpatient record review performed. There is nothing remarkable noted. Subsequent notes discuss an array of topics such as gastritis, chronic pain (the first digit of right hand), and dental. On October 3, 2006, there is the first yellow flag. Chris Purcell is noted to be drinking alcohol and smoking cigarettes. There was medium risk. Health promotion services were recommended: tobacco cessation and nutrition counseling.

In a visit in December 2006, Chris denied use of alcohol. On January 31, 2007, he is diagnosed with "nicotine dependence" and prescribed varenicline (Chantax) to assist with the problem. On August 30, 2007, Chris was complaining of insomnia; he reported that he felt always fatigued. On September 7, 2007, Chris is prescribed zapidem (Ambien) for the insomnia. Yet, at these times, Chris denied increased stress and reported normal mood. He reported being healthy. This changed.

On November 9, 2007, Chris received a suspension for a bottle of liquor in the freezer.

On November 9, 2007, Chris, a self-referral, was seen for alcohol problems. Chris denied using drugs. He did admit to personal issues at home. Chris wanted to escape; he was using the alcohol to self-medicate.

The reason for Chris' self-referral was an incident when Chris had been drinking and caused damage to a friend's property. Chris admitted to alcohol abuse for at least one year. He stated that he was "having trouble cutting back on alcohol." He reported that he started drinking in the Navy. He admitted to binge drinking; he drank 10 liquor shots in 15 minutes.

Chris was asked about trauma. He wrote that his childhood was "good." However, he reported that his family moved a lot. He reported a positive history of alcohol abuse on his mother's side. Chris stated that he was having "emotional problems." He acknowledged being worried about his dying maternal grandmother. Chris was then admitting to some of his problems. His mental status was normal. However, was he dissembling? Keeping secrets?

The doctor, Dr. L, diagnosed the following DSM impairments:

Axis I	Alcohol Abuse
Axis II	NIL
Axis III	Not recorded
Axis IV	Not recorded
GAF	= 81

The Global Adjustment Assessment of Function Scale (GAF) was 81. This suggests minimal symptoms (e.g., depression over grandmother's dying). Overall, it means good functioning in all areas of life. One would be seen as having everyday problems or concerns. However, Dr. L's note suggests Chris' motivation for change was not optimal.

The risk for first alcohol abuse incident was rated as moderately high. Chris questioned the supportive note of his Navy environment; he reported that he did not feel support from his superior commanders. Chris was referred for treatment. It was recommended that Chris be referred to a psychologist.

On November 13, 2007, Chris reported that he first drank at age 15. At 17 to 18, he consumed little; he reported drinking one 12 oz. beer two to three times a year. Between the ages 19 to 20, Chris consumed more, but with social limits, although, of course, the drinking age is 21.

On November 13, 2007, Chris' work performance suffered.

On December 7, 2007, Chris was prescribed alprazolam (Xanax), as needed for anxiety.

On December 10, 2007, one can read progressive regression: Chris was now reporting an array of many painful symptoms: feeling restless, feeling nervous, anxiety interfering with social activities, interfering with work, and insomnia.

Chris reported an increase in anxiety over the past week with a few episodes of shaking, and heart pounding. Chris reported experiencing panic attacks; he reported that the attacks came for no known reason. He had been worrying. He reported being helpless; he reported that he attempted to control the anxiety, but he never stopped it. He attempted strategies such as exercise/jogging and relaxation, but failed. His belief: Nothing will help!

His mental state was not recorded as normal now. He was seen as tired, and his mood was irritable. Chris was diagnosed with a new Axis I disorder: Anxiety Disorder, NOS (Not Otherwise Specified). In the DSM, Anxiety Disorder NOS includes disorders with prominent anxiety or phobic avoidance that do not meet criteria for another specific disorder. Chris' impairments, thus, grew beyond an adjustment disorder. Things got worse!

On December 10, 2007, Chris was known to be attending AA. Not only counseling, but also educational opportunities were provided to Chris.

On December 13, 2007, Chris evaluated the group work as not beneficial. He felt like he was talking to strangers. He felt estranged, cut-off, withdrawn.

On December 13, 2007, Chris had a conflict with Navy authorities; he reported that he feared his commander. He feared that the commander would find out his secret and what he says. Chris was worried about confidentiality.

On December 13, 2007, Chris denied abusing alcohol since initiating treatment. The same on December 14, December 17, December 19, and so on. This was not so on January 7. Chris was drinking.

On January 8, 2008 Chris admitted to some abuse of alcohol.

On January 14, 2008, Chris was in military trouble. Chris had brought a bottle of Jagermeister to the clinic on the weekend and proceeded to drink to intoxication. This would mean an immediate military disciplinary issue; Chris was in legal trouble with the Navy.

By this time, Chris' medical record suggests two diagnoses, alcohol abuse and mood disorder. Obviously, the health professionals were questioning the initial diagnosis. Chris presented more and more symptoms, and now shame and disgrace. He would be ordered to go in front of the command; he would face military court consequences—more loss of honor.

Chris' problems were also growing interpersonally. The alcohol use was causing problems with his peers. He was becoming socially isolated. He reported few sober friends. He had few healthy recreational habits.

Chris also began to present a very different childhood. He reported now that his childhood was "lonely and unstable." The problems were associated with being in a military family. Overall, however, Chris was seen as having historical and current situational problems. From a DSM perspective, he was seen as having a co-morbid disorder: alcohol abuse and a mood disorder. It appears that more and more, health professionals were wondering if Chris had a mood disorder. Yet nothing is specific. Was it Mood Disorder, NOS? Chris was seen as at risk for further substance abuse. The primary reason for the assessed risk was an underlying mood disorder. The mood disorder was seen as contributing to Chris' misery. It was also seen as resulting in a poor (military/green) attitude and poor work performance. Military disciplinary court was likely.

Chris was ongoingly questioned about suicide risk. Chris denied risk. He denied intent, plan, and so on. There was no suggestion of risk. At what point was Chris intentionally dissembling, keeping a mask about his deep howling battle.

Dr. C, a licensed clinical psychologist, offered the following DSM diagnosis:

Axis I	Alcohol Abuse
	Mood Disorder, NOS
Axis II	Deferred
Axis III	None noted
Axis IV	Problems with primary support system

His GAF was now 55–60. That is consistent with moderate symptoms in functioning (e.g., depressed mood, panic attacks) and moderate difficulty in social, and occupational functioning (e.g., few friends, conflict with peers or commanders).

I should also offer a further comment on Mood Disorder, NOS. This includes a wide array of disorders, from manic-depressive (bipolar) disorder to depressive disorder. It is used with mood symptoms that do not meet criteria for any specific mood disorder and when it is difficult to choose between Depressive Disorder NOS and Bipolar Disorder NOS. It is also commonly used by health professionals to classify children to young adults whose symptoms will likely crystallize into a bipolar disorder. A manic-depressive disorder early in life is a developmental disorder. There is a positive family history of a manic-depressive (bipolar) disorder. There is a lot of biology to a lot of this disorder.

Greater intervention was recommended: Recommendation #1: Chris was referred to individual counseling to address not only alcohol use, but also behavioral issues. An appointment was made.

Recommendation #2 was for psychological consultation to further assess and clarify the mood-related problems. Further assessment for mental health needs was planned. An appointment was made.

Recommendation #3 was a referral to a medical doctor to determine whether Chris would benefit from medication to assist in mood regulation.

A day later, January 15, 2008, Dr. C saw Chris again. Chris was seen as cooperative. Dr. C evaluated Chris' mood, problems, and so on, and this included questions about suicide risk. Chris denied suicide ideation and risk. He also denied homicidal ideation, intention, or plan. Chris, in a nutshell, was also denying any significant stressors at that time. Chris was treated; he was attending a group. Chris was receiving individual counseling for substance abuse. Chris was not deemed at risk.

On January 15, 2008, Chris was seen. Dr. C. discussed Chris' mother and her bipolar disorder. His mother's sibling, who also has a mental illness, was discussed. The helpers, I believe, were becoming more and more aware of Chris' underlying pain. He suffered from a developing mental disorder (psychopathology). Yet he denied any current or previous suicide ideation, intent, or plan. Was he wearing a mask? Was he covering his despair?

On January 15, Chris noted that his alcohol abuse and his recent binge drinking was a "stupid mistake."

On January 17, 2008, there was a record review by Dr. L, a medical officer, a counselor, and another clinical staff; the group recommended follow-up counseling, an after-care program supported by his commander. Only a member of a soldier's command office could order the plan. The Navy had concerns, and Chris was aware of the meaning of the concern in a green culture. Did he fear even incarceration? Dishonorable discharge? Involuntary repatriation? Being disenfranchised? Military humiliation? What were Chris' stressors?

On January 22, 2008, Dr. C saw Chris for 60 minutes. This was to be their last visit. There was no suggestion of suicide risk. Chris reported some mood- and adjustment-related difficulties within the past 2 months. A comprehensive psychiatric evaluation was planned. The plan was to continue treatment; of course, sadly, it never occurred. He needed comprehensive care, which would have included psycho-therapy, medication, and hospitalization.

Therefore, mental health professionals, just prior to the tragedy, saw Chris Purcell, and those professionals did not document Chris to be at risk for suicide (or homicide). Although he attended appointments with professionals, overall it appears that he was noncompliant with treatment. He was seen as having a mood disorder; he was seen as depressed, anxious, and abusing alcohol. However, he was not seen as a threat to himself.

The noncompliance reference is in relation to the fact that he was attending counseling but perhaps not discussing the depth of his problems. Was he taking the medication as prescribed? He was known to be concerned about side effects. Did he follow through with the prescribed treatment? He had a history of noncompliance to prescribed medication.

Albeit, based on the health record, this tragedy was not predictable. Was it preventable? That is a very different question, and the questions were raised for the military.

We may never perfectly know why Chris killed himself; however, the personal documents are most revealing. Secrets come alive. In a PA, we can do more. From the interviews, we can get a pretty good idea why Chris died by suicide and why at that particular time.

THE INTERVIEWS

Let us next present the interviews, utilizing Shneidman's empirical basic outline, although one has to let the interview flow. Be that as it may, I routinely conduct the autopsy in a standardized fashion, as Dr. Shneidman taught me. It is an open-ended function. It is not like a physical autopsy or forensic investigation (see Chapter 3).

For the psychological autopsy, the following people were interviewed: Mike Purcell, father; Helene Purcell, mother; Kristin Purcell, sister; Derek Ozawa, best friend.

We had hoped to interview some of Chris' Navy buddies, however, they were not allowed to participate. Thus, a question: are there secrets that we don't know? Before I present the verbatim answers as recorded, I want to mention a travel.

Helene and Mike Purcell live now in Algoma, Wisconsin. It was an old fishing village on the shores of Lake Michigan, a beautiful rural community. On August 26, 2011, I flew to Green Bay, Wisconsin, rented a car, traveled through dairy country and stayed two days in Algoma. Helene and Mike invited me into their home; we did the interviews, we talked, we went to a Friday fish fry, and we shared. I stayed at the Hotel Stebbins, established in 1857. (I had a special Victorian room, with a lake view.) In the evening, I sat in a unique historic bar, watching the Green Bay Packers in a preseason game. There was excitement in the air. On August 27th I walked to the pier, enjoying early morning fishing. It was serene. Later, Helene, Mike, and I went for breakfast at a fishermen's hangout (one can still have breakfast for $3.00). We talked some more. The setting was quite juxtaposed to the reason for being there: Death.

After information identifying Chris, I proceeded with the PA. I have placed my text in italics.

Question 1: Tell me about Chris.
Helene Purcell: Chris was born on December 19, 1986, in Keflavik, Iceland. Mike and I were in the Navy. The birth was a caesarean; there were no complications. However, I had postpartum depression.

What was he like as a baby?
Chris was a good kid; he was sensitive. He was very attached to me. We attempted to get a baby sitter; however, after 6 attempts, she did not want to care for Chris. Chris cried all the time. We were very attached. His death is hard for me. Chris was my heart.
Derek Ozawa: It is hard to say. He was quiet. If you got to know him, he talked. He had to be comfortable. He was a really good kid, super funny.

You were friends?
Like grade 8, I met him. We skateboarded. That was huge then. That is how we met, skateboarding. He moved a lot. He moved to Japan, then San Diego. We visited; I stayed in California. We got close. I remember in the summer, he would come back. He stayed with me and my family. Nothing was really different. It was nice to have a friend like this. Later, he moved back; he moved to the house next door. It was not planned. It was great. Chris did not like high school. He went then to night school. We hung out. We skateboarded.

After graduation, he wanted to go into the Navy. We were surprised. It did not seem like what he would do. He did not like structure, like in school. He was not that kind of person. It was a surprise! Chris went to boot camp and then Maine. We lost touch for a bit. We'd email. He came home, but he was a little bit different.

Different?
He seemed depressed; he seemed to have fallen in a pit. There was something.

Something?
I don't know how to explain it. I recall calling him on his 21st birthday. He never returned the call.

Anything else?
He was drinking. He came here on Thanksgiving; I picked him up. He was drinking. At 11 a.m. he was drinking. He would drink before breakfast. It was weird. He talked about what he was doing. We went to the skate park; but, he did not have his board. I did not know if he was still skating. After that, I did not hear from him.

Question 2: Tell me about the death.
Mike Purcell: The evening that Chris died, I had duty that night [Great Lakes Base, Chicago], from 8 p.m. to 8 a.m. We had eaten, gone for a walk, and were playing cards, when Kristin, our oldest daughter called. She said, "Chris has a gun; he wants to kill himself. He has been drinking." Kristin had called him; they had talked. Therefore, I called his base in Brunswick, Maine. I had told them that my son was suicidal and had a gun. They told me, "We know" and it was "being taken care of."

After the call, I went to work. I thought that I could find out more there. It was a bad night, just waiting. At midnight, the Captain and the Chaplain came in; they said what happened. Chris had killed himself. I had a forewarning.

What I learned from the reports and from people that Chris had been drinking. He was on MySpace. He had a chat about being suicidal. Some were urging him on; some said, "Do it." There was a girl on line; they talked. She called security.

Security arrived; Chris was drunk. They found a gun case and bullets. However, they were supposed to search him but they did not search him. They were there for 45 minutes, the tension escalated. Twelve people had come; there were nine when he died. Someone said, "We need to handcuff him." They did and went outside. They even put him in a head lock. Yet, they did not search him.

Chris wanted to go to the bathroom; they took one handcuff off. There was no security. There should be. A friend went into the bathroom with him. There he pulled out the gun in his waistband and shot himself.

Anything else?
I was upset! They did not follow standard operating procedure. I accept that a suicide; Helene will never get past it. However, I want a proper accounting. They could have done something. Chris did not need to die. They did nothing. They should have taken the gun. That is the biggest issue! I can't change it; maybe for the next Sailor, we can.
Helene Purcell: The night that he died, I was taking care of my mother. Kristin came and said Chris was on the phone. She said that he had a gun. He wanted to kill himself. So I told Mike. I tried to call Chris; he would not answer. I called the Quarter Deck; they said that they knew and said, "We have everything under control." Back then, I was taking care of my mother 24/7. I had no Facebook. I did not text. I did not know.

How did you learn that Chris died?
Mike came home at 1 a.m. with the chaplain and he told me. Mike was on duty at the Great Lakes Base. Chris was in Brunswick, Maine.

What was your reaction?
Shock! Sadness! Confusion! I was confused because they said that they were handling it. I was shocked. They said that he was okay. I was saddened. They said everything was fine. It was shock!
Kristin Purcell: It is so vague. That night, I was on my computer. Someone messaged me on MySpace. I thought that it was Spam; but it was a girl, _____. She said that, "Your brother wants to commit suicide." She got my attention. I then called Chris. We talked. I had no idea that he was suicidal. We were talking for about an hour. I asked if he was okay. He said, "yes." Then the girl messaged me again; she pointed me to a conversation in a chat room. I read it. He said that he had a gun; I had no idea. I would not have hanged up the phone.

When I read the chat on MySpace, I called my boyfriend. We discussed telling my parents, so I talked to them. I would regret if not. So I told them. They contacted the base in Maine. We were in Chicago. Dad contacted base security. My parents and my sister Blair tried to call Chris. I was the last person to talk to him.

What happened next?
Around 1 o'clock, I heard my mother scream. I knew something was not right. There were two men in the living room; one was a chaplain. I had heard the scream and crying; I knew!
Derek Ozawa: His sister called; that is how I learned about his death. I did not get to talk to him.

Were you surprised?
Definitely. It was a shock. A friend had been in that situation; he was a superb help to the friend. He was angry towards the friend. Chris was never suicidal. It was very surprising. He [Chris] said, "Such an idiot." He was always there for the friend and me.

Question 3: Outlining the victim's history.
Mike Purcell: Chris was born in Iceland. There were so many moves. It was my Navy life. Here is where Chris lived: Keflavik, Iceland 1986–1989; Great Lakes, Illinois 1989–1992; Charlotte, North Carolina 1992–1998; Northbrook, Illinois 1998–2000; Sasebo, Japan 2000–2001; San Diego, California 2001–2004; Northbrook, Illinois 2004–2005; Brunswick, Maine 2006–2008.

Chris had problems with the life of a Navy family, the moves. He had problems adjusting to five high schools. He had problems socially. He had friends and then we would have to move. He was not outgoing; he would make one or two friends. For Chris, it was traumatic.

And Helene had a bipolar disorder. As he grew up, Helene would have problems. If she was depressed, it was bad. It was more disruption in the family. There were hospitalizations. It was all hard on the kids. Helene's illness and the moves had a big effect on Chris. In the back of my mind, I never wanted it to be this way. But this is Navy life.
Helene Purcell: One thing about Chris: he did not academically like school. He always struggled. We moved a lot; we left Iceland when Chris was 2. Between 12

to 17, he went to five high schools. It was stressful. In retrospect, Navy life was hard. Chris loved sports, especially baseball and basketball. At 13, he got a skateboard. That was a big thing. He was good. He got a lot of praise.

The Navy life also resulted in problems in socialization. It is hard. At 18, Chris wanted to go into the military. I did not want him to go. However, because all our moves and the lack of jobs, it was a job, so he went into the Navy. It is not easy. I got over that he wanted to join the Navy. He was first at Great Lakes for 6 months, so we got to see him. Then he went to Maine. The separation was difficult.

Anything else about his history?
No, not really. About him being depressed, he never said, "I am depressed." At 15 or 16, I wanted Chris to see a counselor. He had trouble with all the moves. I told him to see a counselor; however, he said no.

Medication?
No. He once saw a psychiatrist and prescribed Adderall. I did not help. When at Great Lakes, he was prescribed Zoloft, but he took it for only one month.

Alcohol abuse?
I never saw it. I never saw him drinking. He did not abuse substances. He started drinking in the Navy; they drink a lot in the Navy. He was clearly having liquor. He drank Jaegermeister and Wild Turkey. They found 20 bottles in his room. We had no idea.

Can you tell me about his siblings?
He had two sisters; Kristin, she is 26; and Blair, she is 19.

How did they react to Chris' death?
Kristin was devastated. She talked. Blair was devastated; however, she never talked about it.

Medical illnesses?
He had a normal medical history; the usual cuts and bruises. Nothing else.

Hospitalizations?
No.

Accidents?
No. Well, with skateboarding, nothing major.

Family?
Navy life is difficult. The moves are very difficult.

Therapy?
No.

Suicide attempts?
No.
Kristin Purcell: Chris always had a hard time adjusting. When he went to Japan, he had problems; he was stuck in the previous place, Illinois. It was really hard for Chris. Letting go was difficult. Yet, for me, I was the exact opposite. I was excited about the moves.

As a brother?
He was a good brother. He was very protecting. He was always looking out for me and Blair.
Derek Ozawa: His parents were in the Navy. I knew it was hard. He never said anything; I asked. He never said anything bad about his father or mother. It was just a Navy family? When I asked, Chris said, "It is the Navy."

Parents?
They are typical. He said, "Oh, my mom is so amazing." There was nothing unusual. I knew his sister.

Friends?
The thing about Chris was skateboarding. Everything was skateboarding. And that is what we did.

Girlfriends?
In grade 8, he hung out with a girl. She was a girlfriend. But later, I knew of no one. No one really.

Did he talk about a girlfriend?
Not much. He didn't talk really.

School?
He graduated from night school. We didn't talk about it. I knew he hated school.

Navy?
Not much. I asked.

Depressed?
Hard to say. Yes, I think that he was a lot of the time.

About what?
About school. If you hate school, and you have to go, it sucks. Chris was not meant to go to school. He would say, "I'm not going anywhere." I tried to tell him, "Bear threw it." But, he was down about it. But he was smart.

Anything else?
Well, Chris came to visit us before his death. When he was leaving, he was upset. He was crying. He would give everyone, my mom and sister, a hug. It was strange; he never cried. He was stone faced. It was weird.

Question 4: Details of victim's family.
Mike Purcell: Helene is bipolar. Other members of her family have similar problems; a sister is depressed, maybe bipolar. But they deny it; that has an effect. And a brother is an alcoholic. My grandfather was an alcoholic.

Any suicides?
No. However, shortly after Chris, another distant relative shot himself.

Did he know about Chris' suicide?
|No.

Illnesses?
Most died of old age. One had cancer.
Helene Purcell: Yes, I'm bipolar. My sister has clinical depression.

Substance abuse?
Alcohol use.

Illness?
My mother died from cancer and a brother died from cancer at 18. However, my family are old school: they don't talk about problems and illness.

Anything else about your family?
I think Chris lacked self-esteem. Who am I? I never realized that he had problems.
Kristin Purcell: Just the moves. The military life was hard for Chris. He longed for Illinois. Oh, substance abuse runs in the family.

Question 5: Description of personality and lifestyle of the victim.
Mike Purcell: As a teen, he was competitive. He would play video games. He would stay up all night. He had friends in the neighborhood. He loved skateboarding. He was a smart person; however, he did not care for school. He was quiet, always respectful, and pleasant. We never had the normal teen issues, like sex or drugs. He was the best of kids. He gave us no issues. No trouble with the law, except once in Japan. He was skateboarding on a railing, so he had to repaint it. He was the best.

Anything about his personality?
He did not like to talk to people. He would keep things inside, bottled-up. Maybe every 6 months or so, he would get emotional and talk about it. However, typically, he kept to himself. He kept stuff to himself.

Anything else?
He was very anti-medicine.
Helene Purcell: Chris had a really good sense of humor. He was always joking. He would make light of things. He was easy going. In hindsight, he was hard to get motivated. He was bright, not academic. But, he was super smart. He loved music.

Music
Anything Van Morrison.

Anything else?|
Just that he loved skateboarding. It calmed him down. However, he stopped when he went into the Navy. It was not acceptable.

Girls?
Chris never dated. He was shy. He had a lot of female friends; one was special. It was hard for him.
Kristin Purcell: As he grew up, he was very active in sports; especially baseball and basketball. He loved skateboarding. It was his thing. But the Navy stopped the skateboarding. He was less active. In the Navy, Chris was drinking. He started smoking cigarettes.

How much?
|About a half pack per day. Not before, maybe to control his weight.
Derek Ozawa: Chris was closed off, if he did not know you. However, if he knew you and trusted you, he would be open, but not pour his heart out. Other than that, he was a rebellious kid. He got in trouble at school. He got detentions. He had a really cool personality.

Lifestyle?
Skateboarding was number 1. He was competitive at it. I would say, "Man, no more competitiveness." He did not go out much, unless skateboarding. It bummed me out that he stopped skateboarding. He stopped doing that.

Question 6: Victim's typical pattern of reaction to stress.
Mike Purcell: He was a lot like me, on even keel. He would see the other side of a thing. Not overreact. Not freak out. He would accept the stress. Analyze it. And do it.
Helene Purcell: Chris would get angry. He would have little bouts of anger. He would yell. Sometimes he would sit and play video games. I think the main stress was the moves. He was afraid. He kept a lot in.

Anything else stressful?
The moves. New situations were stressful, like a new school all the time. For example, he never knew Japanese people, and then suddenly he was in Japan. It was difficult. He was not prejudiced; it was a new situation. That is why I did not want him in the Navy.
Kristin Purcell: Chris was very emotional. Small things could send him off. He would close up and cry.

Sometimes?
Yes, very sensitive.

Drink?
After he joined the Navy. I would say the Navy was stressful.
Derek Ozawa: It seemed that he didn't talk about it. He would get frustrated, but not that stressed. He would brush stress off. If things bugged him, he brushed it off. He would not stew; he would skateboard or go for a walk.

Question 7: Any recent upsets, pressures?
Mike Purcell: Yes, one of the things that started his downward spiral was while I was in Baghdad. It started the alcohol abuse. He grew close to a girl, Sue. She had been married and was separated. He was close to her. Chris wanted to move the relationship forward; she just wanted to be friends. Then, a friend, also a hospital corpsman, who had been in Iraq, returned. He started a relationship with Sue. Chris was very upset; he said, "Fuck it." Then he started drinking more. That got him into trouble. One time, while off duty, he arrived at the clinic drunk. He was arrested and had to go to an alcohol rehabilitation program.

In November, the doctor diagnosed Chris with borderline personality disorder. That really upset him. Chris was prescribed medication. Then another medication. Chris graduated from the program, the day that he turned 21. But he started drinking again.

On December 19, a few weeks later, he bought a gun. He continued to drink. Sue continued to reject him. He was charged for drinking. He had to go in front of the Discipline Review Board. He was disgraced and upset. But that is the routine of the review board. He felt pressure and was upset and overwhelmed.

Do you think that having to go in front of the review board traumatized him?
Yes.
Helene Purcell: Yes, he said his friend, Sue, had a new boyfriend. She just got divorced. He said that, "I love her." She had a daughter and he loved her daughter too. I did not realize that he was in love. She rejected him. She said she did not

know. He wanted a family. He said, "I lost my dream." Sue was his best friend. She started dating someone else. They were sneaky. He was very devastated. It was a huge loss. It was very important. That was the upset.

Kristin Purcell: From what I gather, he was close to a girl, Sue. He and Sue were best friends. He was more interested, not her. That was big. That led to the suicide. It was a loss!

Anything else in the last 12 months?
No. I did not know Sue. We talked a little on MySpace. Chris and I, when he joined the Navy in 2005, did not talk so much. When he joined MySpace, the last 6 months, we talked more. Sue was the loss!

Derek Ozawa: Chris was more comfortable here. The Navy was stressful for him. It was again moves in the Navy. The Navy was stressful.

Any recent upsets?
His mom talked about this girl, but he did not say anything to me. What I know is that the last Thanksgiving, he was drinking, a lot and early. He was also smoking cigarettes.

Question 8: Role of alcohol or drugs.
Mike Purcell: Yes.

What about guns?
Ever since Chris was young, we had guns. I had to shoot guns. They were in the house. We would go to the shooting range. We did in November, when we last saw Chris. We always had guns.

Helene Purcell: Yes, he also started smoking cigarettes. He started drinking in the Navy, not before.

Guns?
We always had guns. We were in the Navy. We did not think anything was wrong.

Kristin Purcell: Yes, but I did not know too much about Chris. After, I learned. (*Guns?*) We always had guns in the house.

Derek Ozawa: Chris used to be a social drinker; we would have a drink. When he last visited, he was abusing alcohol.

Prescription drugs?
No.

Drugs?
No.

Guns?
I never talked about it.

Question 9 (a). Nature of interpersonal relationships.
Mike Purcell: He had a very close friend, Derek. He seemed to make close friends. There was Sue. However, she didn't see it as boyfriend-girlfriend. [We then discussed borderline personality disorder. We discussed, what does it mean? I discussed the DSM definition. "Can they have friends?" Mike asked.]

Helene Purcell: Chris had a few friends. Derek for years. And Sue. He shared music. Laughed. Was funny. However, he was a deep person.

Derek Ozawa: He had a few friends. He had my family. We had skateboarding, but that goes only so far.

Question 9 (b). Nature of ego (Can you give me three adjectives to describe Chris?)
Mike Purcell: Intelligent. Impatient. Empathic.
Helene Purcell: Funny. Kind. Sweet.
Kristin Purcell: Introspective. Emotional. Loyal.
Derek Ozawa: Quiet, Caring as a friend. Felt comfortable with us—within the circle.

Question 10: Fantasies, dreams, thoughts . . .
Mike Purcell: He wanted to be a skateboard pro. He was very good, but not at a pro level. After high school, he said that he wanted to be a fireman. I said, "Great." I took him to a fire station. They showed him around, and he learned that he had to take a college course. Somehow he got sidetracked and decided to join the Navy. He went there to get trained. So he decided to join. That was part of the plan; he could get the college course. That was his goal.

Death or suicide?
He liked odd music. He liked *Donnie Darko* and *Jacob's Ladder*.

His friend's suicide attempt?
He didn't discuss it. He could not believe it. He was already in the Navy; he was not there. He said that he could not believe it. It was over a girl problem. He said, "Why would he?"
Helene Purcell: Dreams? He always wanted to move on his own. He wanted to get an apartment. He had a motorcycle and he wanted to get a car. Finally, he got the money, and wanted to buy a car. He wanted to take care of himself. Be an adult. Be in the Navy. He wanted to be a firefighter. But we didn't discuss it much.

Death or suicide?
Chris thought suicide was not a big deal. He saw a movie, *Donnie Darko*. It is about suicide. I could not watch it. He thought suicide was normal. I believe Chris did not want to die. He wanted help. That is why he called. He wanted the relationship with Sue.

His friend's suicide attempt?
He said that he believed that his friend swallowed pills over a girlfriend. He said, "That is so dumb.. He did not get it. So what happened at 21? Why?
Kristin Purcell: He wanted to be a firefighter or EMT. After the Navy, that is what he planned.

Death?
No.

Suicide?
Not at all, only his friend's suicide attempt. We talked about it. He brushed it off.

Relationship?
Yes.
Derek Ozawa: Not really. I remember before the Navy, he wanted to be a fireman. And, dreams of skateboarding.

Question 11: Changes in the victim before death.
Mike Purcell: The alcohol abuse. It started about 6 months to a year before his death. He was sad!

Helene Purcell: Chris died January 27, 2008. He came here in November, on November 23, 2007, for Thanksgiving. He was unusually quiet. I was then taking care of my mother. However, we talked. I looked at him; he was just lying, looking into space. I asked if he was okay. He said, "Yes, I'm fine." However, he was very quiet. He looked sad. I asked, but I should have said more. You ask, but you don't know.

Alcohol use?
No. He had said in November that he had been drunk and trashed a room. I asked; he said, "I don't remember." Chris was sensitive. He needed protection. He was my buddy.

Kristin Purcell: I was not aware. After, I learned that he was not able to sleep. He had insomnia. He had been excessively drinking and smoking. I didn't know.

Derek Ozawa: The drinking at Thanksgiving. That is it. When he came to visit, he was not the same. He was like defeated. It was weird.

Question 12: Information relating to life-style of victim.
Mike Purcell: He planned to be a fireman.

Anything else?
He tried to take care of himself before. He was a vegan. He exercised. He did good stuff. He tried to stop smoking.

Helene Purcell: Success. He was really proud about his skateboarding. He was proud.
Navy?
Yes, he had told Kristin that he enjoyed the Navy. He felt good about the Navy. He never said otherwise.

Kristin Purcell: He had been chosen to be on the President Bush team. When President Bush was in Maine in 2007, he was chosen to be one of the people to protect him; as EMT. It was a high honor. There were only 14 or 15 or so. He was one!

Derek Ozawa: When he first went to boot camp, he said it was amazing. He was going to be like his dad. He was in the Navy.

Anything else?
The skateboarding.

Question 13: Assessment of intentions.
Mike Purcell: I think that he wanted help. The night that he killed himself, if the right people were there, if they did the right thing, he would be alive. But that night, he planned to do it. He was on MySpace; he wanted help. He wanted to be rescued.

Helene Purcell: Did he want to die? No. He called people; he wanted help. He was going to be disciplined. That was stressful. He was going to the military board. It is a big deal.
Was he aware of such consequences with the board? Someone told him. He was really worried about it. Stressed. It was the last straw. Plus, he had money problems. He had a car, motorcycle, and cell. He never said anything about selling his motorcycle. And Sue. He tried to talk to people; no one listened.

Kristin Purcell: No. He was pushed into a corner.

Who?
The people who were there. The 7 or 9 people in the room. The military police.

Derek Ozawa: I think it was a suicide. Chris kept things to himself. He bottled things up. He needed help.

A cry for help?
He talked to someone on line. He wrote a note. He had asked me on his last visit, "Why do I have to feel like this all the time?"

Question 14: Lethality
Mike Purcell: The gun.
Helene Purcell: He used a gun.
Derek Ozawa: He used a gun, but he did not want to die.

Question 15: Reaction to information of death.
Mike Purcell: I was dumbfounded. How did it happen? They said he died by suicide. We were mesmerized. It was in the newspaper that things were not done right.
Helene Purcell: I want to talk about it. I need to talk. There is such stigma.
Kristin Purcell: Shocked. Devastated. If I had known, I would have done something. It is traumatizing.
Derek Ozawa: First, it was unreal. I was unreal. Shock!

WHY DID CHRIS DO IT?

Like all suicides, and military (or police) suicides are no different, Chris's suicide is complex (Leenaars, 2013). It is a myth, for example, that suicides are due to psychopathology alone, although many (not all) have an inability to adjust—a psychopathological impairment and disability (WHO definition). Suicide is a multidetermined event. This was true for Chris. There are, as you have read, many reasons for Chris' death. It was not simple. One has to take the ecological perspective. I will next explain some core individual, interpersonal, community, and societal factors to his death—some causes. I will discuss the following: The military family and culture, some quantitative factors or characteristics in young adulthood, a comment on Chris' lethal cognitive style, and an assessment of his psychopathology. Afterwards I will turn to the question of why did Chris die at that time, followed by some opinions and a theory of Hospital Corpsman Chris Purcell's suicide. I will end with a concluding thought—actually a survivors'.

THE MILITARY FAMILY AND CULTURE

There is no doubt in my mind; Chris' Navy family was stressful. For Chris, it was traumatic; he says so in his autobiography as a teen. It is probable that he even suffered from PTSD because of the nature and culture of Navy life. In my book, *Suicide Among the Armed Forces* (2013), I highlighted this often overlooked reality; I discussed Lynn Hall's most insightful exegesis (2011). I offer here some thoughts about Chris and his Navy family.

One often perceives families in terms of strengths and weaknesses (Everson & Camp, 2011). Families foster well-being; this is especially demanding for military families. They have to be more resilient than families in the general population. It is simply a fact that they are exposed to and experience more trauma than the average family; it is a family under fire (Everson & Figley, 2011). Like in the general population, of course, some military families are more vulnerable than others. Some family members are more vulnerable. Military families can be vulnerable due to both internal factors (e.g., history of mental health disorder, alcohol abuse, dysfunctional structure), and external factors (e.g., frequent moves, spouse working outside of the home, lower median income, high percentage of divorces). There are endless lists. However, the top three current military at-risk factors (Everson & Camp, 2011) are frequent relocation, previous long-term deployment, and longer separations during combat-related deployment. There is no question that these three traumas were true for Chris. He did not cope well with the Navy lifestyle. It disabled him. I truly believe that he suffered from PTSD. It is a fact in "why Chris died by suicide." The data speak for themselves; just listen to the words of his family and friend. Chris was under fire.

Mike and Helene Purcell attempted to provide a resilient family; however, as R. Blaine Everson and Thomas Camp (2011) note,

> There are limits to which any family system can be taxed emotionally, and any given family's ability to adjust to change and adapt to its circumstances is crucial to the idea of resilience. . . . Inadequate adaptations rendering a family more helpless in the face of adversity and the presence of new stressor events may also lead to increased vulnerability as result of a phenomenon known as "pile-up" (McCubbin, Thompson & McCubbin, 2001). The continued presence of unresolved demands (i.e., pile-up) eventually leads to emotional exhaustion under the tenets of disorders or psychosomatic physical maladies in some family members. (p. 16)

There was secondary traumatization; Chris suffered almost all his life, so I believe. There is so much to his mental pain.

As Hall (2011) noted, it is paramount that the readers understand the military worldview or mindset. This is so for the children. One must take a system or ecological view to understand Chris' death. Military families are more frequently rendered hopeless and helpless by stressors and vulnerabilities (Everson & Figley, 2011; WHO, 2002). That is secondary traumatization. Further, each branch of the military presents its own unique "friction." This is so in the Navy! The Navy culture was a factor (cause) in Chris' suicide. As Hall (2011) argued, unless you understand this fact, you will never understand a suicide in the military (and this is similar to a police suicide, such as Kelly Johnson's), and thus, it is essential consideration in your forensic (DSI) investigation.

There is one more military system cause: Chris joined the Navy. In all probability, Chris identified with the heritage of a Navy life. He wanted to be like his father (identification). He wanted his father and mother to be proud of him. This is not to negate the fact that Chris saw the Navy as a job and as a way to get education; however, I believe that the deep attachment was more central to his choice. He wanted his family to be proud. It was an honor to serve.

The Navy satisfied Chris' needs; at the very least: attachment. Chris wanted to get away from what he experienced growing up, his anxiety, his moods, his pain. He wanted to flee from "a need for dependence" (Hall, 2011). However, Chris could not escape from his intrapsychic pain, what I believe was accurately diagnosed at the end as Mood Disorder, NOS. There was a precursor, I believe, to a diagnosis of manic-depressive (bipolar) disorder. The attempts to flee his problems, however, did not end the problems. The Navy was not a solution; it became a deeper unbearable pain. There was shame and disgrace.

The military has walls—green walls (Leenaars, 2013; Scurfield & Platoni, 2013). This was true for Chris; just listen to the words of his survivors. This is one reason why death investigations are an uncovering of the forensic unknowns. Chris kept things inside. He kept secrets. He lied. Further, the Navy heritage put Chris in a double bind. As Hall (2011) pointed out, military personnel are restricted (at least perceived so) from seeking counseling. They are then also admonished by their chain of command from seeking help. Chris feared his commanders. It is the way of the green culture. Military families foster secrecy, stoicism, and denial (Leenaars, 2013). They do so automatically, not willingly. It is what a soldier and his/her family do. It is expected in the collective culture. This may have dire consequences, and one is suicide. Hall (2011) noted,

> Instead of providing a supportive, nurturing, reality-based mirror, the parents may present a mirror that only reflects their needs, resulting in children who grow up feeling defective. "When one is raised unable to trust in the stability, safety, and equity of one's world, one is raised to distrust one's own feeling perceptions, and worth" (Donaldson-Pressman & Pressman, 1994, p. 18). (p. 47)

This is military life. This has to change. This is the very aim of Mike, Helene, Kristin, and Derek sharing their story. There is a community and societal factor to *all* suicides.

Furthermore, there was the alcohol abuse. There is a last straw incident at the clinic. He was charged. There was a military disciplinary issue, a common factor in military suicide. That was traumatic. It was more shame and disgrace.

There is a further military cause: Chris was to present himself to the Discipline Review Board. Being in a Navy family, Chris knew what that meant. It was a trauma, a Navy humiliation. It was dishonor. As Mike Purcell stated, "He was disgraced and upset." This was *a* cause. Indeed, there is no question that there were multiple Navy causes.

To conclude this discussion of *a* cause, I want you to reflect on what Emile Durkheim (1897/1951) wrote over 100 years ago:

> When he puts on his uniform, the soldier does not become a completely new man; the effects of his education and of his previous life do not disappear as if by magic; and he is also not so separated from the rest of society as not to share in the common life. The suicide he commits may therefore sometimes be civilian in its character and causes. But with the exception of these scattered cases, showing no connections with one another, a compact, homogeneous group remains, including most suicides which occur in the army and which depend on this state of altruism without which military spirit is inconceivable. This is the

suicide of lower societies, in survival among us because military morality itself is in certain aspects a survival of primitive morality. Influenced by this predisposition, the soldier kills himself at the least disappointment, for the most futile reasons, for a refusal of leave, a reprimand, an unjust punishment, a delay in promotion, a question of honor, a flush of momentary jealousy or even simply because other suicides have occurred before his eyes or to his knowledge. Such is really the source of these phenomena of contagion often observed in armies, specimens of which we have mentioned earlier. They are inexplicable if suicide depends essentially on individual causes. It cannot be chance which caused the appearance in precisely this regiment or that locality of so many persons predisposed to self-homicide by their organic constitution. It is still more inadmissible that such a spread of imitative action could take place utterly without predisposition. But everything is readily explained when it is recognized that the profession of a soldier develops a moral constitution powerfully predisposing man to make away with himself. For this constitution naturally occurs, in varying degrees, among most of those who live or who have lived under the colors, and as this is an eminently favorable soil for suicides, little is needed to actualize the tendency to self-destruction which it contains; an example is enough. So it spreads like a trail of gunpowder among persons thus prepared to follow it. (pp. 238–239)

This was true for Chris; Durkheim knew it. It is important for you to be knowledgeable.

YOUNG ADULT SUICIDES ARE PSYCHOLOGICALLY DIFFERENT FROM THOSE OF OLDER PEOPLE

As I stated, a suicide note is the penultimate act. It is the unsolicited production of the suicidal person, usually written minutes before the suicidal death. They are an invaluable starting point for comprehending the suicidal act and for understanding the clues and patterns about people who actually commit suicide (Leenaars, 1988; Shneidman & Farberow, 1957). This is true for Chris.

Like Shneidman and Farberow (1957), my core belief is that a theoretical-conceptual analysis offers the richest contribution in suicide note analysis. I presented an outline for such interpretation, with significant construct validity, in Chapter 1; thus, I will not repeat it here. Essentially, from around the world and decades of study, I presented a psychological theory, with both intrapsychic factors/clusters and interpersonal clusters. They allow us to understand Chris's death better. It allows you to see! And perhaps to *know* for the first time!

The first controlled study of suicide notes indicated that the dynamics or reaction patterns vary with critical demographic variables, notably age (Shneidman & Farberow, 1957). In Chapter 1, I discussed this problem of various definitions of young, old, and the like, and proposed an evidence-based scheme. The three groups with characteristics and age ranges, are Young Adulthood (Intimacy vs. Isolation, age 18–25); Middle Adulthood (Generativity vs. Stagnation, 25–55); and Late Adulthood (Integrity vs. Despair, 55 and up). In this case, we can ask the following question: Are young adults', like Chris Purcell's, suicide notes and, by implication, suicide psychologically different from other adults? This question is important in light of the fact that most soldiers are in young adulthood.

SUICIDE NOTES OF YOUNG ADULTS: THE NOMOTHETIC FINDINGS

My research suggested that it is the age group from 18 to 25 that is most different from other adults in their suicide notes and, by implication, suicide (Leenaars, 1989a & b). Young adults differ from other adults on several essential patterns. This observation is one of more or less, not presence or absence since these patterns occur across the life span. It is simply a matter of degree. It is a continuum; at some point, it is a significant quantitative difference, not qualitative difference. Suicide is suicide. The following observations have been made:

THE INTRAPSYCHIC DRAMA

Indirect Expressions

Complications, ambivalence, redirected aggression, unconscious implications, and other indirect communications (or behavior) are often evident in suicide. There is dissembling; Chris did ("I have suffered in *silence* most of my life" [italics mine]. The person may even confuse what is real and not real, objective and subjective, and such ("It is all meaningless"). The observation of unconscious implications is especially important here. Of note, what was Chris consciously aware of? This is an important phenomenon in suicide—repression, denial, secrecy and so on; that is, unconscious dynamics (e.g., wishes, beliefs) may well be the driving force for an individual who defines an issue for which suicide is perceived as the best solution. Such characteristics are more evident in the suicide notes and, by implication, suicide of young (and middle) adults than late adults. Very often these adults are confused and likely unaware of significant causes that lead to their death. This is true for Chris, I believe.

Inability to Adjust/Psychopathology

Although many suicides may not fit *best* into any specific nosological classification; depression, the "down phase" of manic-depressive (bipolar) disorders, anxiety disorders, PTSD, and other disorders have been related to some suicides. All these disorders can be seen to reflect a maladjustment; the suicidal person himself or herself states in the note that he (she) is unable to adjust. Chris did. Even more than other adults, young adults are diagnosed as exhibiting a disorder; this is because psychopathology begins to crystallize at this stage of life. Considering themselves too weak to function effectively, young adults, more than other adults, reject everything except death—they do not survive *life's* difficulties. Chris could not ("It is just all meaningless"; "I don't want to suffer anymore").

Vulnerable Ego

A consistency in suicide is with lifelong coping patterns ("I've always felt this way"). Like other people, soldiers have enormous consistency in their ego, even during life's timelines. This was evident in Chris at a very early age. The suicidal person consistently does not function effectively ("I just can't go on anymore"). This is especially true of young adults; young adults (compared to middle and late adults) more frequently exhibit in their suicide note a relative weakness in their capacity to develop constructive tendencies (i.e., attachment, love) and to overcome their personal difficulties. Their ego has been weakened by a steady toll of traumas (dose response). This was true for Chris ("I just can't go on anymore").

Identification-Egression

Intense identification (or bond) to a lost or rejecting person or to any ideal (e.g., being in the Navy) is critical in understanding the suicidal person. If this emotional need is not met, the suicidal person experiences a deep discomfort (pain); he is estranged ("never suffer alone"); and he or she wants to be gone, to be elsewhere, to exit—to egress. Such a process is more evident in young adulthood than late adulthood and is clearly related to the crisis of intimacy vs. isolation. It was for Chris ("I'm not escaping any problem, im not running from anything. I'm saving me from me").

INTERPERSONAL STAGE

Interpersonal Relations

The suicidal person across the life span has problems in establishing or maintaining relationships (although it may be to another ideal, the Navy). The suicide is often related to unsatisfied or frustrated affiliation (attachment) needs. Even more than other adults, young adults frequently describe a disturbed, unbearable interpersonal situation in their suicide notes. Ideographically, this is abundantly true for Chris. Minimally, the following needs were frustrated: attachment, abasement, autonomy, harmavoidance, and infavoidance.

It is especially the pain of isolation (i.e., Erikson's crisis of *Intimacy vs. Isolation*) in these young adults, like Chris, that is critical in understanding their suicide. Erikson stated,

> Where a youth does not accomplish such intimate relationships with others— and I would add, with his own inner resources—in late adolescence or early adulthood, he may settle for highly stereotyped relations and come to retain a deep sense of isolation. (1968, p. 138)

What is critical during young adulthood is that these adults develop intimacy, attachment, affiliation, and partnership. One typically develops mutuality with a love partner, although the military sometimes offers a family. The psychosocial strength or virtue or protective factor in young adults is love. It is "mutuality of devotion" that allows young adults, according to Erikson, the increased capacity to function (or adjust) effectively. Without intimacy, one becomes isolated and unable to establish or maintain relationships. In the military, the soldier becomes cut off or disenfranchised. The individual, however, might not only turn away from others, but may turn his/her anger to whatever approaches (Frager & Fadiman, 1984). Indeed, it appears that some young adults (and that includes Chris) may not just settle for a deep sense of isolation but choose death as a permanent solution (identity) to their unbearable interpersonal pain. Chris died because of loss! *"Goodbye life, I have lost all interest in you."*

What is unique in young adults generally was true for Chris as a unique person. His life and suicide mirrored the lives of many young adults. Chris was not that unique; indeed, he is prototypical of suicides in such young heroes.

A DEVELOPMENTAL VIEW OF YOUNG ADULTS' SUICIDES

When one is attempting to understand the suicide of adults, age (time line) is a significant variable to be accounted for, as already noted in Chapter 1. The suicide notes and, by implication, suicides of young adults *are* psychologically quantitatively different from other adults. This is true for our soldiers. There appear to be highly perturbed levels on such psychological issues as "I love you," "I am caving in," "I want to be gone," "I am weakened," and "This is the only thing I can do." Chris simply wrote, "It is just all meaningless."

A life-span developmental perspective is essential in understanding suicidal people. I believe that many of my findings apply to Chris; I believe, Chris died by suicide, and the nomothetic findings help us to understand the why. The idiographic is no different. My current formulation about young adults should not be construed to mean that development is simply discontinuous—development across the life span is both discontinuous and continuous (Piaget, 1970). Adult development is dynamic, ongoing, *and* serial. The suicidal person does not respond anew to each crisis (with a small "c") in his/her adult life, but his/her reactions are consistent in many ways with that individual's previous reaction to loss, threat, impotence, and such. There is an elliptical nature to his/her development (Leenaars, 2004) as well as change. This was Heraclitus' view, thousands of years ago. This was true for Chris. My point here is simply that, within the adult life span, young adults' suicides, like Chris', were quantitatively, not qualitatively (commonalities), different from other adults, despite enormous commonalities across the life span. We need to understand each soldier uniquely and generally.

A COMMENT ON CHRIS' COGNITIVE STYLE

The cognitive style of the suicidal person is unique and lethal. I earlier offered on the topic a comment. What were Chris' major premises (core beliefs)? Why his "therefore"? Based on the PA, we can at least speculate on his cognitive style. He was perturbed. Overpowering emotions intoxicated him. He was drunk! Concurrently, there were constricted logic and core beliefs. His logic can be symbolized by the following:

> All people rejected by the girl whom they loved ought to be dead
> I was rejected by Sue
> Therefore, I ought to be dead.
> Or,
> All disgraced sailors ought to be dead
> I feel shame and disgrace
> Therefore, I ought to be dead.
> Or "All soldiers with a military disciplinary issue and are to go before military court ought to be dead."
> Or "All people with a fucking life ought to be dead."
> Or "All people looking hideous ought to be dead."

He was putting a lot of things into a nutshell. His "therefores" were lethal.

Assessment of Psychopathology

I have never assessed Chris Purcell, therefore, I cannot provide a diagnosis. Based on the above data/evidence, however, I can speculate a likely diagnosis of a mental disorder for Chris Purcell, with numerous cautions about postdiction of emotional disturbances. There were, however, clinical records, including DSM diagnoses. Chris was assessed as depressed and at risk for suicide by age 14. Despite a need for an ecological perspective of violence (WHO, 2002), the worldview of an inability to adjust/psychopathology of individuals who died by suicide is important. The percentage of mental disorders in young adults who die by suicide is very high. This is true for military suicide especially, given the very above-the-norm and increasing rate for suicide in soldiers. Yet it does not adequately explain the death. Suicide is complex; mental illness is only a factor, not *the* factor. There *never* is. With this preamble, the question raised is Did Chris have a mental disorder?

Based on the DSM-IV criteria (American Psychiatric Association, 1994), my best evaluation is as follows:

Axis I	Posttraumatic Stress Disorder, Chronic
	Mood Disorder NOS
	Alcohol Abuse
	Adjustment Disorder, With Anxiety, Acute
Axis II	NIL
Axis III	The first digit on right hand
Axis IV	Relational Problem NOS
	Occupational Problem
	Acculturation Problem
	Phase of Life Problem
	Other psychosocial and environmental
GAF	= 10.

Some may read this as overly "psychiatric"; however, some others would say, "That makes sense." I am only offering some understanding, keeping in mind that there are different points of view. Many people who die by suicide have a mental disorder. We have to get past the stigma of psychopathology.

Based on the interviews conducted for this PA, we know that Chris had significant problems in adjusting to traumatic events as a child and as an adolescent. Navy life, especially the frequent moves, made it so. This raised concerns about PTSD. He showed symptoms of avoidance, dissembling, and so on. There were persistent symptoms of difficulty adjusting, including the following: sleep disturbance, irritability, and even outbursts of anger; difficulty concentrating; hypervigilance; and anxiety. He was anxious throughout his life and was very anxious toward the end of his life. Thus, I believe that he had posttraumatic stress disorder (PTSD), complex or otherwise, chronic and longstanding. I do know that a great deal of trauma(s) occurred when he was young. It did at age 14. He said so. I know that he was acting out early as a young teenager, especially at school. Moreover, he likely then already dissembled (e.g. avoidance, numbing, lying). He was secretive. As a young adult, he felt unbearably rejected by the one girl who he had hoped loved him: Sue. The loss was the final straw. There was probably more trauma; psychological autopsies answer some questions, but not all. We will never know 100% of the barren bones. This is true in almost all suicides.

Chris had anxiety and worry. It must have become unbearable; he could not continue that way. He was restless, irritable, and had sleep disturbance. He like his counselor, identified anxiety, and his family and friends did in the end. His despair raged, especially in the last days of his life. He was highly perturbed.

Chris was depressed; overall he had a mood disorder; his psychologist diagnosed such. After the loss of Sue, there is a depressed mood and anxiety. I would suggest a Mood Disorder, NOS would be most accurate. However, I would predict that a manic-depressive disorder, or if you prefer the term (I do not) bipolar disorder would over time have been diagnosed. (There are construct validity issues, among other real problems, even in the current DSM-V, I believe). It is a developing disorder, and children to young adults' symptoms are not entirely consistent with a clear DSM diagnosis. Chris had a mood disorder; this was evident after the loss of Sue. Chris had such symptoms as insomnia, low self-esteem, irritability, mood fluctuations, and feelings of hopelessness and helplessness. The mood symptoms caused clinically significant distress in relationships and community levels. *It did in the Navy.*

Yet, I think Chris also had an adjustment disorder, with anxiety and possibly depressive symptoms. This inability to adjust is associated to the development of emotional and behavioral symptoms in response to an identifiable stressor; this began possibly with anxiety and depression after the loss of Sue and was quickly followed by alcohol abuse. However, the most proximal identifiable stress was the alcohol abuse charge and the pending Military Review Board hearing. The nomothetic literature discussed in this book is entirely consistent with this belief. Of course, there were historical traumas, ever-increasing traumas. The symptoms were clinically significant, based on the family doctor's and the counselor of LEAC's notes and the reports of the informants. There was marked distress beyond what would be expected, including in the Navy culture, from exposure. There was impairment. The distress was not only due to bereavement, although that too was present, unresolved, and complex (his grandmother). There was a lot of unbearable pain, the common stimuli for suicide.

Chris Purcell abused alcohol; he was reported to be drinking 1 to 2 bottles of hard liquor per day. There was, like in so many military suicides, a maladaptive pattern of alcohol use. There was continual use in the end. He had an alcohol level well above the well-known level of intoxication of 20 mg/dL (On a different measure, a breathalyzer, the U.S. legal limit is 0.08 blood alcohol level [In Canada, 0.05]). The toxicological examination by Dr. P. reported the following item/result for Chris Purcell's level of ethanol in blood; "140" mg/dL (Vitreous fluids was 180!). Chris was highly intoxicated (7x the level) at the time of his death. (Could he be judged not responsible for his suicide at that moment, due to reason of insanity, due to intoxication? Could he be responsible in intent? What would Dr. Litman say about "intention" in this case?) The alcohol abuse started after he went to Maine and after the loss of Sue. The alcohol abuse was a regression; yet, in the end, even the bottle did not numb his pain. He wanted to escape; he wanted to die by suicide.

Now for the controversial; I do not believe that Chris had borderline personality traits; he did *not* have sufficient traits to warrant a diagnosis of the disorder (BPD). Chris functioned well; yet, after the loss of Sue, Chris regressed. His ego weakened. There was a narcissistic injury(ies). He became estranged. He never recovered. The acting-out/alcohol abuse began and forever increased. His fragile ego broke.

Chris had beliefs that deviated markedly from the expectations of his green (military) culture. It led clinically to significant distress and he, as the events revealed, could not adjust. All was colorless and unattractive. Chris was paralyzed. It is easy to trace it back to trauma in his early life in a Navy family.

However, this is not equal to a borderline personality disorder. BPD is a pervasive pattern of instability of interpersonal relationships, self-image and affect, and marked impulsivity by early adulthood. This is not true for Chris. Yet he believed that he was diagnosed with BPD; there is no question about this fact. He told, as you read in the interviews, his parents. However, and this is a key, Chris was never diagnosed with BPD; an adjustment disorder, yes. Chris sometimes jumped to conclusions and held a disabling belief. He was aware of the meaning of the diagnosis and as I noted before, he was aware of the military's deliberate and intentional use (abuse) of the diagnoses (see Leenaars, 2013). He faced the loss of his Navy career and his honor. However, as I have, Mike Purcell went through the documents—there was no evidence of BPD. Chris held a lethal belief, and it added to his demise. The question remains, did someone tell him he did? It was a practice in the military.

Chris had multiple psychosocial and environmental problems; the main ones were Relational Problem, NOS; Occupational Problem; Acculturation Problem; and Phase of Life Problem. The first two are obvious. Acculturation Problem involving adjustment to a different culture (e.g., the green culture). The Phase of Life Problem is associated with a particular developmental phase or life circumstance, such as entering the Navy. Finally, one of the most lethal problems was Noncompliance with Treatment. This category is used when a key focus is noncompliance with important aspects of treatment for his reported emotional disturbances. Chris did not comply with his medical doctor's prescription for medication, such as Zoloft. The reasons may be his belief about medication (e.g., medication side effects), but not only. Chris also did not comply with his counselor. (This is not uncommon with suicidal patients).

The GAF is a global assessment of functioning. Chris Purcell had received a GAF of 55–60, which is consistent with serious impairment. However, a score of 10 is warranted in cases of persistent probability of severely hurting self; Chris killed himself.

Thus, it is easy to discern that Chris suffered so. It was multidetermined and complex; however, psychopathology, some longstanding, was an element in his demise. Indeed, Chris' problems are highly consistent with what we see in the military, whether trauma or suicide (Leenaars, 2013).

HOW DID CHRIS DIE?

"How did Chris die, and when; that is, why at that particular time?" The answer to that question is even easier than the basic one, "What is the most probable mode of death?" *The gun, stupid.* With absolute certainty, the availability of the gun is why Chris killed himself that day, hour, moment, and second. It is predictable. You do not have to be an expert on gun control, like me (at least the WHO [2006] classifies me as a gun control expert), to know that obvious fact. Chris had a gun. Furthermore, if you know the research on means restriction, you see it is evidence-based (WHO, 2014). Gun control works! Mike, Helene, Kristin, and Derek know that.

A basic in SOP intervention: Get the gun! You always have to get the gun. It is difficult in harm's way, but that is why the experts in the battlefield (Bryan, Kanzler, Durham, West, & Greene, 2010) say, "Evacuate." You remove the gun; it is the most effective tactic, environmental control. It works. In the military, you always get the soldier, like Chris, out of harm's way.

I next offer my opinion on *"how"*! Care for the suicidal person should be reasonable and prudent (Leenaars, 2004; Leenaars, Cantor et al., 2000a, 2000b, 2002). What is reasonable and prudent, including in the military (or police service)? The community defines the standard. The writings of Thomas Gutheil (e.g., 1992), one of the most prolific authors on this topic, espouses the community-based perspective. He too takes an ecological view. Gutheil (1992; Gutheil, Bursztajn, Hamm, & Brodsky, 1983) described the elements in more detail in terms of community, jail, hospital, clinic, EMT, police, and health practitioner standards. The community standard refers to what reasonable practitioners similarly qualified would have done. This should be no different in the military. This is the standard for my opinion in this case.

Responsibility for the care is the health professional and in the current setting, the intervention, and most specifically, the health staff. This includes EMT, fire department personnel, police, and other specialized military personnel—all the way to the general and Secretary of Defense (or Minister of Defence in Canada). The basic guide is reasonable and prudent care. Military standards support this principle. Robert Litman (1988, 1994) and Bruce Bongar (1991; Bongar & Greaney, 1994) have written extensively on the topic.

Litman (1994), for example, offers the hospital setting as a prime example of care. Patients in hospitals have a right to receive "reasonable care"; this is true in a military facility. Once more, the prevailing standard in the community should be our guide and the standard, including that of the Navy's applies. Indeed, the military's policy and procedure state so.

The primary responsibility for care, however, is with the primary caregivers; this is true in a military facility. This means the medical doctor, psychiatrist, psychologist, nurse, social worker, and so on are the caregivers, depending on the resources available. In this case, this belonged to the responders and the Navy.

The United Nations Working Group on the Principles for the Protection of Persons with Mental Illness and for the Improvement of Mental Health Care (UN, 1991) has also offered some basic principles. The soldier has rights. Chris had rights. Its first principle on basic rights, the UN, has as its second clause: "2. All persons with mental illness, or who are being treated as such persons, shall be treated with humanity and respect for the inherent dignity of the human person." Responsibility for care implies humanity and respect in care, otherwise it is not responsibility. There are questions about responsibility in this case.

The UN report (1991) describes standards of care: "1. Every patient shall have the right to receive such health and social care as appropriate to his or her health needs . . ." and "2. Every patient shall be protected from harm including unjustified medication, abuse by other patients, staff or others or other acts causing mental distress or physical discomfort." These are standards, I believe, for the first responders' responsibility. The Navy SOP state the same.

There are further problems. Once a health worker, police, and so on, takes a person into care, he or she must assess risk, if that person is suicidal (Bongar & Greaney, 1994). Much of care issues in the United States and Canada, for example, are based on a claim of misdiagnosis or failure to diagnose. The issue of diagnosis is common; this was not a problem. Everyone would know that Chris was at risk. He said so.

An American case, Bell vs. New York City Health and Hospital Corporation (1982), illustrates the point, however. In that case, a psychiatrist was found liable for premature release of an inpatient who committed suicide because the psychiatrist's examination of the patient prior to release was judged to be inadequate. He failed, for example, to request prior treatment records or to inquire about the patient's psychotic symptoms. Thus, he failed in assessment.

There are problems in prediction and assessment of suicide risk (see Chapter 1), but not in this case. This, in fact, was not difficult in this case; everyone knew Chris was at risk.

There are issues in failure of care beyond assessment that are not so relevant here, but are so in many other cases of warriors' suicides (Leenaars, 2013). Gutheil (1992) and Bongar (1991; Bongar & Greaney, 1994) have written extensively on the topic. The most common American failure issues identified are as follows: (a) failure to predict or diagnose the suicide; (b) failure to control, supervise or restrain; (c) failure to take proper tests and evaluations of the patient to establish suicidal intent; (d) failure to medicate properly; (e) failure to observe the patient continuously (24 hours) or on a frequent enough basis (e.g., every 15 minutes); (f) failure to take an adequate history; (g) inadequate supervision and failure to remove belt or other dangerous objects; and (h) failure to place the patient in a secure room (Robertson, 1988, pp. 198–199).

Although there are various proposals that have been advanced for the above failures, typically the results of civil law suits in the United States determine the final version of the standard. In the Bell vs. New York City Health and Hospital Corporation (1982), the psychiatrist was found to have failed in his care. *What about in Chris' case?*

What constitutes wrongdoing? What is suicidogenic? When are mental health workers, police and such, liable? Gutheil (1992) suggested that there are fundamentals of malpractice, related to the following: the existing clinician-patient relationship; negligence or the breach of duty (although negligence itself does not necessarily equate with liability); the negligence results in specific danger or harm; and the fact that the clinician was negligent resulting in the patient committing suicide, if the element of causation is determinable. Demonstrating causation is often difficult; Gutheil offers a metaphoric example that illustrates best the issue. He illustrates:

> Consider a camel with serious osteoporosis of the spine, whose back is laden with straw. A final piece of straw (the proverbial "last straw") is placed on the back, and the camel's back breaks. In utilizing a clinical analysis of the situation, the clinician would consider the pre-existing condition of the camel and its back, the burden posed by the pre-existing straw, and the final straw leading to the condition of clinical compensation. (Gutheil, 1992, p. 150)

The legal viewpoint, at least in the United States, focuses on the last straw, which is called the "proximate cause." The question is a "but for," and we quote Gutheil again, "But for this last straw, the camel's back would not have been broken" (1992, p. 150). In this case, "But for no one taking the gun, Chris Purcell would not have killed himself." The question is, did the (failure in care) (negligence) cause the suicide? The answer lies in the statement "Dereliction of a duty directly causing dangers" (Gutheil, 1992, p. 150). Dereliction has application to in-hospital suicide, outpatient suicide, suicide after release, and military suicide.

In the United States, negligence, as defined by the American Learned Hand rule of 1947, refers to failure to invest resources up to a level commensurate with anticipated saving in dangers (Gutheil et al., 1983). In my opinion, this was the case. There are probably other failures, but there is no question from my area of expertise, this was the case. It is well known that suicide, in a case when the person is known to have a gun, can be predicted and prevented (e.g., suicide watch, controlling availability of means), but someone failed to invest resources up to the level commensurate with anticipated saving in dangers.

To summarize my opinion, let us return in conclusion to Gutheil (1992), with his advice, as it is applicable in this case. He suggests the approach to liability prevention involves responsible and prudent assessment, responsible and prudent intervention, durable documentation and consultation. Regardless of one's setting and thus, military facilities, maintaining the "good" standard of care prevails. And, in my opinion, I do not believe that this is so in this case. Although there may be other "But fors" outside my area of expertise, there is no question from my area of expertise about whether Chris killed himself at that time. He had a gun. Mike says so. Helene says so. Kristin says so. Derek says so. Only a fool would not say so. But for not getting the gun, Chris Purcell would have probably been alive that day. There is no doubt in my mind that this "But for" is not only one of negligence but also of liability. There is a dereliction of duty directly causing dangers. Chris Purcell died. The "But for" meets, without a doubt in my mind, the criteria of deliberate causation, not only in one way, but multiple ways.

However, there is the Feres doctrine. It does not matter if there was a last straw. Why did Chris die at that time? *The gun!* It does not matter if there was dereliction of duty. The doctor, EMT, Hospital Corpsman police; everyone is exempt. Feres controls so (Feres vs. U.S., 1950).

Of course, simply because the government and military declare that you are never responsible, does not mean you are not guilty. You only hide behind the green (or blue) walls.

OPINIONS REACHED AND BASIS THEREFORE

Based on the foregoing, using the PA method of investigation, I have reached the following opinions:

1. Chris Purcell died by suicide. The mode of death is unequivocal.
2. Beyond the question of what, we can answer with little doubt, the why Chris died by suicide, and how Chris died (He shot himself).
3. The PA richly illustrates Chris Purcell life; there was a history of trauma. He was traumatized by the military culture/system; he was distressed, depressed, and suicidal by age 14, if not before. There is a suicidal history and an acute (proximal) suicidal crisis.
4. Further to Purcell's suicide notes, the content and themes in the note, chat on MySpace, and other personal documents illuminate his suicidal mind, and many details of his life are tragically illustrated by the contents of his notes and documents.
5. There is a history of a mental disorder/psychopathology.
6. There is a history of PTSD. He also suffered, among others, from mood disorder, NOS, and alcohol abuse.
7. There were proximal signs of unbearable pain, mood disturbance, and suicide risk. There were distal ones. There are abundant precursors to his lethality; yet it is only in the last month(s) that there is high suicide risk. We know that in his last communications that he was highly lethal and perturbed.

8. In addition to the mental, physical, and spiritual imbalance, he had a most traumatic interpersonal relationship—a deep attachment to Sue, and I believe, the Navy (albeit ambivalent). They were lost! The loss/rejection of Sue, I believe, was a narcissistic injury, the straw that broke his heart.

9. Chris Purcell did experience a number of traumas in his life (e.g., Navy life; frequent moves when young; experiencing, and witnessing injury and death of others, as Hospital Corpsman; and threat to his Navy career). The forthcoming Military Discipline Review Board narcissistically injured him. This should not be a surprise. He came from a Navy family; he wanted his parents to be proud of him. There was shame and disgrace.

10. In the green culture, there is absolute obedience. It is a collective culture. There were military disciplinary issues and conflict(s) with Navy authorities. Chris was charged with violating the law. There was military humiliation. There was loss of honor.

11. Hospital Corpsman Purcell was treated for a number of painful mental impairments, such as severe anxiety and alcohol abuse. The treatments were consistent with community standard, but also unsuccessful. The main reason was noncompliance with treatment. *This is always lethal!*

12. However, on the night of his death, the first responders care was *not* consistent with community standard; there was dereliction of duty causing death! It may well be deliberate indifference!

Thus, there is no doubt in my mind that, at the time of his death, Chris did intend suicide. We knew that before. However, I have also answered why, I believe. It was multidetermined. However to be clear on my opinion in #12; I believe that there was deliberate indifference by the military system; they were not only aware of the suicide cost of service at the time of the civil war, after Vietnam, and 1991 (Scurfield, & Platoni, 2013), but did nothing about it; dissembled about military suicide; intentionally told warriors and doctors to lie and deny (keep secrets); did not provide adequate training; and so on (Leenaars, 2013; Scurfield & Latino, 2013; Silver, 1986). This is called system trauma or *sanctuary trauma* (Silver, 1986).

It has been established since 1830's, first by General Carl von Clausewitz, that war causes "friction". Charles Figley (1985) has suggested that the critical question in care is this one: Is the environment supportive or not? Was it for Chris? These are important questions in our ecological forensic investigations. We must look beyond the individual, say his/her mental disorder. Silver (1986) defined sanctuary trauma as friction which "occurs when an individual who suffered a severe stressor next encounters what was expected to be supportive and protective environment" (p. 215), and is only met with more trauma and its wake. Sanctuary trauma may be suicidogenic, actually causing the death. I opine it did for Chris Purcell. Was it inadequate training? Was it the intentional green belief to keep secrets? Did that secret add to the responders to ignore the deadly gun? Was it stigma? If the answer is yes to any of these questions, it may be deliberate indifference. This is a question that in our justice system, a judge and/or jury decides.

I will next summarize an answer to the question, why did Corpsman Chris Purcell kill himself?

A PSYCHOLOGICAL THEORY OF CHRIS PURCELL'S SUICIDE

Psychologically, Chris Purcell's suicide was complex. It was an intrapsychic drama on a Navy stage. As Durkheim would predict over a century ago, there was loss of honor. There was high perturbation and high lethality. Utilizing evidence available, and an analysis as discussed earlier, I propose the following psychological answer to the question: Why did Chris Purcell die by suicide?

INTRAPSYCHIC DRAMA

Unbearable Psychological Pain

Chris Purcell's mind, based for example, on his suicide note, was permeated with pain. It was a bed of bayonets. Shame and disgrace were paramount. He had lost everything. *All* his dreams were a loss. Although I believe that his suicide was much more, his suicide was a flight from these specters – the loss of Sue, his flawed Navy career, and his disgraced military reputation. He was in great distress. Deprivation, distress, and grief are evident. He felt boxed-in, hopeless, and helpless. He arrived at what he perceived to be the end; suicide became *the* solution, a relief from intolerable psychological pain.

Cognitive Constriction

Chris Purcell's mind was a constricted mind. There was constriction of perception, logic, reason, and conscience. He put things in a nutshell. He only reported permutations of a history of trauma—loss of Sue, a charge, a painful life. He was overwhelmed and overpowered. There was a paucity of thought, focusing only on the traumatizing and grief provoking topic.

Indirect Expressions

Chris felt he was encircled; he was estranged. He submitted to his pain and irrational core belief. He concluded that he had to kill himself. He turned his anger inward. He was, however, not ambivalent. Although we know a lot about his psyche, I believe that there were unconscious dynamics in his death—even the Navy family/culture was a deadly one; some do not survive.

Inability to Adjust (Psychopathology)

Hospital Corpsman Chris Purcell considered himself too weak to cope (or adjust); he gave up the fight. He, without a doubt, believed that his death was best for his reputation and himself. Like his treating psychiatrist and psychologist, I believe that Chris had a mental disorder. He says, in fact, that he was depressed; he may also likely have suffered from posttraumatic stress disorder, mood disorder, and alcohol abuse, among others. There was, without question, a deep psychological pain and an inability to adjust to his life's demands, like he could not as a child and teen in a Navy family.

Vulnerable Ego

Chris' ego was weakened; he lacked constructive tendencies. With the loss of Sue (he talked about her a lot), he felt desolation. This was the final loss toward the end. Then the core belief of the loss of his flawed Navy career was all he could bear. (What was the identification here?) Further, there were unresolved problems, something that he could not change—himself. He saw himself as hideous. Chris became discouraged, to a lethal level. He, thus, felt that he must be punished with death (attribution inward). He was so isolated (even from his best friend, Derek), illogical, and harsh.

INTERPERSONAL STAGE

Interpersonal Relations

Chris' problems were determined by his history (the Navy family; his mother's bipolar disorder) and the current situation that presented itself. He never did transitions well. He was weakened and felt defeated by the loss of Sue, his alcohol abuse, and military disciplinary issues. His needs were unsatisfied, at least attachment, abasement, autonomy, harmavoidance, and infavoidance. The frustration of these core needs became exceedingly stressful; he was not capable of healthy action. He drank. He had hoped for the acceptance of Sue, but such he saw as not forthcoming. He was hopeless about being able to survive (a core belief). Chris was, by all eyewitnesses, under constant strain and frustration; it was so for months. He responded with fear, helplessness, and horror.

Rejection-Aggression

In his suicide note, he wrote about a single traumatic event—his life. His ideal, and dreams were lost. He was rejected. He feared the loss of his Navy reputation. There was Navy humiliation. He was so discouraged in the end and suffered a deep narcissistic injury. Yet his aggression was attributed inward; there was no aggression turned outward in his note; however, it was in his chat. He also expressed such to his family. He was defeated and severely anxious and depressed, not outwardly angry.

Identification-Egression

Hospital Corpsman Purcell deeply identified with Sue, his father, and the Navy culture. *All was lost!* He felt rejected. His life, he now thought, was flawed and lethal. His reputation would be lost. He was unwilling to accept the loss of this ideal—his Navy career. In similar illogical thinking, he reasoned, "Fuck it." His beliefs were traumatizing. Hospital Corpsman Purcell lost his integrity, and the only solution was suicide. He first escaped with his alcohol abuse and then by his death. He escaped!

A CONCLUDING THOUGHT

There are many thoughts that I could conclude this chapter with. None will do the honor that Hospital Corpsman Third Class Chris Purcell deserves. Thus, I will let Mike Purcell, Chris' father, speak. Joe Gould (2011) on May 24, 2011, wrote a piece for *Military Times*, entitled, "Are Suicides Considered Less Honorable?"

> If military leaders want to stamp out the social stigma of psychological illnesses, it has to start with the commander-in-chief, writes vet Mike Purcell.
>
> As suicides rise among service men and women, and the nation comes to grips with the reality of their psychological wounds, why should they be accorded any less honor than those who have died of physical injuries, Purcell asks.
>
> "This Memorial Day please remember those we have lost on 'the other battlefield,'" Purcell writes. "Their service mattered greatly, as did they. Their families deserve to be recognized with dignity and respect, in their time of profound loss."

Purcell is far from alone

CHAPTER 10

Documents in the Courtroom

The suicide note, as I have argued, is of particular forensic interest and importance. In those cases dealing with wrongful death and suicide, the note can shed significant light on other forensic data, just as the other forensic data can shed significant light on the note. It is regrettable, however, that forensic study of suicide notes has been limited. Besides my own, there are only two other publications, to my knowledge, in the forensic literature (Duncan & Edland, 1974; Hanzlick & Ross, 1987). This, in some cases, has resulted in evidence presented to the court by police officers, coroners, psychologists, and so on that has no basis in science. For example, the following has been concluded: All suicide notes mean a suicide. Bill left a note. Therefore, Bill killed himself. This sounds like the classical illogical syllogism about Socrates that I discussed: All men are immortal. Socrates is a man. Therefore, Socrates is immortal. It is the first premise in both arguments that is wrong (see Chapter 1).

Even empirical studies (e.g., Kleck, 1988) that address the miscounting of suicide seem to leave the assumption that if there is a note, it is a suicide. Indeed, a study of coroners' certification procedures (Syer & Wyndowe, 1981) found that 50% of coroners reported wanting a suicide note in a case to determine the mode of death as a suicide. Yet the number of people who kill themselves and leave a note is well below 50% of the population. Studies report rates that range from 12% (Shneidman & Farberow, 1957) to 36%–40% (Leenaars, 2004; Shneidman & Farberow, 1961). This may be a reason for the underreporting of suicide; however, there is also another embedded problem; that is, a false positive: A note but not a suicide. There are, furthermore, other myths held about suicide notes (Leenaars & Lester, 1991). From a clinical/forensic perspective, the issue is how do we establish the true and false, positive and negative in our cases? How do we uncover the true facts? How can we distinguish between a person who intended to commit suicide from a person who did not intend to commit suicide but a note was left? This and other questions have been raised in cases dealing with suicide notes (and related communications) in forensic cases.

In this chapter, I present three cases for which I served as a forensic expert. However, the reader should regress to Chapter 1 to remember the roadmap for a general perspective on suicide, which is a must *a priori* knowledge before beginning forensic digs.

CASE INVESTIGATIONS

I will present two cases in which a suicide note played a pivotal role in the courtroom, illustrating not only how suicide notes can be analyzed in forensic cases but also raising questions and limitations of the same. Facts are not disguised because the records are public, although names are changed, but not for the very public Daniel Beckon case. My reports to the legal system on the cases were based on the discussions below, presented for each case.

Daniel Beckon Inquest

Daniel Beckon, a Canadian premiere jockey, died July 2, 1987. His death resulted in one of Canada's most publicized inquests. Two suicide notes written by Daniel Beckon were found at the scene of his death. The notes are presented in Table 10.1. The question raised in this case is whether Daniel Beckon's mode of death was a suicide. This case was complicated by the fact that a social scientist with no known expertise in suicide notes and suicidology in general reported to the inquest the following: "Based upon an analysis of the content and ideation of the two communications, it is my judgment that they are precisely what they manifestly appear to be; namely messages in certain contemplation of suicide." The expert goes on to say, "The content is archetypically consistent with a state of mind" of shame, self-blame, and enduring hopelessness. He concludes, therefore, that "Mr. Beckon's death was in all likelihood self-inflicted."

How was this judgment made? The expert testified that "both experience and research" led to his conclusion: a note; therefore, suicide. However, there was no reference to research in his testimony, despite frequent reference to "research indicates." A descriptive procedure, utilizing a patchwork of information, appears to

---

Table 10.1

Suicide Note to Sue Beckon

I hearby leave every thing to my loving wife Sue Beckon Farm Ltd. stocks in REFF house. Sue I wish that I could be the husband you deserved for what it's worth I only loved you. Forgive me for all the hurt.

Love
  Daniel

Suicide Note to son, Tom

Tom I love you so much you are the only thing I can be proud of.
Never do drugs son they only hurt the one's you love.
For give me for what Im going to do.

Lovingly only You's
  Daniel Beckon

---

have been used; one that is not documented in the literature. Even more concerning is that the final conclusion was based on an analysis of a note alone. My point is that if one wants to present an analysis of a suicide note in the court, there are a variety of methods in the literature to understand them, and even then, one needs to know their limitations.

An important aspect of the issue at hand is that suicide is an intentional act (see Chapter 1). To repeat, Litman (1984) notes,

> The concept which defines a death as suicide rather than an accident is intention. For example, we assume that when a man shoots himself in the head with a gun, he intended to die. Therefore the death was a suicide. However, if in fact, he intended to survive, for example, if he thought the gun was not loaded, the death was accidental. (p. 88)

In cases in which it is difficult to evaluate a dead person's intention, the death, as you know, is called equivocal. For example, the facts surrounding the case are not known, or because the person's intentions were masked or (if I may add) the only datum is a note alleged to be a suicide note.

In the Beckon case, there were other data questioning whether it was a suicide. It may have been a murder. Daniel Beckon may have been forced to write the note. If that is true, it means that a suicide note does *not always* mean a suicide. The case, already discussed, of Freddie Prinze, is a different example (Litman, 1984). The question was, even if he left a note, was the death intentional? To restate, the question to determine the mode of death as a suicide is Did the person *intentionally* kill him/herself (the NASH question)?

To address the question of intent, the suicide note, as you now know, must be placed within the context of other forensic data. The specific procedure within forensic suicidology that would assist in such situations, as you have learned, is called the psychological autopsy. (Litman, 1984; Rudestam, 1979; Shneidman, 1981). The psychological autopsy is defined as the procedures one has to undertake to clarify the nature of a death and focuses on the psychological aspects of the death. In the psychological autopsy, data are obtained through interviews with persons close to the deceased, including, for examples, family, friends, doctors, and associates at work. Facts and circumstances from anatomical autopsy, suicide notes, police records are obtained and other procedures are utilized. It is on this basis that one can begin to answer the above questions and specifically here, Did Daniel kill himself? All this should not be construed to mean that the suicide note has no place in forensic cases. On the contrary, a suicide note is a "window" to the mind of the decedent. For example, if a note of the deceased is determined by a scientific method of analysis to be a suicide note, one can conclude that in all probability the person at the time of the note had suicide on his/her mind. The note is, indeed, an extremely valuable (invaluable) bit of datum within the larger procedural framework of the psychological autopsy to assess intentionality and to conclude that in all probability the death was a natural death, accidental death, suicide, or homicide (NASH, and of course undetermined).

Within the context of the above limitations, what can we learn from Beckon's notes? It is the purpose here to provide an analysis of Daniel Beckon's notes utilizing the framework discussed in Chapter 1:[1]

INTRAPSYCHIC DRAMA

I) Unbearable Psychological Pain

Daniel Beckon appears to communicate a flight from "hurt," making reference specifically to "hurt the one's you love." However, other motives (elements, wishes) were likely evident. Daniel is distressed, deprived, and forlorn. He communicates that he is boxed in, feeling a sense of hopelessness and helplessness. It appears that if Daniel Beckon killed himself, the suicide was functional; it abolished painful tension.

II) Cognitive Constriction

There is a poverty of thought exhibited by expressing only permutations and combinations of grief-provoking content—"hurt," "love." He uses the classical words of constriction: "everything," "only," "all," "never." Daniel's perceptions were constricted.

III) Indirect Expressions

Daniel expresses themes of humility ("forgive me"), submission ("I hereby leave"), devotion ("for what it's worth I only loved you"), and flagellation ("all the hurt," "never do drugs son they only hurt the one's you love").

IV) Inability to Adjust/Psychopathology

Daniel considers himself too weak to overcome his personal difficulties and therefore appears to reject everything in one fell swoop. He states, "I hereby leave." He makes comments about "all the hurt" and specifically mentions "drugs" in one note. Although it is impossible to ascertain what specific mental disorder is present, the notes do suggest that a serious disorder may well have been present.

V) Ego

One can conclude that Daniel had some relative weakness in his capacity for developing constructive tendencies (e.g., attachment, love). *If* he killed himself, he wished to die.

---

[1] The method itself called for myself and an independent judge to score the notes. The independent judge was provided only with a typed copy of the notes, names were changed, and he was told that the first note was left to the man's wife, the second to his son, Tom. The reason for the use of a blind judge is to address the issue of clinical reliability. Only the agreed-upon scores were used.

INTERPERSONAL STAGE

VI) Interpersonal Relations

Unresolved problems in Daniel are evident. He appears to be defeated—"I wish that I could be the husband you deserved." The stressor appears to be unsatisfied or frustrated needs. Although it is difficult to determine precisely which needs are operating, attachment is clearly one ("love").

VII) Rejection-Aggression

Although Daniel does not state this directly, there is evidence that self-destruction, *if* this occurred, was not the only goal. One can conclude that in the notes he is likely attacking someone else. I find it significant, for example, that he writes to Tom, his son: "You are the only thing I can be proud of." It is impossible from the notes to determine precisely who and/or what Daniel was angry at at the time he wrote the notes. Daniel, *if* he killed himself, may well have turned back upon himself murderous impulses that had been directed elsewhere.

VIII) Identification-Egression

Daniel communicates egression ("I hereby leave," "forgive me for what I'm going to do") and desertion from his closest bonded family ("loving only you's," "I only loved you"). *If* Daniel killed himself, the notes would suggest that he wanted to exit from the "hurt."

The specific protocols scores in the TGSP (see Chapter 1), are as follows: 1, 2, 3, 6, 9, 11, 13, 15g, 16, 20, 21, 29, 30, 31, 32, 35.

The above appears to be, from my view, what we can say in this forensic case from the notes. It gives us a window into Daniel's mind at the time that he wrote the note—or was forced to write the note or so forth. However, we must place the notes within the context of a larger set of data to answer many other pertinent questions. One cannot determine the intent to be dead from a note alone. It may be, to use a colloquial analogy, a smoking gun, but one still needs the body. Although each case presents its own limitations, the best procedure is a psychological autopsy to answer the question "Did the person intentionally kill him/herself?" (see Berman, 1993, Jacobs & Klein, 1993; Litman, 1984, 1993; Shneidman, 1981).

Verdict: The final verdict in the case, based on divergent forensic data, was that Daniel Beckon's death was not a suicide. The mode of death was ruled to be "undetermined."

Adrian Niel Clancy vs. the State of Texas

Adrian Niel Clancy was charged with capital murder regarding the shooting death of Dr. Al Nagy on July 1, 1992. Mr. Clancy was charged with hiring a professional killer to kill Dr. Nagy, who was the former husband of Mr. Clancy's ex-wife, Lynn. The major evidence that the State of Texas had against Mr. Clancy were two admissible letters that expressed suicidal ideation. Table 10.2 presents these notes.

Table 10.2

LETTER ONE

November, 1993

Peter:

I am writing this to you by hand so that you can check and determine that it is indeed from me.

Lynn has asked for a divorce, again, and I am so distraught that I am unwilling to carry on with life. By the time you receive this you will know that I am no longer around. I will be in spirit and I hope you will do what's right and proper with this letter.

First, I attempted to explain the entire mess to Bill Smith but was unsuccessful in having him do anything to turn Lynn's head from self-destruction.

In may of 1992 she was, as you know, involved in one or two affairs, most of all with or most significant, with her attorney (can't remember the SOB's name). We sat one night on the bed and with a very cold stare she asked, "if we get back together, will you get in touch with Jerry and ask him to do something about Al?" Peter, at first was taken aback, but on reflection not nearly as much as I should have been. I told her, "Lynn, If I do this, we will have made a lifelong commitment to remain together no matter what." She said, "All I want is my children and you, that's all."

I told her that she would have to help in getting the children and letting me know when Al was coming and going so I could pass the information on.

Well, I did what she asked. I contacted one of my former clients, whom you may remember as Mr. Jones, and we made the arrangements. During this whole thing, I kept Lynn fully informed as to what was going on and she knew when I was meeting with whom, etc. I even ran a new name in on her to be sure she was aware of everything. Maybe, somewhere in the reaches of my mind, I was doing this (new home, etc.) to protect myself if anything ever occurred as is now going on.

Peter, she doesn't deserve to have these children - she is sick, self-centered and has become the damnest bitch you have ever seen.

I am too old to start over, I am too sick to care, I have never loved before - I have become useless because of her and I am going to take the easy route - let her take the hard one - she deserves it.

You know old buddy, it's hell to be used like this - to be set up - to be shot down - Maybe I am just striking back the only way I know, we made a pledge - she has broken it - its over - but dammit - the bottom line is this.

Lynn and I entered into a conspiricy to have Al killed. We are both Guilty, one as the other - I am gone - and burning in hell for all eternity.

Maybe after she is tried and convicted she will be in prison long enough to think long and hard about what she has done to her friends, family, children and least of all me.

I am making this last request of you Peter - give this to Tony Berger with the Dallas police - and tell him the following - hell - let him read the following, -

The gun was a 9 mm. Browning - the bullets exploding - the shooter - shot once in Dallas that day and later in Houston.

We took the children to Fort Worth so the job could be done that day - Al crossed us up and left town -

We were a little surprised that the job was done that night, but it was -

Table 10.2 (Cont'd.)

LETTER ONE (Cont'd.)

The shooter contacted me through another person about a year ago and asked for another sum ($5,000). I paid him and asked my contacts to insure he was not coming back for more - he has not -
The shooter lives in California - he lived in N.Y. at the time. I do not know how to contact him.
He was paid 2000 up front and 20000 the next week - I paid him a total of nine -
Lynn knows how the money was obtained - if Tony will look carefully at my bank account of Dallas Records he would see that a check to KLM was cancelled and cash withdrawn - neat coverup -
Sorry to burden you - but someone has to stop this woman before she kills another husband - two is enough -

Thanks Peter - so long!!
Adrian

LETTER TWO

Sam:

This may be the strangest letter you have ever received.
Its from a dead man about a dead man.
I have taken my own life, that's over.
Peter Lee has been given (mailed) a letter concerning Al's death -
The bottom line is this.
Lynn and I entered into a conspiricy to have Al killed - the reasons are complex.
The simple fact is that she doesn't deserve to have these wonderful children and she should go to jail for her part in the process. She will never pass a Polygraph Test and she knew when and how he was going to die.
Go get her - I can't hurt any longer and she can't hurt me any longer.

Adrian Clancy

Mr. Clancy wrote the letters in November 1993. He wrote these letters while contemplating taking his life by the use of a shotgun or rifle. He went into the backyard after writing the letters, placed the barrel of the gun into his mouth and started to pull the trigger when his poodle dog, Barika, jumped on his lap and attempted to lick his cheek. He has a long-standing fondness for animals and he realized that the dog needed him to take care of it. It has been reported that he has not been suicidal since then. He was suicidal on that occasion because his wife had asked for a divorce for the second time.

In the notes, Mr. Clancy states that he planned to kill Dr. Nagy. The question though is on, Is it an accurate perception that notes that contain suicidal content are prone to be truthful in content? (Or more simply, Is what a person writes in a suicide note always the truth?) Of course, no expert in a specific court case provides the final opinion of guilt or innocence, since that is in the domain of the collective opinion of the jury (or a judge). The jury decides whether there is proof beyond a reasonable doubt and/or whether there is reasonable doubt. Yet the expert can provide an opinion about what is known about suicide notes in general such as accuracy, truthfulness, and so on. All that is very different in our forensic investigation; we dig for the psychological bones, not dig in the dark.

There is only one, although indirect, study on the question of the truth about the content in suicide notes, presented by Tuckman et al. in 1959 in the *American Journal of Psychiatry*. They studied the reason for suicide in 63 suicide notes and the reason stated by informants. The results indicated a very high (90%) agreement or compatibility between these sources, suggesting that some credibility could be given to suicide notes. However, does this absolutely imply that content in notes is prone to be truthful in content? My opinion is no, not necessarily. We know that both informants and the suicidal individual are prone to present a situation as they see it, full of distortions, projections, and other inaccuracies (Leenaars, 1988, 1989b; Maris, 1981). We discussed this in detail in Chapter 1, under dissembling. This is a recognized problem in the study of personal documents, third-party interviews, and psychological autopsies in general (Allport, 1942). Indeed, the suicidal person him/herself may be, at the moment of decision, the least aware of the essence of reasons for killing him/herself or the truth of what he/she writes.

What is directly relevant to the above question is the fact that the suicidal person is constricted in his/her perception and logic (Leenaars, 1988, 2004, 2010a, 2013; Shneidman, 1985). Synonymous with constriction is a tunneling or focusing or narrowing of the range of options usually available to that individual's conscious mind. The suicidal person exhibits a greater poverty of thought than other people even when these other people imagine being suicidal. The suicidal person, as outlined earlier, expresses only permutations and combinations of grief-provoking content. Can one be truthful in such a state of mind? As a further critical point, Tripodes (1976) has indicated in his studies of suicide notes that the suicidal person often confuses real and not real, objective and subjective, feelings and the outside world, and so on. The suicidal person may see the note as a clear, obvious message, but it is often a confusing, contradictory message. There may be, for example, a confusion of truth, nontruth and more in the suicidal mind.

A very frequent aspect of the cognitive state, for example, in the suicidal person is that the person him/herself believes that the suicide was caused by a single thing (Leenaars, 1988; Menninger, 1938). It might be flight from pain, incurable disease, the threat of senility, loss of honor, and so on. The person may believe with passionate eloquence and with seemingly logical insistence, that it is *this one thing* that caused the death. The suicidal person says something like, "Life is this way and it will always be this way." However, suicide is a multidimensional malaise, more complex than the suicidal mind can understand and communicate. The suicidal person may be least aware of the essentials of his/her torturing despair.

We cannot, thus, know from a note alone that what the person writes is true or false. The suicide note is not like a deathbed confession. Specifically, in the Clancy case, we do not know whether he planned to kill Dr. Nagy or not. An analysis of the notes cannot answer that question by itself; rather, the notes must be placed within the context of other forensic data and then the letters can be invaluable. We need more evidence than a confession in a note to find someone guilty of a crime beyond reasonable doubt. We need convergent validity. This is the place for the PA (see Geberth's informative 5th edition [2015] of his practical guide to tactics, procedures, and forensic techniques in homicide investigation).

As an aside, Mr. Clancy's letters are not strictly suicide notes. If we mean by the word *suicide*, "death arising from an act inflicted upon oneself with the intent to kill oneself" (Rosenberg et al., 1988, p. 1451), then a *suicide note* is written by someone who killed him/herself. Mr. Clancy did not kill himself. Definition of terms is critical in science (and law). At best the notes are parasuicide notes, although, as discussed earlier, IASR and I have real questions about the term *parasuicide*. On this point, it is relevant to understand that even suicide attempters (a form of parasuicide) are different in some ways from the people who kill themselves (Shneidman, 1985). For example, Shneidman (1985) has suggested that the common cognitive state in parasuicide is an "obsessional quality with some planfulness." This is not to say that constriction does not occur in the parasuicidal situation but that it may not have a limiting characteristic. Empirically, there have been only a few differences isolating the writings of nonfatal attempters and completers; yet the main conclusion to date is that the theoretical frame presented appears to be applicable to attempters who made moderate to high lethal attempts (Leenaars et al., 1992). Yet, are such highly lethal attempters different from mild attempters? Of course, attempters are different from ideators and so on. Mr. Clancy, at most, was a contemplator—someone who thought about killing himself.

Much of the above concern regarding completers, attempters, contemplators, and so on has to do with the issue of lethality—the probability of a person killing him/herself (i.e., the intent; see Chapter 1). For example, the question to be asked of a suicidal person is "During the last 24 hours, I felt that the probability of my actually killing myself (committing suicide and ending my life) was: absent, low, medium/fifty-fifty, high, very high (came very close to actually killing myself)." Lethality, as you know, is critical to assess in clinical and, by implication, forensic situations (Leenaars, 1995). In Mr. Clancy's case, we do not know from the letters alone what his lethality was when he wrote the notes. Was it low, medium, or high? Did a dog change the mind of a highly lethal person? (I believe that is possible.)

Within the context of the above, it is the purpose here to provide an analysis of Mr. Clancy's notes utilizing the framework presented in Chapter 1. (The method used was the same as in the Beckon case.)

Letter 1: The first letter is entitled "Peter" and is dated "November, 1993." "Peter" is Peter Lee, his attorney. The following observations can be made:

INTRAPSYCHIC DRAMA

I) Unbearable Psychological Pain

Mr. Clancy appears to communicate a flight from pain, making such references as "I am too sick to care" and "I am so distraught." However, other motives (wishes, needs) were likely evident. He felt rejected, harassed and especially hopeless. Mr. Clancy saw suicide as a solution to an urgent problem—Lynn asking for a divorce.

II) Cognitive Constriction

Mr. Clancy communicates only about a trauma—Lynn asked for a divorce.

III) Indirect Expressions

Mr. Clancy communicates ambivalence; for example, contradictory feelings toward Lynn.

IV) Inability to Adjust/Psychopathology

Mr. Clancy saw himself too weak to overcome his personal difficulties and therefore appears to reject everything. He states, "I am gone," adding "and burning in hell." Although it is impossible to decide what specific mental disorder is present, the letter does suggest that a serious disorder may well have been present at the time of writing the notes.

V) Ego

Mr. Clancy appears to have some relative weakness in his capacity for developing constructive tendencies. He wished to die.

INTERPERSONAL STAGE

VI) Interpersonal Relations

Unresolved problems in Mr. Clancy are evident. His interpersonal relation with Lynn was disturbed. He appears to be defeated: "I am so distraught that I am unwilling to carry on with life." The stressor appears to be unsatisfied or frustrated needs, notably attachment; however, other needs, for example, dominance ("let her take the hard one—she deserves it") are likely evident. It is likely that this stressor has a history but was relatively persistent and his wish ("a lifelong commitment") was not forthcoming.

VII) Rejection-Aggression

Mr. Clancy is preoccupied with a traumatic event—the loss-rejection of Lynn. He is ambivalent, that is, hostile and affectionate, to Lynn. It seems clear, however, that a situation was created in which death is desired, partly in order to attack/hurt Lynn. He wanted revenge. The act may well have been calculated to have a prolonged evil effect on Lynn. He writes, "We are both guilty, one as the other."

VIII) Identification-Egression

Mr. Clancy communicates egression; that is, he wants to depart from a region of distress and to be elsewhere, citing "hell."

The protocol sentences of the TGSP are as follows: 1, 2, 6, 7, 10, 13, 15g, 16, 19, 20, 21, 23, 25, 28, 31, 35.

Letter 2: The second letter is entitled, "Sam." "Sam" is Dr. Sam Nagy, the decedent's brother.

INTRAPSYCHIC DRAMA

I) Unbearable Psychological Pain

Mr. Clancy appears to communicate a flight from pain—"I can't hurt any longer." However, the solution of suicide does not appear to be caused only by such a single thing; other motives are evident. For example, he states, "Go get her," referring to "Lynn and I entered into a conspiracy to have Al killed." Mr. Clancy sees suicide as a solution and relief from suffering—"she can't hurt me any longer."

II) Cognitive Constriction

Mr. Clancy communicates evidence of adult trauma.

III) Indirect Expressions

No observations.

IV) Inability to Adjust/Psychopathology

No observations.

V) Ego

No observations.

INTERPERSONAL STAGE

VI) Interpersonal Relations

Unresolved problems are evident, wherein Mr. Clancy suffered defeat. His interpersonal relations are disturbed.

VII) Rejection-Aggression

Mr. Clancy communicates the existence of a traumatic rejection—"I can't hurt any longer and she can't hurt me any longer." He sees Lynn as a destructive influence on him. He is preoccupied with Lynn, whom he has lost and who rejected him. This, from his view, resulted in the planned suicide, citing "I have taken my own life, that is over" and "This may be the strangest letter you have ever received. It's from a dead man." Yet one can conclude that Mr. Clancy is attacking someone else. Mr. Clancy calculated that the act—and the letter—would have a prolonged evil effect on Lynn—"she doesn't deserve to have these wonderful children," "she should go to jail," "go get her."

VIII) Identification-Egression

There is evidence of egression, noting a letter from a dead man.

The protocol sentences of the TGSP were 1, 2, 7, 20, 25, 27, 31, 32, 35.

As a summing up of this case, let me address the question at hand somewhat differently: What facts are considered to be critical in assessing the accuracy of representations in a suicide note; that is, a note written by someone with suicide on his/her mind? Can one make a statement about the accuracy of representations in a suicide note only from that note? Although one may be able to speculate (i.e., anything is possible), it is probably prudent not to do so, although one can make statements about pain, despair, mental constriction, and so on. We need to know the limitations of our data. After all, the issue in court is what is most probable, not what is possible. In a situation like the case of Mr. Clancy, suicide notes are best understood when examined within the context of the life in which they occur (Shneidman, 1980, 1985, 1993) or with the issue at hand, other forensic data.

Verdict: The verdict in the case was that Adrian Clancy was guilty. However, the evidence raised enough questions in the case, that Mr. Clancy was spared the death penalty, something of a victory in the case, according to a consulting psychiatrist and the lawyers in the case.

MYTHS ABOUT SUICIDE NOTES

What are the common myths about suicide notes? Leenaars and Lester (1991) undertook an evidence-based study to answer that question. I offer a nomothetic answer.

The identification of salient clues to suicide has always been seen as a critical aspect of DSI. Suicide notes are one such clue. However, studies of suicide notes observed that the lay public in general failed to be aware of some of the essential hallmarks of a note. Arbeit and Blatt (1983) reported that most individuals could not distinguish genuine suicide notes from simulated ones. Leenaars and Balance (1984) further reported that some people with clinical expertise were similarly handicapped, although they did note that these individuals were in a minority. These observations led to the question of how people construe a note to be genuine and, thus, it is hoped, will allow an investigator to better know if a note is genuine or simulated.

Lester and Leenaars (1987) first began a systematic investigation of the differentiation of genuine suicide notes. They gave Shneidman and Farberow's 33-matched collection of genuine and simulated notes to a group of undergraduate students to decide which of each pair was "genuine." The range of correct identification was 13% to 83%. Some of the genuine notes ($n = 17$) were consistently identified as obviously genuine (i.e., those notes judged correctly more than 50% of the time) while others were not ($n = 16$). Because genuine notes do differ in being construed as genuine, Lester and Leenaars suggested that research was warranted to isolate what characteristics of suicide notes are salient for people and allow perception of a suicide note as genuine.

Leenaars and Lester (1989) attempted to isolate these characteristics by comparing samples of more obvious and less obvious genuine notes on the basis of a series of patterns and clues that have been identified as characteristic of suicide notes and by implication, suicide. These characteristics were the common characteristics of suicide notes, discussed in Chapter 1. Each of these patterns or characteristics is composed of a number of specific protocol items (or clues). The results indicated that none of the eight patterns distinguished the sets. Furthermore, only 2 specific protocol clues of 35 significantly differentiated the two groups of notes: a limitation of thought and a stimulus-bound focus on a traumatic situation. However, when people distinguish genuine, they do not use evidence-based constructs. The research indeed shows the clues discussed, and thus, the TGSP are useful in distinguishing real from nonreal notes. We will be more accurate. The 1989 Leenaars and Lester results were meager; they suggested that a phenomenological study was warranted. The 1991 Leenaars and Lester study begins such an investigation. The relevance, thus, is for primary forensic investigation.

METHOD

Shneidman and Farberow's collection of matched genuine and simulated notes was given to 32 individuals who were registered in an undergraduate psychology course to decide which of each pair was "genuine." In addition, they were asked, "What aspects of the notes led to your decision?"

RESULTS AND DISCUSSION

Our findings (Leenaars & Lester, 1991) were convergent with Lester and Leenaars (1987) that some notes are consistently identified as obviously genuine and others were not. Nineteen notes were identified as obviously genuine (i.e., those notes judged correctly more than 50% of the time) and 14 as not obviously genuine. The range of correct identification was 25% to 72%. A few notes in the 1991 sample differed from the 1987 choices, however, these were within expected deviation around the criteria (Pearson $r = 0.54$, one-tailed, $p < .005$).

As a basis for our phenomenological analysis, we focused our remarks especially on those notes that were isolated in both studies as correctly or incorrectly genuine. From these notes identified consistently as obviously genuine, we learned that, first, people often looked for a traumatic event in the note to identify that note as genuine. Examples included a rejecting spouse, a lost job, a debt, an affair, or an illness. It appears that the identification of a precipitating event was important to our subjects. As one subject stated about a trauma in a note, "What led me to choose this letter was the fact that he was giving a reason as to why he was killing himself." Yet about the same letter, another subject rejected it because of that reason. Sometimes the wrong letter was chosen by some subjects because the simulated one had a singular preoccupation with a trauma. Yet it is likely that this criterion alone allowed many of our subjects to be successful in selecting genuine notes.

Second, some (a small minority) people saw feelings as important (e.g., hopelessness, depression, anger, ambivalence, desperation, and tiredness). Third, some people looked for a forlorn, hopeless quality. For example, one subject wrote, "He just can't go on any longer." Another remarked that the person wrote, "I have nothing to live for." Fourth, a previous attempt was identified by a number of subjects as an important clue in a note. Fifth, a few subjects simply felt that the notes sounded convincing. These few subjects simply appeared to consistently rely on their sense or feelings about the note such as "sounded good," and "sounded sincere." Indeed, we know that motivational aspects in general affect people's response to suicide notes (Sherman, Presson, & Chassin, 1984). Sixth, aside from our first observation, however, people varied in their response (i.e., in their basis for selection). One subject looked for whether a person stated what he or she was going to do. Another said a suicidal person would tell a wife that she could inherit everything. Indeed, what emerged was that each subject had a theory of suicide notes and suicide in general, often one that was wrong. For example, one subject reported that a suicidal person would not admit that he was not of sound mind and therefore systematically rejected all notes with such communication. As another example, one person indicated that he rejected the (genuine) note because it was addressed to the police ("One doesn't write to police"). As a final example, a couple of subjects rejected (often wrongly) notes that communicated a message such as "God bless you" because "God doesn't like suicide." Seventh, one of the most striking phenomena was that some subjects chose a note for a reason that others used to reject it. Here are some examples: Explanation/too much explanation, reason/too many reasons, too long/too brief, anger/too much anger, instruction/too much instruction, concerned about others/too concerned about others, states method/does not state method, and so on. Obviously there are opposite, contradictory theories of suicide.

From those genuine notes identified consistently but incorrectly as not obviously genuine, we learned that, first, the reason or criterion for selection, as discussed previously, was more evident to them in the simulated note in the pair. It is important to note, as Leenaars (1988) reported, that if one attempts to describe the content of simulated and genuine suicide notes, it becomes evident that individuals under both conditions very frequently describe their behavior as highly similar in some critical aspects (and as significantly different in others). When a person relies on a singular high-frequency clue that occurs in both genuine and simulated notes, there is, of course, no basis to differentiate between them, and the person may simply choose the wrong note (i.e., the simulated one). Highly frequent data in suicide notes are not synonymous with discriminating (or differentiating) data between genuine and simulated suicide notes. For example, a statement about egression is often stated in both, but being figuratively intoxicated by constricted logic and perception is more evident in genuine notes. The communication of trauma, on the other hand, is both a highly frequent and a discriminating clue in genuine notes. All of this may result in the wrong decision for subjects when confronted by a simulated note that has a frequent (common) characteristic of a genuine note. This can be a problem in DSI.

Second, striking contradictory views again emerged: too short/too long, too precise/vague, and so on. Third, as noted earlier, people's own theory of suicide, regardless of how idiosyncratic, resulted in them making wrong choices. For example, suicidal people do not leave a will in their last letter, do not sign the note, do not write dates or times, and are not concerned about survivors. All of these, of course, do occur in genuine notes.

In conclusion, it appears that people have their own theory about suicide notes in particular and suicide in general. One consistent and correct view is that a traumatic event is important in identifying a genuinely suicidal person. Often there is a stimulus-bound focus (i.e., a singular preoccupation) on a trauma, although, as you have learned, there is much more to the suicidal solution than the existence of a precipitating traumatic event. Beyond this, our study did not reveal much consistency in people's views about suicide notes. Often people are idiosyncratic in their perceptions. "Mysterious." (Are you? Or are you evidence-based?) Indeed, we were struck by the extreme contradictions in the views about suicide notes and, by implication, suicide.

Most importantly, we found the results of our phenomenological study to be alarming rather than being revealing about what characteristics of suicide notes are salient for people to judge them as genuine. People hold strikingly opposite views of suicide; often both are wrong. We were especially alarmed by the great number of myths that people hold, such as "If the person believes he was wrong, he would not end his life." It is important to recognize that these are not the fables and facts that are frequently discussed in the literature (see Chapter 1), but clearly myths nevertheless. Such myths may diminish an investigator's classification of a genuine note, and, as I have already discussed, have resulted in erroneous conclusions in a courtroom. Indeed, our series of studies on differentiation of genuine notes allows us to conclude that it may well be helpful to educate forensic investigators specifically about suicide notes. Suicide notes may be a useful tool in DSI.

ACCIDENT OR SUICIDE?

Next, I present a case on the question of mode—accident or suicide? Kees Finn, a 28-year-old married male died in a car accident on January 2, 2000, in Illinois. The MVA was a car-truck accident. Mr. Finn's vehicle, according to a number of witnesses, travelling westbound, suddenly swerved into the path of a semi-truck. Mr. Finn's car hit head on into the truck. Both vehicles drove off to the right side of the road into a ditch striking some trees before coming to rest.

A provisional report from Dr. Bob Sims, the medical examiner, stated that Mr. Finn died from "Multiple fractures and trauma to the extremities, thorax and the abdomen" as well as "apical decapitation." Toxicology reports were negative.

A note was found in the vehicle; it stated,

I'm sorry

Jane
You were the
only one who
understood. The

only one I ever loved. My
only love

• No show & tell
• Bury me
• Bury St. Alfonso

"The only one I ever loved" was partially scratched out.

An investigation uncovered that although Mr. Finn was married; there had been marital stress. He also had been recently charged with sexual harassment in the workplace.

A police investigation uncovered that Mr. Finn was distressed at the time, mainly because of the sexual harassment charge. Tabachnik (1967) documented decades ago that life crises in accident victims were often traumatic. He noted that especially "slights and humiliation were significant in the lives of accident victims, in the period immediately preceding the accident" (p. 409). Despite Mr. Finn having been despondent and described as "depressed," he appeared, according to family informants, to be coping well. No one in the family suspected any problems; yet other informants saw it quite differently. A fellow employee wondered immediately if it was a suicide. On the positive, there was a partial resolution of the complaint and a possible withdrawing of the charge. According to the last witness to see Kees Finn, he was "upset" and "disturbed"; yet he refused to talk. He was leaving for work, going to his car.

Dr. Sims' medical examiner's autopsy report reads: The cause of death is very acute multi-organ and systemic trauma. Drug and alcohol examinations are negative. There is no underlying evidence of organic disease.

On mode, Dr. Sims concluded,

> Based upon failure to find a defect in the automobile, witnesses describing the accident, review of the note found in the vehicle, and investigative information concerning recent incidents in the life of Mr. Finn, I can conclude with a high degree of certainty that the final determination is the manner of death being from suicide and will, unless other information comes forward or is presented, close the case.

Mr. Finn's family could not wrap their head around the suicide classification. They stated that it could not be. Kees was happy; he had a family (Their first faulty premise: "A man with a happy family does not commit suicide"). There was, indeed, the incident at work, but it was resolved. (It was not.) They noted that parts of the note ("Bury me") were humorous. They also asked would a desperate mind edit a suicide note? (Yes). They stated that Kees was just venting. Kees, they reported, never suffered from depression; there is no family history of mental disorder or suicide. Kees was a man of Christian values and morals. Would a Christian kill himself? (Yes) He was planning a Disney vacation. Would a man with a vacation plan kill himself? (Yes) No one is immune to suicide. The family could not believe that it was a suicide and requested an inquest. Of course, in suicide-by-car, it is not quite like pointing a gun at your head. It is often more difficult to discern the mode, but not in this case.

Mr. Sam Vintage hired me to provide an expert opinion on the note. My opinion was only on the note. My answer, thus, was to provide an opinion that Kees' mind was suicidal at the time of writing the note, not if he killed himself. To address the question of mode, the note must be put into the context of other forensic data. I would need to do a PA, which was not the request in this case.

Below is my somewhat flawed report; all identifying detail (e.g., names) have been changed, not the facts:

July 7, 2001
Sam Vintage
100 Main St.
Mosaic O. II
U.S.

Dear Mr. Vintage:
Re: Kees Finn
     DOB: 1971-02-18
     DOD: 2000-01-02

Qualifications
Dr. Antoon A. Leenaars is a registered psychologist in private practice in mental health, public health, and forensic sciences in Windsor, Canada. He is Senior Advisor with the Norwegian Institute of Public Health, Division of Mental Health, Norway, was a member (Researcher) of the Faculty (Dept. of Clinical and Health Psychology) at the University of Leiden, The Netherlands, and was a member (Adjunct Lecturer) of the Faculty (Dept. of Public Health Sciences) at the Karolinska Institutet, Sweden. He is the first Past President of the Canadian Association for Suicide Prevention (CASP), and a Past President of the American Association of Suicidology (AAS), the only non-American to have served in that role to date. He has collaborated with over 100 colleagues in 30 nations, and has published over 200 professional articles/chapters on violence, suicide, suicide notes, homicide, forensic science, psychotherapy, gun control, ethical/legal issues, and related topics. He has published 10 books, including the forthcoming: *Psychotherapy with Suicidal People*, and is the founding/first Editor-in-Chief of *Archives of Suicide Research*, the official journal of the International Academy for Suicide Research (IASR). Dr. Leenaars is a recipient of the International Association for Suicide Prevention's biannual Stengel Award, CASP's Research Award, and AAS's Shneidman Award, for outstanding contributions in research in suicidology. He was awarded the status of Fellow of the Canadian Psychological Association (CPA) for distinguished contribution to the advancement of the discipline of psychology. He has consulted for the World Health Organization (WHO), and institutions, and has served as an expert investigator/witness on cases of wrongful death, suicide, homicide, and homicide-suicide for police services, coroners and lawyers around the world.

A copy of my most recent curriculum vita is attached.

Documents and Data Reviewed
Kees Finn, age 28, died on Jan. 2, 2000. The medical examiner determined the mode of death as suicide. The death occurred in an auto-truck crash. A note was found at the scene of the death. I was asked to offer an opinion on the note.

The following note was found at the scene of the death:

I'm sorry

Jane
You were the
only one who
understood. The
only one I ever loved. My
only love

• No show & tell
• Bury me
• Bury St. Alfonso

Jane was Kees' wife. The phrase, "The only one I ever loved" appeared to be scribbled over.

In performing my analysis, I looked only at the note that reads as above. The note was analyzed, based on a system in the peer-reviewed literature (e.g., Leenaars, 1988, 1989, 1996), using the Thematic Guide for Suicide Prediction (TGSP). The actual method of scoring called for a trained second judge and me to score the note independently. This judge, like me, looked only at the note, and scored along standardized instructions. No other information was looked at until after the note was scored. The reason for consulting with a second, "blind" judge is to address the issue of clinical reliability. In this way, we are "double-rating" everything, a normal practice in forensics. Only the agreed upon scores were used. Below is my analysis within a frame of the suicidal mind, presented in Leenaars (1996).

Opinions Reached and Bases Therefore

The note has the following characteristics of suicide notes (TGSP):

INTRAPSYCHIC

I - Unbearable Psychological Pain
  1. Suicide has adjustive value and is functional because it stops painful tension and provides relief from intolerable psychological pain.
  3. In the suicidal drama, certain emotional states are present, including pitiful forlornness, emotional deprivation, distress and/or grief.
  5. There is a conflict between life's demands for adaptation and the writer's (S's) inability or unwillingness to meet the challenge.
  6. The writer is in a state of heightened disturbance (perturbation) and feels boxed in, harassed, especially hopeless and helpless.
II - Cognitive Constriction
  9. There is poverty of thought, exhibited by focusing only on permutations and combinations of grief and grief-provoking topics.
III - Indirect Expressions
  10. S reports ambivalence; e.g., complications, concomitant contradictory feelings, attitudes and/or thrusts.
  11. The writer's aggression has been turned inwards; e.g., humility, submission and devotion, subordination, flagellation, or masochism, are evident.

IV - Inability to Adjust

13. The writer considers him/herself too weak to overcome personal difficulties and, therefore, rejects everything, wanting to escape painful life events.

15. S exhibits a serious disorder in adjustment.

   f) S's reports are consistent with depression; e.g., depressed mood, diminished interest, insomnia.

V - Ego

16. There is a relative weakness in S's capacity for developing constructive tendencies (e.g., attachment, love).

18. S reports that the suicide is related to a harsh conscience; i.e., a fulfillment of punishment (or self-punishment).

INTERPERSONAL

VI - Interpersonal Relations

20. The writer reports being weakened and/or defeated by unresolved problems in the interpersonal field (or some other ideal such as health, perfection).

21. S's suicide appears related to unsatisfied or frustrated needs; e.g., attachment, perfection, achievement, autonomy, control.

22. The writer's frustration in the interpersonal field is exceedingly stressful and persisting to a traumatic degree.

23. A positive development in the disturbed relationship was seen as the only possible way to go on living, but such development was seen as not forthcoming.

VII - Rejection-Aggression

25. The writer reports a traumatic event or hurt or injury (e.g., unmet love, a failing marriage, disgust with one's work).

27. S is preoccupied with an event or injury, namely a person who has been lost or rejecting (i.e., abandonment).

28. The writer feels quite ambivalent, i.e., both affectionate and hostile towards the same (lost or rejecting) person.

VIII - Identification-Egression

35. The writer wants to egress (i.e., to depart, to flee, to escape, to be gone), to relieve the unbearable psychological pain.

After the analysis of the note, I subsequently looked at the following:

- One-page death certificate
- Supplemental Report of Sgt. Blue
- County Sheriff Dept. Incident Report
- One-page "Medical Examiner Autopsy Report" stating final anatomic diagnosis and final comment, and signed by Bob Sims, M.D./Pathologist
- "Additional Comment and Final Disposition" dated 3/8/00 (one page) signed by Dr. Sims
- Typewritten comments entitled "Information Regarding Notes" prepared by . Jane Finn
- Letter from Peter Finn to Dr. Sims
- Two-page note by Kees Finn
- One-page note by Kees Finn
- One-page note by Kees Finn

Based on the foregoing, I have reached the following primary opinions:

1. Based on my training, experience and research in the field and my review of approximately 2000 suicide notes, there is no doubt in my mind that this is a suicide note, i.e., a note written by someone with suicide in mind.

2. Because the note has many characteristics of a suicide note, Kees Finn's mind at the time of writing this note was suicidal.

3. Based on the reports of the note and the material on the family's comments on the note, I believe that the note is serious and should not be construed as humorous in nature. The note is the writings of a suicidal person.

4. Based on the samples of earlier notes authored by Kees Finn, these are readily distinguishable from suicide notes. However, there are specific elements in some of these notes, such as, "I need you, Jane. Please don't give up on us. I just don't know if I can make it without you" that suggest elements of distress and interpersonal problems, which may be significant in assessing Mr. Finn's ongoing state of mine, before his death.

In addition, I have reached the following additional opinions, based on the note:

Kees Finn's mind, based on the note, was permeated with pain—intolerable pain. He was forlorn and distressed. He needed to adapt, but was unwilling or unable to meet the challenge. He was in a state of heightened disturbance (perturbation).

Kees Finn's mind was a constricted mind of thought, focusing on only one topic—being understood, loved.

Mr. Finn was ambivalent. He was likely overwhelmed and turned his anger inwards (e.g., submission, flagellation)—"I'm sorry."

Kees Finn could not cope; he saw himself too weak to adjust. Indeed, his mind was indicative of depression. Although I have not assessed Mr. Finn, and therefore I cannot provide a diagnosis, I can offer a speculation. Based on the evidence, I can speculate that Mr. Finn likely suffered from, at least, a depressive disorder.

Mr. Finn's ego was weakened; he lacked constructive tendencies (resilience). In fact, there is an element of harshness and self-punishment—"You were the only one who understood"; "I'm sorry"; "Bury me."

Mr. Finn was weakened and defeated, although it is unclear from the note what precisely defeated him. There is, however, a frustration of needs—attachment, being understood. His frustration was in all likelihood exceedingly stressful and persisting to a traumatic degree.

Kees Finn's note is consistent with the experience of a traumatic event or hurt or injury. He is preoccupied with "only" this event—he feels so rejected. And, he feels quite ambivalent, love and hate, towards the same event—only understood by Jane, his "only love."

Mr. Finn wanted to egress—to escape from the pain—"Bury me."

Other Expert Testimony

The cases in which I have testified or provided depositions during the last four years are:

State of Indiana vs. Bei Bei Shuai

Cathy Minix (re: Gregory Zick) vs. Sherriff Frank Canarecci Jr., et al., State of Indiana

The People of California vs. Guy Leslie Barker

Compensation

My fee is $xxx (U.S.) per hour.

Antoon A. Leenaars, Ph.D., C.Psych., CPQ

References

Leenaars, A. (1988). *Suicide notes.* New York, NY: Human Sciences.
Leenaars, A. (1989b). Suicide across the adult life span: An archival study. *Crisis, 10*, 132-151.
Leenaars, A. (1996). Suicide: A multidimensional malaise. *Suicide and Life-Threatening Behavior, 26*, 221-236.

SOME FURTHER REFLECTIONS ON KEES FINN'S SUICIDE

I can let the note speak for itself; yet I wish to remark about some testimony that I heard. The most common suicide by car is a head-on collision between a passenger car and a substantially heavier vehicle, usually a truck (or bus). A tire expert, in forensic evidence-based detail, showed how the tire tracks can be analyzed in a suicide versus accident case. In Mr. Finn's case, there were no brake marks on the road, only tire marks indicative of immediate impact. In almost all cases of accidents the driver applies the brakes or initiates other evasive action; this was not present in Mr. Finn's car-truck accident. The expert concluded that the tire marks were most consistent with a case of suicide. In such cases, presence or absence of skid marks, visibility, road conditions, braking and other evasive actions, and mechanical condition of the vehicle are all essential clues. Identifying suicides among fatalities caused by MVAs is a major challenge. Dr. Curphey faced that challenge, so do all medical examiners or coroners. It is difficult to distinguish, not only because of ambiguity, but also because the person likely dissembled, even the choice of a vehicle is often used intentionally. It allows deception. There may be multiple reasons to cover the intent: insurance, stigma, avoiding secondary harm to family, and so on. Sound forensic investigation, thus, is a must. That same standard applies to suicide note evidence. In a court, like a PA, a jury takes all the evidence together into account and concludes. The suicide note and vehicle/road marks, together with other forensic data (police reports, informants' testimony), result in a final classification in this case of suicide. All the evidence together solved this case; my testimony was part of the larger case presented. It was not an accident. It was suicide.

CONCLUDING REMARKS

Suicide notes are *prima facie* data. Prima facie means "at first sight." It refers to what is known before the fact. In science, this is the nomothetic (Windelband, 1904). The nomothetic is the general, whereas the idiographic is the individual. *Prima facie* and nomothetic are concepts from different sources; the first from law (such as "seems *prima facie* to be guilty") and the second from science (such as seems nomothetic that all suicides are self-inflicted deaths). Operationally they are very close. They are conceptual dimensions, critical to law and science (see Leenaars et al., 1997). With the topics at hand, suicide notes are both in law and science *prima facie*/nomothetic data. Yet we have to dig out the individual evidence, the idiographic data.

Windelband (1904), Shneidman (1980), and Leenaars et al. (1997) suggest that in science, the nomothetic and the idiographic are possible approaches. The idiographic involves the intense study of the individual. This is always the core in DSI. The idiographic, like the nomothetic approach, must follow laws of science. In law, the individual is equally relevant to forensic questions. The general and individual concern both law and science. With these distinctions in our forensic mind, we can conclude that suicide notes may be invaluable to the forensic scientist in addressing a number of questions discussed here: Did this person intentionally kill him/herself?; and, Is it an accurate perception that notes which contain suicidal content are prone to be truthful in content? There are many more questions we can answer in the equivocal case.

Space here does not allow me to address a larger number of relevant questions about suicide notes that have been discussed in the courtroom. Yet, to conclude, my thesis is that suicide notes are invaluable (archival) data— "windows" to the mind of the decedent; if one knows the empirical basis for understanding them and they are considered within the context of other data, regarding some forensic questions. They allow us to uncover the forensic unknowns.

As a final remark, each question about a suicide note in a forensic case has a nomothetic answer; yet each case must also be evaluated independently according to its own idiographic data, some beyond the note. In this way the law and science are alike.

CHAPTER 11

The PA in the Courtroom

John Scott Dell was born the 3rd of March 1951, to parents Myra and John. He died on the 29th of December 1995. His death certificate reads the mode of death as "Undetermined."

What was the mode of death? Was it a suicide or, as some believed, a homicide? This is the question in this chapter. Suicide and homicide are interwoven, as discussed earlier; to assess one is to eliminate the other, although sometimes we meet a person who is both homicidal-suicidal. The homicide-suicide presents a special task for DSI, as discussed in Chapters 1 and 2. To answer the question in the case of Scott Dell, I will follow the principle of *res ipsa loquitur*. The facts—personal documents, letters, psychological autopsy notes, court testimony and the verdict—will be presented verbatim. It uncovers the psychological bare facts. It is a "Who done it?"

The data convey their message. I assembled them here, some two banker boxes, as the case unfolded to me, beginning with a history of Scott Dell. Next I present a note and the analysis of the note. There are, however, limitations, as you have read, to a note. To determine the mode of death, one has to address the central question of intent. Did the person intend to kill him/herself? One cannot conclude from a note alone that this is a suicide (see Chapter 10). The specific procedure within suicidology that would assist is called the psychological autopsy. In the psychological autopsy, data are obtained—personal documents, reports, letters, and third-party interviews. The note is valuable, sometimes essential, within this larger procedure of the psychological autopsy. The note, when placed in the context of that person's life, allows us to answer the question, "Is this a suicide or not?" This is the question about Scott Dell (and is not uncommon in our day-to-day forensic practice).

An outline of the psychological autopsy was provided, following Shneidman's perspective on the technique. There are standard empirical questions (see Chapter 4). The data, beyond the note examined, include newspaper accounts, police reports, letters, and court testimony. The most important technique in the psychological autopsy is the third-party interviews. I plan to present abbreviations of the interviews of Myra Dell, mother; Loretta McCarthy, aunt; Elsa Steenberg, friend; Sue Kwast, friend; and Paul O'Dell, physician. Scott's own story, his autobiography, is presented next, followed by some pretrial accounts. Finally, my court testimony and the verdict are presented in detail. The data are immense—maybe my truncated presentation is too brief, others will see it as too long., When he read the chapter, David Lester noted,

"The biggest point and most interesting is your court testimony verbatim. A verbatim account is most rare." The testimony was a rewarding and historical experience (a first in Canada), especially the cross-examination by a Mr. Bumble (Mr. Selkirk). On a final note, Dr. Lester suggested that I should mention the judge's decision beforehand, but to do so would be to deviate from the classical "Who done it?" It would also detract from the reader's clinical task, that is, to put the pieces of data (the bones) together to make his/her own assessment—is it homicide or suicide? That is the purpose of this chapter. I hope that the case illustrates the roadmap presented in this book.

Let me begin with more history.

HISTORY

To place Scott's death in the context of his life, here is a brief biography of Scott's life: Scott Dell was married to Cherrylle Dell. Cherrylle was born on November 15th, 1954; at age 17 she met Scott in Wilber Force, Ontario, Canada, in 1970. They married on December 31, 1971.

In October of 1974, Scott and Cherrylle moved to Toronto; Cherrylle separated from Scott in April of 1975, while she was employed as an exotic dancer. During the separation, Cherrylle became pregnant by another man and Eden was born in 1976. Scott and Cherrylle reconciled; Scott raised Eden as his own daughter and became employed at General Motors in Oshawa.

In May of 1978 Scott and Cherrylle applied and were approved to be foster parents. They moved to Millbrook in November of 1985 and began a home for special needs children. In 1987, Megan was adopted. In November of 1988, Scott and Cherrylle purchased a farm called Stony Hill Farm near the village of Killaloe. In 1989, their biological son, Frank, was born and Scott left employment with General Motors.

In July of 1992, Cherrylle left Scott, moved in with her female lover, Gay Doherty and commenced a petition for divorce from Scott. Between July and December of 1992, Cherrylle repeated allegations of physical assault by Scott upon her, allegations of physical assault upon a special-needs foster child, and allegations of sexual abuse by Scott upon their children. In January of 1993, the assault charges against Scott were withdrawn; all abuse allegations made by Cherrylle were determined to be fabrications (dissembling). In May of 1993, Scott was awarded sole custody of the children. Cherrylle continued to make allegations of sexual abuse, again determined to be false. Scott owned the farm at this time.

Early in 1994, Scott developed throat cancer. Cherrylle then became pleasant toward Scott in public. Scott underwent traditional treatment under the care of Dr. Paul O'Dell as well as exploring spirituality and medication. He underwent surgery on his throat cancer in September of 1994. This surgery, combined with radiation treatment and Scott's own efforts, resulted in complete remission; however, he completely lost his sense of taste. Scott and his family and friends were happy.

In November of 1994, Gay Doherty left Cherrylle, remaining first in the area, although she moved to Texas in April of 1995. Scott hoped for reconciliation and transferred the farm into joint ownership. In July of 1995, Cherrylle met Nancy Fillmore and they moved into Cherrylle's home. Scott met Susan Kwast in August of 1995 and started dating.

On the 14th of December 1995 Scott attended the clinic of Dr. O'Dell. There were no signs of cancer and Scott was described as having a positive attitude.

Despite Scott dating Susan, he was still quite attached to Cherrylle. Scott had planned to have Susan come to the farm for Christmas, but despite Scott having custody, Cherrylle was upset and stated that Scott could not have the children if Susan was there. Around the 18th of December, Susan terminated the relationship with Scott. Scott continued to plan a Christmas dinner with the family, planning the event of December 30th.

On December 28, 1995, Gay Doherty returned for a visit to Killaloe. She called Scott and went to visit Cherrylle and Nancy. While there, Cherrylle was talking to Scott on the telephone and did so, almost continually, until early evening to 4:00 a.m. on December 29th. Scott was reported to be drinking wine. On December 29th, Gay returned to Cherrylle's house, picked up the children and returned around 4:30 p.m. Scott had planned to pick up the children, but did not show. While waiting, Cherrylle told Gay that Scott's cancer had returned and that he had finally admitted to the sexual abuse. At around 5:00 p.m., Cherrylle called the farm, but received no answer. Gay decided to go to the farm; upon her arrival, she found the door ajar. Gay left the property and returned to Cherrylle's home, asking for help. Cherrylle and Nancy refused, but Cherrylle called a friend, who together with another man, returned to the farm with Gay. A short time later, Scott's body, half-naked, was found. They discovered a partially full bottle of wine, Le Piat Di'Or, with a partially full glass of wine. A note was found. The Ontario Provincial Police (OPP) were called.

OPP officer Wayne Carmaly arrived at the farm at approximately 11:55 p.m. on the 29th. The note, wineglass, and bottle were seized. The coroner was called. Dr. Henry Tiedje the next day viewed the body and issued a death certificate listing the immediate cause of death as Metastatic Carcinoma of the Mouth.

Upon being notified of Scott's death, his parents and family became suspicious. Cherrylle had told everyone that the cancer had returned; however, they contacted Dr. Paul O'Dell who stated that that was not possible. Cherrylle continued to tell people that the cancer had returned and requested a cremation. Yet, because of the family, an autopsy was performed by Dr. Virbala Acharya, and it was learned that cause of death to be acute ethylene glycol poison (or more commonly known as antifreeze). The antifreeze had been found in the bottle of wine. The autopsy report reads as follows:

> Synopsis:
> This 45-year-old male with a previous carcinoma of the pharynx with recent recurrence and surgery on the right side of the neck related to the carcinoma was doing heavy work on the day of death which was December 29, 1995. He was shoveling the snow off the roof and also drinking wine. The exact cause of death is not clear but is thought to be cardiopulmonary. The body of the deceased which was frozen was referred to the Ottawa General Hospital for a post mortem. The date of death was December 29, 1995.

Cause of Death:
1. No residual primary or metastatic carcinoma.
2. No definite anatomical cause of death.

Scott's mother, Myra was informed of the coroner's office decision on April 16, 1996. The letter read as follows: "I am unable to state with any confidence that his death was a suicide. I have elected to mark the death certificate as undetermined."

A NOTE

The cause of death was listed as "Undetermined," yet questions remained—was it suicide or homicide (accident and natural were ruled out.)? The note, found at the scene, was called a "suicide note." The coroner and police officer, for example, had called the note a "suicide note." The note read as follows:

SCOTT DELL NOTE – 29 DEC 95
Dear Mr. Fantasy
Carmelita – Linda Ronstadt – Debbie Quinn
Fun – life would go on forever. Death – suicide
The truth is simple but seldom ever seen.
If Truth is Purity can it ever exist in such an impure world. If it can't what does that mean. Are we all living in the shadows of
I feel like holding you close to me like never before I feel like making love to you I feel like all the bad stuff would go away.
You and I are stuck because of all the bad stuff that has happened to us last 3 years. We need to make it go away.
I'm trying not to think about things I want to think about. I don't know if that is what I should do or not. I can't help it. I Don't want to want you. I don't want to be rejected
If we don't get back together we maybe shouldn't see each other very much.
I thought maybe this wasn't a good night because I was too tired but I think the truth is revealed no matter what.
Sun – before
Lying on a beach with you
We forget all time that our life is a gift that has been given us to enjoy not to waste.
I doesn't last long. It is not a sin to be happy but it may be to be unhappy.
What did you think was going to happen if I drank a bottle wine listening to music we used to listen too
I'm going to think about you and me together
Maybe that's the only way you can except to thru a spiritual vision.
I seems true that is not a sin to be happy so maybe that means that it is to be unhappy
You will have to listen to your heart not your head.
I had a vision of you very briefly you were like some neophyte Angel floating in the air but you were disconnected you head from your body.
1) Mary Akroyd.
2) I was probably supposed to die
   But my life was spared
   I don't know why. That bothers me.

3) Let go theres nothing that you are holding onto now is going to help you
4) Let go. You are holding on tight.
5) Our lives are going by really fast

THE ARREST

Stories continued. Then, beginning in August of 1996, Cherrylle contacted the OPP with a series of suspicious fires; later it was learned that these were fabrications (more dissembling). In March of 1997, the relationship between Cherrylle and Nancy Fillmore ended and Nancy, by arrangement on the 18th of March attended the Killaloe OPP detachment to meet with Sgt. Ken Leppert. She later returned on the 18th and 27th of the same month. In April of 1997 Cherrylle learned that the OPP were investigating Scott's death. Cherrylle continued to contact the police, making allegations of fraudulent behavior of Nancy Fillmore, fires, and so on. A number of harassment's occurred toward Nancy, including a fire in the backyard of her apartment. By the summer of 1997, Nancy became more agitated and feared that Cherrylle intended to kill her. She told Sgt. Leppert, for example, that she feared for her life. On August 18, 1997 she told a number of people about her fear, and then, on the 19th of August 1997, it is alleged that a 16-year-old street youth entered Nancy's home, where she was passed out because she had consumed a lot of alcohol. He set a fire and Nancy died. The cause of death was determined to be carbon monoxide poisoning.

On the 20th of December 1997, Sgt. Ken Leppert, charging her with a number of offenses, most importantly 1st degree murder, arrested Cherrylle. Yet questions remained in the case against Cherrylle, most notably the note that was alleged to be a suicide note. Subsequently Sgt. Leppert contacted me and asked for my opinion: Is the note a suicide note or not? The specific referral question was Is the note found at the scene of Mr. Dell's death on December 19, 1995, a suicide note?

THE ANALYSIS OF THE NOTE

The documents and data reviewed was the note found at the scene. The case, thus, presents a unique opportunity. To postdict a communication as representing suicide risk or not, The TGSP will be used. In performing my analysis, I first looked at the note before any background information was known. The analysis is as follows:

The note has the following characteristics of suicide notes:

INTRAPSYCHIC DRAMA

I. *Unbearable Psychological Pain* (1 out of 6 protocol sentences, PS)
1) In the note, certain emotional states are present, including pitiful forlornness, emotional deprivation, distress and/or grief.
II. *Cognitive Constriction* (1 out of 3 PS)
7) S reports a history of trauma (e.g., rejection by significant other).
III. *Indirect Expressions* (1 out of 3 PS)

10) S reports ambivalence; e.g., complications, concomitant contradictory feelings, attitudes and or thrusts

IV. *Inability to Adjust* (1 out of 3 PS)

15g) S exhibits a serious dysfunction in adjustment. Unable to specify.

V. *Ego* (1 out of 3 PS)

16) There is a relative weakness in S's capacity for developing constructive tendencies (e.g., attachment, love).

INTERPERSONAL STAGE

VI. *Interpersonal Relations* (3 out of 6 PS)

19) S's problem(s) appears to be determined by the individual's history and the present interpersonal situation

20) S reports being weakened and/or defeated by unresolved problems in the interpersonal field.

21) S's suicide appears related to unsatisfied or frustrated needs; e.g., attachment.

VII. *Rejection-Aggression* (3 out of 8 PS)

25) S reports a traumatic event or hurt of injury (e.g., unmet love, a failing marriage).

27) S is preoccupied with an event of injury, namely, a person who has been lost or rejecting (i.e., abandonment).

28) S feels quite ambivalent, i.e., both affectionate and hostile toward the same (lost or rejecting) person.

VIII. *Identification-Egression* (1 out of 3 PS)

35) S wants to egress (i.e., to depart, to flee, to escape, to be gone), to relieve the psychological pain, associated to the traumatic event.

Based on the foregoing analysis, I reached the following primary opinions:

- Based on my training, experience, and research in the field and my review of approximately 2,000 suicide notes, there is no doubt in my mind that this is not a suicide note, that is, a note written by someone with suicide intent in mind.
- The specific protocols scored in the TGSP are, thus, as follows: 3, 7, 10, 15g, 16, 19, 20, 21, 25, 27, 28, and 35. (see Chapter 1)

LIMITATIONS OF A NOTE

More generally on the question raised, based on an analysis of an alleged suicide note alone, one cannot conclude, "This is a suicide" (Leenaars, 1999b). One needs to know one's limitations. Be that as it may, the suicide note is of particular interest and import to forensic scientists/clinicians or officers. To illustrate, I presented in the previous chapter another much-publicized coroner's inquest case in Canada—Daniel Beckon. We need to know the bones' limitations.

Returning to Scott Dell's case, his writing had a few characteristics of a suicide note, having 12 out of 35. The 12 protocol sentences relate primarily to an interpersonal trauma; that is, unmet love, rejection. It lacks in the intrapsychic characteristics; for example, unbearable psychological pain is almost absent and it is *the* stimulus to suicide. There is a lack of mental constriction and so on. It is in the intrapsychic world that people decide (intention) to die by suicide. I will outline in more detail my testimony at the trial. Let it suffice to conclude here: This is not a suicide note.

THE PSYCHOLOGICAL AUTOPSY

After the initial analysis and decision, I subsequently looked at the OPP's condensed synopsis of the John Scott Dell murder, April 25, 2000, which was the basis for most of the background information presented earlier.

In addition to the earlier opinion reached, I reached the following opinion:

> Mr. Dell's note is consistent with the experience of and preoccupation with a traumatic event, the break-up with, who in the Condensed Synopsis, is identified as his ex-wife, Cherrylle Dell. The "bad stuff" in "last 3 years" was painful for Mr. Dell. Mr. Dell has been frustrated and ambivalent. He wished for a positive development in the relation, but feared rejection. Thus, there is a history and a current circumstance that are the focus of the writing. He wished to have relief from the "bad stuff." The note is primarily a note about trauma, that is, the relationship, but it is not consistent with other aspects of a suicide note.

Subsequently the following question was asked: Did Scott Dell intentionally kill himself? This question is on the mode of death; that is, the question of intention—did this person intentionally kill himself? To address this question, as a noted earlier, this case must be placed within the content of further information about Scott's life and death. The specific procedure is the psychological autopsy; we discussed this in detail in Chapter 4.

RES IPSA LOQUITUR

Following Shneidman's lead (see Shneidman, 1993b), the chapter will follow the principle of *res ipsa loquitur*: The bones speak for themselves. The documents, newspaper accounts, letters, autobiography, investigation reports, third-party interviews, court testimony, and so on speak for themselves. Let me begin with a few letters that Scott had written in cards with a letter well before his death to Cherrylle.

> Whenever we are apart, I think back to how you came into my life . . . like a sunrise bright and magical. Setting me aglow with your love I know when we're finally together it will feel just like that first time. . . . You'll never know how much I miss you, babe. No matter what happens, you'll always be my most Precious Angel
>   Love forever Scott

Cherrylle

I guess you know how I feel about you. Milestone events tend to bring out the reflective side of me. Also tends to emphasise that loss I feel I guess when we don't celebrate together I don't usually look at the past with regrets but last couple of days found me thinking about our past wishing I hadn't taken so much for granted, wished I had realised how precious and fragile real love is and held on to you with all my might

    I really wish you happiness,

    Just wish I could share it with you

        Love Scott

These two cards with letters, addressed to Cherrylle, suggest that there is a history to the traumatic (intimate-partner) relationship to Cherrylle Dell. The content and themes in the note and earlier letter are consistent. The note was not a new communication. From the note, letters, and other data, it can indeed be concluded that Mr. Dell loved Cherrylle a lot, but not wisely.

Subsequently, the following question was raised: Did Scott Dell intentionally kill himself?

This question is on the mode of death, that is, the question of intention—did this person intentionally kill himself? To address this question, as we noted, this case must be placed within the context of further forensic data, beyond the note (Litman, 1988; Shneidman, 1999).

For the psychological autopsy, the following people were interviewed:

Myra Dell, mother
Lauretta McCarthy, aunt
Elsa Steenberg, friend
Sue Kwast (by telephone), friend
Paul O'Dell (by telephone), physician.

The following records were requested and reviewed:

Dr. Harris—Statement and transcript from prelim
Dr. O'Dell—Statement and transcript from prelim
Myra Dell—Statement
Elsa Steenberg—Statement and transcript from prelim
Sue Kwast—Statement and transcript from prelim
Loretta McCarthy—Statement and transcript from Prelim
Blair Voyvodic—Interim report from OPP
Francis Murphy—Interim report from OPP
Nancy Peplinskie—Interim report from OPP
Statement of Death
Medical Certificate of Death
Letter re: Scott Dell by Henry Tiedje, Coroner
Anatomical Pathology Report
Report of The Centre of Forensic Sciences
Scott Dell, transcript from divorce petition
Scott Dell, transcript CAS and children

Scott Dell, autobiography from Durham CAS file
CAS foster home study
Scott Dell chronology from Peter Sammon file
Scott Dell GM employment records
Scott Dell records from Dr. O'Dell
Note written from Scott Dell to Eden Dell, October 27, 1992
Christmas card to Eden from Scott Dell, 1995
Two cards with letters, addressed to Cherrylle Dell from Scott Dell
(Exhibits Seized from 18 Mill Street, Killaloe)
Poetry, addressed to Sue Kwast
Photographs, Scott Dell and others
Photographs, farm
Photographs, scene of death

THE INTERVIEWS

Let us begin with the interviews, utilizing Shneidman's (LASPC's leaders) basic outline, although I have tended to add after #9, a question about the nature of the person (i.e., his/her ego), eliciting an array of descriptions to the person. Be that as it may, I routinely conduct the autopsy in a standardized fashion as Dr. Shneidman taught me, although, as strongly espoused, in an open-ended fashion. It is not like a standard police investigation. If it was, there would be no need for this book. Here are the verbatim answers as recorded (I have placed my words/questions in italics):

Question 2: Tell me about the death.
Myra Dell: Well, Cherrylle, his wife, her phone call Saturday morning, said that Scott's body had been found the night before, he died . . .

And Cherrylle added to my daughter, Scott had a bad report at the last visit to the hospital, December 14th or 16th. And he and Eden, [oldest daughter and a friend in K "Killaloe"] Elsa had met at Cherrylle's house, and Scott told them that things looked bad, a bad report. But keep it quiet, and we believed that. So we went up to the funeral and this is what happened. He had a heart attack.
Loretta McCarthy: Well, there were specifics that he had been cleaning snow off the roof, and overdid it, himself, because he had cancer. There was a rumor about that he had a bad report about cancer.
Sue Kwast: I found out through Elsa, she and, she called me and they found him a few days after Christmas. He'd been drinking wine, a friend found him. And then they thought it was cancer. That didn't make sense to me. I just didn't think that, he was fine, you will not go so sudden. He had been planning for Christmas; he was seeing the kids. He was planning to go to school in Ottawa and go to Scotland. It didn't make sense, and because his cancer was in remission. It didn't make sense. The suicide thing, it will be so far from what Scott would do.
Paul O'Dell: I learned about it from a physician in the hospital, who knew the aunt. The aunt had called about the status of the cancer. The doctor called . . . Yes, cancer was under control. The death was, thus, under unusual circumstances.

Question 3: Outline the victim's history.
Myra Dell: Mother is Myra, 77. Father is John, 79. Retired, he was a grounds-keeper. Children six. Richard '52, Catherine '54, Stephen '56, Patricia '58, Marion '60, and Sterling '64. Scott was the oldest, born in '51.

Was he ever suicidal?
   No.

Did he ever make a suicide attempt?
   Never, no.

Was he depressed?
   I don't think so. He did say, after the cancer, I've got different priorities now. It makes you see what is important and not.
Lauretta McCarthy: Scott, mild-mannered man, a thinker, loved music. Was up on a lot of issues. Loved politics also loved land. He was a vegetarian . . . growing on the land. We talked music things, he loved to talk and discuss things. I remember one at the Cuban embassy, we talked with people. He had left U.S. because of Vietnam, the war. Loved discussions.
Elsa Steenberg: Lots, he's a friend, a close friend, very supportive friend, especially, very supportive family, especially his mom, except in his teens years, when rebelling. But he had a real strong commitment to his family, regarding his mom. . . . He felt Cherrylle couldn't be with him. He couldn't deny her. She was so manipulative.

What was he like when he found out about the cancer?
   He was very distraught. He was worried about the kids. Who would look after them? Where will the kids go? That was initially, he just found out. He went to see a social worker for that, he did that . . . he talked to me about Cherrylle, and her affair, her silicone breasts and exotic dancing, getting pregnant by someone else, and pretending it was Scott's child. He was always saying she couldn't help it that it's the way she is. Always making excuses. She would dress very provocative. He would say, fine, but she would push, he would say it's fine, including the affair. Scott wanted her to get it out of her system, and renew the marriage and fix it. His biggest regret was his marriage, didn't work out.

Was he ever suicidal?
   Never.

Did he ever make a suicide attempt?
   Never. He was more determined to stay alive because of the kids.

Was he ever depressed?
   Like depressed? No. I don't think more than a person would be about the cancer. He was upset, depressed about the cancer, but he worked at it.
Sue Kwast: He told me about Cherrylle, difficult, not easy. She appeared to have him wrapped around her finger, manipulative. He was helpful. He still loved her. He knew she was troubled . . .

The relationship?
   We got along fine . . . Broke up at the time? Just before Christmas. I thought it was the best, not a good idea. It was a long distance relationship. I dislike getting in between Cherrylle and Scott.

Reaction to? He was really sad, later he was upset, left a message, angry. He said, "Okay, I'll get on with life." I felt good, better to be angry and I hoped that he had a good Christmas.

Paul O'Dell: He had cancer . . . being on the tongue and in lymph nodes, had treatment, including radiation . . . operation. The response to treatment was excellent, completion . . . cancer not detectable . . . *Some residual effect?* Well. None. He did have a support system. He did have symptoms, dryness of the mouth, due to post radiation, operation of mouth. No evidence of cancer. No evidence of cancer progressing. In Mr. Dell's mind, he was "well."

Question 4: Details of victim's family.
Myra Dell: *Was anyone ever suicidal?*
No.

Were there any deaths of cancer?
Lots of people. It's very prevalent in the family.

Were there any unusual or catastrophic deaths?
No.

Motor vehicle accidents?
No.

Question 5: Description of personality and life style of the victim.
Myra Dell: *Can you tell me something about Scott?*
He came up to Canada to avoid the Vietnam War. It was a lottery, he was never chosen. He went through American school, but we came to Canada in the summer. He stayed in Canada. He was very political. He had lots of friends. Loved sports. Did well in school. Found it very easy, and did well.

Tell me about the kids?
Eden, not his. Cherrylle left and came back pregnant. He said, "I think a lot of her." Adopted a girl Megan, 13. Had a child, Frank, 11.

Describe his personality.
Elsa Steenberg: He's quiet. Once you get to know him, he never stops talking. He was very intellectual. He was open-minded. He'd think about a situation and see it in different ways. He wouldn't be judgmental.
Paul O'Dell: He was pretty upbeat, very robust, big physical man. Had children he felt committed to.

Question 6: Victim's typical pattern of reaction to stress.

What were the typical patterns of reacting to stress or emotional upsets?
Myra Dell: He probably kept it inside. Never told anything.

What about Cherrylle?
Most stressful. Yes.

What kind of reaction?
He was very frustrated. He didn't understand why. She just went out one day, took the car, cleaned out the house and went to Toronto with a woman.

What were his typical patterns of reactions to stress or upsets?
Loretta McCarthy: I think he would internalize them.

How did he react to the cancer?

Strongly, well he'd take it in stride. He was facing it. About suffering, he wasn't a complainer. He had to get through it, and this is how he dealt with it. He had researched it, thinking that he was going to do, he had read and dealt with it.

Elsa Steenberg: *What were his typical patterns?*

He would call me; he'd talk to me for hours. I know, little sleep and he'd still be talking.

Anything else?

He'd talk, go on and on about Cherrylle.

What was he upset about?

Cherrylle, Nancy Fillmore, they were together. He didn't like that. He felt Nancy was trying to maneuver the kids away. She had said bad things and, everything he felt . . . and problems with Cherrylle, he once picked up the kids and Cherrylle was under dressed. Put some clothes on, she said and she just laughed.

What about the cancer?

He talked about it, beating it.

Paul O'Dell: I think he had taken his treatment, his radiation and did well . . . He accepted that he was good.

Depressed?

I can't think of any signs of clinical depression. When first presented himself, he had advanced cancer, it was a great concern. He went into treatment. He was not depressed . . . and responded well.

Depressed?

No. As a doctor I see many patients with clinical depression. I am not an expert, but I see discouragement . . . in people and then refer to psychiatrist to evaluate.

Question 7: Any recent upsets, pressures?

Myra Dell: Well the cancer, he was fighting cancer, recovering from it.

Loretta McCarthy: The cancer, and just the ongoing relationship with Cherrylle. They had been separated for awhile.

Any recent or upsets in the last 12 months?

Elsa Steenberg: The cancer.

Anything else?

The Nancy and Cherrylle thing in the relationship. Cherrylle and Scott were becoming friends again, during the summer before Nancy moved in. It was for the kids. He wanted to make sure there was a positive relationship for the kids . . . The cancer, it was gone in early December, positive. It was clear that, it was under control.

Was he upset?

No, he was happy.

In December?

Yeah, early December.

Sue Kwast: Cherrylle, he had a lot of problems with her. I we talked a long time, it was about Cherrylle . . . That's the reason why we broke up. I didn't want to get involved. There were so many problems with Cherrylle. I didn't want to get involved it.

Anything else about the breakup?
He was upset, like anyone would be.

Question 8: Role of alcohol or drugs.
Elsa Steenberg: *Any drugs or alcohol in his lifestyle?*
Occasionally he'd smoke pot, but stopped, once sick. He had an occasional beer, Sleeman, but after the cancer he stopped, only occasionally.

Question 9a: Nature of interpersonal relationships.

Tell me about his interpersonal relationships with anyone?
Myra Dell: He got along. A lot of people admired him. He was the big brother. My kids thought he was great.
Elsa Steenberg: He wasn't that outgoing. People listened; he had lots of friends. He was a part of a group, a co-counseling group.

Question 9b: Nature of ego.
Myra Dell: Outgoing.

How would you describe his personality?
Loretta McCarthy: Sensitive, protective, tenacious, courageous, hard working.
Elsa Steenberg: One of the most intelligent people that I ever met.
Sue Kwast: Gentle, kind, humble.

Secretive?
I'd think about his health

Cherrylle?
He spoke about her past history, a bit.

Family?
Yes

His health?
Yes

Question 10: Fantasies, dreams, thoughts . . .
Loretta McCarthy: Well we would talk about dreams, about how they relate to our lives. That they were special, how the dreams affect us, if we pay attention to them.
Elsa Steenberg: He wanted to go to Ottawa to take a chef's course. Talked about success.

Ever talk about death?
No.
Sue Kwast: To go to Scotland, to go to learn to find out his history, Scotland and Ireland. That's what he wanted to do.

Death?
No

Suicide?
   No

Question 11: Changes in the victim before death.
Elsa Steenberg: No.

Question 12: Information relating to the life style of the victim.
Myra Dell: He bought the farm, he grew up on a farm.

Was he happy?
   Yes. He spoke to us at Christmas about the kids. He wanted to buy a plow to clean the snow so that the kids could get to the school bus . . . He loved the farm.
Elsa Steenberg: The cancer check, he was excited about it

Question 13: Assessment of intentions.

You think there's any reason why he may have intentionally played a role in his death?
Myra Dell: No. For two reasons. Why would he? He was so happy that he had a good report. He looked at life differently . . . If he had, he would have talked and talked. He never left without talking and talking.
Loretta McCarthy: No. There wouldn't have been any sense after what we had gone through.
Elsa Steenberg: No. We had planned to go out for New Years. He had too many things to do, to talk.
Paul O'Dell: No. If record of any suicidal indications, it would be documented and referred to someone.

Question 14: Lethality.

Did he behave in any kind of destructive fashion?
Myra Dell: No.
Paul O'Dell: No. Not a violent type of person, a passive person, upbeat, not violent. I mean pacifist, not passive.

Question 15: Reaction to information of death:

Any reactions to his death?
Loretta McCarthy: I was shocked. I couldn't believe it, because he went through so much. He went through all this and then to be dead. It made no sense at all. Why did this happen, all the pain and then die?
Elsa Steenberg: I didn't believe it. Scott's death, it couldn't be right. We had planned to go out on New Years. I had talked the night before. Later, I called his number but no answer.
Paul O'Dell: I just saw him within two weeks. I examined him, x-rays, etc. and there was nothing. There was no evidence of cancer. This was complete inconsistency about the cancer story. You can't do assumptions. There was no clinical evidence. He was 2 to 2 ½ years past treatment.

AN AUTOBIOGRAPHY

I believe that the interviews speak for themselves; yet there was much more information. I had requested a long list of documents, cited earlier. And here we learn more; let me begin with an autobiography that Scott had written on April 24th, 1987:

Autobiography – Scott Dell

I was born in Toronto in 1951 and moved to Connecticut with my family near the end of 1954. My earliest memories revolve around living in Toronto and the subsequent events leading up to our move. I am the oldest of seven children, and my brother Richard and sister Catherine were also born in Toronto before we moved.

One of my earliest memories is living on Winter Avenue in Scarboro, which at that time was very rural. As a matter of fact the small house we lived in had no indoor toilet. Two memories from this house are my father accidentally running over our dog in our driveway, and a recurring occurrence which was our neighbour who was a truck driver coming over to our house with his guitar and singing Hank William's Song's with my Dad. When we decided to move to Connecticut we sold this house and we moved in with my aunt in a subdivision in Scarboro. My aunt had just lost my uncle and I remember that things were quite strained. One vivid memory I have of that time is of my older cousin who had been mildly stricken with Polio. When we moved in he was in the process of starting to walk again. Another memory I had was my father, who had left to work on our house that we would live in Connecticut, returning with a brand new 1954 Green Ford Pick Up Truck. As soon as he came home he took me out for a ride around the block. I remember also taking the train to Connecticut with my mother and my brother and sister. My dad drove the truck with what belongings he could carry. I remember repeatedly asking my mother where he was, all the time looking out the window of the train for him.

I have very warm feelings about my childhood. I remember always feeling very secure and loved by my parents. I have a very close relationship with both my parents and brothers and sisters today still, even though separated physically by the distance between Millbrook and Connecticut.

As far as the three main lessons my parent taught me, I would have to say they would be honesty, the ability to share (necessary with six brothers and sisters) and the concept of equality. My parents were very liberal politically and they really stressed the equality of all races and creeds.

My early school years were quite enjoyable as I found schoolwork to come very easily. I got quite bored with school by the time my high school years came to an end. I had a fairly active social life, Scout's when I was younger and Sports and Dances when I was in high school.

I left school after Grade 12 though I had thought of going to University. By the time my grade 12-year came around I just couldn't bear the thought of sitting in a classroom for 4 more years.

I met Cherrylle up in Wilberforce, where my parents had a summer cabin. I had gone up with my family that summer and had decided to stay, because it was my draft year in 1970, and the Vietnam War was at its height.

What has been good about marriage has been having someone to share life's dreams, hopes and concerns. What's not so good I suppose is always having to temper your personal wants and desires to be compatible with your mate. Unless you want to lead a totally narcissist existence, I don't suppose that's so bad though.

The biggest problems I have had to face were probably first deciding at nineteen to leave home and evade the U.S. military draft. It is a decision that I sometimes still question myself. Another problem after being married for only a couple of years agreeing to an abortion for Cherrylle, even though I did want the child. I felt my marriage was more important though. . . . Another big problem we had to face, as a family was the death of a foster daughter, Corien who died in our home last year.

I am already a parent, but I feel that I would enjoy more children, and have more love to give other children besides our daughter. I see some differences in adoption as opposed to natural parenting. As you will be having children with perhaps hostilities, fear and insecurities from very possibly bad experiences.

As far as faith, I was raised a Roman Catholic, though not in a terribly dogmatic fashion. I suppose any faith I have now is very loosely defined fairly flexible. I find myself constantly looking at and questioning spiritual beliefs and very interested in other's beliefs. On that sense it is not the same as when I was a child because it is always changing to some extent. Growing I hope. What I would teach a child is I think as much as possible about many beliefs and what I believe, and to try to install the ability to search for themselves to find their own truth.

Pleasant changes would of course be the addition to our family, which would be more the physical presence, but of collective sharing. Unpleasant could of course be the working out of problems, which a child may bring to us from the past. The positive thing about this of course is that by working through these problems it should bring us all closer together.

A FEW PRETRIAL DOCUMENTS

The information on Scott is now two banker boxes full (and the police have even more boxes). I can thus only highlight a few observations here in the hope of providing a few snapshots of the events.

Dr. Bruce Harris was Scott's family physician since February of 1989; Dr. Harris frequently saw Mr. Dell and his family. In his statement to the OPP and preliminary, we read:

> Mr. Dell was seen as an attentive parent with a sincere interest in his children. His personal visits to my office were relatively infrequent, as he appeared to be healthy. He was seen in July of 1993 requesting support regarding family issues. At that time he was estranged from his wife. His wife had accused him of sexually abusing their three children. The patient suffered intensely over these accusations. The degree of stress was very severe and resulted in considerable sleep disturbance and weight loss. The patient stuck by his children and was able to endure the emotional crisis of this accusation, which was eventually decided to be unfounded. Throughout this the patient remained committed to his children. Despite the stress involving this accusation and the disruption of his family the patient never displayed any signs to me of depression.
>
> 1. In February of 1994, he was noted to have a sore throat. This eventually led to the referral of an ears, nose and throat specialist who found a carcinoma at the base of his tongue. The patient applied himself intensely to getting better. He was referred to literature; in particular, a book by Dr. Bernie Siegel entitled

Love, Medicine and Miracles, which encourages people to dedicate themselves positively to overcome the illness of cancer. Scott did this in earnest and underwent radiation therapy at the Cancer Clinic in Ottawa.

He did very well, going into complete remission. Throughout this time Scott remained very committed to getting well and seems quite inspired in his commitment. He stated that he had to get better in order to meet the needs of his children. Again, at no time was there any suggestion of depression, although, he certainly was under considerable stress and strain, not only from the illness but from the alienation within his family.

Scott worked with his former wife to develop a mutual custody agreement in order that his children are able to see their mother. Again, his commitment was very consistent to his children.

Scott was last seen in my office on September 14, 1995. At that time I could see no indication of depression or suggestion that he was suicidal.

And in the prelim in respect to questions by the Crown attorney (prosecuting) attorney, Peter Barnes, we learn from Dr. Harris:

Q. Was there any indication at that time or any concern that you had that the discomfort that he was suffering was in fact possibly result of cancer returning?

A. There was no indication of that.

Q. And, again, as of the date of that visit was there any indication of him being depressed?

A. No, there was no indication of that.

We thus, learn from Scott's family doctor that there are no records of mental illness, depression, or suicide risks. We also learn that despite Scott having been described as "secretive," he sought help and counseling for traumatic issues in his life; for example, sexual abuse charges, cancer.

From Dr. Paul O'Dell's prelim, we learn the following:

Q. During the time that you saw him then were there any significant milestones chronologically, or dates which would be of particular significance to you in that you might use those occasions then to discuss any change in his prognosis or expectancy?

A. There are no significant milestones to make in following a cancer, but as I said in earlier questioning, the statistical . . . surviving the first year is a definite plus and each year after that brings in it, and if you're looking at survival from cancers it's not a linear thing. It's more logarithmic and so that getting through that first year is a very definite positive step. We will usually mention that to patients and we'll, but usually be realistic. They always want to ask the question "Am I cured yet?" We never said that to him.

Q. At what point would you have been in a position to tell Scott Dell that he appeared to be disease-free?

A. Well, he is always clinically disease-free because that is a term that we use.

Q. Would you, given the nature of the disease that you treat, have any concerns with respect to the patients that you see as to depression or clinical depression, or any suicidal thinking, or ideation?

A. Well, clearly that's a problem. People do get depressed with . . . there are many things that cause you to be depressed. When a diagnosis of cancer is made just the diagnosis would be a source of depression for, to some extent, for many of us. The treatments that you have to go through and some of them quite arduous are a further source of depression. I'm not in the business of, on a day to day basis, recognizing clinical depression, not being a psychiatrist, but in medicine we do see people who are depressed and most of us will recognize significant clinical depressions. Now, what happens in an office encounter is different than what happens when the person goes home and they are in the confines of their own home, and you know, clearly we could miss depression, but in my experience and exposure to this individual, that he did not exhibit clinical depression.

Dr. O'Dell's testimony is entirely consistent with my interview material. Briefly, Scott was cancer free, not depressed, and focused on getting well. At the last office visit on December 14th, a few weeks before Scott's death, Scott was most positive. Scott knew he was well. Dr. O'Dell had made a follow-up visit in 3 months. Of note, Dr. O'Dell's reaction of concern to the unexplained death of one of his success stories makes clear sense, once you learn about Scott and speak to Dr. O'Dell directly. He is clearly a bright and learned physician.

The statements and prelim depositions of Elsa Steenberg and Sue Kwast present basically only more detail to what had been learned in the interview. Ms. Steenberg revealed that Scott was positively involved in meditation and visualization (something he shared with Cherrylle); this fact may make the reference to a vision in his last letter more explainable. Both Elsa Steenberg and Sue Kwast emphasize Scott's obsession with Cherrylle and Ms. Kwast was quite specific that this was the stimulus for Scott's and her breakup. We also learn that Cherrylle was quite upset at Sue's existence. There were a number of writings from Scott to Sue; here is a sample:

Can't wait to see you again!
Out of the blue a warm wind blew
You to me around me surrounding me
A warm blue wind that carried me to this place
I needed to be This place that is you
Your warm blue eyes like clear coral waters
Calling me Home This place that is you
A home I have been missing all my life
Home
To this place called you
Love Scott

Sue
I knew you were gone
Tonight
When I went to bed alone

And smelled you on my sheets
And almost felt you pressed up close
Against me
Your hair all in my face
I knew you were gone
Tonight
When I could almost see you
On top of me
Riding slow up and down up and down
I knew you were gone
Tonight
When I could almost hear you
Moan
And laugh
And tell me once again
You love me
I knew you were gone
Tonight
When I went to bed alone

The content and themes in the letters to Sue are not consistent with those to Cherrylle (as presented earlier). As stated, Scott's last note and previous letter were similar and different from those to Sue (to provide John Stuart Mills Methods of Difference, and Agreement and Difference, to the event). This is critical because the defense had argued that Scott was overwhelmed by the loss of Sue, resulting in the stimulus for his alleged suicide.

CHERRYLLE AND SCOTT

Scott's history is full of positives. For example, even his GM application, when he first began to work there, states, "Strong appearing applicant." These descriptions appear consistent (sameness) throughout his history.

The court material in this case is, from my experience, not common (although it does occur). Here we learn a large array of facts, all made under oath. One fact appears obvious; Cherrylle lied about everything, even in court. She, for example, had lied that she had a degree from the University of Toronto; indeed, records showed that she completed grade 8 and only started grade 9. And of course, all the allegations about Scott, such as the sexual abuse, were ruled to be fabrications. Although it is not my purpose to detail Cherrylle's life but a few facts are critical.

Cherrylle's family was described as "severely dysfunctional." Cherrylle's grandfather molested her and of note, her father was charged and found guilty of sexual molestation of children. Cherrylle's father's guilt is stated to have sparked a major regression in Cherrylle and was the beginning of all the sexual abuse allegations toward Scott.

Cherrylle suffered from mental illness; she was troubled and already hospitalized as a teenager. There are at least three suicide attempts recorded. Cherrylle is described as suffering from low self-esteem, being very, very sensitive to criticism, having a really bad temper, and having physically assaulted Scott on occasion. She accused Scott of physical assault, such as attacking her with a knife; all allegations were judged to be fabricated. Scott did admit to one incident, when he grabbed Cherrylle, after she left him for the first time in 1975, and pushed her against the wall of her father's house. On that occasion Cherrylle was with her lover and Scott was upset. In the court recording, it is noted that Scott immediately let go. There are no other records of physical abuse despite Cherrylle's statements to the contrary. Cherrylle, it is believed, lied about everything, even under oath (dissembling). Cherrylle had many problems including with her children. They preferred Scott and the oldest two testified against their mother at the murder trial of their father. Based on the date, I believe that Cherrylle probably had recurrent depressive episodes and had a history of suicide attempts, and a narcissistic personality disorder.

Scott, on the other hand, is described as coming from a healthy family, although Cherrylle labeled them as dysfunctional. He is seen as quiet, having a slow temper, and being very bright. He was a family man, having strong interest in his children. He often took care of the children; one was described as difficult and Scott often cared for the child, as Cherrylle would get quickly frustrated. For example, he would spend hours with the child in a Fisher Price swing to soothe the child. As another example, during a sexual assault to one of the children by an older boy, he was seen as most supportive (an event that is seen as having added to Cherrylle's regression). He was known to be determined to beat the cancer for the children.

Just before his death, he was planning to buy a snowplow for his truck to clear the snow on the road to make it easier for the children. He was described as "excellent" with children. He had interests and hobbies (e.g., gardening, enjoying music, playing the guitar, and reading). He had future plans; for example, he had bought a New Year's ticket to celebrate with Elsa Steenberg and other friends at a local establishment, the Wilno. His main problem was constantly stated to be "Cherrylle." He was aware of this fact, but felt that he was so in love with Cherrylle. Scott believed Cherrylle needed only support, not criticism.

Based on the psychological autopsy, I developed the following opinion on the question "Did Scott intentionally kill himself,"—"No." Utilizing standard profile from the TGSP as well as an alternative construction (look) with Shneidman's commonalities (see Table 11.1), Scott showed few of the characteristics of suicide; indeed, the note's scores were the same for his life. If one uses Shneidman's prodromal clues in his Terman's studies of gifted suicides, one comes to the same conclusion (Shneidman, 1971). These include some 10 items: early evidence of instability, including dishonesty; rejection by the father; multiple marriages; alcoholism/drug abuse; an unstable occupational history; ups and downs in income; a crippling physical disability; disappointment in the use of one's potential; any suggestions of self-destruction; a competitive self-absorbed spouse. Again, Scott had some markers, but not the large majority. In his review of the Terman cases, Shneidman looked at trauma, instability, recent downhill course, controls (inner and outer) and so on. He was able to identify four of the five cases successfully to be most suicidal that had, in fact, committed suicide (the fifth case was Shneidman's number six pick). This result would be a probability of 1 out of 1131. That is predictability!

Thus, as discussed in chapter 1, an investigation can look at contextual cues, there is more than one method to assist in determining whether a death is natural, accident, suicide or homicide (see Table 11.1).

Based on the psychological autopsy, here are a random number of other opinions that I reached:

- There is no history of mental disorder.
- There is no history of depression.
- There is no history of suicide risk.
- There is no history of depression or suicide in Mr. Dell's family of origin.
- Mr. Dell does not have a history of depression or suicide risk.
- Mr. Dell does not appear to have had a mental disorder, although he did have a problematic relationship (adjustment problem) to Cherrylle Dell.
- Mr. Dell did experience a number of traumas in his life (e.g., marriage/loss of Cherrylle, carcinoma, false accusation about sexual abuse by Cherrylle).
- Mr. Dell adjusted to traumatic events without signs of depression or suicide risk, although reactions were evident, e.g., very severe degree of stress to the (false) accusation of sexual abuse. (Any normal person would. I would.)
- Mr. Dell was diagnosed and treated for carcinoma of the base of the tongue. Mr. Dell adjusted well and positively to the diagnosis and treatment. There was no indication of depression or suicide risk.
- Mr. Dell did not have "persistent cancer" at the time of his death. There was no indication of depression or suicide risk prior to his death, regarding cancer or any other physical condition.
- Mr. Dell did not suffer from depression or suicide risk during the last 12 months before his death.
- There is no indication of recent depression or suicide risk before his death.

Thus, there is no doubt in my mind that in all probability that at the time of his death, Mr. Dell did not intend suicide.

Table 11.1. Shneidman's Ten Commonalities/
Standard Profile of Suicide

I. The common purpose of suicide is to seek a solution.

II. The common goal of suicide is cessation of consciousness.

III. The common stimulus in suicide is intolerable psychological pain.

IV. The common stressor in suicide is frustrated psychological needs.

V. The common emotion in suicide is hopelessness-helplessness.

VI. The common cognitive state in suicide is ambivalence.

VII. The common perceptual state in suicide is constriction.

VIII. The common action in suicide is egression.

IX. The common interpersonal act in suicide is communication of intention.

X. The common consistency in suicide is with lifelong coping patterns.

Thus, my answer to the question, "Did Scott Dell intentionally kill himself?" is "no."

A NEWSPAPER'S STORY

By the time Cherrylle Dell's murder trial came to court, the case had become a national event. The following account appeared on the front page of Canada's national newspaper, *The Globe and Mail*, on Saturday November 18, 2000:

> The Village Vamp and her Two Lovers
> By Erin Anderssen
> Crime Reporter, Killaloe, Ont.
> There once lived in Killaloe, a place of aging hippies, herbal marijuana bust, a comely woman whom most everyone considered charming, if a little odd for the fur coat and high heels she favored on trips to the post office.
> Years from now, when they talk of Cherrylle Dell, as they most assuredly will, the story may start this way, with what everyone first noticed: the Barbie Doll looks and flashy clothes that made her a small-town original even before two of her lovers turned up dead.
> She'd married an American, Scott Dell, when they were still teenagers. They lived outside town in a log farmhouse, raising a family and taking in disabled children.
> About 10 years ago, Cherrylle left her husband for a woman, which, though this was the conservative Ottawa Valley, did not engender the reaction you might expect and was generally accepted among friends.
> It's what happened later that truly earned Ms. Dell her place in valley folklore. Just after Christmas in 1995, Scott Dell was found half-naked in an upstairs bedroom in the farmhouse, poisoned, the authorities would allege by antifreeze-laced wine—quite possibly by his own hand, although in the village there were whispers of something else. Cherrylle had, by then, moved in with Nancy Fillmore, a social worker who a friend says answered an ad to be caretaker to Cherrylle's kids. In 1997, after the two had separated, the apartment building where Ms. Fillmore paid rent, and from where she would have been able to see the red brick of Cherrylle's house across Brennan's Creek, burned to the ground. Trapped inside, Ms. Fillmore died. . . .
> Police eventually arrested and charged a teenage boy with murder in connection with the fire, but their investigation continued . . .
> Five months later, the authorities decided that Scott Dell had not committed suicide after all, but had been poisoned intentionally; Ms. Dell, now 46, was arrested and charged with first-degree murder.
> She'd been in jail awaiting trial for more than two years when the police came calling again. She was accused of instructing the teenager to set the fire that killed her one-time lover and was charged for the second time with first-degree murder . . .
> For pure titillation, the case of Cherrylle Dell has it all: a beautiful defendant, sex and betrayal and a strange, small town rumbling with chatter.
> Gay Doherty, the former lover who discovered Mr. Dell's body, has said she's considering a book, and a Toronto film company has already expressed interest.
> Residents here can be expected to tune into the trials, the first of which, for her husband's death, is scheduled to start on Monday.

COURT TESTIMONY

Before court, I read the testimony of key witnesses. These did not change my opinion; yet I did learn from Gay Doherty that Cherrylle was writing while she was on the telephone and Elsa Steenberg testified the following:

5 ____ Q. So she phoned you between the time of Scott's death and the funeral?
_____A. Yes, she did.
_____Q. How long did the conversation last?
_____A. Not very long.
10____Q. Tell us what you remember of the conversation?
_____A. She told me that she had told Scott that he could let go now and her
angel would take him to heaven.
_____Q. What do you mean she said that he could let go now? What context
was that?
15____A. Well, I was under the impression that she was giving him the right to
let go.
_____Q. When did she say that had happened, that she had said that to him?
_____A. The last time they had spoken together on the
20____telephone.
_____Q. Well, perhaps I've missed it, but I don't think you've told us about a
conversation on the telephone.
_____A. Cherrylle told me that she had been talking with Scott on the
telephone.
25____Q. When did she say she had been speaking with him?
_____A. I don't remember the day. However, I do remember her telling me that
"You can let go. My guardian angel will take you to heaven."
30____Q. During that conversation, do you remember her saying anything else to
you?
_____A. I remember her saying to me, "Now that Scott is dead, I want to be your
friend, I want to take Scott's place."
_____Q. Prior to Scott's death, had you ever been to her home before?
_____A. I've never been to her home.
5____Q. Okay. I want to ask you about some pieces of information. Did Scott
ever tell you that, at the beginning of 1995, that his cancer was no longer
in remission?
_____A. That it was no longer in remission?
_____Q. Yes.
10____A. That his cancer had come back?
_____Q. Yes.
_____A. Never, his cancer had not come back.
_____Q. Did Scott ever tell you or did you ever become aware in 1995, in the
last year of his life, that he was throwing
15____up?
_____A. Never.

Keeping in mind that I had been asked about Scott, not Cherrylle, I enquired about these facts the police provided me with the following notes. These were alleged to be written by Cherrylle the night of December 29th. What is obvious is that the content and themes are identical to Scott's note. Not only is Scott's note not a suicide note, but also there are questions about the author of the note (as there were with the Daniel Beckon case). Did Scott or Cherrylle author the note or parts of the note? I will return to this point in my testimony. Here is Cherrylle's note:

> The sun as a life
> Source
> Staying in the sun
> Laying on the
> Beach
> Staying in the light
> Were not meant to be
> Happy
> Its not sin to be
> Happy
> Maybe it's a sin to be
> Unhappy
> Should live in
> Environment your
> Happy in.
> Looking for guidance
> Not doing this right
> Something's wrong.
> If it's the spiritually right thing to
> Do theirs nothing to
> Be afraid of
> Something has to change
> Mini-brief vision
> Cherrylle floating almost
> Like an angel—but not
> Really an angel—head
> Was not connected to
> My body. Flash vision—
> Wasn't connected.
> Close to each other but
> Not connected.
> I need to let go of something
> I need to let go of something
> How fast our lives are going.

MY TESTIMONY

To turn to my testimony, I shall again use the principle of *res ipsa loquitur*:

> 1766.
> R. v. Cherrylle Dell
> Tuesday, January 16, 2001
> —Upon commencing at 9:30 a.m.
>   MR. BARNES: Good morning, Your Honour.
>   THE COURT: Mr. Barnes.
> 5   MR. BARNES: Your Honour, the purpose of course

this morning was for the Crown to call Dr. Antoon
Leenaars. Mr. Selkirk has indicated that a Mohan
type of voir dire will be required . . .
MR. BARNES: Your Honour, perhaps I can just
articulate for the Court then the purpose that I'm
5   calling Dr. Leenaars. Of course, it's for him to
be permitted to give expert opinion evidence in
two areas in particular. First, as to the
application of a technique to the facts of this
case that is widely or generally accepted and used
10   in the fields of psychology, psychiatry and
suicidology—Dr. Leenaars will tell us what
suicidology is—and used to distinguish between
genuine and non-genuine suicide notes or what are
purported to be suicide notes . . .
MR. BARNES: Secondly, Your Honour, I anticipate
30   his giving evidence as to the application of a
technique known as a "psychological autopsy" to
the case . . .
Q. Can you just briefly describe the subject matter in a little more detail with
respect to your thesis?. . .
A. Yes. Part of the problem in suicide is trying
20   to understand the suicidal person because of course he's
deceased, and so one looks at alternative information, trying to
understand the person. And suicide notes have always been
considered one window to the mind of the deceased.
Studies in this area began much more
25   empirically in the 1950s with Shneidman and Farberow. Through
contacting them . . .
So what we developed was a way of looking at
suicide notes through protocol, by that I mean protocol
sentences, which is a—empirical, it's a positivist procedure
where falsifiability, which is so important in science, is
possible . . .
Q. Are you currently involved or recently
involved with respect to the training of any medical health
professionals?
A. Yes . . .
You see, suicide prediction is very difficult.
There aren't very simple scales available. If you will, there's
5   an old notion of phrenology, looking for a bump on the head.
You're not going to find a bump of suicide on the head. So it's
Complex. . . .
10   So what we do is we try to train psychiatrists
and psychologists into this kind of understanding, trying to
understand the suicidal person from commonalities rather than
simply whether they have depression or not . . .
Q. Now, is there—in the literature of
25   suicidology, have there been any empirical tests—testing that
has been done and published with respect to the analysis of

suicide notes or the technique that you employ?

A. Yes. The very beginning of actually suicide
studies actually sort of coincides with the modern suicidology
30 beginning. Dr. Shneidman had been sent to the V.A. from the V.A.
Hospital to a coroner's office, and to his surprise he discovered
some 700 suicide notes . . .

5   A. And he's a good scientist, and what he
decided to do was not read these notes but rather he decided to
use the technique of science to look for falsifiability by
comparing them to non-genuine notes. This was the very first
beginning studies scientifically of notes . . .

Q. When was that that Shneidman had started this
work?

A. This started in the 1950s. They published a
book in 1957 called "Clues to Suicide". He called on his friend
15 Norman Farberow, who is also one of the grandfathers of the
field. And they started publishing the first study showing that
indeed genuine notes and non-genuine notes were very different,
that if you ask people to simulate a note, that they're not the
same, that there are actually distinguishing features . . .

Q. Have there been any tests of the ability of
lay people to distinguish between genuine and non-genuine or
simulated notes?

10 A. Yes. This has been one of the questions from
the very beginning. In one of the first studies that is
published in a journal by Arbeit and Blatt, he had taken 93
judges with four different levels of clinical training, and—

20 what he found is out of that group only 13
were able to distinguish genuine from non-genuine notes . . .
basically what it showed is that, according to Arbeit, only those

30 with clinical training could distinguish genuine from
non-genuine. Subsequently, David Lester . . . and I have looked at a series of
studies, trying to see, you know, what allows people because we've also
found that most people, even undergraduate students in psychology, cannot
distinguish genuine from non-genuine notes.
What we did is, for example, we gave the

5   sample of genuine and non-genuine and tried to see whether there
was some way of distinguishing what is it that allows a person to
decide a note is genuine . . . And basically we couldn't find any . . .

And basically what we found is that people have
25 very idiosyncratic theories about suicide, their own very
personal belief.

Now, there was one common thing that people
quite consistently looked for a suicide note, and that was a
trauma, that there was some event that was quite traumatic for
30 the person, an unmet love, a physical disease, et cetera. But,
of course, when you ask people to write non-genuine or simulated
note, you also find people being able to simulate or to say "put that
into the note". So it doesn't really distinguish a genuine
from a non-genuine note very well . . .

Generally, what can be concluded is that
there are a lot of myths about suicide and suicide notes that
people have.

Q. On the other hand, in terms of the employment
15 of the 35 protocol sentences and the methodology which you say
you've developed and which has been peer reviewed, what do you
say as to the ability of somebody trained in that method to
distinguish between genuine and non-genuine notes?

A. Quite good actually . . .

Q. What are the limitations, in your opinion, in
individual cases, in trying to apply these protocol sentences and
this methodology to the analysis of individual notes which may or
may not be genuine suicide notes?

5 A. Well, if I may, part of the problem, of
course, in the whole field is that in science, whether it's
sociology or psychology or psychiatry, we're looking at the
general. This is the nomothetic approach. Here you get general
patterns, common patterns, and of course when you look at the
10 individual case, the idiographic approach, if you will, it can be
quite different. This is sort of like—more like what I do
clinically with each individual patient than some of the
research . . .

You have to
look at the individual note and be cautious about, you know, what
you're concluding because there have been cases where people in
court—for example, in the Daniel Beckon inquest that I was
30 involved in, which—

Q. That's the Ontario inquest?

A. Yes, that was the Ontario inquest where the
late Sopinka hired me to take a look at this conclusion where
someone said, you know, "If there's a suicide note, therefore the
person killed himself." From my point of view, of course, you
can't conclude that. What you can conclude from a note is that,
5 you know, the person's mind may have had suicidal intent, there
may have been characteristics of suicide, but then to jump that
the person killed himself seems to me to be a little erroneous.
You have to know the limitation of the data. That's, for
example, why a psychological autopsy comes into play, to give you
10 a wide array to answer the question, "Did the person commit
suicide or not?" . . .

Q. Doctor, in this particular case, in July of
2000 you were approached by the Ontario Provincial Police.
30 A. Yes.

Q. And you were provided with a note?

A. Yes.

Q. And were you at that time provided with any
material other than a note?

A. Yes. I was provided with a synopsis of the
case. However, it should be important for the Court to note that
5 I did not read the synopsis. In fact, I never read anything that

anyone sends me until after I do the note. I let it be, I score
it again, and then I might, after I make my conclusion, start
reading the other material . . .

MR. BARNES: Q. And do I take it that—I think
we've covered this, but I take it that you were asked by the
police, first of all, as to whether or not you had an opinion as
20 to whether or not the note in front of you, Exhibit 8 in the
trial, was a genuine or non-genuine suicide note essentially.

A. Yes. I concluded that it was not a genuine
note, that the person who wrote this did not have suicide intent,
did not have characteristics of a suicidal mind in this note.
25 Q. All right. And did you reach that opinion,
then, by applying the protocol sentences that has become Exhibit A?

A. Yes. I had scored this note, then left it,
and then scored it again not knowing my previous scores, to
30 develop some consistency. And again concluded that, although it
had a few characteristics that you might find in a note,
specifically about a trauma . . .

Q. All right. And perhaps we will go into the
protocol sentences, then, and the basis of the formulation of
your opinion. When you say that you looked for the presence of
10 protocol sentences—

A. Uh-huh.

Q. that is you looked for each of the 35
protocol sentences being present or being evidenced in the note.

A. Yes, that's basically the technique . . .

Q. Go ahead when you're ready.

A. Yes. In terms of the various aspects that I
find in the note, that you might find in a suicidal state, the
5 first one relates to—in the suicidal drama, certain emotional
states are present.

Q. Could you just refer to the protocol sentence
as well to make it easier for counsel to follow what you're
saying?
10 A. Yes, number three.

Q. Yes.

A. In the suicidal drama, certain emotional
states are present, including pitiful
forlornness, emotional deprivation,
distress, . . . or grief.
15 Clearly in this note—keep in mind it says "and/or", so it's
not necessary, and these are including, so they're examples, if
you will. But clearly there's distress in this note and there's
deprivation, the loss of the relationship, which subsequently,
with the synopsis, I concluded was in terms of Cherrylle. . . .
20 Q. Go on.

Q. Are there any elements that you found to be
20 consistent in this note with a mental disorder?

A. Well, there's an item under this category,
number 15(g), which is sort of like when people communicate that

there's something wrong, that there may be a disorder or a
dysfunction, but you can't really specify it. You know something

25 is wrong, but it might be a situational distress. It's sort of
like the category that you use if none of the other ones apply.
    Q. Is a situational distress different than a
mental disorder?
    A. Yes, it would be . . .
what we find is more discussion about
the situation, the context for Scott. For example, 19, the
subject's problems appear to be determined by the individual's
history and the present interpersonal situation. He talks, for

20 example, about a history, three years of bad stuff, so there's a
history to this, plus the current situation. If we can't get
together again, maybe we should leave, you know, maybe we
shouldn't see each other so much.
    Q. And the reference to the three years of bad

25 stuff, and if we can't get together again, perhaps we shouldn't
see each other. Are those phrases that appear in the note?
    A. Yes. Then 20, he discussed being weakened
and/or defeated by the problems in the interpersonal field. This
is that, you know, if we can't really get back together, then

30 maybe we shouldn't see each other that much because, you know,
all the bad stuff, et cetera, that he just seems that he can't
solve this, and if we can't get back together, maybe we shouldn't
see each other.
    21, the suicide appears to be related to
unsatisfied or frustrated needs. Clearly, that's evident in his
need for attachment to Cherrylle, and it's frustrated. It's been

5 thwarted, if you will, unsatisfied.
    23, a positive development in the disturbed
relationship was seen as the only possible way to go on living,
but it was not seen as forthcoming. Again, he talks about the
relationship, if they get back together, but if they can't, and

10 it's likely not going to happen, maybe we shouldn't see each
other.
    Then under "Rejection-Aggression", we find

25 Again, this is that there is a traumatic event, again, the
unmet love kind of thing.

15 And then 27, that he's preoccupied with the
event or injury, namely, the letter is about his preoccupation or
obsession, if you will, with Cherrylle.
    And then 28 he's quite ambivalent, both
affectionate and hostile, angry if you will if we can't get

20 together. So there's an ambivalence towards this. But there's
none of the anger or aggression, the hatred in some of the other
protocols. If I may, it's not only what is in this note, it's
what's not in the note that makes it so important to distinguish
as a genuine or non-genuine.

25 And the last one, in terms of identification,
egression, he says he wants to egress, to escape. Basically,

what he says is, again, maybe we shouldn't see each other so
much, but he never says the ultimate that we find in a suicide
note, "This is the only way out; I need to kill myself. Please
30   forgive me," et cetera. There's none of those kinds of wishing
to escape. It's just simply not to see Cherrylle if they can't
get back together.
    Q. Now, if I can, just in perhaps—further, the
protocol sentences have subheadings.
    A. Yes, they do.
    Q. The first deals with the general heading
5   "Unbearable Psychological Pain", and as I've been counting, there
are six protocol sentences, and you found evidence of one of the
six protocol sentences under the general heading "Unbearable
Psychological Pain."
    A. That's correct. It doesn't have the kind of
10   pain that we look for in a note where the person says, "It's
intolerable and the only thing I can do is escape to kill
myself." It doesn't have the hopelessness and helplessness, for
example, that we find . . .
10   Q. With respect to the second half of the
protocol sentences, then, "Interpersonal Relations."
    A. Four of—I think there's four, yes, four of
six. The ones that are missing is that, you know, the
frustration is to a point that he can't tolerate it anymore, and
there isn't an indication from this note that he's under constant
20   kind of strain or that he's too unhealthy or that he can't do
anything about it. He says basically, you know, "If we can't
work this out, let's not see each other."
    Q. And to what degree are the ones present, in
your opinion, under this heading?
25   A. Well, the four that I find are clearly
evident, that there is an interpersonal problem, and that there's
a history, and that he's been frustrated by his needs in this.
However, you know, if I would write a forlorn love letter, I
would also find these elements in any forlorn love letter . . .
15   Q. The final cluster "Identification -
Egression" . . .
—that he wanted
    to escape from the difficult relationship, but there is none of
    that in the sense of "I'm going to kill myself, this is the only
    way out," which we classically find in suicide notes. And we
25   also might find, you know, "Please forgive me, this is the only
    thing I can do." There's none of those kinds of things. There's
    also no suggestion that, you know, he's unwilling to accept this.
    He's just basically saying, "If we can't work this out, then
    let's not see each other so much." . . .
Q. In any event, as a result of your examining
    this note on those occasions, are you, by employing these
    protocol sentences and the methodology that you have described,"
20   able to express an opinion with respect to whether or not it is a

genuine suicide note?

A. I believe it's a non-genuine note. By that I mean this note does not seem to be consistent with having suicide intent in mind.

25 Q. Now, if I may, I'll just move along. And subsequent—now, you provided that opinion in a letter, doctor. You provided that opinion in a letter?

A. Yes . . .

Q. All right. And, subsequently, then, you were contacted by the Ontario Provincial Police and asked to do a further analysis of additional materials.

A. Yes. They asked me whether I could determine whether the person killed himself or herself, and I said from the note alone, as I've written in some of my articles like Suicide Notes

5 in the Courtroom, that you cannot determine that from a note alone, and that the procedure that's generally accepted in the field is a psychological autopsy that would allow us to give you an answer to that question . . .

Q. All right. What is a "psychological autopsy"?

25 A. A psychological autopsy is a generally accepted procedure in the field . . .

This is a retrospective investigation, a psychological investigation, where you take a look at what occurred. You would examine the coroner's reports. You would examine the autopsies. You would interview typically three or

10 more people whom may have known the deceased. You would read, anything, material that the person might have left, court documents, police records, school records, employment records, maybe they've been hospitalized, looking at clinician notes, whatever. You gather a wide array of information trying to

15 determine whether this person intentionally tried to kill themselves.

Q. Now—

A. Let me go back again. This first started back in the 50s when the coroner in L.A., Curphey, who by the way was

20 a Canadian, asked Shneidman, Dr. Farberow and Dr. Litman—he had a number of cases that were undetermined, and he asked them, "Could you assist me here in whether these cases, because it could not be determined based on the more forensic investigation or police reports, whether they were actually suicides or not."

25 And they assisted Curphey in this kind of technique since the 50s to try to analyses and give a perspective about intention, whether this person intended.

Now, keep in mind people often ask, like bereaved families, "How could you kind of determine that the

30 person intended to do something after they're dead?" Well, we all make assumptions about people's intentions. We don't see them. We constantly, in our relationships, make inferences based on what people say, and maybe what they wrote, et cetera. We do that all the time. The psychological autopsy, the trained person

simple in terms of this knows how to do that better. They're
trained as a psychologist or a psychiatrist or some related field
5   to analyses and understand the intention.
     So it's been used, the psychological autopsy,
since the 50s, but not only in terms of individuals cases like
what was—occurred since the 50s, and some cases are famous
like the Marilyn Monroe case that Litman did, but also in terms
10 of research . . .
     Q. Now, are the protocol sentences that you've
15 described to us applicable to the psychological autopsy?
     A. Yes, absolutely, because these are sort of
like the common characteristics that you might find in suicide.
Ed Shneidman, for example, talks about 10 commonalities. They're
embedded in these protocols . . . So it allows you, if
you will, with these protocols or Shneidman with his
commonalities, or et cetera, to frame, to try to understand the
intent to determine these equivocal cases: Was it a suicide or
not? . . .
     Q. May I stop you there for a moment, please, and
just ask you this. When you were asked to do this by the police,
10 that is perform a psychological autopsy with respect to Scott
Dell, did you employ the 35 protocol sentences?
     A. Yes, I constantly have them in my mind.
They're constantly—they're sort of my protocols. They're my
hypotheses. They're the things that I look for. But certainly
15 would not be the only things that I would look for. I mean,
there's much more to suicide, and each case, each individual case
is unique . . .
     Q. Other than in the fact that in the
psychological autopsy that the individual is deceased, what then
are the similarities or differences between the psychological
autopsy and the diagnosis or treatment of the individual patient?
5   A. Actually, in the psychological autopsy it's
easier because what you are doing is postdiction. When you're
treating a person and trying to predict, you may not have all the
information in front of you. They may not be giving all the
information. You may not be able to speak to their Minister or
10 Rabbi who may be a support system.
     So when you're trying to work with a clinical
patient, it's actually even more difficult. When doing a
psychological autopsy, you can gather all sorts of information . . .
. . . Q. In this particular case, that is relating to
the death of Scott Dell, when the police asked you if you would
be prepared to do this, did you have an opportunity to tell them
what data or what interviews you would like to conduct?
20 A. Yes. I chose the interviews myself, who I
wanted to see. I was very explicit about wanting to speak to Dr.
O'Dell and . . .
Q. Doctor, the questions that you asked during
the interviews, did they cover a specified or pre-specified list

of topics?

30   A. Yes, they do.

Q. And did you record the answers from the
interviews in any way?

A. Yes. There's a fairly standardized kind of
questioning that Dr. Shneidman taught me . . .

Q. You preserved the list of

20 questions?

A. Yes.

Q. And your answers.

A. Yes . . .

the purpose of asking these questions

during the interviews and looking at these materials was to
answer certain questions, if possible.

A. Yes. It would be basically: Did the person
intend to kill themselves? Was this a suicide? That's the basic

10 question.

Q. And having conducted that psychological
autopsy, was the information that you were able to gather
sufficient, in your opinion, for the purposes of answering those
questions?

15   A. Yes . . .

Q. And, again, when you were looking at these
20 documents, do I take it that you're relating them in some way to
the protocol statements with respect to state of mind, that is
intrapsychic as well as interpersonal relations?

A. Yes, you constantly look for these common
features, whether it's, you know, Ed Shneidman's or these

25 protocols, something that gives you some sort of consistency.
Again, Maris' notion of suicidal career, if you will . . .

As a result of conducting

30 this psychological autopsy with these materials, were you able to
form an opinion as to whether or not Scott Dell was suicidal?

A. Yes.

Q. And what was that opinion?

A. That he was not suicidal, that he had never
been suicidal, that he was not suicidal at the time of his death.

Q. You've indicated that subsequently you had an

5 opportunity to review further materials, that is between the time
that you formed that opinion and reported upon that opinion and
today's date in January of 2001.

A. Yes.

presented me with some notes that

were alleged to have been written by Cherrylle Dell. I was most

20 interested in this because Gay Doherty, for example, in her
testimony said that that night Cherrylle was on the phone until
four o'clock in the morning with Cherrylle, which made me
curious. Also Elsa Steenberg reported that she had—Cherrylle
had been speaking to Scott about "letting go, letting go," which

25 is part of what appears in the suicide or what was alleged to be

the suicide note, the non-genuine one, if I may.

Q. The suicide note that's attributed to Scott Dell.

A. Yes.

30   Q. All right. And just if you could, what passages in that note are you referring to about letting go.

A. "Let go, let go." These were things that Elsa Steenberg in this court had said that she had told Scott on the phone. It's concerning to me—

Q. That is that Cherrylle Dell had said?

A. That Cherrylle Dell had said "letting go." It

5   concerns me because "letting go" can mean all sorts of things. For example, some of us may have known people who have a terminal cancer or disease, where we kind of provide guidance, where we kind of assist, you know, "let it go," "it's okay," "relax, be peaceful." You allow the person, if you will, to go peacefully

10   into their death. It's—I mean, I don't see many, but I do work with cancer patients, in helping them assist in their dying.

Q. And those lines that you're talking about are in fact the last lines on the last page of the note.

A. Yes. There's also something else in the note,

15   though, that had always puzzled me, but then Gay Doherty sort of supports it. When he writes:

> What did you think was going to happen if
> I drank a bottle of wine listening to the
> music we used to listen to. I'm going to
> think about you and me together.

20   I mean, it makes then sense that, of course, these notes are notes he's taking probably from the telephone conversations because obviously he's communicating to Cherrylle, and we know from Gay Doherty that she was on the phone that night all night.

Q. So were the Court to find that the notes in

25   fact were the product or made during that conversation, making that assumption, are there any other matters that—would that change or vary your opinions that you've previously expressed in any way?

A. No, it would not change my opinion that this

30   note is not a suicide note, but it would raise the issue of who's the author of this note, which goes back, for example, to the questions that I've been asked for, like Sopinka asked me in the Daniel Beckon case, is "Who's the author of the note?"

CROSS-EXAMINATION BY MR. SELKIRK:

Q. Now, I gather at some point in time, quite recently, that there is a doubt in your mind as to whom authored what we've been referring to as Scott Dell's note.

A. Yes.

15   Q. There is a concern that Mr. Dell, if we accept the fact that Mr. Dell was on the phone with Cherrylle Dell at the time of the writing of this note, there is a concern that Scott Dell was simply writing down what Cherrylle Dell told him,

was saying on the phone.

20   A. If I may, I think there are certain lines in there, because they're consistent with other writings that I've had from Scott such as about the relationship with Cherrylle, I think is clearly his writings, his statements.

Q. Which writings are those, please?

25   A. When he's writing about:
I feel like holding you close to me like
never before I feel like making love to
you . . .

Q. The areas of being preoccupied with an object,

15 in this case a person, and being rejected or abandoned by that person or object. That's a classic scenario for a suicide, I'll suggest to you. Dr. Shneidman will suggest that to you.

A. He will suggest to you that it's more than simply a trauma. All sorts of people have traumas, rejections

20 but don't kill themselves. That's the situation around the event. What you have to look at is the suicidal mind, the events, not simply whether somebody has a disease, lost employment or rejection. You always have to go to the commonalities, the kind of pain, the frustration of needs, the

25 hopelessness and helplessness. The rejection are part of the limbs of the tree, to use that analogy; the core is the trunk. So you're always looking at the mind part, but you also look at the situation around it.

All sorts of people have traumas, difficulties

30 and don't kill themselves. It's not sufficient. It's certainly part of it, although sometimes even for you and I it would make no sense. Like the person in California who wrote a note, killing himself because there's a scratch on the car. For you and I it makes no sense; for him it did . . .

Q. And, of course, whether or not a person left a note or not is determinative of whether the person committed suicide.

A. It should be, at least from my point of view, one part of determining—one part of the facts to determine

5 that.

Q. But if a person did not leave a note, that does not mean—you would not conclude, "Oh, the person did not commit suicide."

A. That's correct.

10 Q. And if he did leave a note, you would not conclude, "Oh, that person committed suicide."

A. I would want—

Q. Based on the note.

A. Just simply based on the note, I would want

15 more evidence. It might be, to use a metaphor, a "smoking gun," but you still want the body and how that body was killed or how he died, if I may say so. Sorry about the word "killed." It's how the person died . . .

Q. Well, let's go back to Scott's family
situation. If the situation is that his family home is broken,
to use the common terminology, it's a broken home, the family
split up; if it's found that the eldest daughter moved out
10 without even telling Scott, snuck out; if it's found that there
are significant custody access problems and in fact Scott might
be losing, gradually losing custody of the children; if Scott's
ex-wife is living with a lesbian partner who strongly dislikes
Scott and made it obvious; in terms of just that one aspect of
15 family, Scott is not coping very well.

A. What we know is that he had a series of
traumas, difficulties, but you certainly would also, before you
look at that family, look at the family of origin. For example,
in his life, the ground that we all have, the building blocks of
20 who we are, that's where you begin in terms of the suicidal
career. You look at—

Q. Let's just stay with your opinion as to
whether or not Scott appeared to be coping, contending
successfully with his family life.

25 A. I think he was doing quite well given the
circumstances. He was seeking help. He went to speak to Dr.
Harris about the problems. He spoke to Dr. O'Dell. He sought
other people for assistance. He spoke to some friends about his
problems. He got help. He persevered. The court cases that he
30 was involved in show that he was receiving support from the
Children's Aid. The Children's Aid tested him. The
psychologists didn't have any concerns. There was a whole host
of support systems, markers. He also had interests, hobbies, the
vegetables—the gardening I should say and the guitar and other
things that would be on the positive side, the protective
aspects. So, again, it's not simply the events but how we cope
5 with them, how we adjust to them.

Q. Objectively looking at Scott Dell's family
life, he was not coping very well.

A. I disagree.

Q. Because you want to read subjective things
10 into Scott Dell's mind, which you have no idea about, right? You
want to say he got this help, therefore he was helped.

A. I, you know, listened to people, I read the
case material of the court and other things which—

Q. And if one gets help for a problem in 1992,
that doesn't necessarily have any relevance to the person's
30 situation in 1995.

A. It shows a career in terms of him getting
help . . .

Q. People who are coping well are not
experiencing trauma at the same time, are they?

25 A. They're not the same.

Q. Of course not, but he can't say, "If I'm
being—if I'm walking down the street, coping very well walking

down the street and people are hitting me on the head," it is the
same, "I'm not coping with going down the street very well
30   because people keep hitting me in the head."

A. It depends on your state of mind, on how you
cope with things. Most—

Q. Right, but that's the subjective element which
you know nothing about.

A. But that's the core of what you look at in
terms of the various data on how we adjust. We also know that he
5   saw various doctors. He saw—

20   Q. And if Scott comes to Dr. O'Dell and says, "My
social situation has improved", it's not very helpful as to
what Scott did or did not do eight months later because his
situation could have unimproved.

A. Yes, of course.

25   Q. Sure. In fact, that's the problem with
relying on all of this stuff from '92 and 93, that his situation
could have changed.

A. But you also look at the beginning of his
life, the consistency over time. That is, again, the life long
30   coping patterns, the consistencies, or the suicidal career, if
you will, or coping career. You never take one thing, Mr.
Selkirk, in isolation. You look at . . .

Q. Okay. When you are doing a psychological
autopsy, the validity of your findings is determined by the
reliability of the information that you receive, is that fair to
30   say?

A. Yes, in that sense it's sort of like what we
do every day. Whether a psychiatrist or a psychologist, you're
kind of trying to make formulations and ideas, and of course in
the everyday clinical world, there's always issues of reliability
and the amount of information. This would not be any different
except in this case we have even more data than usually we get,
5   you know, working as a psychologist or a psychiatrist.

Q. And his relationship with Cherrylle and/or
other females, it would appear that he could not be with the one
he loves, and he doesn't love the one he's with, and no
suggestion that that situation is going to change or improve.

A. I think he always maintained hope about
5   Cherrylle. There's no question that he was very obsessed or, if
you will, in love. I think he loved Cherrylle a lot but not
wisely.

Q. And if the evidence is that he was aware that
Cherrylle was simply manipulating him and that the opportunity or
10   chances for reconciliation are slim and nil, then again helpless,
hopeless.

A. Not necessarily. He had coped with this
problem with Cherrylle from time to time. It wasn't the first
time. I mean, already early on in their marriage, et cetera,
15   they had been separated. So again looking at that, I mean, he

sought people out, he talked to people about it, he tried to
cope. Again, you'd have to look at each individual and the
actual data, whether they're hopeless or helpless or what their
state of mind is . . .
Thoughts of suicide or death, that's
another symptom?
10   A. Yes.
Q. And clearly in Scott's note, if he wrote it,
authored it, he writes "suicide/death."
A. Death/suicide.
Q. Death/suicide. Thank you.
15   A. Yes. But that doesn't mean necessarily he's
thinking about suicide. I mean, Shakespeare wrote about—
Q. Not necessarily.
A. Shakespeare wrote about suicide. He wasn't
necessarily suicidal. So people write about it—
A. All I'm saying is people write about it. It
doesn't necessarily mean that they're suicidal . . .
Q. Would you agree that on this area of cancer
and suicide, that literature on the subject seems to indicate
that the incidents of suicide in males with cancer are increased
in the immediate period following diagnosis and extending perhaps
25   for as long as five years?
A. I've read that in that book. They also said
that the data is ambivalent in that section . . .
A. They say themselves that —in this, that
there is some ambivalence in terms of—however—"Overall
5   however the literature is ambiguous" they say. So it's not
clear. Although generally it would be the case that many medical
conditions, including cancer, place a person at higher risk.
Again, those are the things around, the branches, et cetera, of
each individual person. We've long known since Sainsbury that
10   certain medical conditions place people at risk. I mean, we even
debate here in this country about terminal illnesses, you know,
and suicide . . .
Q. Well, the text goes on to say:
Cancers of the head and neck have an
11-fold increase in suicide rates, as
opposed to cancer generally which has a
relatively modest twofold increase.
5   A. Yes, but they also go—say elsewhere that
gastrointestinal cancers have the highest rates. So the fact is,
yes, cancer is a risk factor, but so are diabetes, so is Lou
Gehrig's disease, so is spinal cord injuries . . . It's axiomatic that
medical conditions put us at risk.
That doesn't mean, though, that everyone with cancer or diabetes
kills themselves. Again, it's how their mind is, how they cope
with things . . .
20   Q. Now, when you're doing the psychological
autopsy and interviewing people that could be described as

survivors, is it fair to say that the survivors can only give
their point of view?

A. That's correct . . .

Q. They have a tendency to see the deceased in a
positive light.

A. Yes, or a very negative light. You always, in
the autopsy but even in your everyday interviewing, have to judge
people in terms of that it's their point of view. We do this in
the clinical setting every day, constantly . . .

Q. Nonetheless, is it your recollection from what
they told you that Scott was secretive about his feelings
25   vis-à-vis Cherrylle and about his health? Is that your
understanding from which you based your conclusion on, or is it
something different?

A. Most of them did not use the word "secretive."
I think that the mother might have used the word, but most of
30   them basically said that he did not talk about, did not want to
share about these kinds of things. He wanted especially, for
example, with Cherrylle, to try to keep a positive appearance of
who Cherrylle was. He didn't want to focus—continually, even
in his court appearances, he discussed about—that she had this
bad background, and he just wanted her to get help and be well.
but he talked about other things. He
talk about his health to doctor—

Q. Unimportant things.
15   A. No, he talked about his health to Dr. Harris,
Dr. O'Dell, to some of the other people. He certainly talked
about the relationship to various people, including Dr. Harris.

Q. He talked about his relationship with
Cherrylle?
20   A. Yes. The issue of the sexual abuse charges,
according to the deposition.

Q. People have killed themselves for less.

A. People kill themselves for a scratch on a car.
The death of a canary is another example. It depends on the
25   person. I'm serious about the canary.

Q. No, I fully appreciate that . . .

Q. Now, let's add to the suggestion that he would
not speak about his feelings or his health. A psychiatric or
25   psychological testing, I guess—did you see Dr. McLean's report
on Scott?

A. No, I did not.

Q. This is done in—the report is dated January
13th, 1994. This is a full family clinic assessment of Scott,
30   Cherrylle and the children. This is something you would have
appreciated seeing had you known of its existence? . . .

MR. SELKIRK: Q. Well, Dr. McLean is a
psychiatrist practicing in the City of Ottawa here and has done
Family Court Clinic for many years. His conclusions were
10   that:

Personality testing suggested that Scott
was quite concerned about presenting an
unrealistically positive image of
himself. In day-to-day living, he would
invest a lot of energy to maintain an
appearance of adequacy, control, and
effectiveness. He may tend to utilize
denial to overlook faults or insecurities
15   in himself or his life situation.
Resultantly, he would likely have a
serious lack of personal insight into or
understanding of his own behavior. His
need to look good may have lowered the
clinical scales to make him appear better
adjusted psychologically. Nevertheless,
the testing did suggest that Scott be
somewhat immature and self-centered. He
would demand attention and approval from
20   others and would be sensitive to
rejection. He would likely blame other
people for his difficulties and if angry
would tend to express his anger
indirectly. Most of the time he would
appear to be overcontrolled but brief
episodes of more aggressive behavior
could occur. Although Scott appears
outwardly socially conforming, inwardly
he may tend to be rebellious.
25

This would have been information that should have been provided
to you, in your expert opinion?
        A. I would have appreciated seeing it . . .
20   Q. And only Scott can tell us if that pain was
unbearable.
        A. Well, I think in a psychological autopsy we
can get a fairly good concept of that . . .
5   There is evidence that he had trauma, crisis,
that he had had these since, I think, the early parts of the
problems in the relationships, but it also shows that he coped
with these, that he handled them that he sought out help
support, et cetera. You can't simply determine, because this
10   person has a crisis, that they're suicidal or in unbearable pain . . .
Keep in mind, when you're looking at anybody,
whether it's in my office or in this kind of situation, you look
5   at the positives and the negatives. You're always going to find
some negatives in anybody's lives, but overall you look at the
positive. He clearly, I don't believe, had a mental disorder or
an underlying mental disorder. I don't think it was discerned or
assessed by anyone that he did so. So I think generally he
10   seemed to have good coping abilities. There are other people,

site documents, like even the job application where he's called a "strong applicant." I think all of that is relevant. Again, you look at the person's history over time, how they coped, adjusted.

    Q. Would you—in terms of being called by some
15   unknown person in GM in the 70s a "strong applicant", would you not agree that that has little relevance to Scott Dell in 1995?

    A. Oh no, it's relevant. It would be relevant when you do a psychological autopsy because you don't simply look at the current event. You look at the person's personality and
20   coping style throughout their life.

    Q. People change.

    A. People change but they stay enormously consistent as well. I mean, the Shneidman study that I mentioned where by the age of 30 he already, from reading the material,
25   could determine which ones would kill themselves by the age of 50 with quite an accuracy . . .

It's a trained element, it's the professional
25   training that make the difference. Even in Arbeit and Blatt's discussion, what is it that allows people to distinguish genuine from non-genuine was the clinical training that these people had . . .

30   Q. There is no standardized form established by the scientific community to do a psychological autopsy?

    A. There's a fairly standard procedure, for example, that Ed Shneidman would teach me, and the kind that they've been using since the 1950s that many of the people use. I don't know what other people are using, but this is the one that I use that is most published and discussed . . .

    Q. But it is not standardized to the point or in a way to give reproducible results.

    A. I think that, from my point of view, this is fairly standardized. The person may ask the questions
20   differently, but generally the psychological autopsy would be looking at the person's intention, looking at precursors, looking at the history, looking to see whether there's been attempts, looking at the people's family of origin, how they cope with stress, whether there's been a mental disorder, et cetera. I
25   think how they might go about it would be different, but generally there would be similar questioning, I think, standardized. . . .

Q. And the testing or analysis that you did, you did not subject it to any form of peer review or independent review to see if others would come up with similar opinions as you?

    A. One would never do this in a specific
5   individual case. You do that for research, in terms of whether people can use this or whether it's peer reviewed. Typically—

    Q. As far as you're aware, you have not asked anybody else to review your work on this case to see if they would come up with a similar opinion.

10   A. I did not give this case or ask Dr. Shneidman

to interview the people . . .

Q. Right. There is no standard profile for a
15 suicide?

A. I think there is genera—it depends on what
you mean by "standard profile". If you mean sociological, like
male, divorced, if you mean the sociological phenomena, I would
say, no, there isn't a standard kind of profile. If you mean in
20 terms of pain, hopelessness, helplessness, ambivalence, yes, I
think there's a fairly common agreement about many of the
factors . . .

15 RE-EXAMINATION BY MR. BARNES . . .

Q. Thank you. During the recess, then, you had
an opportunity to look at the report of Dr. McLean in its
entirety, the 29 pages.

A. Yes, I did.

Q. And having had an opportunity to look at the
5 entire report but more particularly the eight pages that pertain
to Scott Dell, has anything that you've read in the balance of
the material resulted in your wishing to qualify any of the
answers that you gave to my friend and the passage that you were
referred to?

10 A. Well, from my point of view, Mr. Selkirk only
read part of the report and only part of the psychological
testing, not the concluding impression. And so he's just giving
me part of that report that I had not seen. His conclusion is:

It was the writer's impression that Scott
Dell suffers from no major psychiatric
15 illness. I did feel he tends to be a
rather controlled and guarded individual
who is perhaps not as open about his
emotions and feelings as Cherrylle,
somewhat inwardly rebellious [he says].
Appears to be less impulsive or likely to
act out on these tendencies as compared
to Cherrylle. Although Scott has some
personality difficulties, they appear to
be less significant than Cherrylle's.

He then says:

Scott does seem to have an emotional
attachment with the children, and also it
seems they have done well since being in
his primary care over the last eight
months. It would also seem that Scott
would be more supportive of the
25 children's relationship with their
mother's and vice versa . . .

Q. And does that opinion, and giving that opinion
credit, cause you to modify any of the views that you've
expressed today?

5 A. No, it actually continues to support my belief

that, you know, during his career, his life, he did not suffer
from a major psychiatric illness as opposed to Cherrylle Dell who
he says did . . .

VOIR DIRE

My testimony was a *voir dire*. The main question was, Is this testimony admissible? This is important because no expert in suicide has ever testified in a criminal court on such issues in a Canadian court. The *Ottawa Sun* on January 17, 2000, printed the following article:

Witness Makes History

While Dr. Antoon Leenaars has twice testified in California, yesterday marked the first time a suicide expert has ever taken the stand in Canadian court.

It's the opinion of the clinical psychologist that the 1995 death of Scott Dell, 44, was no suicide and that his final hand-written letter was no suicide note.

The Crown is trying to introduce the expert evidence in the murder trial of Cherrylle Dell, 46, accused of poisoning her estranged husband.

Not reliable

But defense lawyers argue the doctor's findings are not scientifically reliable. Moreover, the Supreme Court of Canada has recently cautioned lower courts against allowing expert witnesses to do the judge's job, which, in this case, is to determine the cause of Scott Dell's death.

Leenaars, who has a practice in Windsor, is the past president of the American Association of Suicidology and a member of the International Association for Suicide Research and Prevention. He's also an author and long-time researcher who has examined more than 2000 suicide notes.

The doctor said he believes Scott Dell had been coping with life's problems around the time of his death by trying to maintain a positive attitude, despite his inability to romantically move on after his wife dumped him.

- Caroline Murray

Psychological autopsies have a long history, over 60 years, in the United States, not Canada. Shneidman, Litman, and Farberow are generally credited with introducing the technique in the 1950s to civil matters and coroner's inquests. They pioneered the first standard "empirical" roadmap. PAs are now widely accepted in civil cases (Litman, 1988). This standardized technique was first introduced into criminal cases in an Arizona case in 1976 (Lichter, 1981). They are now widely accepted in American criminal courts.

In the Arizona case, Wendy Jones's murder of her husband, Daniel, appeared to be a simple case of first degree murder (Lichter, 1981). At trial, defense counsel employed the autopsy technique to show that Mr. Jones had been a sadistic paranoid who beat his wife. The jury relied on the autopsy to make a decision. Since then the autopsy has been employed in civil cases in the United States, including by myself. In a most interesting clinical case (Jacobs & Klein, 1993), Jackson v. State of Florida (1987), the appellate ruled,

The expert psychiatrist specialized in suicidology and, for purpose of this trial, performed a psychological autopsy on the appellant's seventeen-year-old daughter who had committed suicide in March of 1986. His testimony explained that a psychological autopsy is a retrospective look at an individual's suicide to try to determine what led that person to choose death over life. In order to make that determination, in this case, the expert reviewed the child's school records, the police records surrounding the case, including all of the state's evidence and all of the defendant's statements and medical records, an incident report from an earlier suicide by the child and various testimony from the witnesses appearing at this trial. However he admitted that he did not personally interview any of the witnesses who appeared at trial nor did he ever meet or interview the suicide victim. His opinion, bounded by reasonable psychiatric certainty, was that the nature of the relationship between the defendant and her daughter was a substantial contributing factor in the daughter's decision to commit suicide.

Having reviewed the record, we are satisfied that the state presented sufficient evidence to establish that the psychological autopsy is accepted in the field of psychiatry as a method of evaluation for use in cases involving suicide and that the trial judge acted within his discretion in admitting this evidence at trial. Sections 90.402; 90.403; 90.704; Fla.Stat. (1987).

With regard to the concerns of the defense that the psychological autopsy was not established as reliable before it was admitted as evidence, we note that such opinions are subjective and therefore the issue of reliability is best left to the jury. Further, we perceive no distinction between the admission of the expert's opinion in this case and, for example, admitting psychiatric opinion evidence to establish a defendant's sanity at the time of committing an offence or to prove the competency of an individual at the time of executing a will. See *Morgan v. State*, 527, So.2d.272 (Fla. 1202), *United Stated vs. Edwards*, 819 F.2d 262 (11th Cir. 1987); see also *Krusa v. State*, 483 So.2d.1383 (Fla. 4th DCA 1986); *Terry v. State*, 467 So.2d 761 (Fla. 4th DCA 1985); In re *Estate of Hammerman*, 387 So.2d 409 (Fla. 4th DCA 1980).

There being no merit to the other arguments raised, we affirm the judgment of conviction.

The technique has also been accepted beyond the court; for example, the congressional hearing of the explosion on the USS Iowa on April 19, 1989. Whereas in the United States, the technique is widely accepted, this is not so in Canada. Bob Selkirk, the defense lawyer deemed it "junk science" and the judge, James Chadwick, agreed. My testimony was not allowed, which is of interest, because the trial was by judge. This then raises a problem: How could Chadwick not have a memory, for example, for what I said suicide is? I fully understand that there are issues in expert evidence (Paciocco, 1999); yet both my suicide note analysis and the psychological autopsy meet not only the Frye test of general acceptance (or the McIntosh test in Canada) but also the Daubert criteria, set in Daubert v. Merrill Dow Pharmaceutical, Inc. (No 92-102 (U.S. 06/28/1993). Once more Canada lags behind.

In the U.S. courts, suicidology (including analyses of notes, psychological autopsies) has been accepted under rules of evidence. The autopsy approach, as I noted, in criminal court dates back to 1976 (Lichter, 1981). The science is not seen as novel, passing the classic Frye test of "general acceptance" (although it is the Federal

Rules of Evidence, not Frye, that provide the standard for admitting expert scientific testimony in a federal trial). Daubert vs. Merrill Dow Pharmaceutical, Inc. set out a reliable foundation for opinion. The foundation calls for a theory or technique to be scientific, that is, "can be falsified" (citing Hempel, 1966), "The statements constituting a scientific explanation must be capable of empirical test." For a science to have a reliable and valid foundation, it must meet the following criteria: (a) theory or technique in question can be and has been tested; (b) theory or technique has been subject to peer review and publication; (c) there is known or has to be a potential for error; (d) the existence and maintenance of a standardized technique or method controlling its operation; and (e) Frye test of general acceptance within a relevant scientific community. Let us examine the Daubert standard, keeping in mind the judge is the only gatekeeper.

STANDARDIZING THE PA: ADDRESSING THE DAUBERT STANDARD

Snider et al. (2006) published an important forensic paper on the issue at hand (it has the title of this section's subheading). Snider et al. rightfully argue that the PA and even the term have become complex. Every suicidologist knows the term; yet this is less so in the forensic fields. It is also a truism that Dr. Edwin Shneidman is credited with a creation of the term, shaping it, contributing to it, and most importantly, catalyzing other competent investigators to invest in it. The PA is the baby of Edwin S. Shneidman.

There are, of course, criticisms, and I address some of those under the second part of this volume. One of the most concerning issues is the lack of standardization in protocols and methods of the PA (Snider et al., 2006), although Shneidman himself was quite clear about the protocols and methods (see Chapter 4). Dr. Shneidman was unequivocal. The reason for the current lack is solely because subsequent investigators and researchers developed their own methods; indeed, some do not cite Shneidman or, for that matter, Farberow and Litman (Shneidman's partners at the Los Angeles County Medical Examiners' Office, under the direction of Theodore Curphey). Everyone wants to reinvent the wheel. Would one discuss relativity theory without mentioning Albert Einstein? (Can you reinvent, say, the telephone? What would Alexander Grahm Bell say?) The answer is obvious; yet I predict people will continue to attempt to create the wheel and thus false roadmaps.

It follows:

> The overall lack of standardization and the problem of determining the procedure's validity and reliability pose significant problems when the psychological autopsy is introduced in legal courts where first may be deemed inadmissible by court standards using the Federal Laws of Evidence. (Snider et al., 2006, p. 512)

This is the Daubert standard, the most rigorous and studied guidelines for admissibility to date. (There is nothing similar in Canada.) Like me, Snider and her team offer some reflections, simply because, they say, the lack of standardization. (Did they read Shneidman, Litman, and/or Farberow?) Snider et al. offer a new direction; they undertook a research study.

Snider and her team (2006) identified 33 suicidologists with known experience in the PA and surveyed the forensic experts. It was not an empirical test, just what is common practice. There were 13 respondents (39%; I want to be visible as one of the 13). The researchers indicated that on testability, most respondents indicated that it would be possible to demonstrate reliability. They concluded that "with a standardized interview template on which interviewers could be trained, users might be expected to make more reliable determinations as to mode of death" (p. 513). This is the very reason why I use Shneidman's guidelines (roadmap); it was the first; it has been standardized; and it has been used reliably. Dr. Shneidman, as you read in Chapter 5, agrees with my opinion.

The research showed that some respondents questioned whether validity can truly be shown. This is so because the conclusion reached is not subject to the deceased's opinion; we cannot ask the dead person. (Of course, we cannot!) We have discussed the issue earlier. There can be no unequivocal statement of the dead person (or would the suicide note and other documents help?). This is the very reason why I discussed construct validity at length in Chapter 1. Yet we are left without the suicide's own observation of the skeleton.

On peer review, although there are articles in peer-reviewed journals suggesting meeting the criteria of peer review, the team argues that only through the acceptance of one standard can the criteria's utility be met. Therefore I argue for Dr. Shneidman's approach.

On error rate, Snider et al. (2006) stated that it is dependent on the issue of testability. Again, we cannot ask the deceased. Does construct validity help?

On standardized procedures, they argue that it has not been met. Dr. Shneidman and I would disagree; it was already met in the 1950s. It is thus well established. Yet to repeat, everyone wants to invent the wheel anew. As I quoted earlier, the philosopher Francis Bacon once noted, "Everyone believes what they prefer to be true." To rephrase him, "Everyone believes the standardization that they prefer to be true."

On general acceptance, Snider et al. (2006) note, "With no standardized procedure, there is little to accept or reject." I disagree. We can accept or reject Dr. Shneidman's (and for that matter, Litman's and Farberow's) procedure. I believe that the retrospective death investigation is well accepted, as evidenced by the fact that many judges in the United States have accepted its admissibility.

The purpose of Snider et al.'s (2006) article is "to aid in the establishment of a standardized protocol." I applaud this effort; however, they offer one more template ("wheel"). I believe that we already have a template—Dr. Shneidman's. It has passed the test of time; at least, here I appeal to the sage of our field. It follows the oldest roadmap in the field. In the end, utility in the courtroom is for the judge to decide.

Of course, the PA should develop, if warranted, by research on specific case issues. One possible factor is the use of peer consultation. When the PA began under Theodore Curphey, case consultation was part of the process. Dr. Shneidman, Dr. Farberow, and Dr. Litman would go out into the field and undertake a PA. They would return to Curphey's office and consult on the case and make a NASH determination and answer the key question (see Chapter 4). It was a "multidisciplinary approach." Recently, Welner, Davey, and Bernstein (2014) have made a similar classification. Prospective, multidisciplinary, peer-reviewed forensic consultation has been agreed-upon to assist in accountability and meeting the courtroom's criteria. Of course, the procedure was used in the 1950s; it is not new, nor 10 years old, as some claim. Welner et al. note, "Such cumulative knowledge inevitably evokes an appreciation of the wisdom of 'three heads are better than one'" (p. 1258). It was "three heads" in the 1950s. It would bolster the reliability and validity of the PA and forensic investigation in general. Shneidman said so decades ago.

THE QUESTIONING OF FORENSIC SCIENCE OR THE QUESTIONABLE FORENSIC SCIENCE

On the more general, the PA is not alone being questioned. Indeed, the whole field of forensic science is in question. Some ask, Is it a questionable science? One grave (pun intended) concern is error: false positives (the concern in courts), and true negatives (the real problem for us in the field). Is that acceptable error? Is that science? Thus, it is not simply the PA in court or for that matter, in DSI, but for *all* of forensic science. Is it "junk science"? Some opine so.

There have, in fact, been many who have questioned forensic science in general; even the classic fingerprinting has been found questionable (at times). Judge Harry T. Edwards of the U.S. Court of Appeals for the District of Columbia, a well-known expert on forensic evidence in court, was in 2009, the lead author of a landmark National Academy Science report, "Strengthening Forensic Sciences in the United States: A Path Forward" (National Research Council, 2009). It called into question the scientific validity of almost all of our forensic methods. Not only validity (such as construct validity), but also reliability was questionable, Judge Edwards concluded. The report's main finding: There are severe problems in forensic science. The science is, indeed, questionable, and there are serious questions in the science. The PA is not alone (and this is most important for the forensic investigator in DSI to know, and a judge in court). Edward's report, in fact, offers hope. It provides guidelines for improving methods, practices, and performances in forensic science. Indeed, I have (and will) attempted to be mindful of the very issues and improvements in the PA.

THE CANADIAN CASE: R. v MOHAN

The place for science of any kind in Canada is most problematic (the situation likely differs in each nation). Behavioral sciences such as suicidology fare the worst. There is a danger seen in relying on expert opinion (Paciocco, 1999). The classical Canadian equivalent to the Frye test is the McIntosh Test; the subject of testing must be generally accepted, scientific knowledge. However, R. v Mohan ([1994] 2 S.C.R.9) was the leading case on the criteria for admission of expert evidence. The

Mohan formula is as follows: (a) relevance, (b) necessity in assisting the trier of fact, (c) the absence of an exclusionary rule, and (d) a properly qualified expert. Mohan raised, for example, the issue of novel science; to be not novel, a science had to be generally accepted in a respected field (e.g., the psychological autopsy in suicidology). Behavioral science, after Mohan, became less accepted. Although the issues are detailed, a consequence of a recent ruling of the Supreme Court of Canada, a warning has been issued about expert testimony (R. vs. D.D. ([2000]) SCC 43). That case in question was about child sexual abuse; yet since the ruling, few social scientists have been granted permission to testify in federal court. In Mohan, the late Chief Judge Sopinka (the attorney then, who hired me for the Daniel Beckon case) stated,

> There is a danger that expert evidence will be misused and will distort the fact finding process. Dressed up in scientific language which the jury does not easily understand and submitted through a witness of impressive antecedents, this evidence is apt to be accepted by the jury as being virtually infallible and as having more weight than it deserves. As La Forest Jr. stated in R. v Beland [1987] 2 S.C.R. 398, at p. 434, with respect to the evidence of the results of a polygraph tendered by the accused, such evidence should not be admitted by reason of human fallibility in assessing the proper weight to be given to evidence cloaked under the mystique of science (p. 21).

The decision has created considerable controversies (Ogloff & Cronshaw, 2001). Mohan (1994) was, however, to be applied on a case-by-case basis; since D.D., it has changed. In R. vs. Dell, Judge Chadwick ruled the following:

> R. vs. Dell
> The crown seeks to introduce the evidence of an expert, Dr. Antoon Leenaars. Dr. Leenaars is a Ph.D. in psychology, with a defined specialty in suicidology. Suicidology was defined by him as "the study of suicide and suicide prevention."
> Approximately 75 to 80% of his practice is clinical. The balance of his practice relates to analyzing suicides and providing professional opinions as to whether the deceased met his or her death by suicide. He uses a method involving protocol sentence to analyse suicide notes and to prepare a psychological autopsy of the deceased.
> In this case he has studied the notes found on deceased, Scott Dell's desk shortly after his death. In addition he has prepared a psychological profile or protocol of Scott Dell.
> The psychological protocol was based upon reviewing statements and transcripts of a number of people, most of whom gave evidence at trial. Dr. Leenaars also reviewed a number of documents, some of which were made exhibits at trial.
> Counsel for the Crown and the defense reviewed with me a number of the leading authorities dealing with the admissibility of expert evidence. In their submissions they also reviewed Dr. Leenaars' evidence.
> The Supreme Court of Canada in their most recent decision on the admissibility of expert evidence, have set forth the criteria a trial judge should apply to determine admissibility. In Regina v. J. 148 c.c.c.(3d) 487 Binnie J., in a unanimous decision of the court,. reviews a number of previous cases, in particular, R. v. Mohan. Binnie J, emphasizes the trial judge should take seriously

the role of a "gatekeeper" He goes on to establish the criteria the gatekeeper should apply to determine the admissibility of evidence.

1. Subject matter of the inquiry.
2. Novel Scientific Theory or Technique.
3. Approaching the Ultimate issue.
4. The Absence of Any Exclusionary Rule.
5. A Properly Qualified Expert.
6. Relevance of the Proposed Testimony.
7. Necessity in Assisting the Trier of Fact.
8. The Discretion of the Trial Judge.

My concerns rest with criteria numbers 1,2,3,6, & 7.
Whether the case is being tried by a judge and jury, or by a judge alone, in my view does not make any difference. The same considerations apply. In this case there is ample evidence, to date, to assess the state of mind of Scott Dell and to determine if he committed suicide. Although Dr. Leenaars' evidence was interesting and informative, a trier of fact would apply many of the same signs in reaching their conclusion.

The field of expertise practiced by Dr. Leenaars has not been recognized to date in the Canadian courts. It has been accepted in a limited number of United States courts. Mr. Selkirk refers to it as "junk science". I would not go that far. New scientific theories have to be carefully scrutinized.

The ultimate issue to be decided is whether the accused Cherrylle Dell killed her husband. If it is found that Scott Dell committed suicide, that would dispose of the ultimate issue. As stated in R.v. Mohan this requires the application of "special scrutiny" As Sopinka J. stated in Mohan; "The closer the evidence approaches an opinion on an ultimate issue, the stricter the application of this principle."

The last concern is whether this evidence is necessary to assist the trier of fact. In this case I am satisfied there is sufficient evidence for the trier to decide the question, without the assistance of an expert.

January 19, 2001

Making Your Opinion Matter

I hereby quote some sound reflections on how you, for example, whether police, psychiatrist/psychologist, military and public safety professional, can become qualified as "experts" (Jeffery, Price, & Gyorfi, 2015). Wayne Jeffrey, Stephen Price, and Darrel Gyorfi formerly worked for the RCMP; they are the real thing—cops that investigated and testified as experts in court. They state,

> Those called to give expert or opinion testimony in court must be impartial—and always seen to be impartial. Although usually called by the Crown, their expertise is also available to the defence. An expert is like a hired-gun in a "B" western—their opinion is based on professional, scientific, and observable facts which don't change and aren't affected by the party which calls them to court. An expert does not choose who their opinion harms or helps.
>
> In the courtroom context, an expert is a witness who has acquired special or particular knowledge about a specific area through study, experience, reviewing

scientific works and/or practical observation. They are allowed to give an opinion in court about evidence—the speed of a vehicle, for example, or the physical condition of an individual who may have been impaired. . . .

Preparing an expert opinion report (will-say)

Bear in mind that, while we and the courts call it a "will-say," the term is not a truly appropriate description. A will say is a factual description of an investigator's observations or involvement, but what you are really preparing is a statement of your opinion and its basis.

The fundamental step is to lay out a basis for your opinion—the facts you rely upon. . . .

Testifying in court

Here's a few simple rules for expert witnesses:

• Crown should identify you as the expert to be called in the case and request the court allow you to sit and listen to the evidence provided by the investigators. Ensure that your opinion is supported by the admitted evidence;
• Crown counsel has a limited ability to lead or induce you to answer. In that situation, you should begin your evidence with an explanation and flow seamlessly into presenting your opinion;
• Keep your opinion within your experience;
• Keep the answers reasonably short to allow the Crown to gently direct you. Crown counsel is making an entire case and may reinforce other elements not adequately explained by the investigators;
• Candidly explain your opinion and the facts supporting it;
• Keep your written opinion in front of you to ensure that you cover all elements;
• You are interpreting the evidence based on your experience and knowledge, not making the case;
• Never underestimate the ability of any counsel to see the trees and miss the forest. Ensure you present your basic opinion early in your evidence;
• Listen to and ensure that you understand the question during cross examination or while defending your opinion. If you don't understand or if there is more than one question, ask for an explanation or which question you should answer. Remember that you are impartial;
• If you understand the question, then answer it, not the question that you think should have been asked. Sometimes a stupid question deserved a stupid or direct answer;
• If there is a series of questions, don't answer the next question in the sequence until it is asked;
• Don't ramble. Once you have answered a question, wait for the next. Don't assume that because you would ask another question, someone else will or should.

THE VERDICT

Chadwick deemed the science of suicide not to be acceptable science in Canadian court. There is, in fact, considerable time consumed these days about whether expert testimony (especially those of psychiatrists, psychologists, and other social scientists) is admissible, especially those said to approach the "ultimate issues" (as in the case of Dell). Yet other judges would differ from Chadwick. Judge J. Saunders (2001) noted that social science experts have an important place in court, quoting Chief Justice Scott (R. vs D.D. ([1998], M.J. No. 322).

> The opinion evidence is deemed necessary not so much because the area is outside the common knowledge of the trier of fact, but because common sense may be wrong! In other words, the evidence is necessary to counteract myth, stereotypes, prejudices and biases lay people and judges may have regarding certain classes of persons or subject. (R v DD, 1998, par 60)

Thus, Saunders (2001) claims (and I agree) that expert evidence is necessary because the trier of fact could draw wrong conclusions. This would certainly be true about suicide. No trier of fact, whether jury or judge (as in the Dell case) could draw the right conclusion beyond doubt. These issues are well beyond this volume, but will need to be resolved in Canada (Ogloff & Cronshaw, 2001) and other countries, whereas these appear to have been resolved in the United States for some time—well maybe (National Research Council, 2009). As for my testimony in the Dell case, it is lost to history. It is here presented as a most insightful learning case for the aspiring and veteran forensic specialist (Kitaeff [2010] offers some rewarding reading on the place of forensic science in the courtroom). It has, at least, a value. It is a meaning making!

On February 2, 2001, Cherrylle Dell was found guilty. I will not comment further; however, it is of note that about the suicide note, Judge Chadwick stated, "This is not a suicide note." How was that judgment made? How was it made beyond a reasonable doubt? I believe it is the judge's *personal equation.* Science tells us that the judge cannot unequivocally make such a decision; Bob Selkirk would state, "That is a junk decision." (It is of note that Judge Chadwick was featured in the *Ottawa Citizen* on February 3, 2001, as a knight of justice.) Yet I believe as a clinical case, Scott Dell's is most useful. On the decision, the *Ottawa Citizen* on February 3, 2001, presented the following:

> "Angel" of Death Gets Life in Prison
> "Cherrylle Dell wanted Scott Dell out of her life forever"
> By Peter Hum
> Cherrylle Dell was found guilty yesterday of murdering her husband, Scott, by poisoning him with antifreeze, to the surprise of onlookers who packed a tense Ottawa courtroom.
>
> "I don't believe it," said Mr. Dell's mother, Myra, immediately after Ontario Superior Court Justice James Chadwick gave his reasons for convicting her daughter-in-law.
>
> "We went in with misgivings. We thought it would go either way . . . even though we knew she was guilty," she said.
>
> The first-degree conviction, which meant that Mrs. Dell was immediately sentenced to life behind bars with no chance of parole for 25 years, concludes a two-month trial that has held rapt the Ottawa Valley, where the Dells lived, because of its bizarre details. It had also been the buzz of the Ottawa courthouse because, to many on-lookers, including Mr. Dell's relatives, it seemed that Mrs. Dell might be acquitted.
>
> The defense had argued that Mr. Dell, 44, who was found dead on Dec. 29, 1995, in his Killaloe farmhouse, and who had ingested wine laced with antifreeze, had committed suicide in a fit of depression. The Crown's

circumstantial case was so bizarre and full of holes as to be unfeasible, the defense argued.

But Judge Chadwick, who presided over the non-jury case, was satisfied beyond a reasonable doubt that Mrs. Dell duped her husband into drinking what he called a "lethal cocktail."

Reading a summary from his 89-page decision, Judge Chadwick said: "I find that from 1992 onward Cherrylle Dell expressed hatred towards her husband Scott Dell and wished him dead," the judge said.

"She wanted the exclusive custody of the children, the sole occupation and possession of the farm, and wanted Scott Dell out of her life forever.

"There is seldom a case where we hear such strong and consistent evidence about the character of a deceased person. Scott Dell . . . was very positive about his life and his love for his children. He wanted to live for his children."

"I am satisfied beyond a reasonable doubt that Scott Dell did not commit suicide but was murdered by poisoning."

CONCLUDING THOUGHT

I believe that this chapter uncovers the very essentials of a forensic case, but not of a suicide's mind. It uncovered murder!

PART FOUR

Discussion

Part 4 offers two chapters. Chapter 12, "What I Have Learned," presents some concluding thoughts on the psychological autopsy. One can see the PA like the Socratic Method—a way to uncover the truth of a death. Our questions are Was it a homicide? Suicide? Accident? The forensic expert may be called to offer an opinion on suicide and death, especially in equivocal cases; this is so because unlike other deaths, the key factor in self-murder is intention. We need to uncover the answer to, "Did the person intentionally die by suicide?" Without a doubt, the psychological autopsy is our best forensic tool in death scene investigation (DSI). Furthermore, the investigators knowledge/skill in suicidology/thanatology will be essential; indeed, the best technique and approach in undertaking a PA is to know what suicide is. "What is suicide?" is always the *a priori* question. Thus, I offer Plato's Allegory of the Cave and some implications for DSI, a few different views on the PA. I summarize what I know. To illustrate my belief, I here present the case of *The State of Indiana vs. Bei Bei Shuai.*

Chapter 13, "Final Forgetting," will be a secret.

CHAPTER 12
What I Have Learned

Socrates (470/469–399 BC) was one of the great classical Greek (Athenian) philosophers. He was unequivocally a founder of Western philosophy. He also served in the Athenian military. He is best known through the writings of his student Plato (428-348 BC). Through Plato's dialogues, Socrates has become renowned in multiple fields, among others, of knowledge (epistemology) (Hamilton & Cairns, 1961). He developed what has become called The Socratic Method.

The Socratic scheme of inquiry is based on asking and answering questions to stimulate critical thinking and illuminate concepts, ideas and theories. The Socratic Method is a method of un-covering the bare bones, by steadily finding truths (facts). The basic form is a series of questions formulated as examinations or tests, to help a person to discover truths. It is not about being told the facts. It is truly about investigation. It is about you seeing (and knowing) for yourself. *It is an autopsy* (OED definition). It is a method to find *logoi* (singular *logos*). Aristotle (384–322 BC), another great Greek thinker, credits Socrates with the discovery of the essence of the scientific method (McKeon, 1941). The scientific method is a method of questioning, whether an individual's belief, or a government's, or a state's. It is a roadmap to the truth, the real, and justice.

In the dialogue, *Theatetus*, the question of what knowledge is, is discussed. There we read, *"Wonder is the feeling of a philosopher, and philosophy begins in wonder."* This dialogue teaches people *not* to think they know, when they do not, but to search for the truth.

The *Phaedo*, a dialogue that I studied as an undergraduate student (I have not only a major in psychology, but also a major in philosophy). It is a narrative of Socrates' dedicated student, Phaedo, who gives an account of Socrates' death. In 399 BC, Socrates was accused by a fellow Athenian of "refusing to recognize the gods recognized by the state," and of "corrupting the youth." From my point of view, he was accused of encouraging people to think wisely. Socrates was found guilty by a jury of 500 Athenians; the vote was 280 to 220. The jury was then asked to dictate his penalty. The jury selected death. Socrates was led to jail; his sentence was carried out. The sentence was *suicide*. Athenian law dictated death by drinking a cup of pure hemlock. Socrates' death was a suicide—and he was his own murderer, or if you prefer, executioner.

In the *Phaedo*, we learn some marvelous things about the Socratic Method; here are a few quotes:

> Then I heard someone who had a book of Anaxagoras, as he said, out of which he read that the mind was the disposer and cause of all . . . and I said to myself: If mind is the disposer, mind will dispose all for the best, and put each particular in the best place; and I argued that if anyone desired to find out the cause of the generation or destruction of anything, he must find out what state of being or suffering or doing was best for that thing, and therefore a man had only consider the best for himself and others, and then he would also know the worse, for that the same science comprised both.
>
> It may be said, indeed, that without bones and muscles and the other parts of the body I cannot execute my purposes. But to say that I do as I do because of them, and this is the way in which the mind acts, and not from the choice of the best, is a very careless and idle mode of speaking. I wonder that they cannot distinguish the cause from the condition, which the many, feeling about in the dark, are always mistaking and misnaming.
>
> . . . this was the method which I adopted: I first assumed some principle which I judged to be the strongest, and then I affirmed as true whatever seemed to agree with this, whether relating to the cause or to anything else; and that which disagreed I regarded as untrue. . . . I want to show you the nature of that cause which has occupied my thoughts, and I shall have to go back to those familiar words which are in the mouth of everyone, and first of all assume that there is an absolute beauty and goodness and greatness, and the like; grant me this, and I hope to be able to show you the nature of the cause . . .

Allow me one more attempt to illustrate the Socratic Method. One of my favorites of Plato's writings is *The Republic*. I recall my professor Martha Husain discussing the *Allegory of the Cave* and was quite inspired till this day. (She taught me the pre-Socratic philosophers, such as Heraclitus, and the Socratic philosophers, such as Socrates, Plato and Aristotle.) It is a parable of the progress of the mind from the lowest state of un-enlightenedness to the deepest true knowledge. Imagine that the condition of human beings is being in a cavernous chamber underground, with after a long passage, an entrance to the light, the sun. The people, since childhood, are chained; they cannot move and can only see in front of them. They are prisoners. There is darkness. At some distance higher up there is a fire burning, which they cannot see, and there are performers, who cannot be seen, acting, with figures of people, animals, and so on. These are projected onto a screen, like a puppet show. People only see the shadows! This is the only reality—a false reality (masking). They only know shadows. The prisoners believe the shadows are real! They believe what they believe to be true. They see little of the objects, fire, performers, etc., just darkness. This is the reflection of human knowledge.

Imagine then, one person released from the chains and seeing the fire, performers, and objects, and . . . he would then see all was meaningless illusion. All was a masking (dissembling). He now sees more reality. And then he sees the barren facts. He then goes to the entrance and sees even more light and wonders. He then travels through the passage and goes outside, to see the sun. He then has an epiphany and discovers the truth, wisdom. And what if then he were to return to the cave; would his fellow prisoners believe him? Or, would they kill him? (They did Socrates.) What would he do with his knowledge of the barren bones of reality? How could he communicate his investigation of the sun, *the golden star*?

This allegory is like our own questioning to the un-covering of the darkness of the suicide's mind. In this book, I use the Socratic Method—Socrates knew that it empowered the person, not the teacher or the state; in this case, I hope *you*. *The PA is like the Socratic Method.* Of course, the forensic investigator is at times confronted with a case that may not call for, or allow for the PA. It may be the best tool, but his/her expertise may be called upon without the PA tool. Yet, we can still be like Socrates and find the truth. After some concluding thoughts about using the PA, what work's best, I will present a case example, *The State of Indiana vs. Bei Bei Shuai.*

A SUMMARY ON THE PA

That the method in Plato's allegory of the cave is like the PA process is obvious. The allegory is a metaphor for the Socratic scheme of inquiry. The PA, in summary, is exactly that method. It is based on asking and answering questions. That is forensics at its best. I can think of no better analogy, the very intent of Socrates and Shneidman. The goal of this forensic volume is also quite simple: to provide readers with the inner most details of death scene investigation (DSI). The concept of investigating deaths which are uncertain as to the mode of death—NASH—is at least as old as the work of John Graunt of England in the 17th century. Mr. Graunt's genius lay in aggregating the mortality data into population estimates and constructing the first mortality tallies. The patterns ('same') in deaths had never been shown before. Police, physicians, and the government found great advantage from Graunt's method, in certifying causes of death; investigations of deaths became a science.

The recent history of death certification and death investigation focuses around the Los Angeles Suicide Prevention Center (LASPC). In the 1950's, the Chief Coroner and Medical Examiner of Los Angeles County, Dr. T. Curphey, asked Drs. E. Shneidman, N. Farberow, and R. Litman—LASPC's leaders—to assist in studying death cases which were ambiguous as to the mode of death—NASH. These were cases that depended on the decedent's intention. The first step in sound forensic science of a suicide's mind is evaluation of intention (see discussion, especially Litman's thoughts, in Chapter 1). The only death that centers on *intention* is suicide. To do DSI well, one has to be an expert in suicide, and all deaths—homicide, accidental deaths. Indeed, the best approach to doing a PA is to know what suicide is. It is epistemology. Of course, this is no different than say, the officer/investigator who becomes a drug 'expert'. I have been asked the question, "Can you summarize your thinking about using the psychological autopsy and reviewing the techniques and approaches that you think works best?" In a nutshell, my answer has always been: "Know suicide!" Needless to say, Shneidman, Farberow, and Litman were suicide experts; this was the very reason Dr. Curphey asked them to assist in death certification of his most difficult cases. The LASPC's three leaders were designated as deputy coroners and went to the scene of deaths where they empirically interviewed a number of key informants, and then reported back to Dr. Curphey. In a strictly non-partisan setting, the mode of death—and why—was discussed and determined. It was/is a multi-disciplinary (system) approach; i.e., it depended on a multi-information context (I am biased toward suicide notes). Shneidman labeled this scientific-clinical procedure the psychological autopsy (PA). The PA is a process of seeing with your own eyes. It is about "personal observation," a key interest of both police officers and forensic specialists. The PA is a roadmap to find a way out of the 'dark cave'; i.e., uncovering the barren evidence of the suicidal mind. Yet, it is more; it is also the journey back into the cave, to teach others the same evidence-based process (in both meanings of the term, science and policing) in DSI. That is the challenge of this book.

The PA, at least in an evidence-based way, answers three distinct questions:

1. Why did the individual do it?
2. How did the individual die, and when—that is, why at that particular time?
3. What is the most probable mode of death?

Of course, each case raises new and ever-challenging questions. That is what forensics is. The main function of the PA is to clarify an equivocal death and to arrive at the correct and accurate mode of death. The PA is a thorough retrospective investigation of the *intention* of the decedent. In general, there is no fixed ('edged-in-stone') outline, or one questionnaire, or one blood sample, while conducting a PA; yet, Shneidman, Farberow, and Litman did provide and used a general "*empirical*" outline (see page 122). The fact is, like in all CSI, one asks open ended questions during a PA. *There is no the standard edged-in-stone PA interview.* It is a narrative process; that is why it is not mysterious. It is truly what an investigation is!

Many people make significant contributions to established fields of knowledge. But few are vouchsafed the rare opportunity to create a new discipline, to name it, to shape it, to contribute to it, and most importantly, to catalyze other competent investigators to invest in it. Socrates, John Graunt, and Edwin Shneidman are such people. All three are first rate in science and scholarship. Socrates' name is synonymous with philosophy and his method, the Socratic Method. John Graunt's name is synonymous with actuary science, and his method of mortality tallies. Edwin Shneidman's name is synonymous with suicidology and his method, the psychological autopsy. All three methods show us the truth—"the sun." The PA, in fact, had its origins at the very beginning of contemporary suicidology. The PA refers to a set of procedures, including systematic interviews of survivors (plural), whose primary purpose is to establish the mode of death of the decedent.

Some people, who pick up a book on psychological autopsies, would expect a different content than what they find in my volume. For example, today many use the PA in quantitative nomothetic studies. Dr. Shneidman, however, was clearly opposed to the use of the PA in this way (see chapter on the conversation with Dr. Shneidman). Indeed, as you read in this volume, there are many problems in what some people call a PA. Dr. Shneidman, as you read in Chapter 5, simply held to the view that there was no law against 'them' calling anything that they did, 'a psychological autopsy.' Yet, he strongly believed that the PA was a scientific-clinically based tool in DSI. Ed did not see the PA as a tool for nomothetic, quantitative study, although he saw value in more qualitative study of PAs for finding commonalities of suicide. Therefore, this book focuses on case studies in forensic/coroner cases. I believe that this will be of great interest to police, mental health specialists, forensic experts and the government.

The idiographic approach is concerned with the individual. The PA is an individual case study. It is a report on a single case. However, I believe that every detailed forensic case study has features that are unique and features that are common. Heraclitus believed this, so did Socrates, Graunt and Shneidman. I believe the reader will gain some useful insights into suicide and death. Ultimately, the task of the investigator or would-be investigator is to develop expertise on a topic, here suicide and death—and NASH. I have attempted to set down some individual observations of that dire topic in this book—suicide. Simply put, to do a PA, you must know what suicide is—and what suicide is in that particular individual suicide's mind. Once you know what suicide is—particular and general (ubiquitous)—the PA will come naturally. It is not mysterious. It is a learned narrative process. You can, indeed, accurately reconstruct the mode of death, suicide or accident or homicide. It is a meaning-making of death—and that particular death, often in a PA, suicide. The PA is an evidence-based tool that has passed the U.S. Fry test and Daubert criteria and, I believe, Canada's Mohan criteria. This book is about the evidenced based, generally accepted, standardized (the Shneidman/LASPC "*empirical*" type PA) method, testable, peer-reviewed published, court accepted, forensic psychological autopsy— it is a roadmap (with a margin of error) for you to uncover the barren bones of a mind's despair.

Thus, in this book, I have been writing about suicide, how to best understand that death. Although this whole book is a definition of suicide, I will take one more attempt at my topic. Again, I quote my professor and friend, Dr. Edwin S. Shneidman (1985):

> Suicide, like all deaths, while occurring in a dyadic setting, is, at bottom, an egotic (individual, solo, private) act. It is a one-person deed relating to that person's conscious and unconscious concern with active mastery—which, at its furthermost remove, is related to omnipotence. At the moment of committing suicide, the individual may feel he controls the world—and by his death can bring it down. At least he controls his own destiny, and realistically typically touches and influences the destinies of at least several others. (p. 238)

Once one understands suicide, the PA becomes your best method in suicide-survivor investigation, part of the DSI. I cannot repeat what I wrote on the pages of chapter 3 to 5; however, let me shed some new "light" on the topic. One person, whom I earlier cited was Avery Weisman. Dr. Weisman was a personal friend of Ed. Dr. Shneidman called him "The dean of American suicidology." Dr. Weisman was another early pioneer of the PA; he wrote a number of books on the PA (1968, 1974). The most recent reflections of Avery can be found in Ed's last book, *Autopsy of a*

Suicidal Mind (2004). In the decade old volume, Dr. Avery Weisman offers his last words on the PA. He writes,

> Because a psychological autopsy extends the range of a regular autopsy, it should also tell us what a person was like and lived *for*. This refers to values, aims, and the problems coped with. In order to flesh out the bare recital of disease or the surrounding facts of suicide, I therefore must make a distinction between *impersonal* information, shown by clinical, laboratory, and pathological findings; *interpersonal* information, which is usually called psychosocial; and the *intrapersonal* dimension, gained secondhand from survivors, that may reveal the dead person's inner life. . . .
>
> . . . What remains is to piece together impersonal, interpersonal, and intrapersonal factors, likely to be fragmentary, but larded with our own prejudices and what we are pleased to call principles. Even wise old men, as we discussants are reputed to be, must be cautious in judgment. I like to believe that with collective experience, we can distinguish objective from subjective information, at least most of the time.
>
> Psychological facts are, after all, not so much facts as low-level theories. Interviews with significant survivors after a death must be conducted circumspectly, allowing for idiosyncratic tendencies to idealize the dead, about whom nothing ill should be said. Not every report deserves equal credence. Some people will unwittingly cloak, rather than reveal, unpleasant and incriminating information. By selection, they have the most to lose and, therefore, are entitled to mitigate what they say. Nevertheless, it does not pay to be ultraskeptical, or we'd have nothing left. We can try to be discriminating and not take the survivors' agenda as factual all the time. (pp. 152-153)

My hope is that these few memories and reflections on suicide and the PA will serve as a useful conclusion—a concluding summary of what I know. I don't know how to summarize my thinking about using the psychological autopsy better than presenting a few different thoughts on our topic. To finalize, when asked to review the teachings and approaches that are best, I would, as stated before, answer, know suicide, generally and specifically, the nomothetic and the idiographic. You need to know suicide to undertake a PA, reliability and validity, rare. Maybe, to review what I think is best, allow me to present a new case, *The State of Indiana vs. Bei Bei Shuai.* This case was all about what suicide is. I hope that in this way, I can make you think and invest in the topics of this book.

ONE MORE BRIEF MATTER BEFORE
OUR CONCLUDING CASE

Of course, understandably in law, the judge here knows better who an expert is than those "experts" who appear before him/her. She/he decides. To quote some veteran police officers, "an expert is a witness who has acquired special or particular knowledge about a specific area through study, reviewing scientific works and/or practical observation. They are called to give an opinion in court about evidence" (Jeffrey et al., 2015). The task of course is how do you get to be an expert? To acquire "expert" status, you have no choice—you have to learn to see the "shadows" and the "sun." What is fact! Once you are accepted as an expert, you must prepare a CV (curriculum vitae). The CV is your DSI story. It is your suicidological story. Of course, one's roadmap is continually being built. Like Sisyphus, it is a lifetime of pushing your boulder up the hill, each and every day. As Homer noted about Sisyphus, who was in the same situation every day, you will then be the wisest of investigators.

THE STATE OF INDIANA vs. BEI BEI SHUAI

Bei Bei Shuai was born on September 6, 1976, in Shanghai, China; in accordance with China's one-child policy, she was raised as a single child by "loving and caring" parents. She excelled and graduated from Shanghai University as an accountant. She worked in a Chinese governmental department. She got married and, with her husband, emigrated to the United States in 2000. Unfortunately, her marriage ended in 2008; she struggled economically. Bei Bei subsequently developed a relationship with an older married man (Zhiliang Quan; his name is a matter of public record), who promised to divorce and marry her. After an 18-month relationship, she became pregnant. She experienced severe depression during the pregnancy; she had three documented episodes of suicidal ideation and attempts. There was intimate-partner dissembling and abuse. Mr. Quan abandoned her in the end, leaving Bei Bei Shuai on her hands and knees, clearly emotional, in a parking lot, throwing money at her as he drove off. He told her he did not want her or the baby.

Bei Bei Shuai had suffered from depression; she became very distraught, felt abandoned, deeply shamed, and was suicidal. In China, there is great shame for being pregnant and unmarried. She wrote the following (translated) suicide note:

[first page]
Zhiliang Guan.
Why is a man's mind so cruel, so unfeeling?
Ah!
At the moment when you threw money and turned away, it made me so sad and desperate.
Why does the man who used to be intimate with me now try to stay away from me like I'm a snake or a scorpion?
Throw all love and justice. [This is a Chinese proverb that describes someone who forgets about love and loyalty to each other in the past.] I am just a dirty rag that you can't wait to get rid of. You even see my sorrow and tears as an act to earn sympathy. Zhiliang Guan, what kind of person you are! Your words are like a knife piercing deeply into my heart. This makes my wounded soul even more painful—and my heart and lungs are in deep sorrow. At the very moment my heart broke into pieces. Zhiliang Guan, have you really forgotten me—a person of flesh and blood with feelings? A woman who is about to give birth to a baby! Zhiliang Guan, I have been working hard with my two hands in this foreign land of America for over ten years. I have been very passionate about helping and caring for everyone around me. I've never given into the temptation to take

How could I be abandoned this way and not feel any sorrow? Am I supposed to pretend?

another person's belongings, I really don't understand why I have become such a bad woman in your family's eyes.

[second page]
I have poured out all the love and caring for you that a woman can give. I always think of you first. I've given you the best and loved you with all my heart. Why would your family see me as a woman with vicious intentions? Why would your family talk about me as if I were a skittish, bad woman?
Zhiliang Guan, right now I know that my existence as well as the child's is a burden, trouble and even a hindrance to your own happy life.
So I choose death to give you a successful and happy life in the future. I am only asking you to have DNA tested or find a parent/child association after my death. Please prove my innocence to your family and show them that half of baby Crystal's genes are your own, Zhiliang Guan.
I am taking this baby, the one you named Crystal, with me. There is no need to find my friends.
Why bother?
On the way to Hades (death), I will take care of her.
Please leave me with a bit of personal dignity after my death.

On December 23, 2010, Ms. Shuai attempted suicide by consuming rat poison. She did not die. With the help of friends, she was offered and accepted medical help and was hospitalized, under psychiatric care, at Methodist Hospital in Indianapolis for 32 days. She was diagnosed with and treated for major depression. She was assessed to be at risk for suicide. Bei Bei Shuai survived her attempt; however, complications occurred with her child (fetal). On December 31, 2010, her baby was delivered by cesarean surgery, but 10 days after the attempt, her daughter, Angel, died on January 3, 2011. Detectives began an investigation and Bei Bei Shuai was arrested on May 14, 2011. She was taken into custody in the high-security Marion County prison. She was charged with murder and feticide. She was in jail for 435 days and faced a sentence of 45 years to life.

Shuai's attorney was Linda Pence, of the well-known law firm, Pence Hensel, of Indianapolis, Indiana. From day one, Pence saw the case as "unprecedented"; indeed, she stated, "There has never been a case like this filed in Indiana." Shuai's case was the first in the history of Indiana in which a woman was prosecuted for murder for attempting suicide while pregnant. There was a law, enacted in 1979, to protect pregnant women from violence by their partner, such as abusive husbands. The American Civil Liberties Union, National Advocate for Pregnant Women, and health groups like the American Association of Suicidology, and the American Medical Association, came to Ms. Shuai's aid. Indeed, international support arose for Bei Bei and all pregnant women who may be suffering from mental illness and suicide risk. Of course, it would be obvious that if Shuai was convicted of murder, women would be discouraged from getting help. Pregnant women would be branded; that is *stigma*!

However, despite national and international protest, the prosecuting team persisted with the murder charge. David Rimstidt, the chief deputy on the team at the time, noted that Shuai wrote a suicide note before attempting to kill herself, stating that she is going to "take this baby with me to Hades." Rimstidt concluded, "It's about this woman having a specific *intent* to cause harm that is against the law." Therefore, he concluded, "She is guilty." (See Chapter 1, "A Note on Cognitive Style")

Among other independent professionals, I was retained by Pence Hensel to provide expert consulting service for Bei Bei Shuai. I was to be a suicide expert at trial. I provided a deposition, actually a recorded statement (I was in Canada; they were in the United States) on June 27, 2013; I will present some verbatim testimony below. I was set to testify at trial in September. However, Marion County Prosecutor Terry Curry dropped the charges of murder and feticide; Linda Pence believed that I was one of the reasons (*"You were wonderful!"*). I received an e-mail from Linda on August 2, stating that "Ms. Shuai accepted an agreement requiring her to plead to a violation of a Class B Misdemeanor, Criminal Recklessness, in exchange for the dismissal by the State of the murder and feticide felony charges." We won. Bei Bei was free!

SUICIDE AND PREGNANCY: THE NOMOTHETIC FINDINGS

As I always do, I undertook a systematic literature review; that is the best evidence-based procedure. We searched the database on PubMed/Medline and PsychINFO. We searched terms such as *pregnancy* and *attempted suicide*, *infanticide* or *feticide*, and *filicide*. We identified all possible articles (no source was excluded). We also searched books and chapters. I always attempt to be as broad as possible. From the search, we identified a number of articles (especially peer reviewed), obtained and read all abstracts, and full-text articles that met inclusion criteria were retrieved. All articles (actually few) were reviewed in detail, summarized, highlighted, and cataloged, a basis for a better general (nomothetic) understanding of suicide during pregnancy. From the search, we identified some of the best nomothetic knowledge on the topic of our case. One *a priori* fact is widely accepted in suicidology: pregnancy is a protective factor in suicide. I hereby offer briefly some general knowledge.

There is a consistency of immigrant and country-of-birth suicide rates (Sainsbury & Barraclough, 1968; Voracek & Loibl, 2008); it's meaning too (Leenaars, 2007, 2009). This is true for people from China. Not only the rates and meaning but also the method shows a consistency (Phillips & Gunnell, 2009). China is the only country in the world where females have higher rates of suicide than males (Pritchard, 1996). The most common method in China is poisoning.

Suicide is a leading cause of maternal death; a maternal death follows a registerable living or stillbirth at more than 23 weeks gestation (Oates, 2003). Of maternal deaths reported, Oates (2003) reported that 12% were due to psychiatric causes and 10% due to suicide. Yet among others, Marzuk et al. (1997) and Hawton (2000) have reported low suicide rates during pregnancy; much is associated to mental illness (Oates, 2003). Depressive disorder is a major risk factor in suicide, even during pregnancy (Melville, Gavin, Guo, Fan, & Katon, 2010). Among studies, 8%–12% of pregnant women met criteria for major depression (Melville et al., 2010). Stewart (2011) reported a rate of 12.7% of depression during pregnancy. Although we know some facts about depression during pregnancy, less is known about other disorders and risk. (Anxiety and schizophrenia are observed mental illnesses with the next-highest risks.) Melville and her team (2010) found that half of the women diagnosed with depression met criteria for major depression; notably, about one third of the depressed women reported suicidal ideation. There are risk factors; a major factor is intimate-partner violence. Melville and her team also reported that population, race, and ethnicity play a role; Asians experience an increased risk of depressive disorder during pregnancy. Culture is believed to be a factor; yet more research is needed.

On our topic of suicide and pregnancy, Marzuk and his team (1997) present one of the best studies (a hallmark of Peter Marzuk). Marzuk and his team investigated 315 female suicides of New York City, 10–44 years of age, from 1990 to 1993. Autopsies and forensic investigations were undertaken. Six cases were found by both autopsies and investigations. The live births, during the study period, was 507,956. The mean annual rate of suicide was calculated to be 3.85 per 100,000; that is low. Thus, despite depression and stresses associated with "pregnancy and impending childbirth, pregnant women have a significantly lower risk of suicide than women of childbearing age who are not pregnant" (Marzuk et al., 1997, p. 122). The low risk is, however, for suicide; pregnant women are at high risk for suicide attempts and suicide ideation!

There are risk factors. Gentile (2011) reported that WHO estimates suggest that 3% to 16% of pregnant women fulfill criteria for depression. Yet, in specific populations, such as marginalized minority groups and unwed women, the rate of depression may be as high as 51% (Gentile, 2011). Gentile reported that studies have reported rates of suicidal ideation from 13.1% to 33% in pregnant women. This is true in Asia too. Illegitimate pregnancies, especially in those societies with strong sanctions, result in condescension (abuse). Moreover, there is a strong association to suicidal behavior. Explanations for the associations are rooted in the culture; for example, Chinese collective culture (see discussion in Chapter 1). Furthermore, Gentile noted a significant association between suicidal ideation in pregnancies and mental disorders, especially (and obvious now) depression. This is true for suicide attempts as well. Almost all pregnant women chose poison ingestion for their suicide attempt. Indeed, Czeizel (2011) has, sadly reported a rise of poisoning during suicide attempts during pregnancy. Pregnancy is a special risk factor for suicide attempts of pregnant women (Czeizel, 2011). Of course, self-poisoning pregnant women need specialized medical care and, even more so, socioemotional assistance, including for the child.

Benute et al. (2011) undertook an exploratory study on risk of suicide in high-risk pregnancy; like previous studies, they found depression to be *the* risk factor. Suicide attempts and suicide ideation occur during pregnancy and high-risk pregnancy. Indeed, as Gavin, Tabb, Melville, Guo, and Katon (2011) note, "pregnancy is not a protective factor against suicidal ideation" (p. 239). They undertook a longitudinal study of 3,347 women and found non-White females were at greater risk than White women. There are nation-of-origin, racial, and economic factors (e.g., low income at greater risk). Substance dependency may be a risk factor too (Hennelly, Yi, Batkis, & Chisolm, 2011). Be that as it may, intimate-partner violence stands out as a major risk factor in every study (Martin, Macy, Sullivan, & Magee, 2007).

Martin et al. (2007) undertook a systematic literature review. They note that the previous research shows that intimate-partner (domestic) violence is "common in women's lives and that femicide and suicide are responsible for many pregnancy-related deaths" (p. 136). Yet they note a lack of study, isolating only nine publications on pregnancy-associated violent deaths. Of course, this is not unusual; there are even fewer studies on PMS and suicide, a topic that I have researched, for example (Leenaars et al., 2009). Martin and her team (2007) noted that out of the nine studies, only three studies examined intimate-partner violence in relationship to pregnancy-associated deaths. Simply stated, like with PMS and suicide, pregnancy and suicide is difficult to study. For example, one needs a very large sample (the reason why I did my studies on PMS in New Delhi, India). Despite this limitation, estimates of intimate-partner abuse and suicide suggest that between 30% and 40% of the women were abused. This is an important nomothetic fact as background to our idiographic studies.

There are a few studies looking at the issue of intimate-partner violence among pregnant (and postpartum) suicide victims. One possible source for facts is the National Violent Death Reporting System (NVDRS). The NVDRS offers new insights by listing multiple data sources and allowing better nomothetic investigation. Gold, Singh, Marcus, and Palladino (2012) and Palladino, Singh, Campbell, Flynn, and Gold (2011) looked at NVDRS data from 2003 to 2007; regrettably, there are only 17 states reporting, and there are problems in consistency of data gathering. Be that as it may, the results replicate the truth that intimate-partner abuse was higher among pregnant suicides (and postpartum suicides). Out of 2,083 women with suicide, 1,169 (56%) had a known mental health problem (95% were mood disordered, such as depression); 576 (28%) had problems with current and former partners. Out of the sample, there were 94 counts of pregnancy-associated suicide and 139 counts of pregnancy-associated homicide. Out of the pregnancy-associated suicides, 43 occurred during pregnancy (45.7%) (51 occurred postpartum). Older women were at higher risk for pregnancy-associated suicide. And of the pregnancy and suicide group, 54.3% of the victims experienced domestic problems (homicide was 45.3%). Thus, there is a general association of intimate-partner abuse with maternal violent death. Samandari, Martin, Kupper, Schiro, Norwood, and Avery, (2011), and Romero and Pearlman (2012) have replicated the findings; it is evidence-based at a nomothetic level (Romero and Pearlman also note a higher incidence of motor vehicle accidents in maternal deaths).

Regrettably, there is a dearth of studies on outcome following self-inflicted poisoning during pregnancy. McClure, Patrick, Katz, Kelsey, and Weiss (2011) noted that fetal, neonatal, and infant death, of course, occurs; however, those data are not definitive yet. Preterm birth, low birth weight, and circulatory system congenital anomalies are also possible outcomes. Mental retardation has also been noted (Petik, Czeizel, Banhidy, & Czeizel, 2012). However, as noted by everyone in the area of suicide and pregnancy, more nomothetic study is needed. That is our current background; it is sparse, which may lead us astray. It is in the detail that we find the truth, I have learned. Of course, as one should, I provided copies of the relevant studies to Bei Bei Shuai's lawyer and the prosecutor. Secrecy only hurts your case.

THE EVIDENCE

There was abundant evidence that Bei Bei Shuai was, at the time of her attempt (and before), at a high level of lethality and perturbation. She was depressed and highly suicidal; her mind was a suicidal mind. One could use her case as a prototype for barren discussions on suicide, as I am. (I would like to thank the prosecutor, Courtney Curtis, in the case, who interviewed me, for the suggestion.) The purpose here is not to detail the idiographic assessment and facts. On the issue in this chapter, there was no question in my mind that she was suicidal and was suicidal at the time she wrote her "genuine" suicide note. If she had died, the mode of death was "Suicide." We also have a good idea why and why at that particular time. As I always do, I scored her note with the TGSP; in Chapter 1 (pp. 52-57), I presented the complete text and protocol sentences (TGSP). Bei Bei's note had the following characteristics of suicide: 1, 2, 3, 4, 5, 6, 7, 8, 9, 11, 12, 13, 14, 15f, 16, 17, 19, 20, 21, 22, 23, 25, 26, 27, 28, 29, 31, 32, 33, 34, 35. (That is a near "perfect" suicide note.) May I suggest that you score Bei Bei's note too with the TGSP and then determine her suicidality, lethality, and perturbation. Of course, one always places the note or any evidence within the larger context of the case, all of the evidence. Yet what is your "therefore"; guilty of the charge(s) or innocent? What would you judge? Why?

MY TESTIMONY

On June 27, 2013, I provided a deposition (actually a recorded statement). Bei Bei's defense was headed by Linda Pence (she had no questions); the prosecutor was Courtney Curtis. I present verbatim (with some editing of oral text to written) my testimony. The interview was 2 hours; I present a very small fraction of the time, the main facts speak for themselves. Thus, for the reader, I have inserted a few remarks in [*insert*]. (I have also placed in **bold** my words, when there was a clear increase in intensity in my voice.) The issue in this case, and all cases: What is suicide? What is suicide in Bei Bei? And my hopeful question for the reader: Does it do it? *Do you understand suicide, homicide, and accident better?* I present the text:

> **Courtney Curtis**: I'm going to assume that you have reviewed the suicide note in this case.
>
> **AL**: Yes.
>
> **Curtis**: OK. Can you tell me I guess, have you reviewed the translation? Or do you speak Chinese sir?
>
> **AL**: No, I don't speak Chinese . . . I was given a translation of the note and I've read it a number of times. There's no question that at the time of writing, this person had suicide on her mind. . . . what I did with Bei Bei Shuai's note. I looked

at this note; I read it a number of times. I did not look at any other information or anything before; that is my practice forensically. And then I scored her note . . . [*I discussed in detail the history, theory, research, peer-reviewed and independent-author(s) publications, reliability/validity, gender, cultural aspects and validation, TGSP, etc.—see Chapter1*] What I find is almost all these 35 factors tend to be evident in her note. There are some that are not, but the majority of the factors that I would expect were in her note. So there's no question in my mind that at that point, when that person wrote it, there was suicidal intent. And I can get into the specific things that I saw in the note if you like, but you know, it depends on what you want.

Curtis: Well you know I don't think that we're contesting that it's a suicide note. I was just curious as far as your review of it . . . Are there, maybe, just a couple of things that stood out for you that struck you as particularly genuine?

AL: I'm concerned about the domestic violence; the bullying that occurred to this woman at the time that she wrote the note. I think she was quite sad and desperate. I think, you know, she didn't understand how he [Zhiliang Quan] could throw away all love and justice, like being a rag. What also struck me was that she felt like a knife was pierced into her heart deeply. She felt wounded and in **pain**. There was a deep sorrow. She was in the pain of pain; the howling tempest of her brain was there, I think . . . I think, she sees herself as a good person, that she's worked hard in this country as an immigrant, like many immigrants do; and she doesn't understand why suddenly his family would call her a bad woman and this and that. I think, therefore, she ends up killing herself. The motivation is because of the proximal cause. If you will, it's sort of "but for the last straw, the camel's back would not have been broken." But for what the man said to her and what he did, throwing the money at her and leaving her there in the parking lot, I don't think this would have happened. I think he, although suicide is multidetermined, was the proximal cause of her suicide attempt. What also struck me was that she felt she was a burden. Thomas Joiner, he is the editor now of *Suicide and Life-Threatening Behavior*, that I'm a consulting editor to, has a whole theory that being a burden is absolutely one of the major reasons why people have killed themselves. Terry Maltsberger, a Harvard psychiatrist, would call it suicidal worthlessness. I was struck that she saw herself as a burden—a trouble and even a hindrance to his life. I think that's why, in a mentally constricted mind, she decided to kill herself—so that, she would not be a burden, a trouble. And of course in the Chinese culture, there are all sorts of things about unmarried women and being pregnant. I think, she must have agonized over his accusation that the baby may not even be his child. I think the straw that broke her back was him. I think if it was not but for him, this would have never occurred . . .

Curtis: Do you have the note in front of you?

AL: Yes.

Curtis: OK. There's that section that's off to the left; even though it's typed, it's almost like as if someone was writing in the margins. Do you see where I'm referring?

AL: Yes

Curtis: Could you just read that aloud to me so I can see which version you have?

AL: "How could I be abandoned this way and not feel any sorrow? Am I supposed to pretend?"

Curtis: Alright, thank you. When you say that her partner, the baby's father, was the proximal cause of her suicide, do you mean their relationship or do you mean his activities on that last day before her suicide attempt?

AL: Usually when we investigate nurses and doctors [*for standards of care and liability*] after a patient died by suicide, we are look at what they did [*e.g., failure to diagnose properly, failure in care*] at that last meeting, that last event, etc. So, I believe it's the relationship over time which was both something she wanted and was [*something she found*] confusing. But I think what really traumatized her was that last event. I don't think she was expecting it, when they're in that parking lot; I believe this because I've read his deposition. I specifically asked for that deposition from Linda. I have not read any other depositions, only his. And so there's no question in my mind from my clinical point of view. You know, if it was a psychologist, doing that [*being liable*], he would lose his licence; he may be criminally charged . . .

Curtis: You reviewed her note, I guess, in a vacuum without looking at any other facts or factors, is that right?

AL: That's correct.

Curtis: OK. And then, you looked at other pieces of evidence or other documents to do what?

AL: Well the main thing I wanted to know was whether this was actually a suicide. People believe there was a suicide attempt, at least from the facts. The information that I've gotten, there seems to be an acceptance that this was a real suicide. I've been involved in cases where there's a note, but no suicide. Some people write a note and then they decide not to kill themselves and they put the note away. In terms of being suicidal, for suicidal-at-risk people, it comes and goes. You know, the best time to kill yourself is when you're not suicidal, because you're not going to kill yourself. **To wait!** Sometimes, waiting a day or two or whatever, makes a huge difference. Therefore, the important thing for me was that it was [*a genuine suicide*], and I wanted to know a little bit about what occurred specifically in the event; so, I got the deposition. . . . I mean, I would love to do a complete psychological autopsy in this case. I would love to interview the people involved, Quan, etc., the police, the doctors, but that is not my responsibility. That's yours in this case.

Curtis: I don't know if I have, I guess, the capacity to do one of those, but, you said that you read her partner's deposition. What other pieces of material did you review? . . .

So, when you reviewed Ms. Shuai's note, it makes no difference that she survived; what you're looking for is her suicidal intention.

AL: That's correct.

Curtis: Can you review a suicide note and determine if someone has a mental disorder from its content?

AL: You know, I can make some inferences, but I would never make a diagnosis simply from the note in terms of, that a person has a mental disorder from simply a note, or from a poem, or from whatever. You'd want, as a clinician, to have much more. Now, for research purposes, you might want to do that. This is where, you know, having more information about Bei Bei Shuai would be helpful to me in terms of understanding her; but, my belief is that she was suicidal. But I would never say, because I'm clinically allowed in this province [*Ontario*] to make a diagnosis, I would never say she clearly has a mental disorder; she clearly has a depressive disorder and give her a DSM number.

Curtis: OK, since we can't make a diagnosis of a mental disorder, we are just speaking about suicide or, I guess, someone who is suicidal in this instance, correct?

AL: Yes, but, you know, I believe she was suicidal, I mean depressed, but I would want more information to say she could have been diagnosed [*with a mental disorder*]. I don't want to do any kind of jumping to conclusions from a factor that I see, and then, the clinical or legal thing of making a diagnosis. I would want much more information. I would want the doctor's notes. I would want to speak to the doctor; I would want whatever information is available. What I do find though, supporting the depression notion, is in the deposition of the partner. In fact, he talks about it in there, that she has been depressed and suicidal . . . to know whether there is a mental disorder, you need more information. . . . In a case, I interviewed the psychiatrist and the doctors and the family members and then determined that that person at the time of writing a note, before he died, was not of sound mind.

Curtis: Do you have enough information in this case to make a similar determination?

AL: All I can say is that based on the note, I think she was extremely mentally constricted and I think she was overwhelmed, traumatized; she felt to be a burden. I can make those kinds of statements. But I can't determine whether she's sane or insane from that note. I mean that's a much larger question. But it's quite clear that she was mentally constricted, in my mind. I mean, I make those kinds of inferences in terms of **intention** every day in my office. I (we) make inferences about what people plan and intend, based on what they say in my office, people's behaviors, what they write and maybe even the books that they ask me about or what they say is their favorite book.

Curtis: Have you prepared or are you prepared to speak about the criminalization of suicide?

AL: Yes, if asked.

Curtis: What would you say?

AL: I have presented to my [*Canadian*] parliament, a parliamentary committee; stigmatization and criminalization were clearly part of that report. I think, it would be a horrible mistake [*to criminalize suicide*] because if you criminalize a small group of people for being suicidal, history shows that you are going to get a lot of people not getting help. If I'm depressed and pregnant and think I might get arrested, I'm not going to go to a doctor. Most of us in the field, and including in associations, the American Association of Suicidology, of which I've been a president, the only non-American, would fight this, would be opposed to this. This would result in many more people not getting help. It's like, in the military, people that were suicidal were put in jail. In police services, if I'm a police officer and I'm depressed, I will lose my gun and my badge. So, we know from studies and from the history that criminalization of depression, being suicidal will result in less people seeking help. . . . The problem is that people who were suicidal used to be seen as, especially women, as witches. They were burned and thrown into the water. I don't want to get back to that kind of thing, where we're going to see pregnant women, because of a natural hormonal, and complications, like witches. And that we go on a witch hunt, towards women who are pregnant and suicidal. We need to get rid of the stigma. Stigma is one of the major killers and not only stigma by the general population but, you know, by people in my profession.

Curtis: If someone attempts to commit suicide and is unsuccessful but others are killed in the process, do you believe that that's an appropriate arena of the criminal justice system?

AL: I think that if you are talking about a person who intends to murder someone and does murder someone and then makes a suicide attempt that also results in other people dying in the process, because he's burning down the evidence, I think that person should be charged. But I think a person who's attempting to kill him/herself; I think, that's very different than in a situation where a person is murdering someone.

Curtis: I guess, what my question was, it's not that these two events occur close in time; but that in effect, the method of suicide is actually what kills other people.

AL: I would have to know the specifics of the case. I think each case has to be evaluated individually. I think there are people who are suicidal and plan to kill themselves and have no intent of hurting anyone else. They don't even think of their children. When people kill themselves, they may have a one-year-old or two-year-old; but they don't even think about the child. They are so mentally constricted, so tunnel-visioned, they don't necessarily think about other people. Therefore, I think, each case needs to be evaluated very differently. I think taking poison is very different than intentionally riding down the wrong side of the road. I've had a case where a man was in the car with his brother. His brother, who was driving, died; but he survived on the major highway from here [*Windsor*] to Toronto. Suddenly [*while driving*], his brother went for a bus and my patient survived. [*What was the intention?*] I think, these questions need to be looked at very individually in each case. There is a world of difference, if I start my car in the garage and I try to kill myself, and not knowing that somebody else is in the house, and the fumes get at the other person. You know, I think, you have to look at intent. What was the person's intent?

Curtis: Is there a huge difference, if you turn on your car in your garage and you have an infant who is not mobile, strapped into the back seat of the car?

AL: I have known women who have contemplated that. A lot of depressed women feel that it would be a burden [*leaving the child behind*] especially in certain cultures. Since you are hitting on that; in China, it would be a dishonor **not**

to take the child with you. It would be believed that it would be a disgrace . . . to leave behind the children; it would be the wrong thing to do. You should not assume a suicide is a suicide, because there are cultural aspects in each event.

Curtis: So I think what you're saying is that you cannot make a blanket statement as to whether or not the criminal justice system should never be involved. You think it is a case-by-case analysis.

AL: It's a case-by-case and you have to evaluate. If I intend to kill the people in the car that I'm planning to hit, and I fully intend them to die, that's very different than if my sole intent is to kill myself; but people accidentally or whatever die. Like the cases that I was involved in, where there was murder and then a suicide attempt; it would be a homicide-suicide attempt; there's a clear **intention**. For example [*in one of my police homicide-suicide psychological autopsy investigations*], Inspector Kelly Johnson [*of the London Police Service*] clearly intended to kill Superintendent David Lucio and then herself. If she had survived that attempt, then I think it would be taken that she really intended; she wanted to kill him. There's no question, and if it hadn't been David Lucio, I believe that it's even possible that she would have killed someone else. I don't want to go into the details of the case because some of it is still private in terms of the police department. They make us swear secrecy.

Curtis: Do you have plans to write an article on pregnancy and suicide?

AL: No.

Curtis: Do you have plans to write a case study about Ms. Shuai?

AL: There may be some fascination in this, and if people later on say, would you like to talk about this case, and Linda and you and I would be on a panel, I mean, I'd be more than willing to work with you guys and do something like that. I think there's a real educational value to this case. I think a lot of people assume that pregnancy saves people from depression and other problems. I have three daughters and one has a year and a half old daughter and she's just pregnant again and the other one has a child that's six months and what I see, is that there are a lot of emotions to being pregnant.

Curtis: Aha!

AL: I think people need to be more understanding of depression and pregnancy. I think people need to understand what suicide is, better. So, as I said, if Linda, you, and whoever else is really important in this case, ever want to sit and educate the public, I'd be more than willing to come to Indiana at my own expense and participate at that.

THEREFORE . . .

What have I learned? *Res ipsa loquitur.* The facts speak for themselves, ideographically and nomothetically. My advice: Your knowledge (*epistemology*) is your best approach and/or tool. My direction: Look at the "sun," the golden star. My opinion: DSI, in NASH investigations, are not mysterious. My belief: The PA is your best guide to uncover the barren facts (or "bones"). My questions: What is the most probable mode of death? Was it suicide? Was it homicide? Or an accident? Undetermined? Why did the death occur? Or why did the individual do it? And how did the individual die, and when—why at that particular time?

CHAPTER 13
Final Forgetting

This chapter is now not a secret; it is a test; it is an examination. It is not a multiple-choice exam, but rather it is in essay format. The OED defines examination as "A detailed inspection. The testing of the proficiency or knowledge of students or other candidates for a qualification by oral or written question." It has been a conscious intention. It is the Socratic Method. This book is not only about the barren bones, but how you understand the bare facts (evidence) once found. It is about theory, to understand the forensic unmapped. It is about knowledge. It is about the *golden star*. I will next present some questions from the beginning of the book to this point; I hope it will help you to uncover the truth in your death (DSI) case. What do you remember? What have you forgotten?

SOCRATES' EXAM QUESTIONS FOR DSI/PA

1. The concept of investigating deaths that are uncertain as to mode of death—natural, accident, suicide, or homicide—is at least as old as the work of John Graunt of London, England, in the 17th century. He showed that the impact of death certification was immense. What do you know about John Graunt? What do you know about historical certification?

2. The recent American history of the death certificate procedure on suicide focuses on the Los Angeles Suicide Prevention Centre (LASPC). In the 1950s the Chief Coroner and Medical Examiner of Los Angeles County, Theodore J. Curphey, asked the leaders of the LASPC to assist him with coroners' cases that were ambiguous as to the mode of death. Who are Drs. Edwin Shneidman, Norman Farberow, and Robert Litman? What is the clinical-scientific "empirical" procedure called the psychological autopsy (PA)?

3. In death scene investigation (DSI), we are interested in a specific, unique case. Was Robin Williams' death a suicide? Sigmund Freud's death? Why did, for example, Robin Williams die by suicide? Why did Freud? Why at that particular time? These are the real questions in the forensic unmapped. What did you learn?

4. No single factor or event explains why so many people are violent, such as suicide and homicide. Violence is multidetermined. They are complex. Suicide, homicide, and also war-related deaths are not like water, where all water

freezes at 32 degrees Fahrenheit. They are multidetermined and need a multiaxal approach to understand them (Meehl, 1986); this is very true about suicide. This is called the *ecological model*. Discuss.

5. An acronym for the four modes of death is NASH: natural, accidental, suicidal, and homicidal. This fourfold classification of all deaths has its problems. What does the NASH classification of death refer to? What is a major deficiency?

6. An important aspect of the issue at hand is that suicide is an *intentional* act. As Robert Litman noted, "The concept, which defines a death as suicide rather than an accident, is intention." Discuss. *How is suicide intent determined?* The DSI question, thus, is How can you reach an opinion about what was in the mind of a person who is now dead?

7. There are views that theory should not play a role in understanding suicide. Suicidology should only be tabular and statistical. However, theory, explicit and implicit, plays a key role in understanding any behavior. Theory is the foundation in science (Kuhn, 1962) (and sound DSI). What do you think?

8. The modern era of the psychological study of suicide began around the turn of the 20th century with the investigations of Dr. Sigmund Freud. Since around 1900, there have been a host of psychological theories besides Freud's that have attempted to define suicide. There are at least four major points of view: psychoanalytic (Freud); cognitive-behavioral (Beck); social learning (Lester); and multidimensional (Shneidman). These theories help in some way to clarify the central issue—understanding why people commit suicide. How? Which theory do you like best? Why?

9. Shneidman (1985) suggests that a psychological theory regarding suicide begins with the question, "What are the interesting common psychological dimensions of committed suicide?"—not what kind of people commit suicide. This question, according to Shneidman, is critical. Why? What did Heraclitus think?

10. Let me ask a fundamental question: Is it possible to understand suicide? Is there logic that we can use in DSI? Is there evidence? Facts? Are there useful psychological experiences (e.g., pain levels, cognitions, behaviors, affects)? Do they cluster together? If they do occur together, are there commonalities? What are they? Do the commonalities make sense? Do they make sense as clusters or patterns? Are they consistencies over time? Sex? Age? Culture?

11. The trick in this difficult business is the question of how the specific instance fits into a more abstract classification (e.g., suicide). The forensic specialist, like all investigators, must make judgments about whether the content of a protocol is understandable within a given classification (say, unbearable pain or lethal mental constriction). The knack in suicide classification is concluding "yes" or "no." This in fact may well be the most difficult task that an investigator faces. Why is this a most difficult task?

12. In science, intrapsychic (in the mind) concepts are known as "open concepts." Like any concept, they must, however, be defined by some reliable and meaningful, albeit diverse, empirical facts or events. For example, the concept of *unbearable psychological pain* may be assessed by the person's own story, his penultimate note, a history of previous attempts, dire social media postings, and

so on. Although the term *unbearable pain* of a person cannot be observed directly, it can be inferred and verified. How?

13. Hempel (1966) has pointed out that theory provides the glue that holds a classification together and gives it both its scientific and its clinical relevance. As Hempel stated, mature sciences progress from an observationally based stage to one that is characterized by abstract concepts and theoretical systemizations. This is a challenge. Why is this challenge important? How can it help you in DSI?

14. In the multideterminant nature of suicide, suicide is intrapsychic (in the mind). It is stress and pain, but not simply the stress or even the pain, but the person's inability to cope with the event or pain. However, from a psychological view, suicide is not only intrapsychic, it is also interpersonal (or stated differently, it is beyond the individual level in the ecological model, it is also relationship(s), community, societal). The suicidal individual is not only depressed, mentally constricted, and so on, but he or she is also cut off from loved ones, ideals, and/or even the community. Suicide occurs in a person and between people (or some other ideal; e.g., being loved by someone, being healthy). What does this all mean?

15. The common stimulus in suicide is unbearable psychological pain. The enemy of life is pain. The suicidal person is in a heightened state of perturbation, an intense mental *psychache*. Discuss.

16. The common cognitive state in suicide is mental constriction. The person is figuratively "intoxicated" or "drugged" by the constriction. This constriction is one of the most dangerous aspects of the suicidal mind. Why? What would A. "Tim" Beck say? Discuss.

17. Ambivalence, complications, redirected aggression, unconscious implications, and related indirect expressions (or phenomena) are often evident in suicide. There may be masking (dissembling). Yet there is much more. What the person is conscious of is only a fragment of the suicidal mind. Discuss. In what cases in this text was this concept/observation important? Why?

18. People with all types of pains, problems, and such are at risk for suicide. Psychological autopsy studies suggest that 40% to 90% of people who kill themselves have some symptoms of psychopathology (mental disorder) and/or problems in adjustment. The person may be simply paralyzed by pain that life, a future, and the like, are colorless and unattractive. Discuss.

19. The ego ("The part of the mind that reacts to reality and has a sense of individuality," according to the OED), with its enormous complexity, is an essential factor in the suicidal scenario. Ego strength is a protective factor against suicide. Suicidal people frequently exhibit a relative weakness in their capacity to develop constructive tendencies and to overcome their personal difficulties. There is, to put it in one simple word, vulnerability. There is a lack of resilience. Discuss.

20. The suicidal person has problems in establishing or maintaining relationships (with a person[s] or other ideal[s]). The person's psychological needs are frustrated. Suicide appears to be related to an unsatisfied or frustrated attachment need, although other needs may be equally evident. The possible needs that are

frustrated or blocked are expansive. What do you think may be some of the most common needs from "Harry" Murray's list? Discuss.

21. Loss is central to suicide; it is, in fact, often a rejection that is experienced as an unbearable narcissistic injury. Discuss. Aggression is a common emotional state in suicide. Suicide may be veiled aggression; it may be murder in the 180th degree. Discuss.

22. Intense identification with a lost or rejecting person or with any lost ideal (e.g., health, promotion, employment, gun ownership) is crucial in understanding the suicidal person. Identification is an attachment (bond). Discuss. If the suicidal person's emotional need is not met, the suicidal person experiences a deep pain and wants to egress, that is, to escape. Suicide is escape. Discuss.

23. In concluding, to begin to address the question, "Why do people kill themselves?" or more specifically, "Why did the person die by suicide?" we need a psychology of suicide. We must answer the question, What are the important common psychological dimensions of suicide? The question is critical, for these common dimensions (or "sameness") are what suicide is. What was Heraclitus's view? What did you learn on theory of suicide?

24. Are suicide martyrs (bombers/terrorists) the same and/or different than suicide? What intrapsychic elements are critical for predicting a to-be martyr to kill him/herself? To kill you? Are interpersonal (and/or community and/or society) protocols relevant? What elements? Is ambivalence salient? Rage? Grandiose fury? Extremism in the mind? What is most important?

25. Perception is in the eye of the beholder (Kuhn, 1962). Yet, do we accept the core beliefs of the suicidal soldier suffering from mild cognitive disorder from a TBI? The man with the scratched Ferrari? The student who received a B+? Discuss. Many of us can be relatively sure—no, absolutely sure—that at least the scratch on the Ferrari is not cause to therefore kill oneself. It is also not cause to therefore kill someone else too. However, the dead person did. Why is all this important in DSI?

26. "How it is that some people who are on the verge of suicide . . . can hide or mask their secretly held intentions?" This is called *dissembling*. To dissemble means to conceal one's motives. These people wear "masks." Kurt Cobain dissembled; he stated in his note that he is, "faking it and pretending as if I'm having 100% fun." Most investigators encounter such people—not only suicidal people. Their stories are invalid; sometimes, they even intentionally produce or feign a behavior (or symptom). They fabricate; there is even self-deception. What are the implications for DSI? What can and must you do?

27. Suicide, homicide, homicide-suicide, and other violence have probably always been part of the human experience. Why? Will they? What could we do?

28. The case of Acting Inspector Kelly Johnson and Superintendent David Lucio was a homicide-suicide. What did you learn about this unique case? What did the forensic investigation report reveal? How would a PA investigation and report help you to understand Kelly better?

29. A most important question that arises, including for DSI: On a continuum, when does a discrete event of suicide, such as that of Robin Williams, become a

relationship one, from suicide pacts, ranging from co-equal involvement, such as lovers, to one of pressure and coercion, such as the author Arthur Koestler's and his wife, to unwilling victim and a perpetrator as in Dave Lucio and Kelly Johnson or even mass murder-suicide bombers/terrorists, such as 9/11?

30. Within the NASH categorization (natural, accident, suicide, and homicide), what are accidental deaths? An accident is unplanned and mostly unanticipated. This general attribute must obviously be modified, however, if some accidents are suicides. In such cases, the event would seem to be unplanned and unanticipated to the outside observer. However, the victim knew very well what would happen. In this case, we would have a suicide masquerading as an accident. Discuss. What are possible solutions to the masking?

31. Each year death certificates are filled out by thousands of different certifiers. On each death certificate the manner of death must be indicated. This is the NASH category. There are many factors that affect valid and reliable certification of suicide. The determination of suicide requires establishing that the death was both self-inflicted and intentional. *Intentionality is central.* It would be a truism to state that establishing intentionality is the most difficult task that is inherent in the determination of the mode of suicide. Discuss. What are common errors? How can we be more accurate? What criteria?

32. Allport (1962) provides the following thought:

> Suppose we take John, a lad of 12 years, and suppose his family background is poor; his father was a criminal; his mother rejected him; his neighborhood is marginal. Suppose that 70 percent of the boys having a similar background become criminals. Does this mean that John himself has a 70 percent chance of delinquency?

What were Allport's answers? Why is this always important to be mindful of, in your DSI case?

33. My core belief is that documents such as suicide notes give us the philosopher's (investigator's) gold in our forensic digs. It is the *aurum philosophorum.* It illuminates the roads to the psychological barren bones. Why might I believe this core belief? Are suicide notes *prima facie?* What do you see in suicide notes? Or is DSI all mystery?

34. The psychological autopsy (PA) is the work of Dr. Edwin Shneidman. What did he do? (What did his co-pioneers and he do?) How did the PA get standardized? The main function of the psychological autopsy is to clarify an equivocal death and to arrive at the correct or accurate mode of that death. In essence, what is the psychological autopsy? How is a psychological autopsy performed?

35. There are at least three distinct questions that the psychological autopsy can help to answer:
    1. Why did the individual do it?
    2. How did the individual die, and when, that is, why at that particular time?
    3. What is the most probable mode of death?
    Discuss.

36. Shneidman's paper, "An Example of an Equivocal Death Clarified in a Court of Law" (1993b) is an example of a PA. This one was done in the adversarial setting of a court of law, specifically an Army court martial. The bare facts were that an army officer, Captain Joseph Campbell, was charged with the murder of his wife and faced a lifetime sentence in Leavenworth federal prison. What do you remember about the case? What might you forget?

37. Of course, from the very beginning, it was known that the PA had problems. What were they? What was a key? What did the pioneers do to address the problem? Have we today advanced the PA? How?

38. Somewhere along the way, the PA became the primary approach in studying risk factors. It is espoused that the PA is the best general, authoritative way to study the relationship between particular antecedents and suicide. Almost always, mental disorders, especially mood disorders, are found to be the most strongly associated variable with suicide. A causal link is accepted. All suicides are caused simply by mental illness. It is simple; thus, all DSI is simple. Occam's razor is best! What do you think?

39. Pouliot and De Leo (2006) note that the PA approach has offered an opportunity to provide people with a great deal of information on suicide. Yet there are inconsistencies in the findings due to four main problems. What are Pouliot and DeLeo's concerns? Do you agree? From your view, are there other problems? What can we do to address the questions (and maybe even the questionable)?

40. Hjelmeland, et al. (2012) examined a major flaw in most nomothetic PAs: how psychiatric diagnoses are assigned to the deceased in PA studies. How are the studies flawed?

41. We are told by many of the researchers on the PA that mental disorders cause suicide. They state, We studied it in the psychological autopsy. We showed in the questionnaire that the informant (singular) filled out that there was a mental disorder. Therefore, mental disorder causes suicide. Shneidman, Litman, Farberow, and I would add, "But my dear researchers, there is no evidence in your PA studies of mental disorders." The answer provided, "Precisely, because we believe it; it is therefore true. There are 'pink' mental disorders." (LOL) What does this mean to every cop and forensic investigator?

42. "One sees what one can best see oneself" (Jung, 1971). This fact is often called the personal equation. What is the personal equation? Your equation? How is it relevant in DSI?

43. Shneidman stated that a PA "is done by talking to some key persons—spouse, lover, parent, grown child, friend, colleague, physician, supervisor, co-worker—who knew the decedent." Shneidman, Litman,, and Farberow never talked to only one person. Yet somehow this has become a common practice—a fatal flaw! Why? The solution and thus a standardized procedure: Interview many informants. What did the study by Dieserud et al. (2015) show?

44. It has been argued, despite the observations already in the 1950s, that the PA will evoke painful memories. Thus, should we believe the belief, held by many, or should we research the actual or real facts? What is your experience? (What does an officer do in a CSI?)

45. The mode of death in the Hospital Corpsman Chris Purcell case was unequivocally suicide. Answer the following questions: Why did Chris kill himself? How did Chris die and where; that is, why at that particular time?

46. Chris Purcell left two suicide notes. I hereby present the notes.

(Note 1)
Mom, Pop, Kristin, and Blair
I'm so sorry . . .
Laugh as much as you
breathe
and love as long as you live
I love you
    Chris

(Note 2)
Suicide Note
Mother, Father, Kristen, and Blair: I'm sorry . . . I don't know what else to say. You all mean so much to me . . . I just can't go on anymore . . . I love you all more than you could ever imagine.

I feel it is only right to state my reasons for what I am about to do. First and foremost, this has nothing to do with anyone or anything. I just no longer have the desire to live. Life bores me. Blame it on whatever you want, the season, depression, alcohol abuse . . . it makes no difference, because in the end it is just me. I've always felt this way. I have suffered in silence most of my life . . . and I don't want to suffer anymore. I could go off on a philosophical tangent but in the end it doesnt matter. I appreciate everyones help and guidance . . . I really do.

I've learned a lot from everyone, people I like, people I loathe . . . it's been an experience. I also want to apologize to anyone I may have caused issues with..im not a bad guy..im really not. . . . I have the purest intentions inside my heart . . . I think they just come out all wrong. I think saying I've felt pretty misunderstood my whole life would be an understatement. I don't expect anyone to understand why I did this..I'm sure most will see it as the easy way out...me being a coward, etc. I'm not escaping any problem, im not running from anything. I'm saving me from myself. I came from nothingness and I will return to nothingness. This is probably making a pretty shitty suicide note, but I don't care, I'm just trying to convey my reasoning to who ever might care. It is all just meaningless to me . . . wake up . . . work, eat, masturbate, get drunk, pointless conversation..rinse and repeat. It's fucking madness.

I'm done with it. I'm not sure what kind of emotion this will ellicit to people I know . . . anger, denial, sadness, guilt . . . but just know that there was absolutely nothing anyone could have done Like I said, this is about no one. It is about me. You can see it however you want . . . this has been the hardest decision of my life but it has also been the most liberating one as well. At only 21 I realize I never will . . . meet the love of my life, hear my favorite song, play the best videogame, have sex . . . hear the best joke, have the best original idea . . . etc . . . I will also never disappoint myself or anyone else, never fail at anything again, never suffer alone, never watch life pass me be, never wonder what the fuck my problem is, never be rejected again, and ultimately . . . never live. Goodbye life,
    I have lost all interest in you.

Analyze the notes. (Please, use the TGSP.) What did you learn? What else would you want to see?

47. For the psychological autopsy of Chris Purcell, the following people were interviewed: Mike Purcell, father; Helene Purcell, mother; Kristin Purcell, sister; and Derek Ozawa, best friend. From the interviews, what did you learn? Why did Chris do it?

48. Daniel Beckon—a Canadian premiere jockey—died July 2, 1987. His death resulted in one of Canada's most publicized inquests. What do you know? What more would you like to see? What would be your classification of mode of death?

49. What issues or problems does the case Adrian Niel Clancy vs. the State of Texas raise? What do you think?

50. Kees Finn, a 28-year-old married male died in a car accident on January 2, 2000, in Illinois. Was it an accident or suicide? What is your opinion?

51. John Scott Dell was born the 3rd of March 1951. He died on the 29th of December 1995. His death certificate reads the mode of death as "Undetermined." What was the mode of death? Was it a suicide or, as some believed, a homicide? What is your opinion?

52. The cause of death for Scott Dell was listed as "Undetermined"; yet questions remained: was it suicide or homicide? The note found at the scene was called a "suicide note." The coroner and police officer, for example, had called the note a "suicide note." The note read as follows:

SCOTT DELL NOTE- 29 DEC 95
Dear Mr. Fantasy
Carmelita—Linda Ronstadt—Debbie Quinn
Fun—life would go on forever. Death—suicide
The truth is simple but seldom ever seen.
Dear Mr. Fantasy
Carmelita—Linda Ronstadt—Debbie Quinn
Fun—life would go on forever. Death—suicide
The truth is simple but seldom ever seen.
If Truth is Purity can it ever exist in such an impure world. If it can't what does that mean. Are we all living in the shadows of
I feel like holding you close to me like never before I feel like making love to you I feel like all the bad stuff would go away.
You and I are stuck because of all the bad stuff that has happened to us last 3 years. We need to make it go away.
I'm trying not to think about things I want to think about. I don't know if that is what I should do or not. I can't help it. I Don't want to want you. I don't want to be rejected
If we don't get back together we maybe shouldn't see each other very much.
I thought maybe this wasn't a good night because I was too tired but I think the truth is revealed no matter what.
Sun—before
Lying on a beach with you
We forget all time that our life is a gift that has been given us to enjoy not to waste.
I doesn't last long. It is not a sin to be happy but it may be to be unhappy.

What did you think was going to happen if I drank a bottle wine listening to music we used to listen too

I'm going to think about you and me together

Maybe that's the only way you can except to thru a spiritual vision.

I seems true that is not a sin to be happy so maybe that means that it is to be unhappy

You will have to listen to your heart not your head.

I had a vision of you very briefly you were like some neophyte Angel floating in the air but you were disconnected you head from your body.

1) Mary Akroyd.

2) I was probably supposed to die
   But my life was spared
   I don't know why. That bothers me.

3) Let go theres nothing that you are holding onto now is going to help you

4) Let go. You are holding on tight.

5) Our lives are going by really fast

Analyze the notes. (Please, use the TGSP.) Is this a genuine suicide note? Simulated? How did you reach this opinion? What did you learn from the analysis of the suicide note? How can the TGSP help? What are your opinions? What are the limitations of this note? What else would you like to see for yourself?

53. For the PA on Scott Dell, the following people were interviewed: Myra Dell, mother; Lauretta McCarthy, aunt; Elsa Steenberg, friend; Sue Kwast (by telephone), friend; and Paul O'Dell (by telephone), physician. What did we learn? What did you see as the most important facts? What else would you ask the informants?

54. To turn to my testimony in the Scott Dell case, I used the principle of *res ipsa loquitur*. What does that mean? What did you learn? What do you think of my testimony? What else would you have said? Did I err? When? How? What could I have done better?

55. Daubert vs. Merrill Dow Pharmaceutical, Inc. set out a reliable foundation for opinion in U.S. court. What is the Frye test? What is the Daubert formula? What do you think? Solutions?

56. Snider et al. (2006) published an important forensic paper on the issue that there are serious criticisms for the PA to go to court. One of the most concerning issues is the lack of standardization in protocols and methods of the PA, although Shneidman himself was quite clear about the protocols and methods. Dr. Shneidman was unequivocal. What was his opinion? What were Snider et al.'s recommendations? Your opinions?

57. On the more general, the PA is not alone being questioned. Indeed, the whole field of forensic science is in question. Some ask, Is it a questionable science? One grave concern is error: false positives (the concern in courts), and true negatives (the real problem for us in the field). Is that acceptable error? Is that science? Discuss.

58. Unlike in the United States, the place for science of any kind in Canada in the court is most problematic. The classical Canadian equivalent to the Frye test is

the McIntosh Test—the subject of testing must be generally accepted, scientific knowledge. What is the McIntosh test? However, R. v Mohan ([1994] 2 S.C.R.9) was the leading case on the criteria for admission of expert evidence. What is the Mohan formula? What do you think? Solutions?

59. What have you learned? What did you learn in the case of *The State of Indiana vs. Bei Bei Shuai*? Why is this case important for us in DSI, ranging from the police officer at the death scene to the judge in court? What have you *forgotten*?

60. Socrates was one of the great classical Greek (Athenian) philosophers. He was unequivocally a founder of Western philosophy. He developed what has become called the Socratic Method. Does the method help you? In DSI? In uncovering the barren bones of a suicide's mind? In your life? What do you need to learn next?

References

Aaron, D. (Ed.) (1985). *The Inman diary: A public and private confession.* Cambridge, MA: Harvard University Press.

Allen, N. (1980). *Homicide.* New York, NY: Human Sciences Press.

Allen, N. (1983). Homicide followed by suicide: Los Angeles, 1970–1979. *Suicide and Life-Threatening Behavior, 13,* 155–165.

Allport, G. (1942). *The use of personal documents in psychological science.* New York, NY: Social Science Research Council.

Allport, G. (1962). The general and the unique in psychological science. *Journal of Personality, 30,* 405–422.

American Psychiatric Association (APA). (1994). *DSM-IV: Diagnostic and statistical manual of mental disorders* (4th ed.). Washington, DC: Author.

American Psychiatric Association (APA). (2014). *DSM-5: Diagnostic and statistical manual of mental disorders* (5th ed.). Washington, DC: Author.

Andreason, N., & Grove, W. (1982). The classification of depression: A comparison of traditional and mathematically derived approaches. *American Journal of Psychiatry, 139,* 45–52.

Arbeit, S., & Blatt, S. (1983). Differentiation of simulated and genuine suicide notes. *Psychological Reports, 33,* 283–293.

Asberg, M., Traskman, L., & Thorien, P. (1976). 5-H1AA in cerebrospinal fluid: A biochemical suicide prediction? *Archives of General Psychiatry, 33,* 1193–1197.

Asgard, U., & Carlsson-Bergstrom, M. (1991). Interviews with survivors of suicides: Procedures and follow-up of interview subjects. *Crisis, 12,* 21–33.

Atran S. (2010). *Talking to the enemy.* New York, NY: HarperCollins.

Attig, A. (2010). *How we grieve: Relearning the world.* Oxford, UK: Oxford University Press.

Ayer, A. (Ed.). (1959). *Logical positivism.* New York, NY: Free Press (Original work published 1931)

Barak, A., & Miran, O. (2005). Writing characteristics of suicidal people on the Internet: A psychological investigation of emerging social environments. *Suicide and Life-Threatening Behavior, 35,* 507–524.

Barnes, J. (2007). Murder followed by suicide in Australia, 1973–1992: A research note. *Journal of Sociology, 36,* 1–14.

Barraclough, B. (1986). Illness and suicide. In J. Morgan (Ed.), *Suicide: Helping those at risk* (pp. 61–69). London, UK: King's College.

Beck, A. (1963). Thinking and depression: I. Idiosyncratic content and cognitive distortions. *Archives of General Psychiatry, 9,* 324–335.

Beck, A. (1967). *Depression: Clinical, experimental and theoretical aspects.* New York, NY: Hoeber.

Beck, A. (1976). *Cognitive therapy and the emotional disorders.* New York, NY: International Universities Press.

Beck, A., Beck, R., & Kovacs, M. (1975). Classification of suicidal behaviors: 1 Quantifying intent and medical lethality. *American Journal of Psychiatry, 132*, 285–287.

Beck, A., & Greenberg, R. (1971). The nosology of suicidal phenomena: Past and future perspectives. *Bulletin of Suicidology, 8*, 10–17.

Beck, A., Kovacs, M., & Weissman, A. (1979). Assessment of suicide intervention. The scale of suicide ideation. *Journal of Consulting & Clinical Psychology, 47*, 343-352.

Beck, A., Resnik, H., & Lettieri, D. (Eds.). (1974). *The prediction of suicide risk.* Bowie, MD: Charles Press.

Beck, A., Kovacs, M., & Weissman, A. (1975). Hopelessness and suicidal behavior: An overview. *Journal of the American Medical Association, 234*, 1146–1149.

Beck, A., & Rush, A. (1978). Cognitive approaches to depression and suicide. In G. Serban (Ed.), *Cognitive defects in the development of mental illness* (pp. 235–257). New York, NY: Brunner/Mazel.

Beck, A., Rush, A., Shaw, B., & Emery, C. (1979). Cognitive therapy of depression. New York, NY: Guilford Press.

Begley, M., & Quayle, E. (2007). The lived experience of adults bereaved by suicide: A phenomenological study. *Crisis, 28*, 26–34.

Bell vs. New York City Health and Hospital Corporation (1982) 90. A.D. 2nd 270.456 N.Y.S. 2d 787.

Benute, G., Nomura, R., Jorge, V., Nonnenmacher, D., Junior, R., De Lucia, M., & Zugaib, M. (2011). Risk of suicide in high-risk pregnancy: An exploratory study. *Revista Da Associacao Medica Brasileira, 57*, 583–587.

Berg-Cross, L. (Ed.). (2000). *Basic concepts in family therapy: An introductory text* (2nd ed.). New York, NY: Hawthorne.

Berman, A. (1993). Forensic suicidology and the psychological autopsy. In A. Leenaars (Ed.), *Suicidology: Essays in honor of Edwin Shneidman* (pp. 248–266). Northvale, NJ: Aronson.

Berman, A. (2006). The other 10 percent. *Newslink, 33*(3), 3.

Berman, A., & Jobes, D. (1991). *Adolescent suicide: Assessment and intervention.* Washington, DC: American Psychological Association.

Bjerg, K. (1967). The suicidal life span: Attempts at a reconstruction from suicide notes. In E. Shneidman (Ed.), *Essays of self-destruction* (pp. 475–493). New York, NY: Science House.

Blum, A., & McHugh, P. (1971). The social assumption of motives. *American Sociological Review, 36*, 98–109.

Bongar, B. (1991). *The suicidal patient: Clinical and legal standards of care.* Washington, DC: American Psychological Association.

Bongar, B., & Greaney, S. (1994). Essential clinical and legal issues when working with the suicidal patient. In A. Leenaars, J. Maltsberger, & R. Neimeyer (Eds.), *Treatment of suicidal people* (pp. 179–194). Washington, DC: Taylor & Francis.

Boismont, B. de (1856). *Du suicide et la folie suicide.* Paris, France: Germer Bailliere.

Bossarte, R., Simon, T., & Barker, L. (2007, September 11). Characteristics of homicide followed by suicide incidents in multiple states, 2003–04. *Injury Prevention, 12*, ii33–ii36.

Bostwick, J. (2000). Affective disorders and suicide risk: A re-examination. *American Journal of Psychiatry, 157*, 1925–1932.

Bowlby, J. (1980). *Attachment and loss: Loss, sadness and depression* (Vol. 3). New York, NY: Basic Books.

Brent, D. (1992, April). *Psychiatric effects of exposure to suicide among friends and acquaintances.* Paper presented at the conference of American Association of Suicidology, Chicago, IL.

Breshears, R., Brenner, L., Harwood, J., & Gutierrez, P. (2010). Predicting suicidal behavior in veterans with traumatic brain injury: The utility of the Personality Assessment Inventory. *Journal of Personality Assessment, 92,* 349–355.

Bronfenbrenner, U. (1979). *The ecology of human development: Experts by nature and design.* Cambridge, MA: Harvard University Press.

Bryan, C., Kanzler, K., Durham, T., West, C., & Greene, E. (2010). Challenges and considerations for managing suicide risk in combat zones. *Military Medicine, 175,* 713–718.

Buteau, J., Lesage, A., & Kiely, M. (1993). Homicide followed by suicide: A Quebec case series, 1988–1990. *Canadian Journal of Psychiatry, 38,* 552–556.

Callahan, V., & Davis, M. (2009). A comparison of suicide note writers with suicides who do not leave notes. *Suicide and Life-Threatening Behavior, 39,* 558–568.

Canetto, S. (1994). Gender issues in the treatment of suicidal individuals. In A. Leenaars, J. Maltsberger, & R. Neimeyer (Eds.), *Treatment of suicidal people* (pp. 115–126). Washington, DC: Taylor and Francis.

Canetto, S., & Lester, D. (1995). *Women and suicidal behavior.* New York, NY: Springer.

Carnap, R. (1959). Psychology in physical language. In A. Ayer (Ed.), *Logical positivism* (pp. 165–197). New York, NY: Free Press. (Original work published 1931)

Cavanagh, J., Carson, A., Sharpe, M., & Lawrie, S. (2003). Psychological autopsy studies of suicide: A systematic review. *Psychological Medicine, 33,* 395–405.

Centers for Disease Control and Prevention (CDC). (2009, December 5). *WISQAR website and fatal injury reports.* Retrieved December 5, 2009, from http://www.cdc.gov/TraumaticBrainInjury/index.html

Chavez, A., Paramo-Castillo, D., Leenaars, A., & Leenaars, L. (2006). Suicide notes in Mexico: What do they tell us? *Suicide and Life-Threatening Behavior, 36,* 709–715.

Chavez-Hernandez, A., Leenaars, A., Chavez-de Sanchez, M., & Leenaars, L. (2009). Suicide notes from Mexico and the United States: A thematic analysis. *Salud Publicda de Mexico, 51,* 314–320. [In Spanish]

Colarusso, C., & Nemiroff, R. (1981). *Adult development.* New York, NY: Plenum.

Conner, K., Beautrais, A., Brent, D., Conwell, Y., Phillips, M., & Schneider, B. (2011). The next generation of psychological autopsy studies. Part 1. Interview content. *Suicide and Life-Threatening Behavior, 41,* 594–613.

Conner, K., Beautrais, A., Brent, D., Conwell, Y., Phillips, M., & Schneider, B. (2012). The next generation of psychological autopsy studies. Part 2. Interview procedures. *Suicide and Life-Threatening Behavior, 42,* 86–103

Connolly, J., Cullen, A., & McTigue, O. (1995). Single road traffic deaths: Accident or suicide? *Crisis, 16,* 85–89.

Cook, A., & Bosley, G. (1995). The experience of participating in bereavement research: Stressful or therapeutic? *Death Studies, 19,* 157–170.

Cronbach, L., & Meehl, P. (1955). Construct validity in psychological tests. *Psychological Bulletin, 52,* 281–302.

Curphey, T. (1961). The role of the social scientist in the medicolegal certification of death by suicide. In N. Farberow & E. Shneidman (Eds.), *The cry for help* (pp. 110–117). New York, NY: McGraw-Hill.

Czeizel, A. (2011). Attempted suicide and pregnancy. *Journal of Injury & Violence Research, 3,* 45–54.

Dahlberg, L., & Krug, E. (2002). Violence—A global public health problem. In WHO (Ed.), *World report on violence and health* (pp. 1–21). Geneva, Switzerland: WHO.

Darbonne, A. (1969). Suicide and age: A suicide note analysis. *Journal of Consulting and Clinical Psychology, 33*, 46–50.

Daubert v. Merrill Dow Pharmaceuticals, Inc. N092-102 (US 06/28/1993).

Demirel, B., Akar, T., Sayin, A., Candansayar, S., & Leenaars, A. (2008). Farewell to the world: Suicide notes from Turkey. *Suicide and Life-Threatening Behavior, 38*, 122–127.

Diamond, G., More, D., Hawkins, A., & Soucar, E. (1995). Comment on Black's (1993) article "Comparing genuine and simulated suicide notes: A new perspective." *Journal of Consulting and Clinical Psychology, 63*, 46–48.

Diekstra, R. (1996). The epidemiology of suicide and parasuicide. *Archives of Suicide Research, 2*, 1–29.

Diekstra, R. (1997). Parasuicide: Is it a distinct phenomenon? In A. Botsis, C. Soldatos, & C. Stefanis (Eds.), *Suicide: Biopsychsocial approaches* (pp. 177–186). Amsterdam, The Netherlands: Elsevier.

Diekstra, R., & Van der Loo, K. (1978). Attitudes toward suicide and incidence of suicidal behavior in a generalized population. In H. Winnick & L. Miller (Eds.), *Aspects of suicide in modern civilization* (pp. 79–85). Jerusalem, Israel: Jerusalem Academic Press.

Dieserud, G., Leenaars, A., & Dyregrov, K. (2015). The importance of many informants in PA studies. *Suicidology Online, 6*, 47–55.

Dogra, T., Leenaars, A., Raintji, R., Lalwani, S., Girdhar, S., Wenckstern, S., & Lester, D. (2007). Menstruation and suicide: An exploratory study. *Psychological Reports, 101*, 430–434.

Donaldson-Pressman, S., & Pressman, R. (1994). *The narcissistic family: Diagnosis and treatment.* San Francisco, CA: Jossey-Bass.

Douglas, J. (1967). *The social meaning of suicide.* Princeton, NJ: Princeton University Press.

Duncan, C., & Edland, J. (1974). Suicide notes. *Legal Medicine*, 113–120.

Durkheim, E. (1951). *Suicide: A study in sociology* (J. Spaulding & G. Simpson, Trans.). London, UK: Routledge & Kegan Paul. (Original work published 1897)

Dyregrov, K. (2004). Bereaved parents' experience of research participation. *Social Science & Medicine, 58*, 391–400.

Dyregrov, K., Dieserud, G., Hjelmeland, H., Straiton, M., Rasmussen, M., Knizek, B., & Leenaars, A. (2011). Meaning making through psychological autopsy interviews: The value of participating in qualitative research for those bereaved by suicide. *Death Studies, 35*, 685–710.

Dyregrov, K., Dieserud, G., Straiton, M., Rasmussen, M., Hjelmeland, H., Knizek, B., & Leenaars, A. (2011). Motivation for research participation among people bereaved by suicide. *Omega, 62*, 149–168.

Erikson, E. (1963). *Childhood and society* (2nd ed.). New York, NY: Norton.

Erikson, E. (1968). *Identity: Youth and crisis.* New York, NY: Norton.

Erikson, E. (1980). *Identity and the life cycle.* New York, NY: Norton.

Estate of Hammerman, 387 So.2d 409 (Fla. 4th DCA 1980).

Everson, R., & Camp, T. (2011). Seeing systems: An introduction to systemic approaches with military families. In R. Everson & C. Figley (Eds.), *Families under fire* (pp. 3–29). New York, NY: Routledge.

Everson, R., & Figley, C. (Eds.). (2011). *Families under fire.* New York, NY: Routledge.

Farberow, N. (Ed.). (1980). *The many faces of suicide.* New York, NY: McGraw-Hill.

Farberow, N., MacKinnon, L., & Nelson, F. (1977). Suicide. *Public Health Reports, 92*, 223–232.

Fawcett, J. (1997). The detection and consequences of anxiety in clinical depression. *Journal of Clinical Psychiatry, 58*(Suppl. 8), 35–40.

Feigl, H. (1970). The "orthodox" view of theories: Remarks in defense as well as critique. In M. Radner & S. Winakur (Eds.), *Minnesota studies in philosophical science* (Vol. 4, pp. 3–16). Minneapolis, MN: University of Minnesota.

Feres vs. U.S. 340 U.S. 135, 146 (1950). U.S. Supreme Court.

Ferri, E. (1917). *Criminal sociology*. Boston, MA: Little, Brown.

Figley, C. (Ed.). (1985). *Trauma and its wake*. New York, NY: Brunner/Mazel.

Fishbain, D. (1994). Homicide followed by suicide. Letter to the editor. *Canadian Journal of Psychiatry, 39*, 385–386.

Fishbain, D., Rao, V., & Aldrich, T. (1985). Female homicide-suicide perpetrators: A controlled study. *Journal of Forensic Sciences, 30*, 1148–1156.

Foster, T. (2003). Suicide note themes and suicide prevention. *International Journal of Psychiatry in Medicine, 33*, 323–331.

Frager, R., & Fadiman, J. (1984). *Personality and personal growth* (2nd ed.). New York, NY: Harper & Row.

Frederick, C. (1969, March). Suicide notes: A survey and evaluation. *Bulletin of Suicidology*, 27–32.

Freeman, K. (1971). *Ancilla to the pre-Socratic philosophers*. Oxford, UK: Blackwell.

Freud, S. (1974). Psychopathology of everyday life. In J. Strachey (Ed. & Trans.), *The standard edition of the complete psychological works of Sigmund Freud, Vol. VI* (pp. 1–310). London, UK: Hogarth. (Original work published 1901)

Freud, S. (1974). A case of obsessional neurosis. In J. Strachey (Ed. & Trans.), *The standard edition of the complete psychological works of Sigmund Freud, Vol. X.* (pp. 153-318). London, UK: Hogarth Press. (Original work published 1909)

Freud, S. (1974a). Mourning and melancholia. In J. Strachey (Ed. & Trans.), *The standard edition of the complete psychological works of Sigmund Freud, Vol. XIV* (pp. 239–260). London, UK: Hogarth Press. (Original work published 1917)

Freud, S. (1974b). General theory of neurosis. In J. Strachey (Ed. & Trans.), *The standard edition of the complete psychological works of Sigmund Freud, Vol. XVI* (pp. 243–483). London, UK: Hogarth Press. (Original work published 1917)

Freud, S. (1974). A case of homosexuality in a woman. In J. Strachey (Ed. & Trans.), *The standard edition of the complete psychological works of Sigmund Freud, Vol. XVIII* (pp. 147–172). London, UK: Hogarth Press. (Original work published 1920)

Freud, S. (1974). Group psychology and the analysis of the ego. In J. Strachey (Ed. & Trans.), *The standard edition of the complete psychological works of Sigmund Freud, Vol. XVIII* (pp. 67–147). London, UK: Hogarth Press. (Original work published 1921)

Freud, S. (1974). The ego and the id. In J. Strachey (Ed. & Trans.), *The standard edition of the complete psychological works of Sigmund Freud, Vol. IXX* (pp. 3–66). London, UK: Hogarth Press. (Original work published 1923)

Freud, S. (1974). The economic problem of masochism. In J. Strachey (Ed. & Trans.), *The standard edition of the complete psychological works of Sigmund Freud, Vol. XIX* (pp. 157–170). London, UK: Hogarth Press. (Original work published 1924)

Freud, S. (1974). Civilization and its discontent. In J. Strachey (Ed. & Trans.), *The standard edition of the complete psychological works of Sigmund Freud, Vol. XXI* (pp. 64–145). London, UK: Hogarth Press. (Original work published 1930)

Freud, S. (1974). New introductory lectures. In J. Strachey (Ed. & Trans.), *The standard edition of the complete psychological works of Sigmund Freud, Vol. XXII* (pp. 3–182). London, UK: Hogarth Press. (Original work published 1933)

Freud, S. (1974). Moses and monotheism. In J. Strachey (Ed. & Trans.), *Standard edition of the complete psychological works of Sigmund Freud, Vol. XXIII* (pp. 3–137). London, UK: Hogarth Press. (Original work published 1939)

Freud, S. (1974). An outline of psycho-analysis. In J. Strachey (Ed. & Trans.), *The standard edition of the complete psychological works of Sigmund Freud, Vol. XXIII* (pp. 137–207). London, UK: Hogarth Press. (Original work published 1940).

Friedman, P. (Ed.). (1967). *On suicide.* New York, NY: International Universities Press. (Original work published in 1910).

Garbarino, J., & Crouter, A. (1978). Defining the community context for child-parent relations: The correlations of child maltreatment. *Child Development, 49*, 604–616.

Garrison, C., Lewinsohn, P., Marsteller, F., Langhinrichsen, J. & Lann, I. (1991). The assessment of suicidal behavior in adolescents. *Suicide and Life-Threatening Behavior, 21*, 217–230.

Gavin, M., & Rogers, A. (2006). Narratives of suicide in psychological autopsy: Bringing lay knowledge back in. *Journal of Mental Health, 15*, 135–144.

Gavin, M., Tabb, K., Melville, J., Guo, Y., & Katon, W. (2011). Prevalence and correlates of suicidal ideation during pregnancy. *Archives of Womens Mental Health, 14*, 239–246.

Geberth, V. (2015). *Practical homicide investigation, 5ᵗʰ. Edition.* New York, NY: CBC Press.

Gentile, S. (2011). Suicidal mothers. *Journal of Injury & Violence Research, 3, 90–97.*

Gergen, K. (1977). Stability, change and chance in understanding human development. In N. Daton & H. Reese (Eds.), *Life span developmental psychology: Dialectical perspectives on experimental research* (pp. 135–158). New York, NY: Academic Press.

Gillies, J., & Neimeyer, R. (2006). Loss, grief and the search for significance: Toward a model of meaning reconstruction in bereavement. *Journal of Constructivist Psychology, 19,* 31–65.

Girdhar, S., Leenaars, A., Dogra, T., Leenaars, L., & Kumar, G. (2004). Suicide notes in India: What do they tell us? *Archives of Suicide Research, 8*, 179–185.

Goffman, E. (1974). *Frame analysis.* New York, NY: Harper Colophon.

Gold, K., Singh, V., Marcus, S., & Palladino, C. (2012). Mental health, substance use and intimate partner problems among pregnant and postpartum suicide victims in the National Violent Death Reporting System. *General Hospital Psychiatry, 34,* 139–145.

Goldblatt, M. (1992). *Richard Cory suicides: Diagnostic questions.* Paper presented at the annual conference of the American Association of Suicidology, Chicago, IL.

Goldney, R., Winefield, A., Tiggemann, M., Winefield, H., & Smith, S. (1989). Suicidal ideation in a young adult population. *Acta Psychiatrica Scandinavica, 79*, 481–489.

Goodyear-Brown, P. (Ed.). (2012). *Handbook of child sexual abuse.* New York, NY: Wiley.

Gould, J. (2011, May 24). Are suicides considered less honorable? *ArmyTimes: OUTSIDE THE WIRE.* Retrieved August 28, 2011, from http://outsidethewire.armytimes.com/2011/05/24/are-suicides-considered-less-honorable/

Gutheil, T. (1992). Suicide and suit: Liability after self-destruction. In D. Jacobs (Ed.), *Suicide & clinical practice* (pp. 147–167). Washington, DC: American Psychiatric Press.

Gutheil, T., Bursztajn, H., Hamm, R., & Brodsky, A. (1983). Subjective data and suicide assessment in light of recent legal developments. Part 1: Malpractice prevention and the use of subjective data. *International Journal of Law and Psychiatry, 6,* 317–329.

Hall, L. (2011). The military culture, language, and lifestyle. In R. Everson & C. Figley (Eds.), *Families under fire* (pp. 31–52). New York, NY: Routledge.

Hamilton, E., & Cairns, H. (Eds.). (1961). *The collected dialogues of Plato.* Princeton, NJ: Princeton University Press.

Hanzlick, R., & Ross, W. (1987). Suicide far from home: The concept of transjurisdictional suicide. *Journal of Forensic Science, 32*, 189–191.

Harper, D., & Voight, L. (2007). Homicide followed by suicide: An integrated theoretical perspective. *Homicide Studies, 11*, 293–318.

Hawton, K. (2000). Sex and suicide: Gender differences in suicidal behaviour. *British Journal of Psychiatry, 177*, 484–485.

Hawton, K., Appleby, L., Platt, S., Foster, T., Cooper, J., Malmberg, A., & Simkin, S. (1998). The psychological autopsy approach to studying suicide: A review of methodological issues. *Journal of Affective Disorders, 50*, 269–276.

Hawton, K., Harris, L., Casey, D., Simkin, S., Harrison, K., Bray, I., & Blatchev, N. (2009). Self-harm in UK armed forces personnel: Descriptive and case-control study of general hospital presentations. *The British Journal of Psychiatry, 194*, 266–272.

Hawton, K., Houston, K., Malmberg, A., & Simkin, S. (2003). Psychological autopsy interviews in suicide research: The reactions of informants. *Archives of Suicide Research, 7*, 73–82.

Hawton, K., & van Heeringen, C. (Eds.). (2000). *The international handbook of suicide and attempted suicide.* Chichester, UK: Wiley.

Hempel, C. (1966). *Philosophy of natural science.* Englewood Cliffs, NJ: Prentice-Hall.

Henken, V. (1976). Banality reinvestigated: A computer-based content analysis of suicidal and forced death documents. *Suicide and Life-Threatening Behavior, 6*, 36–43.

Hennelly, M., Yi, J., Batkis, M., & Chisolm, M. (2011). Termination of pregnancy in two patients during psychiatric hospitalization for depressive symptoms and substance dependence. *Psychosomatics, 52*, 482–485.

Henry, A., & Short, J. (1954). *Suicide and homicide.* New York, NY: Free Press.

Hjelmeland, H., Dieserud, G., Dyregrov, K., Knizek, B., & Leenaars, A. (2012). Psychological autopsy studies as diagnostic tools: Are they methodologically flawed? *Death Studies, 36*, 605–626.

Hjelmeland, H., & Knizek, B. (2010). Why we need qualitative research in suicidology. *Suicide and Life-Threatening Behavior, 40*, 74–80.

Ho, T., Yip, P., Chiu, C., & Halliday, P. (1998). Suicide notes: What do they tell us? *Acta Psychiatrica Scandinavica, 98*, 467–473.

Hoge, C., Auchterlonie, J., & Milliken, C. (2006). Mental health problems, use of mental health services, and attrition from military service after returning from deployment to Iraq or Afghanistan. *Journal of the American Medical Association, 295*, 1023–1032.

Hughes, S., & Neimeyer, R. (1990). A cognitive model of suicidal behavior. In D. Lester (Ed.), *Current concepts of suicide* (pp. 1–28). Philadelphia, PA: Charles Press.

Hum, P. (2001, February). 'Angel' of death gets life in prison: 'Cherrylle Dell wanted Scott Dell out of her life forever.' *Ottawa Citizen.*

Husserl, E. (1973). *The idea of phenomenology* (W. Alston & G. Nakgnikian, Trans.). The Hague, The Netherlands: Martinus Nijhoff. (Original work published 1907)

Hutchinson, S., Wilson, M., & Wilson, H. (1994). Benefits of participating in research interviews. *IMAGE: Journal of Nursing Scholarship, 26*, 161–164.

Imajo, T. (1983). Suicide by motor vehicle. *Journal of Forensic Sciences, 28*, 83–89.

Imber-Black, E. (1993). *Secrets in families and family therapy.* New York, NY: Norton.

Isacsson, G., & Rich, C. (2003). Getting closer to suicide prevention. *British Journal of Psychiatry, 182*, 455–459.

Jackson v. State of Florida (1987). Case No. 86-6502. Circuit Court of the MM Judicial Circuit.

Jacobs, D., & Klein, M. (1993). The expanding role of the psychological autopsy. In A. Leenaars (Ed.), *Suicidology: Essays in honor of Edwin Shneidman* (pp. 209–247). Northvale, NJ: Aronson.

Jacobs, J. (1971). A phenomenological study of suicide notes. In E. Geddens (Ed.), *The sociology of suicide* (pp. 332–348). London, UK: Cass.

Jeffery, W., Price, S., & Gyorfi, D. (2015, June/July). Making your opinion matter. *BlueLine,* 16–17.

Jenkins, R., & Singh, B. (2000). General population strategies of suicide prevention. In K. Hawton & K. van Heeringen (Eds.), *The international handbook of suicide and attempted suicide* (pp. 597–615). Chichester, UK: Wiley.

Johnson, H., & Hotton, T. (2003). Losing control. *Homicide Studies, 7,* 58–84.

Jung, C. (1957). *The undiscovered self.* Boston, MA: Little, Brown.

Jung, C. (1971). Psychological types. In R. Hull (Trans.), *The collected works of C. G. Jung* (Vol. 6). Princeton, NJ: Princeton University Press.

Kahane, H. (1973). *Logic and philosophy* (2nd ed.). Belmont, CA: Wadsworth.

Kargon, R. (1963). John Graunt, Francis Bacon, and the royal society: The reception of statistics. *Journal of Historical Medicine, 18,* 337–348.

Kavanaugh, K., & Ayres, L. (1998). Not as bad as it could have been: Assessing and mitigating harm during research interviews on sensitive topics. *Research in Nursing & Health, 21,* 91–97.

Keats, J. (1970). *You might as well live.* New York, NY: Simon & Shuster.

Kelly, T., & Mann, J. (1996). Validity of DSM-III-R diagnosis by psychological autopsy: A comparison with clinician ante-mortem diagnosis. *Acta Psychiatrica Scandinavica, 94,* 337–343.

Kendler, K., & Zachar, P. (2008). The incredible insecurity of psychiatric nosology. In K. Kendler & J. Parnas (Eds.), *Philosophical issues in psychiatry: Explanation, phenomenology and nosology* (pp. 368–383). Baltimore, MD: Johns Hopkins University Press.

Kerkhof, A., Schmidtke, A., Bille-Brahe, U., DeLeo, D., & Lonnquist, J. (Eds.). (1994). *Attempted suicide in Europe.* Leiden, The Netherlands: DSWO Press.

Kerlinger, F. (1964). *Foundations of behavioral research.* New York, NY: Holt, Rinehart & Winston.

Kimmel, D. (1974). *Adulthood and aging.* New York, NY: Wiley.

Kirk, G., & Raven, J. (1971). *The presocratic philosophers.* London, UK: Cambridge University Press.

Kitaeff, J, (Ed.). (2007). *Malingering, lies, and junk science in the courtroom.* Youngstown, NY: Cambria House.

Kitaeff, J. (2010). *Forensic psychology.* Upper Saddle River, NJ: Pearson. Prentice-Hall.

Klass, D., Silverman, P., & Nickman, S. (1996). *Continuing bonds. New understanding of grief.* Washington, DC: Taylor & Francis.

Kleck, G. (1988). Miscounting suicides. *Suicide and Life-Threatening Behavior, 18,* 219–236.

Klerman, G. (Ed.). (1986). *Suicide and depression among adolescents and young adults.* Washington, DC: American Psychiatric Press.

Koren, D., Hilel, Y., Idar, N., Hemel, E., & Klein, E. (2007). Combat stress management: The interplay between combat, physical injury, and psychological trauma. In C. Figley & W. Nash (Eds.), *Combat stress injury* (pp. 119–135). New York, NY: Routledge.

Kreitman, N., Philip, A., Greer, S., & Bagley, C. (1969). Parasuicide. *British Journal of Psychiatry, 115,* 746–747.

Krusa v. State, 483 So.2d.1383 (Fla. 4th DCA 1986).

Kubawar, H., Shioiri, T., Nishimura, A., Abe, R., Nushida, H., Ueno, A., Akazawa, K., & Someya, T. (2006). Differences in characteristics between suicide victims who left notes or not. *Journal of Affective Disorders, 94,* 145–149.

Kuhn, T. (1962). *The structure of scientific revolutions.* Chicago, IL: University of Chicago Press.

Leenaars, A. (1988). *Suicide notes.* New York, NY: Human Sciences.

Leenaars, A. (1989a). Are young adult's suicides psychologically different from those of other adults? (The Shneidman Lecture). *Suicide and Life-Threatening Behavior, 19,* 249–263.

Leenaars, A. (1989b). Suicide across the adult life span: An archival study. *Crisis, 10,* 132–151.

Leenaars, A. (1990). Do the psychological characteristics of the suicidal individual make a difference in the method chosen for suicide? *Canadian Journal of Behavioural Science, 22,* 385–392.

Leenaars, A. (1991). Suicide in the young adult. In A. Leenaars (Ed.), *Life-span perspectives of suicide* (pp. 121–136). New York, NY: Plenum Press.

Leenaars, A. (1992). Suicide notes, communication and ideation. In R. Maris, A. Berman, J. Maltsberger, & R. Yufit (Eds.), *Assessment and prediction of suicide* (pp. 337–361). New York, NY: Guilford Press.

Leenaars, A. (Ed.). (1993). *Suicidology: Essays in honor of Edwin S. Shneidman.* Northvale, NJ: Aronson.

Leenaars, A. (1995). Clinical evaluation of suicide risk. *Psychiatry and Clinical Neurosciences, 59*(Suppl 1), 561–568.

Leenaars, A. (1996). Suicide: A multidimensional malaise. *Suicide & Life-Threatening Behavior, 26,* 221–236.

Leenaars, A. (1997). Rick: A suicide of a young adult. *Suicide and Life-Threatening Behavior, 27,* 15-27.

Leenaars, A. (Ed.). (1999a). *Lives and deaths: Selections from the works of Edwin S. Shneidman.* Philadelphia, PA: Brunner/Mazel.

Leenaars, A. (1999b). Suicide notes in the courtroom. *Journal of Clinical Forensic Medicine, 6,* 39–48.

Leenaars, A. (2004). *Psychotherapy with suicidal people: A person-centred approach.* Chichester, UK: Wiley.

Leenaars, A. (2006). Psychotherapy with suicidal people: The commonalities. *Archives of Suicide Research, 10,* 305–322.

Leenaars, A. (2007). Suicide: A cross-cultural theory. In F. Leong & M. Leach (Eds.), *Suicide among racial and ethnic minority groups* (pp. 13–37). New York, NY: Routledge.

Leenaars, A. (2009). Death systems and suicide around the world. In J. Morgan, P. Laungani, & S. Palmer (Eds.), *Death and bereavement around the world.* (Vol. 5, pp. 103–138). Amityville, NY: Baywood.

Leenaars, A. (2010a). *Suicide and homicide: Suicide among police.* Amityville, NY: Baywood.

Leenaars, A. (2010b). Lives and deaths: Biographical notes and selections from the works of Edwin S. Shneidman. *Suicide and Life-Threatening Behavior, 40,* 476–491.

Leenaars, A. (2010c). Edwin S. Shneidman on suicide. *Suicidology Online, 1,* 5–18.

Leenaars, A. (2013). *Suicide among the Armed Forces: Understanding the cost of service.* Amityville, NY: Baywood.

Leenaars, A., & Balance, W. (1984). A logical empirical approach to the study of the manifest content in suicide notes. *Canadian Journal of Behavioural Science, 16,* 248–256.

Leenaars, A., Balance, W., Pellarin, S., Aversano, G., Magli, A., & Wenckstern, S. (1988). Facts and myths of suicide in Canada. *Death Studies, 12,* 191–210.

Leenaars, A., Cantor, C., Connolly, J., EchoHawk, M., Gailiene, D., He, Z., et al. (2000a). Ethical and legal issues in suicidology. *Archives of Suicide Research, 6,* 185–197.

Leenaars, A., Cantor, C., Connolly, J., EchoHawk, M., Gailiene, D., He, Z., et al. (2000b). Legal and ethical issues. In K. Hawton & K. van Heeringen (Eds.), *International handbook of suicide and attempted suicide* (pp. 421–435). London, UK: Wiley.

Leenaars, A., Cantor, C., Connolly, J., EchoHawk, M., Gailiene, D., He, Z., et al. (2002). Controlling the environment to prevent suicide: International perspectives. *Canadian Journal of Psychiatry, 45,* 639–644.

Leenaars, A., De Leo, D., Diekstra, R., Goldney, R., Kelleher, M., Lester, D., & Nordstrom, P. (1997). Consultations for research in suicidology. *Archives of Suicide Research, 3,* 139–151.

Leenaars, A., De Wilde, E., Wenckstern, S., & Kral, M. (2001). Suicide notes of adolescents: A life span comparison. *Canadian Journal of Behavioural Science, 33,* 47–57.

Leenaars, A., Dogra, T., Girdhar, S., Dattugata, S., & Leenaars, L. (2009). Menstruation and suicide: A histopathologic study. *Crisis, 30,* 2002–2007.

Leenaars, A., Fekete, S., Wenckstern, S., & Osvath, P. (1998). Suicide notes from Hungary and the United States. *Psychiatrica Hungarica, 13,* 147–159. [In Hungarian]

Leenaars, A., Gailiené, D., Wenckstern, S., Leenaars, L., Trofimova, J., Petravičiūtė, I., & Park, B. (2014). Extreme traumatisation and the suicide notes from Lithuania: A thematic analysis. *Suicidology Online, 5,* 33–46.

Leenaars, A., Girdhar, S., Dogra, T., Wenckstern, S., & Leenaars, L. (2010). Suicide notes from India and the United States: A thematic comparison. *Death Studies, 34,* 426–440.

Leenaars, A., Haines, J., Wenckstern, S., Williams, C., & Lester, D. (2003). Suicide notes from Australia and the United States. *Perceptual and Motor Skills, 92,* 1281–1282.

Leenaars, A., & Lester, D. (1989). What characteristics of suicide notes are salient for people to allow perception of a suicide note as genuine? *Death Studies, 14,* 57–62.

Leenaars, A., & Lester, D. (1991). Myths about suicide notes. *Death Studies, 15,* 303–308.

Leenaars, A., & Lester, D. (1994). Suicide and homicide rates in Canada and the United States. *Suicide and Life-Threatening Behavior, 24,* 184–191.

Leenaars, A, & Lester, D. (1995). Assessment and prediction of suicide risk in adolescents. In J. Zimmerman, D. Grosz, & G. Asnis (Eds.), *Treatment approaches with suicidal adolescents* (pp. 47-70). New York, NY: John Wiley & Sons.

Leenaars, A., & Lester, D. (Eds.). (1996). *Suicide and the unconscious.* Northvale, NJ: Aronson.

Leenaars, A., & Lester, D. (1998). Social factors and mortality from NASH in Canada. *Crisis, 19,* 73-77.

Leenaars, A., Lester, D., Lopatin, A., Schustov, D., & Wenckstern, S. (2002). Suicide notes from Russia and the United States. *Social and General Psychiatry, 12,* 22–28. [In Russian]

Leenaars, A., Lester, D., Wenckstern, S., & Heim, N. (1994). Suicide notes from Germany and the United States. *Suizidprophylaxe, 3,* 99–101. [In German]

Leenaars, A., Lester, D., Wenckstern, S., McMullin, C., Rudzinski, D., & Brevard, A. (1992). A comparison of suicide notes and parasuicide notes. *Death Studies, 16,* 331–342.

Leenaars, A., & Maltsberger, J. (1994). The Inman diary: Some reflections on treatments. In A. Leenaars, J. Maltsberger, & R. Neimeyer (Eds.), *Treatment of suicidal people* (pp. 227–236). Washington, DC: Taylor & Francis.

Leenaars, A., Park, B., Collins, P., Wenckstern, S., & Leenaars, L. (2010). Martyrs' last letters: Are they the same as suicide notes? *Journal of Forensic Science, 55,* 660–668.

Leenaars, A., Sayin, A., Candansayar, S., Akar, T., Demirel, B., & Leenaars, L. (2010). Different cultures, same reasons: A thematic comparison of suicide notes from Turkey and the United States. *Journal of Cross-Cultural Psychology, 41,* 253–263.

Leenaars, A., & Wenckstern, S. (1991). Posttraumatic stress disorder: A conceptual model for postvention. In A. Leenaars & S. Wenckstern (Eds.), *Suicide prevention in schools* (pp. 173–195). Washington, DC: Taylor & Francis.

Leenaars, A., & Wenckstern, S. (Eds.). (2004). Altruistic suicide: From sainthood to terrorism. *Archives of Suicide Research, 8,* 1–136.

Leenaars, A., Yang, B., & Lester, D. (1993). The effect of domestic and economic stress on suicide rates in Canada and the United States. *Journal of Clinical Psychology, 49,* 918–921.

Lester, D. (1974). Demographic versus clinical prediction of suicidal behaviors. In A. Beck, H. Resnik, & D. Lettieri (Eds.). *The prediction of suicide risk* (pp. 71-84). Bowie, MD: Charles Press.

Lester, D. (1987a). *Suicide as a learned behavior.* Springfield, IL: Thomas.

Lester, D. (1987b). Murders and suicides: Are they polar opposites. *Behavioral Science & The Law, 5,* pp. 49-60.

Lester, D. (Ed.). (1988). *Why women kill themselves.* Springfield, IL: Thomas.

Lester, D. (1992a). The dexamethasone suppression test as an indicator of suicide. *Pharmacopsychiatry, 25,* 265–270.

Lester, D. (1992b). *Why people kill themselves* (3rd ed.). Springfield, IL: Thomas.

Lester, D. (1993). *Suicide in creative women.* Commack, NY: Nova Science.

Lester, D. (1994). A comparison of fifteen theories of suicide. *Suicide and Life-Threatening Behavior, 24,* 80–88.

Lester, D. (1997). Suicide in an international perspective. *Suicide and Life-Threatening Behavior, 27,* 104–111.

Lester, D. (Ed.). (2004). *Katie's diary.* New York, NY: Routledge.

Lester, D. & Beck, A. (1976). Completed suicides and their previous attempts. *Journal of Clinical Psychology, 32,* 553-555.

Lester, D., & Hummel, H. (1980). Motives for suicide in elderly people. *Psychological Reports, 47,* 870.

Lester, D., & Leenaars, A. (1987). Differentiation of genuine suicide notes. *Psychological Reports, 61,* 70.

Lester, D., Perdue, W., & Brookhart, D. (1974). Murderers who have attempted suicide. *Psychological Reports, 35,* 238.

Lester, D., & Reeve, C. (1982). The suicide notes of young and old people. *Psychological Reports, 50,* 334.

Levinson, D. (1986). Development in the novice phase of early development. In G. Klerman (Ed.). *Suicide and depression among adolescents and young adults* (pp. 1-15). Washington, DC: American Psychiatric Press.

Lewinsohn, P., Garrison, C., Langhinrichsen, J., & Marsteller, F. (1989). *The assessment of suicidal behavior in adolescents: A review of scales suitable for epidemiological clinical research.* Rockville, MD: National Institute of Mental Health.

Lichter, D. (1981). Diagnosing the dead: The admissibility of the psychiatric autopsy. *American Criminal Law Review, 18,* 617–635.

Litman, R. (1984). Psychological autopsies in court. *Suicide and Life-Threatening Behavior, 14,* 1988–1995.

Litman, R. (1988). Psychological autopsies, mental illness and intention of suicide. In J. Nolan (Ed.), *The suicide case: Investigation and trial of insurance claims* (pp. 69–82). Chicago, IL: American Bar Association.

Litman, R. (1993). A voice of death. In A. Leenaars (Ed.), *Suicidology: Essays in honor of Edwin Shneidman* (pp. 267–278). Northvale, NJ: Aronson.

Litman, R. (1994). Responsibility and liability for suicide. In E. Shneidman, N. Farberow, & R. Litman (Eds.), *The psychology of suicide* (pp. 187–199). Northvale, NJ: Aronson.

Litman, R., Curphey, T., Shneidman, E., Farberow, N., & Tabachnick, N. (1963). Investigations of equivocal suicides. *Journal of the American Medical Association, 184,* 924–929.

Lomas, D., & Lester, D. (Eds.). (2011). *Understanding and preventing college student suicide.* Springfield, IL: Thomas.

Lund, L., & Smorodinsky, S. (2001). Violent death among intimate partners: A comparison of homicide and homicide followed by suicide in California. *Suicide and Life-Threatening Behavior, 31,* 451–459.

MacDonald, J. (1964). Suicide and homicide by automobile. *American Journal of Psychiatry, 121,* 366–370.

Mallon, T. (1984). *A book of one's own: People and their diaries.* New York, NY: Ticknor & Fields.

Malmquist, C. (1996). *Homicide: A psychiatric perspective.* Washington, DC: American Psychiatric Press.

Maltsberger, J. (1986). *Suicide risk: The formulation of clinical judgment.* New York, NY: New York University Press.

Maltsberger, J. (2001). Grandiose fury. *Crisis, 22,* 144–145.

Maltsberger, J. (2002). Letters across the Pacific. *Crisis, 23,* 86-88.

Mann, J. (1996, April). *Neurobiological regulation of the threshold for suicidal behavior.* Dublin Award paper presented at the conference of the American Association of Suicidology, St. Louis, MO.

Mann, J., Waternaux, C., Haas, G., & Malone, K. (1999). Toward a clinical model of suicidal behavior in psychiatric patients. *The American Journal of Psychiatry, 156,* 181–189.

Maris, R. (1981). *Pathways to suicide.* Baltimore, MD: Johns Hopkins University Press.

Maris, R., Berman, A., Maltsberger, J., & Yufit, R. (Eds.). (1992). *Assessment and prediction of suicide.* New York, NY: Guilford Press.

Martin, G. (1998). Media influence to suicide: The search for solutions. *Archives of Suicide Research, 4,* 51–66.

Martin, S., Macy, R., Sullivan, K., & Magee, M. (2007). Pregnancy-associated violent deaths: The role of intimate partner violence. *Trauma, Violence, & Abuse, 8,* 135–148.

Marzuk, P. (1989, April). *AIDS-related suicides.* Paper presented at the American Association of Suicidology conference, San Diego, CA.

Marzuk, P. (1994). Suicide and terminal illness. In A. Leenaars, J. Maltsberger, & R. Neimeyer (Eds.), *Treatment of suicidal people* (pp. 127–138). Hampshire, UK: Taylor & Francis.

Marzuk, P., Tardiff, K., & Hirsch, C. (1992). The epidemiology of murder suicide. *Journal of American Medical Association, 267,* 3179–3313.

Marzuk, P., Tardiff, K., Leon, A., Hirsch, C., Portera, L., Hartwell, N., & Iqbal, M. (1997). Lower risk of suicide during pregnancy. *American Journal of Psychiatry, 154,* 122–123.

Maslow, A. (1966). *The psychology of science.* New York, NY: Harper & Row.

McClure, C., Patrick, T., Katz, S., Kelsey, S., & Weiss, H. (2011). Birth outcomes following self-inflicted poisoning during pregnancy, California, 2000 to 2004. *Journal of Obstetric, Gynecologic, & Neonatal Nursing, 40,* 292–301.

McCubbin, H. L, Thompson, A. I., & McCubbin, M. A. (2001). *Family measures: Stress, coping, and resiliency: Inventories for research and practice.* Honolulu, HI: Kamehameha.

McKeon, R. (Ed.). (1941). *The basic works of Aristotle.* New York, NY: Random House.

Meehl, P. (1978). Theoretical risks and tabular asterisks: Sir Karl, Sir Richard, and the slow progress of soft psychology. *Journal of Consulting and Clinical Psychology, 46,* 806–834.

Meehl, P. (1986). Diagnostic taxa as open concepts. Metatheoretical and statistical questions about reliability and construct validity in the grand strategy of nosological revision. In T. Millon & G. Klerman (Eds.), *Contemporary directions in psychopathology* (pp. 215–231). New York, NY: Guilford Press.

Meehl, P. (1990). Appraising and amending theories: The strategy of Lakatosian defense and two principles that warrant it. *Psychological Inquiry, 1,* 108–141.

Meehl, P. (1993). Philosophy of science: Help or hindrance. *Psychological Reports, 72,* 707-733.

Melville, H. (1930). *Moby Dick.* New York, NY: Random House. (Original work published 1851)

Melville, J., Gavin, A., Guo, Y., Fan, M., & Katon, W. (2010). Depressive disorders during pregnancy. *Obstetrics & Gynecology, 116,* 1064–1070.

Menninger, K. (1938). *Man against himself.* New York, NY: Harcourt, Brace.

Menninger, K. (1963). *The vital balance.* New York, NY: Viking.

Middleton, W., Raphael, B., Burnett, P., & Martinek, N. (1998). A longitudinal study comparing bereavement phenomena in recently bereaved spouses, adult children and parents. *Australian and New Zealand Journal of Psychiatry, 32,* 235–241

Mill, J. S. (1984). *Systems of logic.* London, UK: Routledge. (Original work published 1892)

Miller, M. (1999). Suicide-prevention contracts: Advantages, disadvantages, and an alternative approach. In D. Jacobs (Ed.), *The Harvard Medical School guide to suicide assessment and intervention* (pp. 463–481). San Francisco, CA: Jossey-Bass.

Millon, T. (2010). Classification considerations in psychopathology and personology. In T. Millon, R. Krueger, & E. Simonson (Eds.), *Contemporary directions in psychopathology* (pp. 149–173). New York, NY: Guilford Press.

Millon, T., Krueger, R., & Simonson, E. (Eds.). (2010). *Contemporary directions in psychopathology.* New York, NY: Guilford Press.

Milroy, C. (1998). Homicide followed by suicide: Remorse or revenge? *Journal of Clinical Forensic Medicine, 5,* 61–64.

Mistler, S. (2008, Feb. 1). Navy investigating apparent suicide at BNAS. *Forecaster.* Brunswick, Maine.

Morgan v. State, 527, So.2d.272 (Fla. 1202).

Morselli, E. (1882). *Suicide: An essay in comparative normal statistics.* New York, NY: Appleton.

Murphy, G. (1992). *Suicide in alcoholism.* New York: Oxford University Press. M

Murray, H. (1938). *Explorations in personality.* New York, NY: Oxford University Press.

Murray, H. (1967). Death to the world: The passions of Herman Melville. In E. Shneidman (Ed.), *Essays in self-destruction* (pp. 3–29). New York, NY: Science House.

National Center for Health Statistics. (1967). *Eighth revision International Classification of Diseases, adapted for use in the United States.* PHS Pub. No. 1693. Public Health Service, Washington, DC: U.S. Government Printing Office.

National Research Council. (2009). *Strengthening forensic science in the United States: A path forward.* Washington, DC: National Academies Press.

Nadeau, J. (1997). *Families making sense of death.* Newbury Park, CA: Sage.

Neimeyer, R. (2000). Searching for the meaning of meaning: Grief therapy and the process of reconstruction. *Death Studies, 24,* 541–558.

Neimeyer, R. (2001) (Ed.). *Meaning reconstruction and the experience of loss.* Washington, DC: American Psychological Association.

Neimeyer, R., Klass, D., & Dennis, M. (2014). A social reconstructionist account of grief: Loss and the narration of meaning. *Death Studies, 38,* 485–498.

Neugarten, B., Moore, J., & Lowe, J. (1965). Age norms, age constraints, and adult social-ization. *American Journal of Sociology, 70,* 710–717.

Neuringer, C. (1976). Current developments in the study of suicidal thinking. In E. Shneidman (Ed.), *Suicidology: Contemporary developments* (pp. 229–252). New York, NY: Grune and Stratton.

Nolan, J. (1988). Suicide, sane or insane and suicidal intent. In J. Nolan (Ed.), *The suicide case* (pp. 51–65). Chicago, IL: American Bar Association.

Oates, M. (2003). Suicide: The leading cause of maternal death. *British Journal of Psychiatry, 183,* 279–281.

O'Connor, R., & Leenaars, A. (2004). A thematic comparison of suicide notes drawn from Northern Ireland and the United States. *Current Psychology, 22,* 339–347.

O'Connor, R., Sheeby, N., & O'Connor, D. (1999). A thematic analysis of suicide notes. *Crisis, 20,* 106–114.

Ogilvie, D., Stone, P. & Shneidman, S. (1969). Some characteristics of genuine versus simulated suicide notes. *Bulletin of Suicidology,* March, 9-26.

Ogloff, J., & Cronshaw, S. (2001). Expert psychological testimony: Assisting or misleading the trier of fact? *Canadian Psychology, 42,* 87–91.

Osgood, C., & Walker, E. (1959). Motivation and language behavior: A content analysis of suicide notes. *Journal of Abnormal and Social Psychology, 59,* 58–67.

Owens, C., Lambert, H., Lloyd, K., & Donovan, J. (2008). Tales of biographical dis-integration: How parents make sense of their sons' suicides. *Sociology of Health & Illness, 30,* 237–254.

Paciocco, D. (1999). Coping with expert evidence about human behaviour. *Queen's Law Journal, 25,* 305–346.

Palladino, C., Singh, V., Campbell, J., Flynn, H., & Gold, K. (2011). Homicide and suicide during the perinatal period. *Obstetrics & Gynecology, 118,* 1056–1063.

Palmer, B., Pankrantz, V., & Bostwick, J. (2005). The lifetime risk of suicide in schizophrenia: A reexamination. *Archives of General Psychiatry, 62,* 247–253.

Palermo, G., Smith, M., Jentzen, J., Henry, T., Konicek, P., Peterson, G., et al. (1997). Murder-suicide of the jealous paranoid type: A multicenter statistical pilot study. *The American Journal of Forensic Medicine & Pathology, 18,* 374–383.

Pap, A. (1953). Reduction sentences and open concepts. *Methodos, 5,* 3-30.

Pavese, C. (1961). *The burning brand: Diary 1935–1950* (A. Murch, Trans.). New York, NY: Walker.

Perdue, W., & Brookhart, D. (1974). Murderers who have attempted suicide. *Psychological Reports, 35,* 238.

Petik, D., Czeizel, B., Banhidy, F., & Czeizel, A. (2012). A study of the risk of mental retardation among children of pregnant women who have attempted suicide by means of drug overdose. *Journal of Injury & Violence Research, 4,* 10–19.

Pfeffer, C. (1986). *The suicidal child.* New York, NY: Guilford Press.

Phillips, D. (1974). The influence of suggestion on suicide: Substantive and theoretical implications of the Werther effect. *American Sociological Review, 39,* 340–354.

Phillips, D. (1986, April). *Effects of the media.* Paper presented at the conference of the American Association of Suicidology, Atlanta, GA.

Phillips, M., & Gunnell, D. (2009). Restrictions of access to pesticides in suicide prevention. In D. Wasserman & C. Wasserman (Eds.), *Oxford textbook of suicidology and suicide prevention* (pp. 583–587). Oxford, UK: Oxford University Press.

Piaget, J. (1970). *Structuralism.* (C. Mahler, Trans.). New York, NY: HarperCollins Publishers.

Platt, S. (1984). Unemployment and suicidal behavior. *Social Science & Medicine, 19,* 93–115.

Pokorny, A. (1983). Prediction of suicide in psychiatric patients. *Archives of General Psychiatry, 40,* 249–257.

Pompili, M., Girardi, P., Tatarelli, G., & Tatarelli, R. (2006). Suicidal intent in single-car accident drivers. *Crisis, 27,* 92–99.

Pompili, M., & Tatarelli, R. (Eds.). (2010). *Evidence-based practice in suicidology.* Gottingen, Germany: Hogrefe.

Pouliot, L., & De Leo, D. (2006). Critical issues in psychological autopsy studies. *Suicide and Life-Threatening Behavior, 36*(5), 491–510.

Pritchard, C. (1996). Suicide in the people's Republic of China categorized by age and gender: Evidence of the influence of culture on suicide. *Acta Psychiatrica Scandinavica, 93,* 362–367.

Quine, W. (1977). Natural kinds. In S. Schwartz (Ed.), *Naming, necessity and natural groups* (pp. 30–41). Ithaca, NY: Cornell University Press.

Raina, A., Dogra, T., Leenaars, A., Yadov, B., Bhera, C., Lalwani, S., & Leenaars, L. (2011). Identity of victims from fragmented and decomposed remnants by DNA profiling in a case of serial killings. *Medicine, Science and the Law, 50,* 220–223.

Regina v. J 148 c.c.c. (3d) Binnie J. (2001).

Richman, J. (1991). Suicide and the elderly. In A. Leenaars (Ed.), *Life span perspectives of suicide* (pp. 153–167). New York, NY: Plenum Press.

Rickgarn, R. (1994). *Perspectives in college student suicide.* Amityville, NY: Baywood.

Ritchie, E. (2010, April). *Suicide prevention: Valuable information learned from Army surveillance and research.* Plenary presented at the American Association of Suicidology Conference, Orlando, FL.

Robertson, J. (1988). *Psychiatric malpractice.* New York, NY: Wiley.

Robins, E. (1981). *The final months: A study of the lives of 134 persons who committed suicide.* New York, NY: Oxford University Press.

Robinson, E. (1953). Richard Cory. In L. Thompson (Ed.), *Tilbury Town: Selected poems of Edwin Arlington Robinson.* New York, NY: Macmillan.

Romero, V., & Pearlman, M. (2012). Maternal mortality due to trauma. *Seminars in Perinatology, 36,* 60–67.

Rosen, A. (1954). Detection of suicidal patients: An example of some limitations in the prediction of infrequent events. *Journal of Consulting Psychology, 18,* 397–403.

Rosenberg, M., Davidson, L., Smith, J., Berman, A., Ganter, G., Gay, G., et al. (1988). Operational criteria for the determination of suicide. *Journal of Forensic Sciences, 32,* 1445–1455.

Rosenblatt, P. (1983). *Bitter, bitter tears.* Minneapolis, MN: University of Minnesota Press.

Rourke, R., & Fisk, J. (1981). Socio-emotional disturbances of learning disabled children: The role of central processing deficits. *Bulletin of the Orthopsychiatry Society, 31,* 77–78.

Rourke, R., Young, G., & Leenaars, A. (1989). A childhood learning disability that predisposes those afflicted to adolescent and adult depression and suicide risk. *Journal of Learning Disabilities, 22,* 169–175.

Rudd, M., Joiner, T., & Rajab, M. (1996). Relationships among suicide ideators, attempters, and multiple attempters in a young-adult sample. *Journal of Abnormal Psychology, 105,* 541–550.

Rudestam, K. (1979). Some notes on conducting a psychological autopsy. *Suicide and Life-Threatening Behavior, 9,* 141–144.

Rudofossi, D. (2007). *Working with traumatized police officer-patients: A clinician's guide to complex PTSD syndromes in public-safety professionals.* Amityville, NY: Baywood.

Rudofossi, D. (2009). *A cop doc's guide to public safety complex trauma syndrome: Using five police personality styles.* Amityville, NY: Baywood.

Rudofossi, D. (2015). *Dealing with the mentally ill person on the street.* Springfield, IL: Thomas.

Runyan, W. (1982a). In defense of the case study method. *American Journal of Orthopsychiatry, 52,* 440–446.

Runyan, W. (1982b). *Life histories and psychobiology.* New York, NY: Oxford University Press.

Runyan, W. (1983). Idiographic goals and methods in the study of lives. *Journal of Personality, 51,* 413–432.

R. v Beland (1987). 2 S.C.R. 398.

R. v Cherrylle Dell (2001).

R. v D.D. (1998). M.J. No 322.

R. v D.D. (2000). S.C.C. 43.

R. v Hawkins (2001) NSWC 420

R. v Mohan (1994). 2 S.C.R.9.

Sainsbury, P., & Barraclough, B. (1968). Differences between suicide rates. *Nature, 220,* 1252.

Samandari, G., Martin, S., Kupper, L., Schiro, S., Norwood, T., & Avery, M. (2011). Are pregnant and postpartum women at increased risk for violent deaths? Suicide and homicide findings in North Carolina. *Maternal Child Health Journal, 15,* 660–669.

Saunders, J. (2001). Experts in court: A view from the bench. *Canadian Psychology, 42,* 109–118.

Scurfield, R., & Platoni, K. (Eds.). (2013). *War trauma and its wake.* New York, NY: Routledge.

Selkin, J. (1976). Rescue fantasies in homicide-suicide. *Suicide and Life-Threatening Behavior, 6,* 79–85.

Selkin, J. (1987). *The psychological autopsy in the courtroom: Contributions of the social sciences to resolving issues surrounding equivocal deaths.* Denver, CO: Author.

Selkin, J. (2005). *Suicide and the law: Cases, theories and strategies for prevention.* Buffalo, NY: Hein.

Shaffer, J., Perlin, S., Schmidt, W., & Himelfarb, M. (1972). Assessment in absentia: New directions in the psychological autopsy. *Johns Hopkins Medical Journal, 130,* 308–316.

Shaughnessy, J., Zechmeister, E., & Zechmeister, J. (2000). *Research methods in psychology.* New York, NY: McGraw-Hill.

Sherman, S., Presson, C., & Chassin, L. (1984). Mechanisms underlying the false consensus effect: The special role of threats to self. *Personality & Social Psychology Bulletin, 10,* 127–138.

Shneidman E. (1963). Orientations toward death. In R. White (Ed.), *The study of lives* (pp. 200–227). New York, NY: Atherton.

Shneidman, E. (1967). Sleep and self-destruction: A phenomenological approach. In E. Shneidman (Ed.), *Essays in self-destruction* (pp. 510–539). New York, NY: Science House.

Shneidman, E. (1969). Suicide, lethality, and the psychological autopsy. In E. Shneidman & M. Ortega (Eds.), *Aspects of depression* (pp. 225–250). Boston, MA: Little, Brown.

Shneidman, E. (1971). Perturbation and lethality as precursors of suicide in a gifted group. *Suicide and Life-Threatening Behavior, 1,* 23–45.

Shneidman, E. (1973a). *Deaths of man.* New York, NY: Quadrangle.

Shneidman, E. (1973b). Suicide. In *Encyclopedia Britannica, 21,* 383–385. Chicago, IL: Williams Benton.

Shneidman, E. (1977). The psychological autopsy. In L. Gottschalk, F. McGuire, E. Dinovo, H. Birch, & J. Heiser (Eds.), *Guide to the investigation and reporting of drug-abuse deaths* (pp. 42–56). Washington, DC: U.S. Department of Health, Education and Welfare.

Shneidman, E. (1980). *Voices of death*. New York, NY: Harper & Row.

Shneidman, E. (1981). The psychological autopsy. *Suicide thoughts and reflections 1960–1980* (pp. 133–147). New York, NY: Human Sciences Press.

Shneidman, E. (1982a). On "Therefore I must kill myself." *Suicide and Life-Threatening Behavior, 12,* 52–55.

Shneidman, E. (1982b). The suicidal logic of Cesare Pavese. *Journal of the American Academy of Psychoanalysis, 10,* 547–563.

Shneidman, E. (Ed.). (1984). *Death: Current perspectives* (3rd ed.). Palo Alto, CA: Mayfield.

Shneidman, E. (1985). *Definition of suicide*. New York, NY: Wiley.

Shneidman, E. (1991). The commonalities of suicide across the life span. In A. Leenaars (Ed.), *Life span perspectives of suicide* (pp. 39–52). New York, NY: Plenum Press.

Shneidman, E. (1993a). *Suicide as psychache: A clinical approach to self-destructive behavior*. Northvale, NJ: Aronson.

Shneidman, E. (1993b). An example of an equivocal death clarified in a court of law. In E. Shneidman (Ed.), *Suicide as psychache* (pp. 209–246). Northvale, NJ: Aronson.

Shneidman, E. (1994). Clues to suicide reconsidered. *Suicide and Life-Threatening Behavior, 24,* 395–397.

Shneidman, E. (1996). *The suicidal mind*. New York, NY: Oxford University Press.

Shneidman, E. (1999). On "Therefore I must kill myself." In A. Leenaars (Ed.), *Lives and deaths: Selections from the works of Edwin S. Shneidman* (pp. 72–76). Philadelphia, PA: Brunner-Mazel.

Shneidman, E. (2001). *Comprehending suicide: Landmarks in 20th century suicidology*. Washington, DC: American Psychological Press.

Shneidman, E. (Ed.). (2004). *Autopsy of a suicidal mind*. New York, NY: Oxford University Press.

Shneidman, E., & Farberow, N. (1957). *Clues to suicide*. New York, NY: McGraw-Hill.

Shneidman, E., & Farberow, N. (1961). Statistical comparison between attempted and committed suicides. In N. Farberow & E. Shneidman (Eds.), *The cry for help* (pp. 19–47). New York, NY: McGraw-Hill.

Shneidman, E., & Mandelkorn, P. (1967). *How to prevent suicide*. Public Affairs Pamphlet. New York, NY: Public Affairs Pamphlet, No. 406.

Silver, S. (1986). An inpatient program for post-traumatic stress disorder: Context as treatment. In C. Figley (Ed.), *Trauma and its wake*, Vol. II (pp. 213-231). New York, NY: Brunner/Mazel.

Slaby, A. (1995). Suicide as an indica of biological based brain diseases. *Archives of Suicide Research, 1,* 59-73.

Smith, E., & Medin, D. (1981). *Categories and concepts*. Cambridge, MA: Harvard University Press.

Smith, K., Conroy, M., & Ehler, P. (1984). Lethality of suicide attempt rating scale. *Suicide and Life-Threatening Behavior, 14,* 215–242.

Snider, J., Hane, S., & Berman, A. (2006). Standardizing the psychological autopsy: Addressing the Daubert Standard. *Suicide and Life-Threatening Behavior, 36,* 511–518.

Stack, S. (1997). Homicide followed by suicide: An analysis of Chicago data. *Criminology, 35,* 435–453.

Stack, S., & Bowman, B. (2011). *Suicide movies*. Gottingen, Germany: Hogrefe.

Steer, R., & Beck, A. (1988). Use of the Beck Depression Inventory, Hopelessness Scale, Scale of Suicide Ideation and Suicide Intent Scale with adolescents. *Advanced Adolescent Mental Health, 3,* 219–233.

Stengel, E. (1964). *Suicide and attempted suicide*. Baltimore, MD: Penguin Books.

Stenger, E., & Stenger, E. (2000). Physical illness and suicidal behaviour. In K. Hawton & C. van Heeringen (Eds.), *The international handbook of suicide and attempted suicide* (pp. 405–420). Chichester, UK: Wiley.

Stevenson, R., & Cox, G. (Eds.). (2008). *Perspectives on violence and violent death.* Amityville, NY: Baywood.

Stewart, D. (2011). Depression during pregnancy. *New England Journal of Medicine, 365,* 1605–1611.

Stoff, D., & Mann, J. (Eds.). (1997). *The neurobiology of suicide: From the bench to the clinic.* New York, NY: New York Academy of Sciences.

Styron, W. (1990). *Darkness visible.* New York, NY: Random House.

Sullivan, H. (1962). Schizophrenia as a human process. In H. Perry, N. Gorvell, & M. Gibbens (Eds.), *The collected works of Harry Stack Sullivan, Vol. II.* New York, NY: Norton.

Sullivan, H. (1964). The fusion of psychiatry and social sciences. In H. Perry, N. Gorvell, & M. Gibbens (Eds.), *The collected works of Harry Stack Sullivan.* New York, NY: Norton.

Syer, D., & Wyndowe, J. (1981). How coroner's attitudes towards suicide affect certification procedures. In J. Soubrier & J. Verdinne (Eds.), *Depression et suicide* (pp. 36–39). Paris, France: Pergamon Press.

Tabachnik, N. (1967). The psychology of fatal accidents. In E. Shneidman (Ed.), *Essays in self-destruction* (pp. 399–413). New York, NY: Aronson.

Tabachnik, N. (Ed.). (1973). *Accident or suicide?* Springfield, IL: Thomas.

Teasdale, T., & Engberg, A. (2001). Suicide after traumatic brain injury: A population study. *Journal of Neurology, Neurosurgery, and Psychiatry, 71,* 436–440.

Terrio, H., Brenner, L., Ivins, B., Cho, J., Helmick, K., Scally, K., et al. (2009). Traumatic brain injury screening: Preliminary findings regarding prevalence and sequelae in a US Army brigade combat team. *Journal of Head Trauma Rehabilitation, 24,* 14–23.

Terry v. State, 467 So.2d 761 (Fla. 4th DCA 1985).

Thoresen, S., & Mehlum, L. (2004). Risk factors for fatal accidents and suicides in peace-keepers: Is there an overlap? *Military Medicine, 169,* 988–993.

Thoresen, S., & Mehlum, L. (2006). Suicide in peacekeepers: Risk factors for suicide versus accidental death. *Suicide and Life-Threatening Behavior, 36,* 432–442.

Tomlinson-Keasey, C., Warren, L., & Elliot, J. (1986). Suicide among gifted women. *Journal of Abnormal Psychology, 95,* 123–130.

Toolan, J. (1981). Depression and suicide in children: An overview. *American Journal of Psychotherapy, 35,* 311–322.

Tripodes, P. (1976). Reasoning patterns in suicide notes. In E. Shneidman (Ed.), *Suicidology: Contemporary developments* (pp. 203–228). New York, NY: Grune and Stratton.

Tuckman, J., Kleiner, R., & Lavell, M. (1959). Emotional content of suicide notes. *American Journal of Psychiatry, 116,* 1104–1106.

Tversky, A. (1977). Features of similarity. *Psychological Review, 84,* 327–352.

United Nations (UN). (1991). *Human rights and scientific and technological developments.* Report of the working group on the principles for the protection of persons with mental illness and for the improvement of mental health care. Resolution 98B. New York, NY: Author.

United States vs. Edwards, 819 F.2d 262 (11th Cir. 1987).

Unnithan, C., Huff-Corzine, L., Corzine, J., & Whitt, H. (1994). *The currents of lethal violence.* Albany, NY: State University of New York Press.

Van Praag, H. (1997). Some biological and psychological aspects of suicidal behavior: An attempt to bridge the gap. In A. Botsis, C. Soldatos, & C. Stefanis (Eds.), *Suicide: Biopsychosocial approaches* (pp. 73–92). Amsterdam, The Netherlands: Elsevier.

Violanti, J. (2007). *Police suicide*. Springfield, IL: Thomas.

von Bertalanffy, L. (1967). *Robots, men and minds*. New York, NY: George Braziller.

von Bertalanffy, L. (1968). *General systems theory* (Rev. ed.). New York, NY: Braziller.

Voracek, M., & Loible, L. (2008). Consistency of immigrant and country-of-birth suicide rates: A meta-analysis. *Acta Psychiatrica Scandinavica, 118,* 259–271.

Wagner, F. (1960). Suicide notes. *Danish Medical Journal, 7,* 62–64.

Warden, D. (2006). Military TBI during the Iraq and Afghanistan wars. *Journal of Head Trauma Rehabilitation, 21,* 398–402.

Weisman, A. (1968). *The psychological autopsy: A study of the terminal phase of life*. New York, NY: Human Sciences Press.

Weisman, A. (1974). *The realization of death: A guide to the psychological autopsy*. New York, NY: Aronson.

Weisman, A. (2004). Consultation by Avery Weisman, MD. In E. Shneidman (Ed.), *Autopsy of a suicidal mind* (pp. 151–157). New York, NY: Oxford University Press.

Welner, M., Davey, E., & Bernstein, A. (2014). Peer-reviewed forensic consultation in practice: Multidisciplinary oversight in common practice. *Journal of Forensic Sciences, 59,* 1254–1259.

West, D. (1966). *Murder followed by suicide: An inquiry carried out for the Institute of Criminology*. Cambridge, MA: Harvard University Press.

Windelband, W. (1904). *Geschichte und naturwissenschaft* (3rd ed). Strassburg, Germany: Heitz.

Wolff, H. (1931). Suicide notes. *American Mercury, 24,* 264–272.

Wolfgang, M. (1958). An analysis of homicide-suicide. *Journal of Clinical and Experimental Psychopathology, 19,* 208–218.

World Health Organization (WHO). (1957). *Manual of the international statistical classification of diseases, injuries, and causes of death*. Based on the recommendations of the Seventh Revision Conference, 1955. Geneva, Switzerland: Author.

World Health Organization (WHO). (2002). *World report on violence and health*. Geneva, Switzerland: Author.

World Health Organization (WHO). (2006). *Preventing disease through healthy environments*. Geneva, Switzerland: Author.

World Health Organization (WHO). (2014). *Suicide prevention: A global imperative*. Geneva, Switzerland: Author.

Yufit, R., & Lester, D. (Eds.). (2005). *Assessment, treatment and prevention of suicidal behavior*. New York, NY: Wiley.

Zachar, P., & Kendler, K. (2010). Philosophical issues in the classification of psychopathology. In T. Millon, R. Krueger, & E. Simonson (Eds.), *Contemporary directions in psychopathology* (pp. 127–148). New York, NY: Guilford Press.

Zhang, J., Conwell, Y., Zhou, L., & Jiang, C. (2004). Culture, risk factors and suicide in rural China: A psychological autopsy case control study. *Acta Psychiatrica Scandinavica, 110,* 430–437.

Zilboorg, G. (1936). Suicide among civilized and primitive races. *American Journal of Psychiatry, 92,* 1347–1369.

Zilboorg, G. (1937). Considerations on suicide, with particular reference to that of the young. *American Journal of Orthopsychiatry, 7,* 15–31.

Index

Page numbers in **bold** refer to tables. Page numbers in *italics* refer to figures.